New Perspectives on Agri-environmental Policies

Significant advances have occurred in recent years in Europe and in North America in addressing agri-environmental policies. Land use issues tend to be more pressing in Europe than in the United States as a whole because of different spatial exigencies. Because these advances have taken place within individual academic disciplines, there has been something of a loss of synergy and often efforts are duplicated.

While important institutional and legal differences still exist between the two continents, the sharing of recent scientific advances will benefit scientists on both sides of the Atlantic and this is the main purpose of this book. The primary features of the book are threefold. First, the authors aim to identify options for policy to overcome the challenges ahead related to future agri-environmental policies. Second, they synthesize existing knowledge and identify gaps in current knowledge along with future research needs. Finally, they explicitly compare agri-environmental interactions and approaches to their resolution in Europe and in the United States.

This is the only major book of its kind that focuses specifically on the intersection between agricultural and environmental policies and issues. Furthermore, the multidisciplinary approach taken in the volume, as well as the inclusion of authors from both sides of the Atlantic Ocean, makes the book unique. This book will be of most value to university faculty and students interested in agriculture and the environment on both sides of the Atlantic, the text should also be of interest to informed laypersons as well as policy-makers.

Stephan J. Goetz is Professor of Agricultural and Regional Economics at The Pennsylvania State University and Director of the Northeast Regional Center for Rural Development. **Floor Brouwer** is Head of Research Unit Management of Natural Resources at LEI (The Agricultural Economics Research Institute) in the Netherlands, with responsibility for the coordination and management of research on management of natural resources.

Routledge explorations in environmental economics

Edited by Nick Hanley

University of Stirling, UK

New Perspectives on Agri-environmental Policies

A multidisciplinary and transatlantic approach

Edited by Stephan J. Goetz and Floor Brouwer

Routledge
Taylor & Francis Group

LONDON AND NEW YORK

First published 2010
by Routledge
2 Park Square, Milton Park, Abingdon, Oxon OX14 4RN

Simultaneously published in the USA and Canada
by Routledge
711 Third Ave, New York, NY 10017

Routledge is an imprint of the Taylor & Francis Group, an informa business

First issued in paperback 2011

British Library Cataloguing in Publication Data
A catalogue record for this book is available from the British Library

Library of Congress Cataloging in Publication Data
New perspectives on agri-environmental policies: a multidisciplinary and
transatlantic approach/edited by Stephan J. Goetz & Floor Brouwer.
p. cm. – (Routledge explorations in environmental economics; 22)
Includes bibliographical references.

1. Environmental policy–Europe. 2. Environmental policy–United States.
3. Agriculture and state–Europe. 4. Agriculture and state–United States. I.
Goetz, Stephan J. (Stephan Juergen) II. Brouwer, Floor. III. Series:
Routledge explorations in environmental economics; 22.

GE170.N495 2009
333.76–dc22

2009015747

ISBN13: 978-0-415-77702-5 (hbk)
ISBN13: 978-0-203-86780-8 (ebk)
ISBN13: 978-0-415-51688-4 (pbk)

Contents

Figures

Tables

1 A multidisciplinary and transatlantic approach to agri-environmental policies

Motivation and overview

Stephan J. Goetz and Floor Brouwer

Introduction

Significant advances have been made in recent years both in Europe and in North America in the analysis and understanding of agri-environmental policies. By agri-environmental policies we refer to the wider set of instruments that transcend beyond traditional price or income support policies to include explicitly environmental dimensions of agriculture and alternative land use patterns. While land use issues in some ways tend to be more pressing in Europe than in the United States as a whole because of different spatial exigencies overall as well as major institutional (legal) and cultural differences, we contend that this setting makes a comparative analytical perspective across the Atlantic especially valuable. Fundamentally, the biophysical and ecological relationships of interest to scientists are essentially identical on these two different continents.

Furthermore, because the advances described here tend to occur within individual academic disciplines, an important loss of synergies occurs and efforts often are duplicated. Thus, while important institutional and legal differences exist between the two continents, we believe that the sharing of recent scientific advances will benefit scientists on both sides of the Atlantic. The primary features of the book are threefold. First, we identify options for policy to overcome the challenges ahead related to future agri-environmental policies. Second, we synthesize existing knowledge and identify gaps in current knowledge along with future research needs. Finally, we explicitly compare agri-environmental interactions and approaches to their resolution in Europe and in the United States.

Some basic comparisons

As already noted, significant differences exist among the European Union (EU) nations and the United States on a number of geophysical measures. Perhaps most striking to the European visitor to the United States are the large distances across the country in comparison to the denser European settlement patterns. With 9,376,000 km^2 the United States is nearly three times larger than the EU-15 nations combined (3,242,000 km^2) but has slightly less than one-quarter the population density, with 32 versus 119 inhabitants per km^2 (OECD 2008a). Of course, these averages conceal enormous variations within the two continents as well. For US visitors to Europe, the compact style of farming and housing development or containment is often most remarkable, with agricultural areas abutting rural towns and villages, and having done so for centuries. This is in sharp contrast to the typical US agricultural scene, where farmers actually live on the land that they own. At the same time, and in contrast to the perception of nearly unlimited land resources, less than 20 percent of US territory is actually devoted to crops. Further, especially in the west with its wide open and "big sky" country, urban development is in fact nearly as compact as it is in the more densely settled northeast. The reason for this is largely the result of water limitations in that part of the country. These limitations have given rise, in recent years, to calls for moving agricultural production back to the northeastern parts of the United States, where rainfall is more abundant.

A potentially important difference between these two regions is the gap in population growth rates over time. The US population expanded by 1 percent between 2004 and 2005, for example, compared with only 0.5 percent in the EU-15 and 0.1 percent in Germany, one of the slowest-growing nations. In the United States, the Brookings Institution had predicted just prior to the ensuing financial decline that an additional 25 percent of the housing stock would have to be built over the next 30 years both to replace deteriorating housing stock and to accommodate new international migrants. Most of this construction would likely occur on the urban fringe, which is also the locus of over 50 percent of the sales of agricultural production. It is here that the greatest conflicts between agriculture and housing development, and arguably the environment, are likely to occur. And, in the northeast United States at least, space limitations are in many ways similar to those found in Europe.

Despite the perception of seemingly vast differences in terms of land area and utilization between the EU and the United States, it is noteworthy that very similar shares of total national land are devoted to agriculture (OECD 2008b: 17). In particular, about 45 percent of all land is used agriculturally in the United States and across the EU-15 countries on average. The range for this statistic is from 67 percent in the United Kingdom to only around 7 percent in Canada. The countries considered here also are similar in terms of nitrogen efficiency (OECD 2008b: 21); this is "the percentage ratio of total nitrogen uptake of crops and forage (tonnes) to the total nitrogen available from fertiliser, livestock manure, and other nitrogen inputs (tonnes)," although the EU has on average managed to make some improvement on this score between 1990–1992 and 2002–2004, to nearly 60 percent.

On the policy side, both the United States and the EU increasingly use incentive payments to enhance agro-environmental quality. Trading of rights is used both in the United States (at least regionally) and in the Netherlands (OECD 2008b: 553). In terms of environmental measures tracked by the OECD, one-quarter of the total land area in the United States is "protected." This compares with an average of 15 percent for the EU-15, but the range here is from nearly

32 percent in Germany to 19 percent in the Netherlands and only 3.4 percent in Belgium. While such casual inferences need to be drawn with great care, because of the lack of scientific controls (such as protected lands), the selection of countries shown, and the presence of rival explanatory causes, it is interesting to note the relationship between pesticide use and the share of endangered bird species shown in Figure 1.1 for a select group of countries.

Thus, one of our key goals is to examine and understand whether the environment and agriculture necessarily are in competition with one another, and whether or where complementarities and even synergies may be present.

About the rest of this book

The remainder of this book is divided into three parts, starting in Part I with a collection of chapters by authors from both sides of the Atlantic Ocean that is intended to improve our understanding of current and emerging relationships between agriculture and the environment. Part II presents new perspectives on the modeling of agri-environmental relations, while Part III focuses explicitly on the scope for emerging agri-environmental policies.

Part I: understanding current relations between agriculture and environment

In Chapter 2, Findeis *et al.* explore the question of how important demographic trends influence shifts in land use which create major environmental impacts. This is an issue not only in member nations of the OECD, but in countries around the world as population continues to grow and, more often than not, increasingly settles in urban agglomerations. Land use outcomes depend not only on the demand for land but also on the supply of developable land and, in regions experiencing population pressure, allocation of land to agricultural

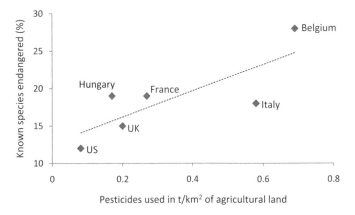

Figure 1.1 Pesticide use and threatened bird species, selected countries (source: OECD 2008b data).

purposes has in part delayed land development. Farmers hold land as a retirement asset or more permanently for purposes of intergenerational transfer. At the
same time, with rapid aging of the population in many countries land use transitions may accelerate in the near future. This trend is already being observed in
some areas according to the authors, leading to transitions in lifestyles and perceptions or sense of place among residents.

Three interrelated demographic trends influence the transition process from
rural to exurban to urban places: global population growth, greater mobility, and
growth of the world's elderly population (both in absolute numbers and as a proportion of total population). The authors focus on rural–exurban–urban transition
zones in the United States, identifying hotspots of transition in states historically
viewed as major agricultural states. In the middle of this transition, important
new opportunities are arising for agriculture, creating forms of new agriculture
that are now more dominant. A key aspect is the growing importance of off-farm
employment and non-farm income for US farmers, more so than in Europe for
reasons largely attributable to policy differences, which often is made possible
by easy access to jobs and increased mobility. Because this increase in off-farm
labor supply affects farm program participation and specific farming practices,
Findeis *et al.* argue that it is critical for agri-environmental policies to consider
these interrelationships. A second key aspect is the imminent transfer of land
from the elderly US farm population to other farmers or to land development.
Again, agri-environmental policies can influence the transition process, and the
environmental impacts that result across transition zones.

In Chapter 3, Legg outlines a comparative perspective from the OECD on the
role for government in providing payments for environmental services from
farming. He compares key agri-environmental policies of the United States and
the EU. Arguing that agriculture and other activities support a number of land-
based services for the environment, Legg explores agriculture's environmental
benefits and the contribution of payments to farmers for the delivery of services
from farming. Legg also presents trends in market and price support and argues
that the findings from valuation studies are often not shared sufficiently with
policy-makers.

Legg suggests that more research is required to understand the demand for
agri-environmental goods and services, and what happens once the public payments to landowners cease. Details of the implementation of such programs need
to be thought through carefully. Finally, markets for agri-environmental services
are critical, and if market efficiency goals are to be met carefully defined reference levels and property rights are needed.

Von Haaren and Bills in Chapter 4 compare agri-environmental programs in
two specific regions: Germany and New York State. They argue that compiling
inter-country comparisons and taking advantage of experiments with policy
implementation are great challenges for researchers. Their chapter starts with a
brief literature synopsis, which includes a discussion of the efficacy of agri-
environmental programs in the EU and the United States along with key definitions and performance measures. They then provide examples from the

northeastern United States and Germany. The authors argue that an especially critical issue, given the ongoing World Trade Organization (WTO) negotiations, is the merging of compensatory and regulatory incentives to provide agri-environmental goods and services.

In Germany current agri-environmental programs are seen as suboptimal both in terms of environmental results and cost-effectiveness. Given uncertain prospects for future EU subsidies, improved targeting of payments and better motivating of farmers are required to ensure sustainability. In the United States, policy efforts designed to balance agriculture with environmental goals have developed along two distinct paths since World War II. These include most notably soil erosion/water quality management and farmland protection. According to Van Haaren and Bills, discussions surrounding northeast agriculture and the environment tend to occur in parallel universes, to benefit the particular needs of academics and program managers. An additional complication in policy discourse in the United States is that agri-environmental programs often are implemented and funded by state and local governments. This "layering" of federal, state and local efforts is usually ignored in international comparisons, which capture only federal policy interventions. The comparisons presented in this chapter of the US and German experiences are not only timely but beneficial to the unfolding policy debates across OECD nations.

In Chapter 5, Lynch *et al.* examine whether agricultural preservation programs in the United States are paying "too much" to protect land. They write that more than 124 governmental units in the United States have sponsored farmland preservation programs, preserving over 1.67 million acres. These programs seek to prevent the conversion of farmlands to alternative uses, primarily residential development via perpetual restrictions on the farmland parcels. Programs compensate the landowners who agree to such restrictions. The authors ask: what are the opportunity costs to enrolling farmland owners, i.e. how much does their land value change when restricted? Or in other words, what is the right compensation to be paid to landowners? The authors employ a database of farmland transactions in Maryland to analyze how easement restrictions affect the sale prices of land.

Using a hedonic and a propensity score approach, Lynch *et al.* find that sale prices of preserved parcels were 10–20 percent lower than similar non-restricted agricultural parcels. Compensation to farmland owners in the state farmland preservation program averages three times the reduction in land values. A key finding is that farmland preservation programs may be able to achieve the programs' objectives with lower incentive payments.

Chapter 6, by Foulke *et al.*, presents an innovative approach toward modeling the economic impacts of critical habitat designation on the economy of southeastern Wyoming. Here, too, the primary goal is to improve our understanding of the relationship between agriculture and the environment. The authors' work is based on listening sessions that were held to determine how land is used locally, and what specific agricultural practices prevail. These results are used to construct a representative ranch model. Using GAMS they then simulate how different levels of critical habitat designation affect ranch profitability, by altering the amount of land in production. Using Census of Agriculture data and IMPLAN, they aggregate their results from the firm to the regional levels.

The results show that the agricultural sector is significantly impacted even if the amount of land designated as critical habitat is modest, particularly if that land is used as a hay meadow. The reason for this is that hay is critical for ranch operations in terms of maintaining local carrying capacity year-round. This work also raises important questions about who should bear the costs of species preservation, i.e. the distribution of property rights.

Part II: new perspectives on modeling agri-environmental relations

In the first chapter of Part II (Chapter 7), Willemen *et al.* present an integrated analysis of land use change at different scales. They point out that land cover changes or the rearrangements of landscapes over space affect not only the landscapes themselves but also species diversity, entire watersheds and even the climate. The authors then simulate various future land use change scenarios and discuss the role of land use policies and the importance of making policy-makers aware of landscape function as a tool of analysis. One of their goals is to show the potential complementarity between landscape functionality and land use/land cover change analysis.

This chapter presents scenario-based simulations conducted at different scales of analysis, in the form of two case studies. The first is based on the EURURALIS project (www.eururalis.eu), covers the entire EU, and represents a high-resolution analysis of land use change. Environmental impacts associated with various policy options are also considered. In some regions, abandonment of farmland is shown to have potentially large effects on landscape functions and the environment. In these regions, both commodity and non-commodity production are affected. Other regions, notably those subject to peri-urban development, experience different environmental impacts. The authors' second case study focuses on the Gelderse Vallei of the Netherlands, which represents the small region counterpart that is studied at a high level of detail. The authors show how effects on landscape function of structural adjustment in agriculture along with peri-urban development can readily be examined in great detail.

In Chapter 8, Duke and Johnston examine issues of land use policy and multifunctionality. They evaluate farmland and forest preservation efforts using non-market valuation techniques. One tenet of multifunctionality, according to the authors, is that farmers and farmland should be compensated for providing non-market benefits (amenities) in the same way as they are paid for providing market goods. Fundamental differences exist between European and US approaches to multifunctionality. European policy-makers generally rely on regulatory and entitlement programs that stress multifunctional benefits and their preservation. US policy-makers on the other hand tend to focus on market incentives and values, even though they appear to be increasingly accepting of non-market values. The authors argue that both the US and European approaches could be improved if more evidence about public values and willingness to pay (WTP) for them were compiled and compared. Most importantly, US policy would then better reflect multifunctional benefits while European policy would achieve efficiency gains by balancing the public benefits of agricultural with competing land uses.

Duke and Johnston illustrate how WTP estimates can improve policy discussions surrounding multifunctionality of land use. They present a table of WTP data for preserving farmland and forest parcels, which is derived from statewide and community-level surveys in rapidly growing Sussex County, Delaware. WTP varies depending on the multifunctional attribute considered, and their study clearly shows how parcels could be prioritized in preservation policy so as to deliver maximum benefits. The discussion of the results suggests the conditions under which multifunctional uses may survive a benefit–cost test.

Berger and Schreinemachers in Chapter 9 present agent-based land use models that are designed for teaching, extension and collaborative learning. The authors point out that multi-agent systems involving land use/land cover change (MAS/LUCC) have recently been applied to land use change analyses in both developing and industrialized nations. A critical advantage of these models is the fact that they are able to combine biophysical and socioeconomic processes at very fine resolutions with spatial modeling techniques, including cellular automata. MAS/LUCC can flexibly represent land use decisions and, according to the authors, this fact accounts for their ready acceptance by scholars in various disciplines, including sociologists, geographers and economists. According to the authors these models appeal even to those who distrust quantitative models of human behavior because researchers can directly observe and interpret simulation results in a manner that is both intuitive and allows for interactivity.

In their chapter Berger and Schreinemachers discuss how MAS/LUCC can be used interactively not only in learning situations generally but also for the purpose of participatory simulation. They concede that even though initial applications of MAS/LUCC in interactive settings show some promise, more research is necessary to understand how MAS/LUCC can be fully incorporated into teaching and extension efforts.

Chapter 10, by Seidl *et al.*, examines trade-offs between using land to build castles or to raise cattle, in the context of competition for open space values. They write that pressure to develop working lands for residential housing or commercial purposes is often significant when rural communities attract tourists or so-called amenity migrants. The reason for this is that the market value of the farmland is usually much lower than the value of the land when developed. Yet the externalities associated with such development are usually not considered in the conversion decision, so that social welfare is not maximized. In other words, non-market values of farmland need to be incorporated so that land uses are socially efficient at the community level.

Seidl *et al.* compare how local residents and tourists in Routt County, Colorado, value open space on ranchland. They provide welfare estimates derived from alternative policies designed to manage this space. These options range from zoning to various types of taxes that affect tourists disproportionately. They use the Input–Output Analysis Program (IMPLAN) to simulate the economic effects of these alternative policies. This allows the authors to test a number of competing hypotheses in addition to projecting the possible changes in local income associated with alternative development strategies that are currently being considered in the county.

Part III: the scope for emerging policies

In Chapter 11, Jongeneel and Brouwer analyze the EU's policy framework from the perspective of responsive regulation and the economics of compliance theories as well as from a competitiveness perspective. Indicative best-estimates of degrees and costs of compliance at regulation level are provided. The EU's approach is contrasted with approaches followed in other countries, notably the United States, Canada and New Zealand. As such the chapter aims to provide further insights into the relative impacts of various pieces of regulation on EU agriculture and provides a crude assessment about impacts on costs and the competitiveness of EU agriculture vis-à-vis its main competitors. Moreover, further insight is gained in how different countries might approach similar problems with different regulatory strategies.

Regulations and standards are introduced in agriculture to control agricultural practices and by that assure food safety, improve their sustainability and reduce its potentially harmful effects on biodiversity, soil, water and air. Other measures are implemented to improve land management practices. Obligatory cross-compliance was introduced in the European Union with its 2003 CAP reform, the main objective of the instrument being to improve compliance with standards that were previously insufficiently adhered to. In addition, rules for Good Agricultural and Environmental Conditions (GAECs) need to be respected.

In Chapter 12 Bell focuses on public preferences for protecting working landscapes in order to help inform emerging land use policies. She begins with a comparison across the Atlantic of different programs and approaches that have been used to protect open space and working lands. In the process she considers differences in natural features and regulatory regimes as well as public perceptions of and support for alternative land uses.

Bell then presents the results of two public referenda in the state of Maine surrounding land use management. One involves current use value taxation to protect working waterfront space and the other land acquisition using public bonds. Explanatory factors determining these voting results are identified through regression analysis, with a particular emphasis on how perceived net returns are influenced by where the voters are located in the state and attributes of their local landscape. The author then relates the empirical results to more general debates of how best to protect open space and working lands, and what factors may determine differences of these kinds of programs around the world.

In Chapter 13 Matzdorf *et al.* examine how agri-environmental benefits can be improved under pillar II of the Common Agricultural Policy (CAP). Farmers are rewarded under this pillar with additional premiums if they practice "environment-friendly agriculture" or maintain landscapes in certain ways. Even though agri-environmental measures are mandatory elements of rural development programs, recent evidence suggests that the measures may be falling short of their targets. Using environmental data from the federal state of Brandenburg (Germany), Matzdorf *et al.* examine agri-environmental measures aiming at biodiversity under the Convention on Biological Diversity and at water quality under the European Water Framework Directive.

Most European agri-environmental measures attempt to change specific behaviors: farmers are encouraged to use farming techniques that are specified in contracts with the government. To attain environmental goals, the authors of this chapter recommend that a results-oriented or performance-based approach be used instead. Here, payments are made only when specific agri-environmental conditions are met. The key distinction is that in this case the farmer is free to choose how the condition is to be met, rather than being forced into a specific behavior. The authors conclude their chapter by illustrating how such results-oriented schemes may be designed and implemented using grassland plant species as an indicator for biodiversity and simulated nitrate leaching figures as an indicator for water quality.

In Chapter 14 Khanna *et al.* examine the economics of carbon sequestration from the environment through the use of biomass crops. This topic is in many ways at the heart of the intersection between agricultural and environmental policies and issues and, as the authors point out, land use management practices can increase the amount of carbon sequestered. The chapter investigates the costs associated with alternative management techniques designed for carbon sequestration, and optimal land use patterns over space to ensure that sequestration targets are met.

Using data and simulations from the state of Illinois, Khanna *et al.* find that substantial subsidies are needed to ensure profitability for landowners. Further, sequestration costs rise quickly as targets are increased, especially up to ten million metric tons. Carbon sequestration costs can be reduced using biomass crops, primarily when targets are very high, but this requires substantial subsidies for bioenergy. The chapter concludes with a number of policy implications, including those related to public payments, as well as the interaction among conservation, energy and land retirement policies.

In Chapter 15 Adelaja *et al.* examine the future of farmland preservation programs in the context of moving from retention and viability to resiliency. The authors start from the premise that farmland preservation is potentially a critical strategy to reposition US agriculture. Preservation programs have been adopted by numerous state and local governments as well as non-profit organizations, and most share the goals of preserving productive and viable farms. Productivity is based on suitable natural and regulatory conditions while viability depends more on the business savvy of the farmland operator, as well as the local or state business climate.

In this context, and using lessons from Europe, Adelaja *et al.* focus on emerging societal goals for land retention. They review criteria used to select farmland to be preserved in the United States, and identify the emerging socioeconomic and ecological factors that need to be included to ensure that such programs find more widespread acceptance. The authors then present a wide array of resiliency measures that can be used to prioritize land for preservation purposes. They apply these measures to the state of Michigan and find that their criteria would lead to the selection of different parcels for preservation than would otherwise have been selected. The authors conclude by evaluating the distributional effects of alternative future visions for agriculture and discuss how these could result in varying farmland preservation dynamics.

With this last chapter in the volume, we in some ways come full circle with the work of Findeis *et al.* in Chapter 2, who start out by examining how population demographics drive land use changes over time. This final chapter examines specifically how policy can be used to attenuate the impacts of such population pressure.

To conclude this introductory chapter, we point out that this book is targeted primarily at university faculty and students interested in the topics of agriculture and the environment on both sides of the Atlantic. The book could be used in graduate courses on environmental and agricultural policy and modeling. Given the renewed interest in both local and global sustainability in the United States especially, we believe that the book is timely. Although it is written for academic audiences primarily, the text should also be of interest to informed laypersons as well as policy-makers.

While a number of books exist on agricultural and environmental policy and issues, we are not aware of any major book that focuses specifically on the intersection between these two areas in the manner presented here. Furthermore, the multidisciplinary approach taken in the volume, as well as the inclusion of authors from both sides of the Atlantic Ocean, makes the book unique.

References

Organization for Economic Co-operation and Development (2008a) *OECD in Figures 2008*, Paris: OECD.

Organization for Economic Co-operation and Development (2008b) *Environmental Performance of Agriculture at a Glance*, Paris: OECD.

Part I

Understanding current relations between agriculture and environment

2 Demographic change and land use transitions

Jill L. Findeis, Kathryn Brasier and Rodrigo Salcedo Du Bois

Introduction

Humans increasingly dominate the landscape, a force largely driven by human population growth and distribution (Vitousek *et al.* 1997; Grimm *et al.* 2000; MEA 2005). In many contexts, rural landscapes are transitioning to exurban and eventually urban places, as human population spreads across the land (Brown *et al.* 2004, 2005). The rural to exurban to urban transformation is being observed in the United States, Canada and other OECD countries (see Lubowski 2002; Irwin and Bockstael 2002; Jobin *et al.* 2003, as examples).[1] In other countries and regions worldwide (e.g. Southeast Asia, South Asia, Latin America and Africa), humans are concentrating into urban centers (UNFPA 2007), creating substantial environmental impacts but also eventually spilling population into the countryside as population growth continues. Understanding the impacts of human population growth and dispersion, and how to effectively attenuate the negative impacts of these processes, are among the most important challenges of our time (Vitousek *et al.* 1997).

Three interrelated demographic trends influence the transition process from rural to exurban to urban places. Continued global population growth together with higher levels of consumption in some places, greater mobility of the human population, and growth of the world's elderly population (both in absolute numbers and as a proportion of total population) are expected to affect patterns of rural–exurban–urban transformation, rates of transition and specific socio-economic and environmental impacts and their global distribution. Demographic trends affect food production for growing urban populations, provision of ecosystem services, and use of natural resources including land proximate to population centers (MEA 2005; Entwisle and Stern 2005). Food availability and regional and local food production capacity represent major global issues, particularly given higher energy and rapidly increasing food prices (FAO 2008) coupled with public concern related to food and bio-security. Issues of food security for developing nations are paramount.

Recent demographic trends raise a host of challenges: how to efficiently and equitably feed the human population concentrated in urban centers; how to maintain human health and well-being in these places in the long run; how to sustain the natural resource base in populated spaces; and how to design appropriate policies to balance social, economic and environmental goals. Addressing these challenges requires understanding the complexity of human systems and the larger ecosystem that underlies the population-induced transition process (Axelrod 1997; Miller and Page 2007; Liu *et al.* 2007; Robinson *et al.* 2007; Parker *et al.* 2008).

In this chapter we present demographic trends and interrelated changes in the structure of agriculture and land use, first briefly in a world context and then focusing on the United States. This is followed by an examination of selected state clusters in the United States where agriculture has been a key economic sector but is now under significant pressure from human population growth and dispersion. We cite selected recent literature that has expanded our understanding of factors influencing the process of (farm) land conversion in the United States, particularly from the land demand side. We also examine two trends affecting land use, the structure of agriculture, and potentially the design of agri-environmental policy and programs:[2]

1   significantly more off-farm employment by US households engaged in farm production, a trend enabled in part by proximity to population-employment centers and greater population mobility; and
2   the graying of the US farm population, a trend that raises questions regarding the likelihood of farm transfer to the next farming generation.

In both cases, variation is expected across the transition zone (rural–exurban–suburban–urban) gradient. Demographic data are presented and compared across the transition zone (t-zone) gradient first for the United States and then for Pennsylvania, a state particularly challenged by sprawl (The Brookings Institution 2004; Alter *et al.* 2007).[3] Pennsylvania also has one of the oldest populations in the United States, creating potential for very significant changes in land ownership and land use in the next 20 years.

Urban concentration, spillover and an aging farm population

Comparing the United States to other countries, the population-driven changes taking place across transition zones are in some respects remarkably similar. The concentration of now over half of the world's population in urban centers reflects domestic and international migration fueled by GDP concentrations in city centers (OECD 2007). Unless checked by geography or policy, population eventually spreads over the surrounding landscape. In some cases, consumption drives the transition (Pendall 2003). Greater mobility of the human population also contributes to the spillover onto nearby landscapes, for consumption of natural resource amenities, for perceived healthier lifestyles and safety, but also for lower costs of living. In China, India and in much of the developing world, population is becoming more concentrated in urban centers, which by necessity continually extend their boundaries (Entwisle and Stern 2005; OECD 2007; UNFPA 2007). Countries are at different stages in this process, but the process itself appears to be essentially the same.

The population of the United States has now surpassed 300 million persons, with population estimated at 301,621,157 persons as of July 1, 2007. Projections for the United States show a population of almost 420 million by the year 2050 (US Census Bureau 2004). Population growth in the United States over the last decade reflects a combination of prevailing birth rates and increased longevity, predicted by the Population Reference Bureau at 77.9 years for a child born in 2005, coupled with a positive net migration rate. In the European Union population growth rates are similarly positive; net international migration rates have risen in most OECD countries (OECD 2006). Population growth statistics over the 1993–2006 period for countries in the EU, the OECD countries, and other selected countries are compared in Figure 2.1.

The distribution of the US population between urban and rural residence is approximately three to one, with roughly 75 percent of the US population living in areas defined as metropolitan (metro). National population growth in the United States coupled with greater concentrations in metro areas have necessitated reclassification of rural into urban and nonmetro into metro with successive US population censes. Over the last several decades, long-term trends show that the US population and per capita GDP have become even more concentrated in metro areas, an international trend shared by the OECD countries and most countries worldwide (OECD 2007). Combes and Overman (2004) observe that while the United States and EU appear to differ in the spatial distribution of economic activity due to greater labor mobility in the United States and more product market integration there as well, the United States and the EU share "marked similarities."

Recent migration trends show that US domestic mobility patterns are now favoring metro-to-nonmetro migration over nonmetro-to-metro movement (Schachter *et al.* 2003). However, this represents the "spilling over" of urban population into nonmetro places proximate to metropolitan counties, as well as metro-to-nonmetro migration of retirees whose decisions regarding where to live no longer depend on proximity to a workplace. Recent data bear out the urban spillover effect: Schachter *et al.* (2003) report that "nonmetropolitan counties with high rates of net domestic migration gain were especially prominent near metropolitan areas that experienced relatively high growth rates" (p. 3). The United States also has experienced regional shifts in population, with in-migration of population into amenity-rich places that do not fit the urban spillover model. These trends (long-term urban concentration, urban expansion into nearby suburban and exurban areas, and amenity migration) have significant consequences for the ways in which land is used and developed across the landscape, particularly for working lands (agricultural, forested and range land).

Population aging

In developed and developing countries the increasing absolute numbers and proportions of total population who are elderly are expected to influence the transition; the growing elderly population will constitute a major global challenge

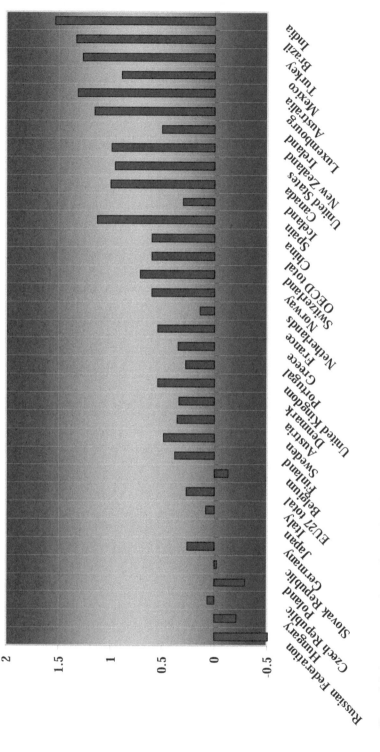

Figure 2.1 Average annual growth rates in selected countries (source: OECD 2006 rates, given as percentages, are for 2006 or 1993–2006 latest available).

over at least the next two decades, straining economic and social systems (OECD 2006). The lifecycle transition from working age to elderly shifts dependency on labor assets to nonlabor assets (including wealth stored in landholdings) and to public safety nets (if they exist). From a land-use perspective, mortality ultimately results in land transfers, creating thresholds for transfers of land out of agriculture when farming is no longer profitable or profitable enough. From a lifecycle perspective, assets typically are built up over working ages and drawn down during retirement. Vesterby and Heimlich (1991) document the relevance of demographics for land-use change in US urbanizing places (see also NASS 2007). Global–spatial impacts will depend on a wide set of variables that bear watching (FAO 1999).

For farms in many countries, rural-to-urban migration of the working-age population reduces the well-documented labor underemployment in agriculture but can leave behind a largely elderly rural population. This is still occurring not only in the United States but also in developing countries; we see this now in South China, a rapidly developing transition zone (Zhang and Findeis 2007). In China but also elsewhere, remittances and access to land are becoming the safety net for an aged population who finds it more difficult to care for itself (Zhang and Findeis 2007). Younger family members accustomed to urban living will eventually face the question of the future use of household land for agriculture. Some villages in China are experiencing return migration, fueling the transition process in the countryside. Rising incomes are also contributing to population spillover from urban centers undergoing extremely rapid growth, transforming farm land to residential use.

The US population is becoming strikingly older, a trend that is consistent with most developed countries. As observed by the OECD (2007), "Over the last 30 years the elderly population (those aged 65 years and over) has increased dramatically in all OECD countries" (OECD 2007: 20), reflecting increases in longevity and total fertility rates below replacement rates in most, but not all, OECD countries. Notable exceptions include Mexico, Turkey, Iceland and the United States (OECD 2006). In 2003, 12 percent of the US population was 65 years of age or older, but the aging of comparatively large middle-aged cohorts will result in rising percentages of the US population classified as elderly and/or retired, and in the elderly dependency rate (ratio) over the next two decades.[4] Population distributions (pyramids) for the US population for 2000 and projected to 2030 are quite different, with the projected pyramid being significantly more top-heavy attributable to the projected greater percentages of the elderly in 2030 than in 2000.

The aging trend is important for understanding the processes playing out across US rural–exurban–urban transition zones. For elderly landowners in the United States, land represents a major retirement asset, i.e. a store of wealth that can be sold off in whole or piecemeal for retirement or old-age security. The transfer of land assets (and potential change in land uses) necessarily has implications for food production, space, landscape and ecosystem services. For rural and exurban places, population aging is a more significant problem than in urban locations, since the elderly population is more concentrated there due to out-migration of the young (e.g. see NASS 2007). Typically, the problem is greatest in rural areas; in the United States, Japan, Canada and Australia, for example, the rural elderly dependence rate exceeded rates in urban and intermediate regions in 2003 (OECD 2007).

The current population age structure in countries such as the United States means that time is critical; land has a greater probability of turnover in coming decades than in the recent past. The greater concentrations of the elderly in rural–exurban places will accelerate the turnover there, although longer lifespans are expected to attenuate the rate. In some regions in the United States, farms will expand into larger operations as the turnover occurs; rental of farmland to other farm producers is already a common landholding strategy employed by elderly farm households. In US transition zones, landscape fragmentation will continue, with new farm household-firms being largely supported by off-farm employment and nonfarm income. For agriculture, the big question today is whether bio-energy/energy development will counter-balance anticipated land transitions from agriculture in those places where the next generation and entering farm operators have shown hesitance to farm.

Transition zones in the United States: hotspots for ag transitions

National statistics showing limited aggregate change in farmland have tended to obscure the regional shifts in land use for farming and farm transition that have taken place, particularly over the 1990s. The aggregates also obscure hotspots of transition, for instance, exurban places, the rural–urban fringe and landscapes of high natural amenities (see discussions in Sharp and Clark 2008, for example). Much of what is considered prime farmland is concentrated in the east and midwest (Ahearn and Alig 2006). The fact that the United States lost ten million acres of prime farmland over the 1982–1997 period, as documented by Ahearn and Alig (2006), is not surprising.

Regions and states particularly affected include states in the northeast corridor (e.g. southeastern Pennsylvania, parts of New York, Delaware, New Jersey, among other states), the mid-Atlantic and north central states surrounding the Great Lakes population expansion (northwestern Pennsylvania, Ohio, Michigan, Indiana, Illinois, Wisconsin and parts of Minnesota), the southeast triangle (North Carolina, South Carolina, Georgia), the Pacific northwest (Oregon, Washington) and large parts of California, Florida and, increasingly, Texas and Colorado. Lubowski *et al.* (2006b) report that land in places defined as urban quadrupled between 1945 and 2002, a much higher rate than the growth rate of the US population over this period.[5] Rural land used for residences increased by 29 percent (21 million acres) between 1997 and 2002, and 30 percent (17 million acres) between 1980 and 1997 (Lubowski *et al.* 2006b). Population growth across landscapes under increased population pressure precipitates conversion of land from agricultural to residential, influencing food production and local food access; land cover and natural resources; and ecosystem function and services (Batie 2003; Rindfuss *et al.* 2004; Brown *et al.* 2004, 2005). For example, water quality impacts from erosion and coastal water quality damage from fertilizer runoff are highest in those US regions where human population is most dense[6] (Claassen *et al.* 2001).

When measured in the aggregate, the total amount of farmland has not changed to the extent that some had predicted in the 1970s and 1980s. But this belies the regional impacts on land use and the structure of agriculture that have affected particular regions in the United States, especially those states and counties with prime agricultural land and strong historical ties to agriculture. In the last two decades in particular, hotspots have developed along the urban–exurban–rural gradient that represent places undergoing structural change. Comparing land use in the United States in 1945 and 1997, Hellerstein *et al.* (2002) report that urban land share has increased in all regions (northeast, southeast, Appalachia, lake states and western), and that "the heaviest urbanization between 1982 and 1992 occurred in the Northeast and the Lake States, with California, Florida, Texas, and Appalachian States also undergoing extensive urbanization" (p. 3). Crop land over the 1945–1997 period has remained largely stable in the western United States, with the largest declines in crop land occurring in the northeast, southeast, Appalachian and lake states (in that order) (Hellerstein *et al.* 2002; Vesterby and Krupa 2001).

The Economic Research Service (ERS) at the US Department of Agriculture (USDA) has developed alternative classifications of the US landscape. The ERS Population-Interaction Zones for Agriculture (PIZA) classification system is particularly useful for assessing variations across transition zones.[7] The ERS PIZA classification shows the extent to which urban activities exert influence on agriculture, affecting production practices, land values, enterprises and the likelihood of conversion of land from agriculture to other uses (Barnard 2005). Figure 2.2 maps the four levels of PIZA classification for the United States, with PIZA 1 representing the most rural and PIZA 4 the most urban (high or developed). The ERS/USDA classification of population-interaction zones involves clustering of census tracts based on population density, commuting patterns and proximity to an urban center.

Certain areas of the United States show strong urban influence; Figures 2.3 and 2.4 identify selected clusters of states where agriculture is strongly influenced by proximity to urban locations. For example, Figure 2.3 shows the New York, Pennsylvania, Delaware and New Jersey cluster. These states, as expected, have large tracts of land classified as PIZA 2, 3 or 4 (refer to Figure 2.3a).

Looked at in another way, those places classified as PIZA 1 are not now influenced by urban proximity. But not all PIZA 1 areas in the United States are remote "rural" either; instead they include places with towns and small urban centers exerting only low influence on agriculture. This raises the following question: once places affected by urban influence and towns and small urban centers are accounted for, how much land actually remains where human impact, as proxied by population density, is still very low? This question can be

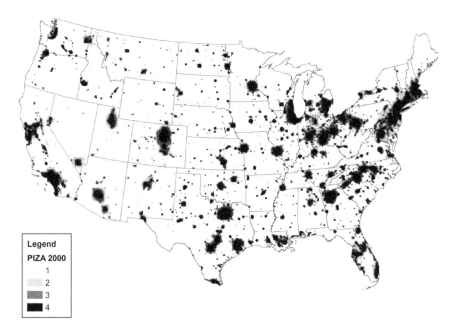

Figure 2.2 Population-interaction zones for agriculture (PIZA) in the United States, 2000
(source: developed based on maps available from the Economic Research
Service, US Department of Agriculture).

answered by examining landscapes classified as more rural under USDA's
Rural-Urban Commuting Area Code (RUCA) system. When places left "unset-
tled" (codes 8–10) are layered on the PIZA 2, 3 and 4 (urban-influenced agricultural) places as in Figure 2.3b, it shows that relatively little low-population
density space is left in the New York, Pennsylvania, New Jersey and Delaware
cluster.[8]

Other selected state clusters where agriculture is influenced by urban proximity are identified in Figure 2.4, to emphasize that states now under population
pressure include many that historically rank among the nation's leading agricultural states. Figure 2.4 shows the extent to which agriculture in the southeast
cluster (Georgia, South Carolina, North Carolina and Virginia), the Great Lakes–
central cluster (Ohio, Indiana and Michigan), the Great Lakes–west cluster (Illinois, Wisconsin, Missouri and Iowa), and the south central cluster (Texas and
Oklahoma) is now influenced by urban proximity.

Characteristics of transition zone farms and population-influenced adjustments in agriculture

The irreversibility of land conversion from farmland to residential and commercial development has led to a rapidly expanding literature in multiple disciplines

(a)

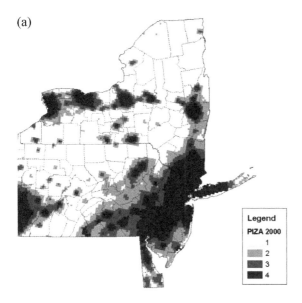

PIZA classifications.

(b)

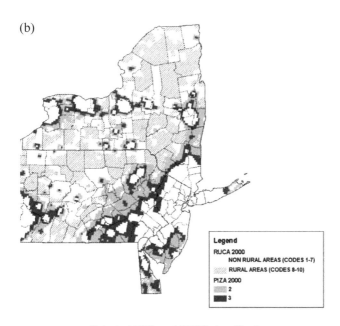

Selected PIZA and RUCA classifications.

Figure 2.3 Population-interaction zones for agriculture (PIZA) and RUCA low population density places in Pennsylvania, New York, New Jersey, Delaware cluster, 2000 (source: developed based on maps available from the Economic Research Service, US Department of Agriculture).

(a)

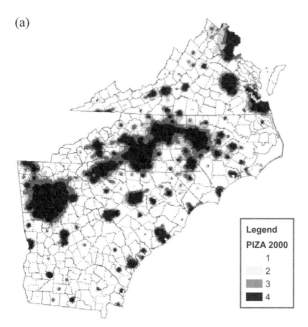

Georgia, South Carolina, North Carolina, Virginia cluster.

(b)

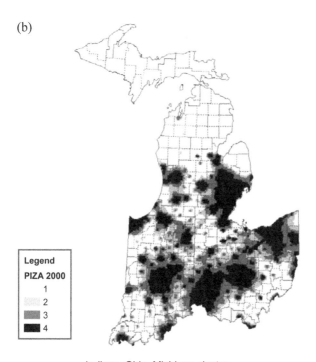

Indiana, Ohio, Michigan cluster.

(c)

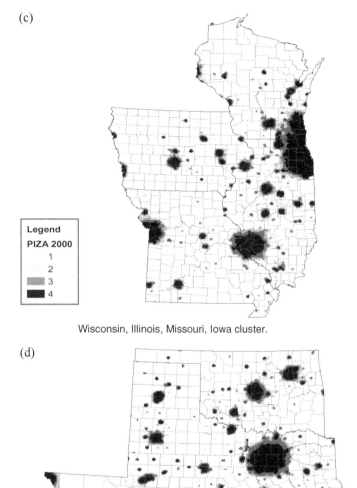

Legend
PIZA 2000
1
2
3
4

Wisconsin, Illinois, Missouri, Iowa cluster.

(d)

Legend
PIZA 2000
1
2
3
4

Texas, Oklahoma cluster.

Figure 2.4 PIZA classification for selected state clusters undergoing significant population-induced transition, 2000 (source: developed based on maps available from the Economic Research Service, US Department of Agriculture).

focusing on the land conversion process (see, for example, Miller and Plantinga 1999; Irwin and Geoghegan 2001; Bell and Irwin 2002; Irwin and Bockstael 2002; Carrion-Flores and Irwin 2004; Pfeffer *et al.* 2006),[9] on policies to reduce conversion rates (e.g. Pfeffer and Lapping 1994; Daniels 1999; Larson *et al.* 2001; Croissant and Munroe 2002; Lynch and Lovell 2003), and on integrating human activities with ecological measures of landscape to understand the dimensions of change (e.g. Jobin *et al.* 2003). From a theoretical perspective, the land conversion process exhibits multiple dimensions that lend complexity to understanding the process and its social, economic and environmental consequences (Parker *et al.* 2001, 2008). Additionally, the conversion process shapes the emerging new structure of agriculture; farms, food production systems and farm households by necessity must be adaptive. In this section, summaries of literature and data will be presented that identify key dimensions of the conversion process, related particularly to the interaction of population changes and the demographics of farms and farm households in transition zones.

In the United States, farms are heterogeneous in size as well as level of production. There is considerable concentration of commodity production, with about 10 percent of farms producing 75 percent of farm output (Hoppe *et al.* 2007). Almost all US farms are considered family farms, with a wide range of farm types: very large or large family farms (7.5 percent of total farms in 2004), medium-sales farming-occupation farms (6.3 percent), low-sales farming-occupation farms (18.8 percent), residential lifestyle farms (39.7 percent), retirement farms (16.1 percent), limited resource farms (9.4 percent) and nonfamily farms (2.2 percent) (Hoppe *et al.* 2007).[10] Shrestha and Findeis (2005) and Shrestha *et al.* (2006) show spatial clustering of US farms by type, scale and proximity to more densely populated centers (clustering of farms with more days of off-farm employment by the principal farm operator). Clustering is also apparent among farms receiving government payments.

As the US population increases, some states continue to have almost all state land in farms (e.g. Nebraska 93.6 percent of state land as farm land, Kansas 90.1 percent, South Dakota 89.6 percent in 2002); in such states, farm payments from government programs are comparatively large (Womach 2004). Farm land in states with urban populations typically covers less than 30 percent of state land (e.g. California 27.5 percent, Florida 29.7 percent, New York 25 percent and North Carolina 29 percent in 2002). Farms in population-influenced states are much smaller by multiple measures of farm size, and even when only "large farms" are compared. Farm land is fragmented, the likelihood of receiving farm subsidies is much lower, and average payments to farms receiving federal farm payments are substantially less (Womach 2004).

Figure 2.5 provides a broad characterization across the US landscape of variations in average farm size, state land in farm land, and receipt of farm subsidies. Data are from the 2002 Census of Agriculture and Womach (2004), with averages computed using state-level census data for states differentiated by longitude in five-degree increments; curves are fitted to averages across the states on the same longitude, taken across the United States (west–east orientation). Indicators include:

1   average farm size at the state level in hectares;
2   average percent of land at the state level classified as farm land; and
3   average percent of farms at the state level receiving farm subsidies (based on Womach (2004) statistics).

Figure 2.5 emphasizes the bifurcated structure of US agriculture between the US central midwest (where the demographics are such that population in many counties is being lost) and the east–west coastal zones, where the US population is concentrated and small- and medium-sized farms predominate the landscape. Documented farm numbers in some populated states have not declined, reflecting growth in small farm numbers, but also a concerted effort by the USDA National Agricultural Statistics Service to provide broader farm coverage in the national Census of Agriculture, particularly in recent years (2002, and again in 2007).

Differences in the structure of agriculture (farm size distribution) are evident coast-to-coast (Figure 2.5). This is also true across rural–exurban–urban transition gradients. The discussion that follows focuses on two important trends that influence agriculture and land use across transition zones. First, since the mid-twentieth century there has been strong growth in off-farm employment and income among the US population operating farms (Hallberg *et al.* 1991; Gardner

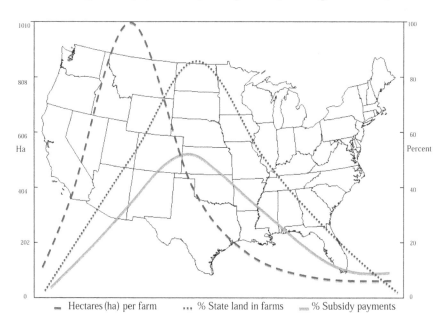

— Hectares (ha) per farm   ••• % State land in farms   ══ % Subsidy payments

Figure 2.5 Geospatial variations in farm land, farm size and percentages of farms receiving US farm subsidy support, 2002 (west–east orientation).

Note
Left axis indicates hectares per farm; right axis indicates the percent of state land in farms as well as the percent of farms receiving US farm subsidy payments as measured by Womach (2004).

1992; Corsi and Findeis 2000; Mishra *et al.* 2002; Findeis *et al.* 2005). This trend is attributed to greater population mobility, proximity to population and employment growth centers, and agricultural labor-saving technology diffusion (Hallberg *et al.* 1991; Gardner 1992; OECD 2001). Off-farm employment has absorbed underemployed farm household-firm labor, and off-farm income now financially supports almost all US farms, even large family-farm operations (Mishra *et al.* 2002). Trends toward substantially more off-farm employment and greater off-farm income dependence (nonfarm income from all sources) likely influence the use of environmentally sustainable farm practices targeted by agri-environmental policies and programs (Jayaraman and Findeis 2003). Whether there is variation along the transition zone gradient is an open question.

Second, we discuss the presence of a relatively large segment of the elderly US farm population that does not expect to be followed by a generation willing to farm. The presence of this population in population-influenced zones creates potential thresholds of farm transition from agriculture to other uses. The story becomes one not only about the emergence of a spatially bifurcated structure of agriculture where a significant proportion of the farm population works off-farm; it is also one in which farms operated by an aging population may transition out of agriculture and create irreversible changes in land and natural resource use in spaces proximate to where most of the US population lives.

To analyze these trends, we compare selected attributes of farms across the rural–exurban–urban transition gradient. We match household-level survey data collected from a 2001 Penn State survey ($n=2,661$) to PIZA classifications. The telephone survey, using the National Agricultural Statistics Service (NASS/USDA) sampling frame for US farms, was conducted by researchers at Pennsylvania State University in collaboration with the NASS and researchers at the Economic Research Service (ERS/USDA). The farm survey includes questions related to work choice and intensity (farm, off-farm, nonfarm business), intra-household decision-making, farm enterprise choice, use of farm practices that reduce environmental impact, land ownership and rent behaviors, intergenerational transfer of farm, and off-farm income dependence. Appended to these data are census and other secondary data on population growth (rate and absolute change), population density and other measures of urban pressure. We also use a 2001 survey of Pennsylvania agricultural household-firms ($n=1,250$) to gain additional insight into intentions for intergenerational farm transfer, farm sale and potential uncertainty over the farm's future. As shown previously by Figure 2.2, Pennsylvania is under significant urban influence and is a hotspot of agricultural transition that may provide important insights and lessons for the future.

More off-farm employment

Theoretically, there is a strong positive relationship between population density and access to off-farm employment (OECD 2001). Population growth and employment growth are known to be strongly correlated, and expected to lead to forms of agriculture in population-interaction zones that reflect a greater dependence of farm households on farm and nonfarm work, i.e. a higher degree of integration of farm and nonfarm economic activity (OECD 2001). This integration implies an agricultural sector in which decisions are especially complex. For example, the goal of farm profit maximization may not come first, followed by other farm household-firm decisions including off-farm labor supply. Under such conditions, a behavioral model that considers the integration of on-farm and off-farm activities is appropriate and even necessary to understand the decisions of people who farm, especially in transition zones (OECD 2001).

This raises important questions directly related to farm household-firm response to agri-environmental policies and programs: to what extent is farm response to policy influenced by the time dimensions of off-farm work? Does off-farm income influence decision-making regarding environmental outcomes in agriculture? Is compliance influenced by off-farm labor considerations, i.e. time constraints on management or capital differences? Jayaraman and Findeis (2003), Nehring *et al.* (2005) and Chang and Boisvert (2006a, 2006b) have found relationships between off-farm work, off-farm income, farm programs (including agri-environmental programs) and use of specific farm practices. Additionally, variations in agricultural and environmental practices and program participation are expected across the transition zone gradient, likely related to the population growth and diffusion processes.

Off-farm employment can be measured in several ways, resulting in some confusion in the policy dialogue. Measurement of an individual's off-farm employment can include:

1   off-farm work as the principal occupation or not (typically as opposed to farming as principal occupation);
2   participation in off-farm employment; or
3   time allocated to off-farm work.

Each measure provides a different perspective. Table 2.1, based on the Penn State national survey data, presents mean percentages for these measures across the PIZA classification for the United States. We report the average percentages of males and females in the surveyed US farm households classified by principal or main occupation as farming, hired farm manager, off-farm or nonfarm job, retirement or other (primarily homemaker, in school, unable to work or disabled); percent participating in off-farm work; and time allocated to off-farm work (weeks per year and hours per week). The means in Table 2.1 are pair-wise tested (t-tests), with means in those PIZA codes influenced by population interaction (i.e. PIZA = 2, 3, 4), each being tested against the mean value for PIZA 1 (most rural). The statistically significant results are indicated in Table 2.1 at alternative levels of significance.

Table 2.1 shows that for US males that operate farms (of any size), the response of "farming" as main occupation declines over the t-zone gradient, reflecting:

1   the greater likelihood of off-farm or nonfarm work as the principal form of work among males in urban-influenced places; and
2   the greater percentage of farms in t-zones operated by males who are retired and farming (retirement farms).

In the most urbanized places (PIZA 4), the percentage of males who consider off-farm work as their main occupation is 12 percentage points higher than in rural places not yet influenced by urban populations (PIZA 1). Slightly over one in five males living on farms in the most urbanized places are now retired, repre-

Table 2.1 Distribution of labor choices across PIZA gradient, based on 2001 US farm household survey data (full sample; not restricted to working-age population)

	PIZA gradient classification			
	1 %	*2* %	*3* %	*4* %
Main occupation				
Farming				
Male	46.8	39.3***	37.6***	30.3***
Female	31.9	25.9**	29.3	26.9
Hired farm manager				
Male	0.8	0.5	0.4	0.0
Female	0.4	1.1**	0.4	0.0
Off-farm or nonfarm job				
Male	29.8	36.5***	33.9*	41.8***
Female	40.9	44.7*	40.7	41.8
No male spouse present	5.8	6.1	10.4	9.0
Retirement farm				
Male	16.1	17.1	20.7**	22.1**
Female	12.4	12.4	17.0**	14.9
Other				
Male	6.5	6.8	7.4	5.7
Female	14.4	15.1	12.6***	16.4*
Off-farm participation rate				
Male	46.9	50.2	50.4	54.9**
Female	53.7	53.5	48.5*	51.5
Off-farm labor weeks (average weeks/year)				
Male	44.9	47.4***	47.9**	48.5**
Female	45.0	45.3	44.7	44.7
Off-farm labor hours (average hours/week)				
Male	41.2	41.6	42.1	44.0*
Female	35.7	35.4	35.1	33.1**

Notes
1 = minimal population interaction, 4 = most population interaction
Mean tests compare the PIZA class indicated to the most rural zone (PIZA = 1). Levels of significance are: * = 0.10, ** = 0.05, *** = 0.01.

senting a potential cohort of working farms among the elderly that will turn over in the relatively near future. Nine percent of farms in the most urbanized places are operated by women, in some cases widows holding onto farms. For females, there is little variation across the t-zone in the percentages of those reporting off-farm employment as their principal work. Only in PIZA 2 are the percentages higher for farm women reporting off-farm work as their principal occupation and lower for farming as primary. PIZA 2 roughly corresponds to "exurban." Women in urban areas are as likely to consider their main occupation "farming" as those in the most rural places. Note, however, the percentage (17 percent) of women who are retired, and who have farms in PIZA 3, suburban areas. This too represents a cohort of farms that could potentially turn to other uses as these women age and population pressure increases in suburban areas.

Differences across the PIZA gradient are generally less pronounced for males and females when the probability of off-farm employment is measured. Roughly half of males and females living on farms in the United States hold off-farm jobs, with these percentages even higher when the sample is restricted to the working-age population. The off-farm participation rate among all US male farm operators ranges between 46.9 percent in PIZA 1 (most rural) to 54.9 percent in PIZA 4 (most urban). When the sample is restricted to working ages (less than 65 years, by Department of Labor standards), the range is 55.9 percent (PIZA 1) to 68.97 percent (PIZA 4). For farm women, off-farm work rates range from 48.5 percent (PIZA 3) to 53.7 percent in PIZA 1; women are more likely to report off-farm work in the most rural places. Restricting the sample to working-age women on US farms, the percentages range from 60.98 percent (PIZA 3) to 66.67 percent (PIZA 4).

Finally, Table 2.1 includes means of weeks and hours per week of off-farm work (measures of off-farm work intensity, for those reporting off-farm work). Differences in means are again observed across the transition zone gradient for males; on average, males operating farms in PIZA 2, 3 or 4 work more weeks per year off the farm as compared to PIZA 1; in PIZA 4 they work more hours per week (an average 44 hours per week). For females, there is no statistically significant variation in number of weeks per year across the t-zone (averages range from 44.7 to 45 weeks per year), but females living on farms in the most urbanized places work fewer hours per week off-farm as compared to the most rural places of the United States. These inverse trends (males reporting more off-farm work in urban areas and females reporting more in rural areas) raise questions concerning the relationships among the types of farms located in urban areas, the family labor requirements of these farms, and household decision-making related to income sources.

Although many farm households now work off-farm, work intensity and principal occupation in particular appear to differ across the population-driven transition zone gradient. Why this is important is that engagement in off-farm work likely influences the amount of time available for farming (management and labor time), timing of work time on the farm, ability to borrow capital and participation in government farm programs, both in general and in specific programs (Jayaraman and

Findeis 2003; Chang and Boisvert 2006a, 2006b). The strong interrelationships between proximity to and interactions with human populations and off-farm work mean that the design of agri-environmental programs should take off-farm employment into consideration, particularly those programs most critical to urbanizing places. Chang and Boisvert (2006b) report "substantial evidence" that off-farm work decisions and the decision to participate in the Conservation Reserve Program (CRP) are made simultaneously, not independently. Jayaraman and Findeis (2003) find that selected farm practices are made jointly with off-farm work decisions. The male's off-farm work decision and utilization of most sustainable practices are jointly determined. The female's off-farm work decision is generally less likely to be made simultaneously with specific farm practices. Both male and female decisions to work off-farm are correlated with use of manure on cropland and rotation of livestock on pasture (Jayaraman and Findeis 2003).

More aged farmers and more retirement farms

Hoppe *et al.* (2007) argue that "One of the most striking characteristics of US agriculture is the advanced age of principal farm operators compared with other self-employed workers" (p. 12). In 2004, 27 percent of farm operators were 65 or older in the United States; this compares to 8 percent of self-employed workers, according to the US Department of Labor in 2005 (as reported in Hoppe *et al.* 2007). Furthermore, USDA's Economic Research Service has shown that "Each farm type – except residential/lifestyle farms – had a larger share of operators who were at least 65 than was true for the nonfarm self-employed" (Hoppe *et al.* 2007: 12). Gale (2002) observes that farmers are farming into old age, influenced by better health, increased longevity and the potential for farming as a part-time retirement activity in the United States. Improvements in technology have also affected the ability to farm into old age. Each year the age of US farm operators increases (Allen and Harris 2005). Phimister (1994), Kimhi (1994), Keating (1996), Stover and Helling (1998), Pesquin *et al.* (1999), Rangel (2000), Fan (2001), Errington (2001), Glauben *et al.* (2004) and Kimhi and Nachlieli (2001) have demonstrated the complexity of the intergenerational transfer process and effects.

There is debate as to whether these differences could have negative implications for US agriculture, with researchers on both sides of the argument (see Hoppe and Banker 2006; Gale 2002). While in aggregate the impacts on farm production may not be large (due to the multigenerational structure of many large farms in the US midwest), the impacts may be strongly differentiated by location and farm size. The age structure of the farm population raises concern in urban, suburban and exurban places where farms provide open space. The National Agricultural Statistics Service recently estimated that up to 50 percent of farm land in Oregon will turn over in the next 10–15 years (NASS 2007). But, again, continued high farm prices could turn the situation around.

In Pennsylvania, one-third of farm households report that they do not expect their children to eventually operate the farm or report having no children (Table

2.2). Another one-fifth "don't know" when asked if they expect the next generation to operate the family farm. Only about 40 percent of farms in Pennsylvania (about two in five) expect their children to eventually operate the farm. Means tests across PIZA classifications show that farm families in Pennsylvania's most urban places are the most unlikely to expect the next generation to farm (50.5 percent responded "unlikely" or "no children"). Interestingly, farm households in PIZA 2 (exurban zones) report being more likely to expect their children to continue operating the farm than farms in the most rural locations in the state (PIZA 1). Farms in PIZA 2 are located where off-farm work is more likely than in the most rural places in Pennsylvania. It is the combination of farm and off-farm work and income across the farm household-firm that is maintaining the vast majority of family farm operations in the United States.

When reporting that the next generation is unlikely to farm, respondents were also asked to supply reasons for this prediction; Table 2.2 also documents these reasons. The effects of urban pressure are apparent for the highest population-interaction zones; operators of farms found in PIZA 3 and 4 are more likely to report that urban pressure is among the important reasons why the next generation is unlikely to continue farming their farm. In the most urban locations, declining farm numbers coupled with future plans for farm sale are also frequently cited as a major reason (see Lynch and Carpenter 2003 for discussion of

Table 2.2 Expectations of Pennsylvania farm land intergenerational transfer, based on 2001 Pennsylvania farm household survey data

	PIZA gradient classification			
	1 %	*2* %	*3* %	*4* %
Expectation of farmland transfer to next generation (own children)				
Not likely/no children	37.9	33.9	33.5	50.5**
Likely	40.1	48.3***	42.9	33.7
Don't know	22.0	17.8	23.6	15.8
Reasons why next generation may not take over farm (multiple answers allowed)				
Urban pressure	6.9	12.1	14.4**	51.2***
Declining farm numbers in local area/plan to sell land	25.2	27.7	26.5	55.0***
Potential for higher returns to labor in other occupations	71.9	73.3	70.7	62.5
Low returns to farming	62.1	69.4	66.4	61.0
Lack of interest by next generation	61.5	57.3	61.3	52.6
Other, including children, already own other farm	11.9	16.3	11.8	15.0

Notes
1 = minimal population interaction, 4 = most population interaction.
Mean tests compare the PIZA class indicated to the most rural zone (PIZA = 1). Levels of significance are: * = 0.10, ** = 0.05, *** = 0.01.

the agriculture critical mass issue). But perhaps even more importantly, regardless of location, low returns to agriculture, the potential for higher returns in other occupations, and lack of interest (in farming) by the next generation are overwhelmingly given as reasons that some Pennsylvania farms will not be operated by the next generation.

In places like Pennsylvania where the population is among the oldest in the nation and where the farm landscape in many of the state's counties is population-influenced, the turnover in farm ownership that could take place over the next two decades will provide opportunities for farm entrepreneurs, but the turnover could also as likely result in land conversion from agricultural to residential or commercial, and additional fragmentation of an already fragmented landscape. Growth and diffusion of the population coupled with the aging of the farm population creates the incentive for land conversion on a scale that could be significant. Pennsylvania is not the only state in the United States where this turnover could occur.

Concluding discussion

Three demographic trends are expected to strongly influence land use and the structure of agriculture in places proximate to urban populations worldwide:

1   growth of human population coupled with increases in consumption in some places;
2   greater population mobility; and
3   an increasingly aged population in many parts of the world.

Human demographic trends pose a major threat to global ecosystems and landscapes, as human population concentrates in urban centers but eventually spreads across the land. Issues of how to feed the growing urban population arise, amid concern over environmental impacts. The need for well-designed agri-environmental policies and programs is clear.

The United States shares in population growth and spillover impacts from urban centers, high levels of population mobility and continual year-by-year increases in the average age of the population and of farmers. Aggregate statistics on changes in farm land and in the structure of agriculture obscure regional and local hotspots of rural–exurban–urban transition. Historically, the transition process has characterized coastal states in the United States. But transition zone hotspots are now being increasingly observed in states long considered as important agricultural states – Indiana, Illinois, Pennsylvania and Michigan, as examples. Under conditions first of population interaction and then of population pressure for other land uses, the structure of agriculture and land use across the nation's transition zones is undergoing significant change.

Agriculture in population-influenced places is challenged to be "adaptive," i.e. willing to seize new opportunities as the transition unfolds. On population-influenced landscapes, a new structure of agriculture has emerged and continues to develop. This new structure is focused on niche markets, short supply chains, direct marketing to consumers, provision of services, multifunctional uses of farm land. Some argue that this new environment presents agriculture with the most significant opportunities in the past 50 years. Further, as documented in this chapter, many farms operating across transition zones in the United States routinely combine farm and off-farm work and income to maintain economic viability. The trend toward more dependence on off-farm employment by US farm households represents a shift attributable to population growth, associated employment growth and higher off-farm wages. Because decisions regarding off-farm work, farm program participation and use of specific farm practices are closely interrelated, the design of agri-environmental policies and programs must take this key dimension of farm household-firm behavior into account.

Finally, in regional and local hotspots of rural–exurban–urban transition, the aging of the US farm population raises the potential of near-future higher rates of farmland turnover. Across transition zones, the current population-age structure constitutes a major threat. As shown in this chapter, in states like Pennsylvania, a significant number of farms report that the next generation is unlikely to take up farming. In part this expectation is attributed to population pressure and the exit of other local farms, but the most commonly given reasons relate to low returns to farming and the potential for better jobs elsewhere. The unanswered question is whether recent higher farm prices, new bio-energy alternatives, and/ or farm policy reforms can reduce the century-long exodus from US agriculture. Additional policies should focus on agriculture in population-influenced areas, and support the affordable transition of farms to young and beginning farmers not necessarily related to current owners.

Notes

1 For simplicity, the term "exurban" will be used throughout the chapter to represent places at the rural–urban interface – peri-urban, suburban, exurban. It is recognized that definitional differences exist.
2 See discussion in Lambert *et al.* (2006) on agri-environmental program participation.
3 For alternative definitions and measures of sprawl, see Torrens and Alberti (2000).
4 The elderly dependency rate is defined as the ratio of the population aged 65 years and above to the working-age population.
5 The overall rate of growth of urban land area was reported to be about twice the rate of population growth (Lubowski *et al.* 2006a).
6 For statistics, see figures 9 and 10 (pp. 34, 35) in Claassen *et al.* 2001.
7 Berube *et al.* (2006) for The Brookings Institution identified exurban places in the United States, providing an in-depth analysis of the exurbs that included demographics, change and regional comparisons. See also Clark *et al.* (2006) for exurban typology based on the US Department of Energy's Oak Ridge National Laboratory LandScan population distribution model.
8 Note that PIZA 4 areas have been fully removed to more clearly show the remaining areas.
9 Also, refer to the land-use literatures of geography, planning, regional science and rural sociology. See also Axelrod (1997), Berger (2001) and Parker *et al.* (2001).
10 The Economic Research Service uses $250,000 annual farm sales or more as the cut-off between large and small farms. Medium-size farms are included in the small category.

34   *J.L. Findeis* et al.

References

Ahearn, M. and Alig, R. (2006) "A Discussion of Recent Land-use Trends," in K. Bell, K. Boyle and J. Rubin (eds.), *Economics of Rural Land-Use Change*, Aldershot: Ashgate. Online, available at: www.ashgate.com/default.aspx?page=637&seriestitleID =149&calcTitle=1&forthcoming=1&title_id=5953&edition_id=6343.

Allen, R. and Harris, G. (2005) "What We Know About the Demographics of US Farm Operators," *Agricultural Outlook Forum 2005*, Washington, DC: US Department of Agriculture, National Agricultural Statistics Service, 12 pp. Online, available at: http:// ageconsearch.umn.edu/bitstream/32823/1/fo05al01.pdf.

Alter, T., Bridger, J., Findeis, J., Kelsey, T., Luloff, A., McLaughlin, D. and Shuffstall, W. (2007) "Strengthening Rural Pennsylvania: an Integrated Approach to a Prosperous Commonwealth," *Research Brief*, Washington, DC: The Brookings Institution, Metropolitan Policy Program. Online, available at: www3.brookings.edu/metro/pubs/ruralpa.pdf.

Axelrod, R. (1997) *The Complexity of Cooperation*, Princeton: Princeton University Press. Online, available at: http://press.princeton.edu/titles/6144.html.

Barnard, C. (2005) "Population Interaction Zones for Agriculture," *Amber Waves*, June. Washington, DC: Economic Research Service, US Department of Agriculture. Online, available at: www.ers.usda.gov/AmberWaves/June05/Indicators/behinddata.htm.

Batie, S. (2003) "The Multi-function Attributes of Northeastern Agriculture: a Research Agenda," *Agricultural and Resources Economics Review*, 32(1): 1–8. Online, available at: http://findarticles.com/p/articles/mi_qa4046/is_200304/ai_n9189249/print.

Bell, K. and Irwin, E. (2002) "Spatially Explicit Micro-level Modeling of Land Use Change at the Rural–Urban Interface," *Agricultural Economics*, 27: 217–232. Online, available at: www.sciencedirect.com/science?_ob=MImg&_imagekey=B6T3V-472BJ99-1-17&_ cdi=4956&_user=209810&_orig=search&_coverDate=11%2F30%2F2002&_ sk=999729996&view=c&wchp=dGLbVzb-zSkzV&md5=9737f5598086cdd0040db0c3a 8952ca6&ie=/sdarticle.pdf.

Berger, T. (2001) "Agent-based Spatial Models Applied to Agriculture: a Simulation Tool for Technology Diffusion, Resource Use Changes and Policy Analysis," *Agricultural Economics*, 25: 245–260. Online, available at: www.blackwell-synergy.com/ action/showPdf?submitPDF=Full+Text+PDF+%281%2C845+KB%29&doi=10.1111 %2Fj.1574-0862.2001.tb00205.x.

Berube, A., Singer, A., Wilson, J. and Frey, W. (2006) "Finding Exurbia: Americas Fast-growing Communities at the Metropolitan Fringe," Washington, DC: The Brookings Institution, Metropolitan Policy Program. Online, available at: www.brookings.edu/~/ media/Files/rc/reports/2006/10metropolitanpolicy_berube/20061017_exurbia.pdf.

Brookings Institution, The (2004) "Back to Prosperity: A Competitive Agenda for Renewing Pennsylvania," Washington, DC: The Brookings Institution. Online, available at: www.brookings.edu/reports/2003/12metropolitanpolicy_pennsylvania.aspx.

Brown, D., Johnson, K., Loveland, T. and Theobald, D. (2005) "Rural Land-use Trends in the Conterminous United States, 1950–2000," *Ecological Applications*, 15(6): 1851–1863. Online, available at: www-personal.umich.edu/~danbrown/papers/ecolapps_reprint.pdf.

Brown, D., Walker, R., Manson, S. and Seto, K. (2004) "Modeling Land Use and Land Cover Change," in G. Gutman, A. Janetos, C. Justice, E. Moran, J. Mustard, R. Rindfuss, D. Skole and B. Turner (eds.), *Land Change Science: Observing, Monitoring, and Understanding Trajectories of Change on the Earth's Surface*, Dordrecht, Netherlands: Kluwer Academic Publishers, pp. 395–409. Online, available at: www.springerlink. com/content/w6576387v7n63631/fulltext.pdf.

Carrion-Flores, C. and Irwin, E. (2004) "Determinants of Residential Land-use Conversion and Sprawl at the Rural–Urban Fringe," *American Journal of Agricultural Economics*, 86(4): 889–904. Online, available at: www.blackwell-synergy.com/doi/pdf/10.1111/j.0002–9092.2004.00641.x.

Chang, H. and Boisvert, R. (2006a) "Does Participation in the Conservation Reserve Program and Off-farm Work Affect the Level and Distribution of Farm Household Incomes?" selected paper prepared for presentation at the American Agricultural Economic Association Annual Meetings, Long Beach, California, July 23–26, 2006. Online, available at: http://ageconsearch.umn.edu/bitstream/21277/1/sp06bo01.pdf.

Chang, H. and Boisvert, R. (2006b) "Participation in the Conservation Reserve Program and Off-farm Work: Implications for Farm and Farm Household Productivity," selected paper prepared for presentation at the American Agricultural Economic Association Annual Meetings, Long Beach, California, July 23–26, 2006. Online, available at: http://ageconsearch.umn.edu/bitstream/21147/1/sp06ch04.pdf.

Claassen, R., Hansen, L., Peters, M., Brenneman, V., Weinberg, M., Cattaneo, A., Feather, P., Gatsby, D., Hellerstein, D., Hopkins, J., Johnston, P., Morehart, M. and Smith, M. (2001) *Agri-environmental Policy at the Crossroads: Guideposts on a Changing Landscape*, Agricultural Economic Report Number 794, Washington, DC: US Department of Agriculture, Economic Research Service. Online, available at: www.agecon.lsu.edu/WebClasses/AGEC7603/Literature/Claassen%20et%20al%20introduction.pdf.

Clark, J., Munroe, D. and Irwin, E. (2006) "Exurban Settlement Pattern and the Exurban Condition: A Typology of US Metropolitan Areas," paper presented at the 53rd Annual North American Meetings of the Regional Science Association, Toronto. November.

Combes, P. and Overman, H. (2004) "The Spatial Distribution of Economic Activities in the European Union," in V. Henderson and J. Thiese (eds.), *Handbook of Urban and Regional Economics*, Volume 4, Amsterdam: Elsevier, pp. 2845–2909. Online, available at: http://team.univ-paris1.fr/teamperso/mayer/Cours/DEA_geo/combes_overman.pdf.

Corsi, A. and Findeis, J. (2000) "True State Dependence and Heterogeneity in Off-farm Labour Participation," *European Review of Agricultural Economics*, 27(2): 127–151. Online, available at: http://papers.ssrn.com/sol3/papers.cfm?abstract_id=231739.

Croissant, C. and Munroe, D. (2002) "Zoning and Fragmentation of Agricultural and Forest Land on Residential Parcels in Monroe County, Indiana," *Geography Research Forum*, 22: 91–109. Online, available at: www.geog.bgu.ac.il/grf/files/vol. 22.pdf.

Daniels, T. (1999) *When City and Country Collide: Managing Growth in the Metropolitan Fringe*, Washington, DC: Island Press. Online, available at: http://thegreenpages.ca/portal/ca/2006/10/when_city_country_collide_mana.html.

Entwisle, B. and Stern, P. (2005) "Population, Land Use and Environment: Research Directions," *National Research Council*, The National Academies Press. Online, available at: www.nap.edu/catalog.php?record_id=11439#toc.

Errington, A. (2001) "Handing Over the Reins: a Comparative Study of Intergenerational Farm Transfers in England, France, Canada and the USA," paper presented at the Agricultural Economics Society Annual Meeting, Aberystwyth, UK, April. Online, available at: www.rics.org/NR/rdonlyres/18AE8D09-C5AC-42D4–97C4-BCC286484EBD/0/handing_over_the_reins_2001016.pdf.

Fan, C. (2001) "A Model of Intergenerational Transfers," *Economic Theory*, 17: 399–418. Online, available at: www.springerlink.com/content/ula0dx4ntuxu68r5/fulltext.pdf.

FAO (1999) "Linkages Between Rural Population Ageing, Intergenerational Transfer of Land and Agricultural Production: Are They Important?" (web resource). Online, available at: www.fao.org/sd/wpdirect/wpan0039.htm.

FAO (2008) "Soaring Food Prices: Facts, Perspectives, Impacts and Actions Required." High Level Conference on Food Security: The Challenges of Climate Change and Bioenergy, Rome, June (web resource). Online, available at: www.fao.org/fileadmin/user_upload/foodclimate/HLCdocs/HLC08-inf-1-E.pdf.

Findeis, J., Swaminathan, H. and Jayaraman, A. (2005) "Agricultural Households in the US: Participation in Labor, Decision-making, and the Effects of Farm Asset Control," *Economie Rurale*, 289/290: 44–62.

Gale, F. (2002) "The Graying Farm Sector: Legacy of Off-farm Migration," *Rural America*, US Department of Agriculture, Economic Research Service, 17(3): 28–31. Online, available at: http://ers.usda.gov/publications/ruralamerica/ra173/ra173e.pdf.

Gardner, B. (1992) "Changing Economic Perspectives on the Farm Problem," *Journal of Economic Literature*, 30(1): 62–101. Online, available at: www.jstor.org/stable/2727879.

Glauben, T., Tietje, H. and Weiss, C. (2004) "Intergenerational Succession in Farm Households: Evidence From Upper Austria," *Review of Economics of the Household*, 2(4): 443–462. Online, available at: www.springerlink.com/content/g152770k41v56v38/fulltext.pdf.

Grimm, N., Grove, J., Redman, C. and Pickett, S. (2000) "Integrated Approaches to Long-term Studies of Urban Ecological Systems," *Bioscience*, 50(7): 571–584. Online, available at: www.bioone.org/archive/0006–3568/50/7/pdf/i0006–3568–50–7–571.pdf.

Hallberg, M., Findeis, J. and Lass, D. (1991) *Multiple Job-Holding Among Farm Families*, Ames, Iowa: Iowa State University Press. Online, available at: www.fao.org/agris/search/display.do?f=./1993/v1901/US9181334.xml;US9181334.

Hellerstein, D., Nickerson, C., Cooper, J., Feather, P., Gadsby, D., Mullarkey, D., Tegene, A. and Barnard, C. (2002) "Farmland Protection: The Role of Public Preferences for Rural Amenities," *AER-815*, Washington, DC: US Department of Agriculture, Economic Research Service. Online, available at: www.ers.usda.gov/publications/aer815/aer815.pdf.

Hoppe, R. and Banker, D. (2006) "Structure and Finances of US Farms: 2005 Farm Family Report," *EIB-12*, Washington, DC: US Department of Agriculture, Economic Research Service. Online, available at: www.ers.usda.gov/publications/EIB12/EIB12.pdf.

Hoppe, R., Korb, P., O'Donoghue, E. and Banker, D. (2007) "Structure and Finances of US Farms: Family Farm Report, 2007 edition," *EIB-24*, Washington, DC: US Department of Agriculture, Economic Research Service. Online, available at: www.ers.usda.gov/publications/eib24/eib24.pdf.

Irwin, E. and Bockstael, N. (2002) "Interacting Agents, Spatial Externalities and the Evolution of Residential Land Use Patterns," *Journal of Economic Geography*, 2: 31–54. Online, available at: http://joeg.oxfordjournals.org/cgi/reprint/2/1/31.

Irwin, E. and Geoghegan, J. (2001) "Theory, Data, Methods: Developing Spatially Explicit Economic Models of Land Use Change," *Agriculture, Ecosystems and Environment*, 85: 7–23. Online, available at: www.sciencedirect.com/science?_ob=MImg&_imagekey=B6T3Y-433P6Y4-G-T&_cdi=4959&_user=209810&_orig=search&_coverDate=06%2F30%2F2001&_sk=999149998&view=c&wchp=dGLzVzz-zSkWW&md5=c4edcbc854c3a2fcc60e2ec087d5db1e&ie=/sdarticle.pdf.

Jayaraman, A. and Findeis, J. (2003) "His Work, Her Work, and the Operation of the Farm: Making Adjustments to Off-farm Employment," paper presented at the 2003 American Agricultural Economics Association (AAEA) Annual Meeting, Montreal, July. Online, available at: http://ageconsearch.umn.edu/bitstream/22218/1/sp03ja02.pdf.

Jobin, B., Beaulieu, J., Grenier, M., Belanger, L., Maisonneuve, C., Bordage, D. and Filion, B. (2003) "Landscape Changes and Ecological Studies in Agricultural Regions, Quebec, Canada," *Landscape Ecology*, 18: 575–590. Online, available at: www.spring-erlink.com/content/v762413016373v6p/.

Keating, N. (1996) "Legacy, Aging and Succession in Farm Families," *Generations*, 20(3): 61–64.

Kimhi, A. (1994) "Optimal Timing of Farm Transferal from Parent to Child," *American Journal of Agricultural Economics*, 76(2): 228–236. Online, available at: www.jstor.org/stable/pdfplus/1243624.pdf.

Kimhi, A. and Nachlieli, N. (2001) "Intergenerational Succession on Israeli Family Farms, 1971–1988," *Journal of Agricultural Economics*, 52(2): 42–58. Online, available at: http://departments.agri.huji.ac.il/economics/noga4.pdf.

Lambert, D., Sullivan, P., Claassen, R. and Foreman, L. (2006) "Conservation-compatible Practices and Programs: Who Participates?" *ERR-14*, Washington, DC: US Department of Agriculture, Economic Research Service. Online, available at: www.ers.usda.gov/publications/err14/err14.pdf.

Larson, J., Findeis, J. and Smith, S. (2001) "Agricultural Adaptation to Urbanization in Southeastern Pennsylvania," *Agricultural and Resource Economics Review*, 30(1): 32–43. Online, available at: http://ageconsearch.umn.edu/bitstream/31609/1/30010032.pdf.

Liu, J., Dietz, T., Carpenter, S., Alberti, M., Folke, C., Moran, E., Pell, A., Deadman, P., Kratz, T., Luchenko, J., Ostrom, E., Ouyang, Z., Provencher, W., Redman, C., Schneider, S. and Taylor, W. (2007) "Complexity of Coupled Human and Natural Systems," *Science*, 317(14 Sept.): 1513–1516. Online, available at: www.sciencemag.org/cgi/reprint/317/5844/1513.pdf.

Lubowski, R. (2002) "Determinants of Land-use Transitions in the United States: Econometric Analysis of Changes Among the Major Land-use Categories." PhD dissertation. Cambridge: Harvard University.

Lubowski, R., Bucholtz, S., Claassen, R., Roberts, M., Cooper, J., Gueorgieva, A. and Johansson, R. (2006a) "Environmental Effects of Agricultural Land-use Change: The Role of Economics and Policy," *Economic Research Report Number 25*, Washington, DC: US Department of Agriculture, Economic Research Service. Online, available at: www.ers.usda.gov/Publications/ERR25/.

Lubowski, R., Vesterby, M., Bucholtz, S., Baez, A. and Roberts, M. (2006b) "Major Uses of Land in the United States, 2002," *EIB-14*, Washington, DC: US Department of Agriculture, Economic Research Service. Online, available at: www.ers.usda.gov/publications/EIB14/eib14.pdf.

Lynch, L. and Carpenter, J. (2003) "Is There Evidence of a Critical Mass in the Mid-Atlantic Agriculture Sector Between 1949 and 1997?" *Agricultural and Resource Economics Review*, 32(1): 116–128. Online, available at: http://ageconsearch.umn.edu/bitstream/31348/1/32010116.pdf.

Lynch, L. and Lovell, S. (2003) "Combining Spatial and Survey Data to Explain Participation in Agricultural Land Preservation Programs," *Land Economics*, 79(2): 259–276. Online, available at: www.jstor.org/stable/pdfplus/3146870.pdf.

Millennium Ecosystem Assessment (MEA) Assessment Board (2005) R. Hassan, R. Scholes and N. Ash (eds.), *Ecosystems and Human Well-being: Current State and Trends, Vol. 1*, Washington, DC: Island Press. Online, available at: www.nhbs.com/ecosystems_and_human_well_being_current_state_and_tefno_140381.html.

Miller, D. and Plantinga, A. (1999) "Modeling Land Use Decisions with Aggregate Data," *American Journal of Agricultural Economics*, 81(1): 180–194. Online, available at: www.jstor.org/stable/pdfplus/1244459.pdf.

Miller, J. and Page, S. (2007) *Complex Adaptive Systems: An Introduction to Computational Models of Social Life*, Princeton: Princeton University Press. Online, available at: http://press.princeton.edu/titles/8429.html.

Mishra, A., El-Osta, H., Morehart, M., Johnson, J. and Hopkins, J. (2002) "Income, Wealth, and the Economic Well-being of Farm Households," *Agricultural Economic Report Number 812*. Washington, DC: US Department of Agriculture, Economic Research Service. Online, available at: www.ers.usda.gov/publications/aer812/aer812b.pdf.

National Agricultural Statistics Service (NASS/USDA) (2007) "Aging Farm Population and Implications for Land Use," The State of Oregon Agriculture, pp. 89–91. Online, available at: http://oregon.gov/ODA/docs/pdf/bd_rpt_age.pdf.

Nehring, R., Fernandez-Cornejo, J. and Banker, D. (2005) "Off-farm Labour and the Structure of US Agriculture: The Case of Corn Soybean Farms," *Applied Economics*, 37(6): 633–649. Online, available at: http://dx.doi.org/10.1080/0003684042000323582.

Organization for Economic Cooperation and Development (2001) *Agricultural Policy Reform and Farm Employment*, Paris: Organization for Economic Cooperation and Development (OECD) (AGR/CA/APR(2001)10/FINAL). Online, available at: www.olis.oecd.org/olis/2001doc.nsf/c707a7b4806fa95dc125685d005300b6/c1256985004c66e3c1256a9b003a5ab6/$FILE/JT00111306.PDF.

Organization for Economic Cooperation and Development (2006) *Society at a Glance: OECD Social Indicators*, Paris: Organization for Economic Cooperation and Development (OECD). Online, available at: www.oecd.org/document/24/0,2340,fr_2825_4971 18_2671576_1_1_1_1,00.html.

Organization for Economic Cooperation and Development (2007) *Regions at a Glance*, Paris: Organization for Economic Cooperation and Development (OECD). Online, available at: www.oecd.org/document/61/0,3343,en_2649_37429_38690301_1_1_1_3 7429,00.html.

Parker, D., Berger, T. and Manson, S. (2001) "Agent-based Models of Land-use and Land-cover Change," Report and Review of an International Workshop, October 4–7. *LUCC Report Series No. 6*, Irvine, California. Online, available at: www.globalland-project.org/Documents/LUCC_No_6.pdf.

Parker, D., Entwisle, B., Rindfuss, R., Vanwey, L., Manson, S., Moran, E., An, L., Deadman, P., Evans, T., Linderman, M., Rizi, S. and Malanson, G. (2008) "Case Studies, Cross-site Comparisons, and the Challenge of Generalizations: Comparing Agent-based Models of Land-use Change in Frontier Regions," *Journal of Land Use Studies*, 3(1): 41–72.

Pendall, R. (2003) *Sprawl Without Growth: The Upstate Paradox*, Washington, DC: The Brookings Institution. Online, available at: www.brookings.edu/es/urban/publications/200310_Pendall.pdf.

Pesquin, C., Kimhi, A. and Kislev, Y. (1999) "Old Age Security and Inter-generational Transfer of Family Farms," *European Review of Agricultural Economics*, 26(1): 19–37. Online, available at: http://erae.oxfordjournals.org/cgi/reprint/26/1/19.

Pfeffer, M. and Lapping, M. (1994) "Farmland Preservation, Development Rights, and the Theory of the Growth Machine: The Views of Planners," *Journal of Rural Studies*, 10(3): 233–248. Online, available at: www.sciencedirect.com/science?_ob=MImg&_imagekey=B6VD9–469WW5S-1–1&_cdi=5977&_user=209810&_orig=search&_coverDate=07%2F31%2F1994&_sk=999899996&view=c&wchp=dGLbVtz-zSkzk&md5=9c09c2c5f3ac5197e272d8106aa4e8ac&ie=/sdarticle.pdf.

Pfeffer, M., Francis, J. and Ross, Z. (2006) "Fifty Years of Farmland Change: Urbanization, Population Growth, and the Changing Farm Economy," in W. Kandel and D. Brown (eds.), *Population Change and Rural Society*, pp. 103–129. Netherlands: Springer. Online, available at: www.springerlink.com/content/u71486531782vku0/fulltext.pdf.

Phimister, E. (1994) "The Impact of Intergenerational Farm Asset Transfer Mechanisms: an Application of a Life Cycle Model with Borrowing Constraints and Adjustment Costs," in F. Caillavet, H. Guyomard and R. Lifran (eds.), *Agricultural Household Modelling and Family Economics*, pp. 169–189. Developments in Agricultural Economics, volume 10. Amsterdam: Elsevier.

Rangel, A. (2000) "Forward and Backward Intergenerational Goods: a Theory of Intergenerational Exchange," NBER Working Paper No. 7518, Cambridge: National Bureau of Economic Research. Online, available at: www.nber.org/papers/w7518.pdf.

Rindfuss, R., Walsh, S., Turner, II, B., Fox, J. and Mishra, V. (2004) "Developing a Science of Land Change: Challenges and Methodological Issues," *Proceedings of the National Academy of Sciences (PNAS)*, 101: 13976–13981. Online, available at: www. pnas.org/cgi/reprint/101/39/13976.

Robinson, D., Brown, D., Parker, D., Shreinermachers, P., Janssen, M., Huigen, M., Wittmer, H., Gotts, N., Promburom, P., Irwin, E., Berger, T., Gatzweiler, F. and Barnaud, C. (2007) "Comparison of Empirical Methods for Building Agent-based Models in Land Use Science," *Journal of Land Use Science*, 2(1): 31–55. Online, available at: www.public.asu.edu/~majansse/pubs/robinson2007.pdf.

Schachter, J., Franklin, R. and Perry, M. (2003) "Migration and Geographic Mobility in Metropolitan and Nonmetropolitan America: 1995 to 2000," Census 2000 Special Reports. Washington, DC: US Department of Commerce, US Census Bureau, Census 2000. Online, available at: www.census.gov/prod/2003pubs/censr-9.pdf.

Sharp, J. and Clark, J. (2008) "Between the Country and the Concrete: Rediscovering the Rural Urban Fringe," *City & Community*, 7(1): 61–79. Online, available at: www. ingentaconnect.com/content/bpl/cico/2008/00000007/00000001/art00005.

Shrestha, S. and Findeis, J. (2005) "Space, Government Payments, and Off-farm Labor Response of Principal Farm Operators: A County Level Analysis," selected paper presented at the Annual Meetings of the American Agricultural Economics Association, Providence, RI, August. Online, available at: http://ageconsearch.umn.edu/bitstream/19511/1/sp05sh04.pdf.

Shrestha, S., Findeis, J. and Smith, S. (2006) "Spatial Aspects of Government Farm Payments and Farm Structure in the US," paper presented at the 2006 Annual Meetings of the Southern Regional Science Association. St. Augustine, Florida, March/April.

Stover, R. and Helling, M. (1998) "Goals and Principles of the Intergenerational Transfer of the Family Farm," *Free Inquiry in Creative Sociology*, 26(2): 201–212.

Torrens, P. and Alberti, M. (2000) "Measuring Sprawl," Working Paper 27, Centre for Advanced Spatial Analysis (CASA). Online, available at: www.casa.ucl.ac.uk/working_papers/Paper27.pdf.

United Nations Population Fund (UNFPA) (2007) "State of World Population 2007: Unleashing the Potential of Urban Growth." Online, available at: www.unfpa.org/swp.

US Census Bureau (2004). Online, available at: www.census.gov.

Vesterby, M. and Heimlich, R. (1991) "Land Use and Demographic Change: Results from Fast-growth Counties," *Land Economics*, 67(3): 279–291. Online, available at: www.jstor.org/stable/pdfplus/3146423.pdf.

Vesterby, M. and Krupa, K. (2001) "Major Uses of Land in the United States, 1997," *SB-973*, Washington, DC: US Department of Agriculture, Economic Research Service. Online, available at: www.ers.usda.gov/publications/sb973/sb973.pdf.

Vitousek, P., Mooney, H., Luchenko, J. and Melillo, J. (1997) "Human Domination of Earth's Ecosystems," *Science*, 277: 494–499. Online, available at: http://magmo.typepad.com/VitousekHumanDomination.pdf.

Womach, J. (2004) "Average Farm Subsidy Payments, by State, 2002," Washington, DC: Congressional Reporting Service Report for Congress (web resource). Online, available at: www.ncseonline.org/NLE/CRSreports/04Sep/RL32590.pdf.

Zhang, L. and Findeis, J. (2007) "Agent-based Modeling of Household Migration and Land Use Decisions in South China," paper presented at the Transatlantic Land Use Change Conference, Washington, DC. September 2007.

3 Payments for agri-environmental services

An OECD perspective[1]

Wilfrid Legg

Introduction

Agriculture in the 30 countries that are members of the Organization for Economic Cooperation and Development (OECD) accounts on average for less than 5 percent of employment and GDP, but for around 40 percent of the total area of land and water used. Agriculture therefore has a close and significant relationship with the sustainability of natural resources. While agriculture draws heavily on natural resources and generates pressure on the environment, it also contributes to the provision of land-based environmental services. This chapter focuses on the role that policies can play in providing payments to farmers in return for the delivery of environmental services from farming.

Context

In order to better understand the rationale for policies to remunerate farmers for providing environmental services (sometimes termed ecological goods and services), and to identify other alternative approaches, it is necessary to outline some key characteristics of the agricultural sectors in OECD countries and the existing policy framework.

First, governments have intervened in the agricultural sector for a considerable period of time. Concerns about food security, commodity price volatility, the level and stability of farm incomes and rural employment, and food safety led many OECD countries to implement a complex web of policy measures that generally involved interventions in commodity markets and regulations throughout the whole supply chain. Historically, those interventions invariably meant insulating domestic markets through trade barriers, which generated surpluses that had to be domestically stockpiled or sold on world markets. That put downward pressure on commodity prices and added to this volatility.

At the same time, technological advances combined with such policies exacerbated the problem. The crisis in world agricultural markets came to a head in the late 1970s and early 1980s and led to an agreement in 1987 among OECD governments to tackle this problem through a gradual and balanced reduction in the support measures causing the problem. A key aim of the Uruguay Round (in the General Agreement on Tariffs and Trade, the forerunner of the World Trade Organization) was to bring agricultural trade into the multilateral trading system rules. The upshot has been a process of agricultural policy and trade reform that has reduced overall agricultural support gradually but to differing degrees across countries and commodity sectors. More significantly, the process has started to sever the link between farm income support and commodity production (decoupling).

Nevertheless, despite these reforms, commodity-linked support (accounting for over 60 percent of overall support as measured by the OECD's Producer Support Estimates) still predominates in many OECD countries, with impacts on the environment and resource sustainability. These developments have been regularly monitored and evaluated by the OECD since 1988 (OECD 2007a, 2007b, 2008a). Figure 3.1 shows the evolution of producer support over the last two decades for the OECD as a whole. Although there has been a notable shift toward policy measures with weaker links to commodity production, this has been a relatively slow and incomplete process. Moreover, the progress has been variable across OECD countries.

Second, over the last two decades concern about the environmental perform-ance of agriculture has increased. This is partly a consequence of a richer and more knowledgeable society that spends a small and decreasing share of its income on primary food and fiber products and places a higher priority on how food is produced and what its impacts are on the environment, animal welfare, and the countryside and rural areas. It is also a consequence of more scientific evidence and better communication of the results of research on the environ-mental impacts.

Third, some of the environmental impacts generated by farming, whether they pollute and deplete resources (reducing environmental capital) or provide ecolo-gical services and enhance the environment (increasing environmental capital) affect farmers directly (such as loss of soil quality or erosion) or indirectly (such as watershed pollution, depletion of groundwater, or the provision of attractive countryside and rural amenities that attract tourists and urban residents). One way or another, these impacts are to some extent internalized by the farming community.

But many of the impacts are not taken into account in farmers' decisions, namely environmental externalities (outputs from activities that either raise an individual's welfare through a bonus or lower it though an imposition) or public goods (outputs from activities that change the welfare of all people but for which no producer is able to extract any payment because they are by definition not exclusive to any potential purchaser). In other words, in such cases farmers are not held to account for the pollution or resource depletion they cause, or are not remunerated for the environmental services they provide. With such imperfect signals (incentives or disincentives) facing farmers, they tend to "over produce" environmental pollution and resource depletion and to "under supply" environ-mental services.

Establishing reference levels and property rights that articulate what is meant

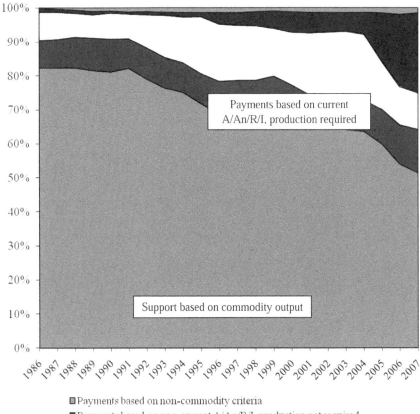

□ Payments based on non-commodity criteria
■ Payments based on non-current A/An/R/I, production not required
▨ Payments based on non-current A/An/R/I, production required
□ Payments based on current A/An/R/I, production required
■ Payments based on input use
□ Support based on commodity output

Figure 3.1 Composition of producer support estimates (percentage share in PSE): 1986–2007 (source: OECD, PSE/CSE database 2008).

Notes
A = area planted, An = animal number, R = receipts, I = income.

in a country or region by "good farming practices" (the minimum conditions that farmers need to implement to reach production and environmental objectives) allows governments to define the line between generation of environmental harm (practices or outcomes that are below the reference level and for which farmers should be held accountable at their own expense to remedy the situation) and provision of environmental services (practices or outcomes that are above the reference level and for which farmers should be rewarded). The OECD has produced seminal work on the issue of reference levels (OECD 1996).

Reducing commodity-linked support has beneficially affected the environment by:

1   reducing the pressure to over-exploit natural resources and farm on environmentally sensitive land; and
2   lowering the application of farm chemicals that spill over into the environment.

But it also has reduced the environmental services associated with some agricultural production systems to the extent that the systems are no longer profitable (such as farming in areas that are economically marginal but have high nature values). Moreover, high levels of support have masked the "need" to remunerate farmers for environmental services provided (it could be argued that this was, albeit crudely and in a non-targeted way, happening as an unintended consequence of commodity support). Reducing support in effect exposes the gap between dealing with environmental pollution or resource depletion and dealing with environmental service provision.

Agriculture's environmental footprint

Before looking at the role of governments in paying for agriculture's environmental services, it is necessary to look in more detail at the impacts of agriculture on the environment in order to highlight some problems and challenges in designing and implementing effective policies. Agriculture's environmental pressures relate mainly to water depletion and pollution, soil quality depletion and erosion, loss of habitats, air pollution and greenhouse gas emissions. On the other hand, the services provided concern biodiversity and ecosystem preservation, landscape conservation, flood and drought control, and carbon sequestration.

A major OECD study tracking the environmental performance of agriculture in OECD countries was published in May 2008 (OECD 2008b). The main finding is that performance across and within countries is mixed, but pressure on water supplies will increase in the future if projected higher global demands for food, fiber and renewable fuels are to be met. In brief, OECD agricultural output has risen about 5 percent since 1990, using more water (3 percent) and energy (6 percent), but less land (4 percent) and labor (10 percent). More specifically, soil erosion and loss have decreased, as has nutrient runoff into the environment (see Figure 3.2), easing pressure on water quality, but pockets of high concentrations remain. Pesticide applications have decreased, but the environmental risks are unclear. Biodiversity loss appears to have halted or slowed, but the data are patchy. Finally, greenhouse gas emissions have been reduced. It is difficult to assess trends in aesthetic countryside landscapes associated with farming because a robust, objective indicator that can be compared across countries remains elusive.

Agricultural production and practices thus generate a complex mix of environmental benefits and damage and are marked by a high degree of diversity in

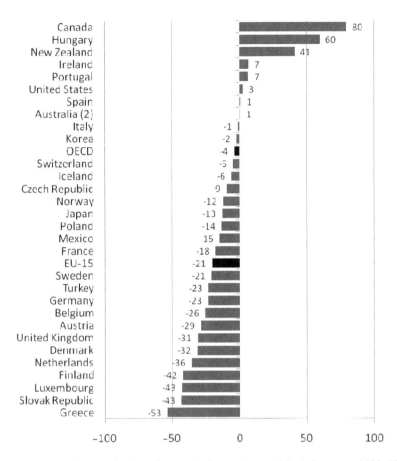

Figure 3.2 Change in the nitrogen balance (tonnes N) 1 between 1990–1992 and 2002–2004 (source: OECD 2008*b*: 20).

Notes
1 The gross nitrogen balance calculates the difference between the nitrogen inputs entering a farming system (i.e. mainly livestock manure and fertilizers) and the nitrogen outputs leaving the system (i.e. the uptake of nutrients for crop and pasture production).
2 Averages for the period 2002–2004 are an OECD estimate.

space (across and within countries) and time (some effects, such as soil carbon or wildlife species take a long time to appear following a change in farming production, land use or techniques). Care needs to be exercised in attributing particular environmental phenomena as "harmful" or "beneficial:" reducing "harmful" environmental effects (such as water pollution) is "beneficial," but reducing "beneficial" effects (such as biodiversity) is "harmful."

It should be stressed that agriculture is not always the sole activity providing land-based environmental services, although farming creates specific patterns of biodiversity and cultural landscapes. Moreover, the relationship between environmental service provision and agriculture varies with respect to production intensity, farm systems, scale of production and site location. While some services result from the actions of individual farms (such as carbon sequestration and some water management and habitats), others arise from the collective activity of farming in an area (such as landscape, watershed management and biodiversity), which could be termed "spatial jointness" or "non-point sources of benefits."

In other words, the links between agriculture and environmental service provision involve questions related to the *supply-side* (the degree of uniqueness of various agricultural activities, scale and intensity of production, site specificity, and the results of collective activity of farming in an area on landscape) and the *demand-side* (the character and location of environmental services that societies wish to have from agricultural activities). Crucial to such a discussion is the issue of prices: at what price (or remuneration) would farmers supply environmental services over and above what they provide as a consequence of current agricultural activity, and what price (or user charge) would society be willing to pay for having those services?

The policy challenges

The challenge for society is to determine and move toward the level and mix of agricultural production and practices that are both economically and environmentally efficient. The risk is that production is economically efficient but does not deliver the "right" amount of environmental outputs (or vice versa). Finding the best balance between farming profitability, competitiveness and resource conservation is a complex issue. The challenge for policy-makers is to identify the existing market or policy failures causing the problem, establish the extent to which markets could be created or policy intervention is needed to address the problem, define the most cost-effective policy approach and choice of instrument, and implement, monitor and evaluate those policies.

Essentially, policy-makers in most OECD countries have at least two broad sets of objectives and instruments in this area: one related to agricultural production and farm incomes, the other related to environmental performance. Given the integrated nature of the relationship between agriculture and the environment (joint agricultural and environmental production, as well as dynamic interactions) such that targeting one set of objectives inevitably leads to consequences for the achievement of the other, the appropriate policy instruments cannot be viewed in isolation. In the few OECD countries where there is little agricultural production support (as in Australia and New Zealand), the policy challenge is in principle simpler: agri-environmental harm can be targeted through environmental policies and regulations, and environmental service provision that is not remunerated through markets or quasi-markets could be targeted through payments from local or national authorities. There could be some consequence on agricultural production as environmental regulations constrain production, but payments that only compensate for the extra costs involved in the provision of those environmental services could be production neutral.

Measuring the demand and supply of environmental services

Accounting for environmental externalities in policy design requires calculation of the harm created and the benefits generated. Environmental services arising from agricultural activities provide such benefits as watershed management, biodiversity, carbon sequestration and maintenance of landscapes. In analyzing benefits, it is necessary to clearly define the relevant property rights (where farmers should be held liable at their own cost for environmental damage, and where they could be remunerated for providing environmental services that go beyond usual "good farming practices" and for which markets are absent or poorly developed), and to measure the demand for the environmental services in question as well as the costs of providing them.

A number of tools and data are available to estimate the costs of providing environmental services and the extent of demand for those services. The overall trend in the provision of services can be obtained from indicators of the state of the environment or the driving forces such as farm systems, management practices and types of land use associated with specific environmental service provision. But the measurement is often difficult. It is necessary to understand the linkages between policies, practices and service provision, and how the lack of monetary values limits their usefulness as policy tools when cost-effectiveness is an issue.

Estimates of the opportunity cost of farmers providing environmental services over and above what is already supplied from their activities (for example, in terms of agricultural output or farm income foregone) can be obtained from farm accounting information. Farmers should best know the extra costs incurred in providing extra environmental services, but there are risks if this information is not independently verifiable. The actual costs of investment by farmers that may be necessary to deliver services, or the costs of alternative investments (such as the cost of building dams to replace water management from agricultural systems such as rice paddies) have been frequently used, but the elements included in such cost comparisons need careful scrutiny.

Some progress has been made in estimating the demand for environmental services using techniques such as contingent valuation (willingness to pay for the provision or avoidance of loss of a specified environmental service) or choice experiments (comparison of willingness to pay attached to the provision of different bundles of services or attributes of a composite environmental service). Other methods include estimating the amount visitors pay to visit sites characterized by agriculturally related landscapes (travel cost method) or the extra value of land and rents adjacent to areas of agri-environmental service provision (hedonic price method) (Pearce *et al.* 2006). But, as outlined below, some of the most promising approaches involve the establishment of auctions (bidding arrangements), ordinal ranking of environmental benefits and tradable permit systems.

Policy approaches in OECD countries

In OECD countries, a wide range of policy measures are used to address environmental services from agriculture. These include:

1   command and control approaches such as designating areas with high nature values where agricultural practices are strictly specified (e.g. national parks or "green zones") or mandating codes of practice, standards and certification of products;
2   economic instruments such as payments for targeted environmental service provision;
3   market facilitation such as provision of market information, setting up tradable permit schemes and auctions, or encouraging agri-tourism and voluntary and cooperative efforts among farmers; and
4   publicly funded research and development and extension services to provide and disseminate information on farm practices delivering environmental benefits.

The approach adopted in many OECD countries (for example, the United States, the European Union and Switzerland) consists of various combinations of environmental cross-compliance, payments for environmental services rendered, conventional production and farm income support mechanisms, and environmental regulations. Environmental cross-compliance obliges farmers to adopt practices or observe regulations that are considered beneficial for the environment in order to be eligible to receive existing farm support or to benefit from payments for environmental service provision. The systems vary in the way they are implemented across countries, but in all cases there is a link between agricultural and environmental policy instruments and objectives.

A closer look at policies in the United States and European Union

In the United States, in 1986–1988, on average 63 percent of support to farmers (as measured by the OECD's Producer Support Estimate) was from budgetary payments, of which only 2 percent was based on historical variables (such as area of land or animals providing support entitlement) or for the production of non-agricultural commodities (such as hedges, walls, coppices and wetlands), while in 2004–2006 the respective figures were 77 percent and 31 percent. In the European Union, in 1986–1988, on average 14 percent of support to farmers was from budgetary payments, of which none were based on historical variables or for non-agricultural commodities, while in 2004–2006 the respective figures were 52 percent and 15 percent (OECD 2007a).

Moreover, there has been a significant change in the share of support measures that include "input constraints," a large part of which are for undertaking farm practices with the aim of improving environmental performance. These include limiting fertilizer and pesticide applications, installing manure waste storage facilities, adopting environmental conservation practices, keeping environmentally valuable land from commodity production or other development, and providing field margins and riparian strips. In brief, such support is provided to pay farmers not to use the amount of purchased inputs or adopt farm practices that would otherwise be the case if there were no constraints. In the United States the share of support with input constraints more than doubled from 23 percent to 48 percent from 1986–1988 to 2005–2007, while in the EU the share rose dramatically from under 2 percent to 44 percent over the same period (OECD 2008a).

In the United States, agri-environmental policy is aimed at maintaining soil quality, preserving farm and ranch lands, improving water and air quality, and increasing wildlife habitat and carbon sequestration. US policy relies on a range of voluntary subsidies and cross-compliance mechanisms. The goal is to design programs to enroll eligible farmers who will deliver under contract the greatest benefit at the least cost.

In this respect, the Environmental Benefits Index (EBI) in the United States is an interesting example in the context of implementing agri-environmental policy. EBIs are indexes to prioritize multiple environmental objectives and rank applications, which were introduced in 1990 for the Conservation Reserve Program. Farmers voluntarily submit offers to provide environmental services and agree to implement certain practices or retire land from production in return for the receipt of annual payments. Applications are ranked in terms of weighted environmental benefits. The given budget for a program is then allocated to the farmers whose applications balance the highest environmental benefit against the costs of adopting conservation practices.

In the European Union, agri-environmental policy is aimed at improving water, soil and air quality; preserving cultural (aesthetic) agricultural landscapes; preserving biodiversity and wildlife habitats; and ensuring viable farms that contribute to countryside stewardship in rural communities. EU policy relies on environmental protection legislation, payments to farmers for participation in voluntary programs, and cross-compliance mechanisms. The goal is to ensure that farmers deliver environmental benefits based on the general concept of good farming practice (keeping the land in "good agricultural and environmental condition").

In both regions, 15–20 percent of farmland is under specific agri-environmental programs and about US$5–6 billion of public support is spent annually on *specific* agri-environmental programs in both areas (although many other programs include environmental elements).

EU policy has stressed the benefits that working farms provide to the environment, while US policy has tended to stress the benefits of idling environmentally sensitive land. However, there is now more convergence of the policies as the United States gives increasing focus to the environmental benefits of working farms. The United States relies more heavily on voluntary approaches and places emphasis on bidding (auction-style) systems. Both the EU and the United States try to influence farm-management practices in achieving environmental goals. In fact, while the *actual* harmful environmental outcome of agricultural practices is often the target for fines and charges ("polluter pays" principle) it is less common to find policies that reward the *actual* outcome of providing environmental services. Rather, it is the *practice* that is considered to lead to environmentally beneficial services that is targeted.

Conclusion and outlook

What are the implications of valuing environmental services for policy design? Although considerable knowledge is available from empirical studies concerning both the costs of providing and the demand for environmental services, great care needs to be exercised in interpreting and using the estimates. The evidence would suggest that a key challenge is to have a better understanding of the demand for agri-environmental services. An important issue concerns the provision of environmental services after the expiration of contracts that involve payments from governments (including budget constraints). Other issues relate to identifying:

1   effective schemes under different systems of land tenure and where benefits are non-point (single farmer) sourced;
2   co-benefits or trade-offs among the various services provided;
3   relationships between environmental services and different farm systems, scale of farming activity, and time period for delivery of services; and
4   the lowest cost provider of a given service.

An issue that has become more prominent in the policy debate concerns the trade-offs between tailored payments (to avoid under- or over-remuneration for environmental service provision) and the transactions costs incurred. However, the evidence shows that tailored and targeted payments are more efficient at transferring funds to the farmers to deliver environmental services and thus save financial resources compared to uniform payments across the agricultural sector (OECD 2007c, 2008c).

Market creation for the provision of environmental services still has much unexploited potential. In this context, providing market information, offering tradable permit schemes, encouraging agri-tourism and facilitating voluntary and cooperative efforts among farmers has much to offer. Research and development initiatives, along with extension services that disseminate information on good farm practices, can complement such activities.

The overall message for policy design is a mixture of carrots and sticks to "get the prices right" by internalizing externalities, accounting for environmental public goods, and providing as much transparency and evidence as possible on which to justify chosen policy measures. The corollary is a clear definition of property rights and reference levels.

Note

1 The chapter is written under the responsibility of the author and does not necessarily reflect the views of the OECD or its member countries.

References

OECD (1996) *The Environmental Benefits of Agriculture (Helsinki Seminar)*, Paris, France.

—— (2007a) *Agricultural Policies in OECD Countries: Monitoring and Evaluation 2007*, Paris, France.

—— (2007b) *Agricultural Policies in Non-OECD Countries 2007*, Paris, France.

—— (2007c) *Effective Targeting of Agricultural Policies*, OECD, Paris, France.

—— (2008a) *Agricultural Policies in OECD Countries: At a Glance 2008*, Paris, France.

—— (2008b) *Environmental Performance of Agriculture in OECD Countries since 1990*, Paris, France. Online, available at: www.oecd.org/tad/env/indicators.

—— (2008*c*) *Agricultural Policy Design and Implementation: A Synthesis*, Paris, France.

Pearce, D., Atkinson, G. and Mourato, S. (2006) "Cost–Benefit Analysis and the Environment: Recent Developments," Paris: OECD.

4 Comparing agri-environmental programs in the United States and the EU

Christina von Haaren and Nelson Bills

Introduction

The effectiveness of agri-environmental programs (policy interventions designed to improve environmental performance on farms and rural landscapes) is a continuing policy issue in all developed nations. However, it is especially difficult to accumulate inter-country comparisons and capitalize on experiences with policy implementation. The purpose of this chapter is to summarize the literature and the debate over agri-environmental program effectiveness in the European Union (EU) and the United States. Closer attention will then be given to examples in the northeastern United States and Germany. Of particular concern, especially in the context of evolving World Trade Organization (WTO) negotiations, are arrangements for blending regulatory and compensatory incentives for providing environmental goods and services on farms and in rural communities.

In the EU, and especially in Germany, current agri-environmental efforts are not cost-effectively related to effects on the environment (see analysis of Société Oréade-Brèche 2005). Considering future prospects for the EU system of payments to farmers, solutions are needed to enlarge the budget for agri-environmental payments, to better target them and to motivate farmers to promote sustainability. New approaches should include concepts that combine environmental planning that targets agri-environmental measures (referred to throughout this chapter as "AEM"), alternative models of remuneration and advisory schemes that better integrate environmental services into the technical assistance provided for farm operators.

While EU agri-environmental schemes were introduced in the early 1990s, the US effort to improve environmental management on farms dates back to the 1930s and concerns with rain and wind erosion. After World War II, US conservation policy evolved into two distinct tracks:

1   soil erosion/water quality management; and
2   farmland protection (maintenance of farmland in its current use).

Each policy track has developed its own constituency and programs that feature a fairly exclusive list of policy tools. Often missing in this fragmented policy environment, however, is the broad view of the rural, working or "multifunctional" landscape that considers the implications of farm and food production for landscape diversity, biological resources, wildlife habitat and open space land interests. Also, US, state and local governments are aggressively promoting and funding AEM programs. This layered approach – featuring federal, state and local initiatives – is often masked in international discussions because commentators almost invariably dwell on federal agri-environmental policies and even more narrowly on programs administered by the USDA.

The motivation for this chapter is that broader comparisons of the US and German experience with agri-environmental programs are both timely and beneficial to the evolving policy debate in the two countries. However, inter-country comparisons present formidable challenges because of wide institutional differences. With these challenges in mind, the first section of this chapter will identify potential or emergent interests in landscape management. The second section deals with agri-environmental policies in the EU, Germany and the United States. The third section examines payments for agriculture and environmental services. Emphasis is placed on achieving comparisons of public support in the EU and the United States, with attention to investments made by all levels of government. In a concluding section, we discuss opportunities for advancing the strategic interests in the working landscape management and the options for providing financial incentives needed for the provision of environmental goods and services.

Definitions and performance measures

There is general agreement that farm and food production yields many non-commodity outputs. Most agricultural commodities are traded in markets, while most non-commodity outputs are provided by other means. The term "multifunctionality" has been coined to describe concerns about the provision of both commodity and non-commodity outputs. Non-market goods and services are now a prominent part of the debate on agricultural policy in rich nations and an integral part of international negotiations on reducing trade barriers for farm and food commodities. As Blandford and Boisvert (2004) point out, views on how to reconcile multifunctionality with freer international movements of agricultural commodities appear to divide along two relatively distinct lines. One can argue that without the continuation of current agricultural policies, freer trade will jeopardize the provision of public goods and positive externalities provided by agriculture. The opposing view is that such policies are primarily designed to protect agriculture from international competition, alter commodity prices and perpetuate trade distortions.

Blandford and Boisvert (2002) also argue that the issues surrounding multifunctionality are too complex in their global, country-specific and local dimensions to be resolved within the traditional domestic/international trade policy paradigm. In such a paradigm, welfare-maximizing taxes and subsidies applied to the non-commodity outputs of agriculture would internalize their external benefits and costs. They conclude that, while forceful on conceptual grounds, attempts to measure such external benefits and costs are faced with obstacles that cannot be overcome empirically. Instead, a workable solution might be to specify conditions and actions that are likely to lead to an increase in the supply of desired non-commodity outputs or attributes, e.g. a set of production standards that will result in improved animal welfare or standards for maintaining areas of wildlife habitat. The cost-effectiveness of alternative combinations of regulation and monetary incentives to achieve an increase in the supply of such desired outputs could then be evaluated.

Following Batie and Horan (2002), these evaluations turn on several design issues, which will now be discussed.

Establishing program objectives

What are the objectives of the program? Is the objective only the enhancement of environmental services, or are farm income support and other program objectives also important? What are the inherent trade-offs between income support and environmental objectives? What environmental services are to be the focus of the program? How are these services to be measured? Will there be different objectives for different regions or enterprises?

Identifying target recipients

Who should be paid? Who is eligible? Should payments go to areas of intensive agricultural production or to areas where the provision of the services affect many people or have significant environmental impacts? Should payments be targeted, and what selection criteria should be used? Which lands should be targeted, those with significant actual or significant potential environmental problems? Or should certain regions or types of crops be targeted?

Determining payment amounts

How much will farmers and landowners be paid? Will payments exceed producer costs? Will payments vary spatially? Will total payment amounts be limited?

Identifying and measuring target activities

What should farmers and landowners be paid to do? Should payments be based on performance (e.g. on a set of criteria that combine several environmental services, perhaps based on an environmental impact index), on the adoption of specific management practices, or on a holistic farm conservation plan? What is the appropriate baseline from which to evaluate payments? Should payments be made only for improvements from the status quo, or for past stewardship? Will constraints be imposed on which lands are eligible for payments? How should compliance with program requirements be monitored and enforced?

Agri-environmental policies in the EU, Germany and the United States

Evolving policies in the EU and the United States respond to these broad issues. The European Union (EU) features a common agricultural policy (CAP) for member countries. The CAP was initiated in 1957 to integrate markets across the boundaries of member countries while securing income for farmers, managing farm product supplies and arranging for common financing of farm subsidies. Subsidy arrangements have included agricultural price support, direct payments to farmers, supply controls and border measures.

The EU instituted several major policy reforms in the early 1990s that included the introduction of green or AEM payments into the CAP. More recent reforms, in 2000 and 2003, initiated the decoupling of farm subsidies from commodity production and placed additional emphasis on environmental concerns. Farmers must now comply more fully with environmental regulations, along with allied provisions for improving animal welfare, food safety and food quality, as a precondition for receiving direct subsidy under the CAP. These latest reforms, along with requiring compliance with more exacting environmental standards, also represent some devolution of farm policy. Each member state now receives more discretion over the timing and implementation of agri-environmental programs (Gunderson *et al.* 2004: 836).

The 2003 provisions for decoupled payments are generally referred to as single farm payments (SFP). The EU-15 member states opted for different models to distribute the SFP, but most are based on past payment history for each farmer and landowner; the new EU accession states do not have that history and introduced flat-rate payments. Germany chose a hybrid model which will gradually change into regionally differentiated flat-rate payments by 2013. Land eligible for support in Germany but not farmed, i.e. arable land set aside from active farm use, must be maintained in "good agricultural and environmental condition" as a precondition for EU support (Council Regulation 1782/2003, Art. 5 and Annex IV).

Also noteworthy in the recent reforms is a marked shift in the way rural development initiatives are treated. The recent CAP reforms established two "pillars," or program pathways, in the budget: Pillar I for market and price-support policies and Pillar II for rural development policies. Rural development, in EU parlance, will embody increased attention to production of environmental goods and services by incentivizing the use of agri-environmental practices. And, using a concept called "modulation," member states have obligations to transfer SFP subsidy funds from Pillar I into Pillar II: SFP payments greater than €5,000 are reduced by 5 percent, while farmers whose SFP is less than €5,000 are not penalized. The budget funds saved through modulation are transferred to the Pillar II Rural Development Fund. At least 80 percent of the funds from the penalties will remain in the country where the SFPs were reduced and are to be used for rural development purposes. The member states can voluntarily increase the modulation share.

Design of agri-environmental measures in the EU and Germany

As noted above, EU farmers can now voluntarily participate in agri-environmental programs within the framework of the CAP's Pillar II. Embedded in such programs is the fundamental concept of good farming practice (GFP). Agri-environmental measures are conceptualized in Europe as environmental services beyond the baseline GFP. GFP are generally understood to be a set of mandatory, threshold levels of environmental obligations for the farm operator. These GFP are defined by basic environmental standards established by European or national legislation (GACE 2002). National law can define additional or more ambitious rules for GFP than the EU can. The GFP standards can be interpreted to mean the "polluter pays principle." Every farmer must comply with these obligations without financial compensation. In addition to compulsory use of GFP, farmers who receive direct payments from the CAP Pillar I will be subject to "cross compliance" (CC) obligations under the 2003 CAP reforms, which link good baseline farming practices to receipt of direct payments.

Agri-environmental measures in Pillar II of the CAP

Pillar II of the CAP stresses rural development and has numerous implications for agri-environmental measures (European Commission 2005). Major thrusts under this pillar will include programs that support improving the competitiveness of the agricultural and forestry sectors (Axis 1), the environment and the countryside (Axis 2), the quality of life in rural areas and diversification of the rural economy (Axis 3) and cross-sector bottom-up projects and initiatives integrating the goals of the other axes (Axis 4 or LEADER). While provisions for the environment are the most important for financing AEMs, it is also expected that others, rationalized in terms of business structure, quality of life and diversification, will also offer possibilities for co-financing environmentally relevant measures. On the other hand, it appears that other axes may support measures which are at cross purposes with environmental goals. Nevertheless, it seems clear that net gains have been made in policy design under the 2003 reforms. Environmental concerns are more clearly separated from other rural development issues, and prospects for moving funds in that direction are improved.

Despite this optimism, the funding situation is extremely dynamic in the EU at present as member states implement the reforms with a large variety of measures and match EU funding with co-financing decisions. Some indication of the similarities and differences across the EU can be obtained from the AEM portfolio of the member states (Table 4.1). Noteworthy is the emphasis given to AEMs characterized as biodiversity measures. These measures are rated in meta evaluations as especially effective in addressing natural resource values and may be considered as multifunctional (Société Oréade-Brèche 2005).

A clear emphasis in all EU member states is the measure of working land. Set-aside measures have not been very well accepted as AEM by farmers. Until recently between 10 and 15 percent of the arable land in active crop rotation had

Table 4.1 Share of different types and objectives of agri-environmental measures in the member states of EU-15, 2000–2005

Objectives and examples of AEM	Number of AEM	%
Water: e.g. reduction of fertilizer and pesticide, reversal of drainage	597	32
Soil: e.g. erosion control, maintenance of organic matter	308	16
Biodiversity: e.g. habitat conservation, landscape structures, habitat networks, conversion of arable land into grassland, species conservation, cultivation of areas where extensive agriculture is retreating	754	40
Others: e.g. organic agriculture, rural landscapes	224	12

Source: Société Oréade-Brèche 2005 (summarized).

to be taken out of production to conform with EU market policies. However, this mandate has been suspended at present because of the increased land demand for producing energy crops. Beyond energy concerns, the preference for working land programs may be partly but not completely explained by environmental factors. Biodiversity and recreation interests in Europe depend more on extensively farmed land than in the United States. On the other hand, in many areas where nature conservation interests would wish for more "wilderness," farmers are not inclined to opt for set-aside programs.

Due to the federal structure of governance in Germany, planning, implementation and control of agri-environmental measures are ultimately the responsibility of the Federal States. The States also have to seek approval and co-financing directly from the EU for their program portfolio. This portfolio includes basic measures developed by the Federal Ministry of Agriculture, which are identical in all states but also include additional programs for each state. The basic AEMs are primarily aimed at improving farming techniques; these programs offer flat-rate payment without taking into account the site-specific conservation issues. The federal government is helping to co-finance these AEMs by topping off the funding each state gets from the EU. This is why most German states assign the bigger part of their AEM budgets to these federally designed measures: it reduces their exposure to environmental support in the state budget. An unfavorable side-effect is that environmental funding is poorly targeted and not necessarily directed to areas with particular environmental needs. Adequate technical assistance for farmers is also problematic. Up to now, EU schemes have not offered financial support for single, farm-oriented consultancies. However, in the 2007 budget period, farm consultancy can be supported financially from Pillar II of the CAP.

Contrasts with the United States

US agri-environmental policy has its origins in the Great Depression and the attendant farm crisis of the 1930s. The 1936 Soil Conservation and Domestic

Allotment Act not only provided for the protection of land resources against soil erosion but also established a framework for direct transfers of federal funds to support the income of US farmers and landowners (USDA 1984). Over the years, the US Congress has perpetuated and elaborated on this dichotomy of supporting farm income and instituting programs that protect natural resources. Concern over the environment accelerated in the late 1970s and early 1980s. In response, federal farm legislation in 1985 featured, for the first time, a major title (section) devoted to conservation issues. Congress instituted conservation cross-compliance, which made acceptable control of soil erosion on highly erodible land with a conservation plan a precondition for access to virtually all USDA farm program benefits. In addition, such program benefits were denied to farmers or landowners who converted fragile grasslands to rotation agriculture (sodbusting) or installed drainage works that permit crop production on wetlands (swampbusting). Congress also provided for a Conservation Reserve Program (CRP), to retire or set-aside land vulnerable to excessive soil erosion. This initiative echoed experimentation with a Soil Bank in the 1950s and 1960s, which set aside nearly 29 million acres (11.7 million ha) under long-term contracts for conservation purposes (USDA 1984). The CRP reinvented the Soil Bank program with vastly improved provisions for targeting land resources that are especially vulnerable to excessive soil erosion from rainfall or wind.

The 1985 federal legislation ushered in a new era of agri-environmental policy initiatives. Congress has revisited this legislation at five-year intervals over the past two decades to tweak program administration and to recalibrate AEM funding. At present, the USDA administers a suite of compensatory programs centered either on land retirement or on providing incentives for improved conservation management on working (actively farmed) lands (see Table 4.2). The CRP dominates these outlays and presently has running costs equivalent to more than €1.5 billion. More than 60 percent of direct USDA conservation payments target specific environmental concerns, principally highly erodible cropland, restorable farmed wetlands or prime farmland (Claassen *et al.* 2004).

Additionally, the US Congress commits significant resources to producer education and technical assistance to farmers and landowners. Most of this education and technical assistance is delivered to rural communities through a nationwide system of local soil and water conservation districts. These districts usually follow the political boundaries of more than 3,100 counties across the United States. State and local governments also appropriate funds to support the efforts of soil and water conservation districts. District staff often deal with broader community problems associated with land and water management, including those that arise from urban land use.

An interesting question of particular relevance to US–EU comparisons relates to the matter of conservation compliance. As noted above, compliance means that US farmers and landowners can only remain eligible for federal farm program benefits when they comply with certain environmental practices (Claassen *et al.* 2004). These restrictions target soil erosion and attendant water quality concerns.

Compliance with environmental standards, however, extends well beyond the reach of USDA programs. Regulatory requirements are also used as agri-environmental policy tools by other federal agencies. The Environmental Protection Agency (EPA) administers the Federal Water Pollution Control Act of 1972, commonly referred to as the Clean Water Act, which focuses on reducing the water quality impact of both point and non-point sources of pollution. In the early 1990s, the focus of the Clean Water Act turned to non-point sources, including runoff from agricultural operations (Claassen 2003). The EPA began aggressive efforts to work with individual state governments in crafting regulatory measures that would control agricultural point source pollution from confined animal feedlot operations (CAFOs). As of 2001, over 6,000 livestock operations were large enough to be classified as CAFOs under the Clean Water Act (Claassen 2003). This designation requires CAFOs to manage both crop and animal enterprises to eliminate discharges of manure and nutrients to surface waters. Details of CAFO regulation vary from state to state, but in New York

Table 4.2 Compensatory AEM programs administered by the USDA

AEM program/program description	*2008 budget*	
	Mil. euro	*%*
Conservation Reserve Program (CRP) and the Conservation Reserve Enhancement Program (CREP): annual payments and cost-sharing to establish long-term, resource-conserving cover, usually grass or trees, on environmentally sensitive land.	€1,529	54.7
Wetlands Reserve Program (WRP): cost-sharing and/or long-term or permanent easements for restoration of wetlands on agricultural land.	€203	7.3
Environmental Quality Incentives Program (EQIP): technical assistance and cost-sharing or incentive payments to assist livestock and crop producers with conservation and environmental improvements on working lands.	€782	28.0
Wildlife Habitat Incentives Program (WHIP): cost-sharing to landowners and producers to develop and improve wildlife habitat.	€33	1.2
Conservation Security Program (CSP): payments and cost-sharing for implementing appropriate land-based practices on working lands that address one or more resources of concern, such as soil, water or wildlife habitat.	€199	7.1
Farm and Ranch Lands Protection Program (FRPP): funds to state, tribal or local governments and private organizations to help purchase development rights and keep productive farmland in agricultural use.	€39	1.4
Grassland Reserve Program (GRP): long-term contracts and easements limiting use to haying and grazing activities while restoring/maintaining native grass and shrub species.	€12	0.4

Source: Cattaneo *et al.* 2005 and US Department of Agriculture 2007.

State, a precondition for operating a large CAFO is the preparation of a whole-farm nutrient management plan by a state-certified nutrient management planner. New York State nutrient management plans for livestock and poultry operations are very comprehensive and extend to managing manure, balancing nutrient applications on cropland and installing facilities to control discharges of waste water from livestock and feed-handling facilities (New York State Department of Environmental Conservation 2004). Producers must review and update this plan annually to obtain a permit renewal.

Several other US federal laws impose environmental standards. The Coastal Zone Act Reauthorization Amendments (CZARA) of 1990 provide a federally mandated program requiring specific measures to deal with agricultural non-point source pollution in order to restore and protect coastal waters. The program requires each of the 29 coastal states with approved coastal zone management plans to utilize voluntary incentives that encourage farmers to adopt measures that control non-point source pollution. If voluntary measures fail, however, then states must enforce adoption (Claassen 2003). The Endangered Species Act of 1973 was enacted to conserve endangered or threatened species and their eco-systems. Under this law, farmers are prohibited from "taking" a member of a species determined to be endangered or extinct. And in some cases, habitat destruction, cropping practices or the use of certain pesticides can be prohibited. The Federal Insecticide, Fungicide, and Rodenticide Act (FIFRA) of 1947 regulates the use of farm chemicals. Certain chemicals can be banned if they pose unacceptable risks to human health or the environment (Claassen 2003).

Agricultural payments in the United States and the EU

In this section, we present estimates of direct financial support to farmers and landowners in the United States and the EU. These comparisons are provisional and subject to much interpretation. One problem is fashioning accurate inter-country comparisons after accounting for wide differences in farm structure and the spatial dimensions of commodity production. The second problem centers on environmental support because funding for AEM comes from more than one level of government. This layering of government support greatly complicates inter-country comparisons because comprehensive data to describe AEM support by individual EU member states or by state and local governments in the United States are not easily accessible.

To achieve a broader and hence more useful policy context, we assembled EU and US data on farm support and arranged comparisons in an area basis for a single currency in calendar year 2006 (US) and 2007 (EU). Results are shown in Figure 4.1 using total USDA direct payments (across-the-board and inclusive of AEM payments) and total crop and pasture acreage as reported by the USDA (Lubowski *et al.* 2006). These crop and pasture data are judged to be equivalent to the EU designation of utilized agricultural area or UAA. When applied, they suggest that, on average, the overall US federal subsidy is €29.3 per hectare. This compares to an estimate of €289.4 per hectare of UAA for all member

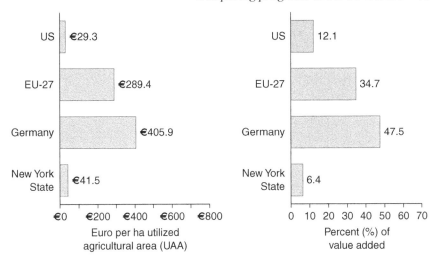

Figure 4.1 Estimated federal direct farm payments for the United States and New York State (2006) with comparisons with EU single farm payments and rural development funds for the EU-27 and Germany (2007) (source: Eurostat, 2007 and US Department of Agriculture 2008).

states, on average, in the EU-27. A comparable figure for Germany is €405.9. Finally, USDA data show that New York State farmers and landowners realize direct federal payments that amount to €41.5 per UAA on average.

These comparisons are arbitrary because of exchange rates but also because of the metric used to account for spatial and structural differences between the EU and the United States. With respect to land area, one could argue that agricultural subsidies should be more appropriately weighted by intensively utilized cropland area, rather than the more inclusive UAA comprised of land in crop rotation, permanent grassland and permanent crops. These alternative area weights can make a profound difference in the numbers and the impressions conveyed on both absolute and relative amounts of subsidy because of wide variation in land-use patterns.

Regardless of distinctions between cropland, pasture and rangeland, Figure 4.1 helps illustrate the preferential dimensions of US farm policy. Income support is concentrated in ten major program crops.[1] New York State is among several other states that produce relatively few of these supported commodities. In addition, outlays for AEM in the United States tend to pool in localities where farms receive relatively high commodity payments, thus further exacerbating state-to-state and region-to-region differences in levels of federal support.

Another way to make inter-country comparisons is to arrange farm subsidy data against value added, measured in producer prices. These comparisons are also on display in Figure 4.1 and show that, in the United States, total federal farm subsidy amounts to about 12 percent of value added in the farm sector.[2] The comparable value for New York State is less than 7 percent. Comparable values for the EU and Germany are 35 percent and 48 percent, respectively.

Expenditure for AEM in the United States and New York State

Turning to AEM support, according to recent USDA data (USDA 2007), annual direct subsidies for conservation purposes are presently about €2.7 billion. These outlays are dominated by rental and cost-sharing payments for long-term land retirement under the Conservation Reserve Program (CRP) (see Table 4.2). Treasury costs for the CRP are in the vicinity of €1.5 billion each year with little trend because enrollment is capped and aggregate annual rental payments are flat. This land-retirement program accounts for about 55 percent of total federal support for AEM and retires 39.2 million acres (15.9 million ha) from active crop production.

Arranging these federal AEM subsidies on a per-hectare cropland basis is instructive (see Figure 4.2). Federal outlays for AEM have ranged from seven to ten euros per hectare since the mid 1990s. Comparable values for New York State are in the range of two to three euros per hectare. This wide difference between the US average and New York State graphically demonstrates the unequal distribution of federal AEM support. The overriding reason is that AEM subsidies are dominated by land-retirement programs, principally the CRP. As noted above, participation in the CRP tends to be correlated with income support payments for a small collection of federal program crops, crops that are under-represented in New York State.

Looking beyond the USDA, state and local support for AEM measures is significant but not widely discussed. A portion of state and local funding is directed to assist with water-quality improvement on farmland, but no comprehensive information on funding from these sources is available. State and local funding to protect farmland from conversion to developed uses, however, is well understood (AFT 2007a, 2007b). Along with direct money outlays, which

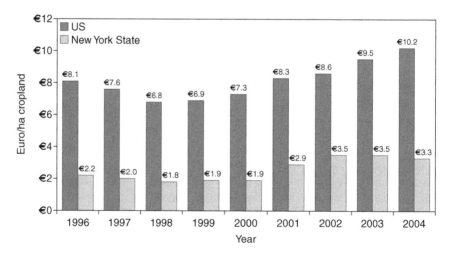

Figure 4.2 Direct federal AEM payments for the United States and New York State, 1996–2004 (source: US Department of Agriculture 2008).

provide financial assistance by topping off federal program support (through the USDA's Farm and Ranchland Protection Program), state legislatures in all 50 states have passed legislation that generate agri-environmental benefits through reduced *ad volorem* taxes on farm real estate (Freedgood 1997). These benefits, "tax expenditures" in economic parlance, are the property tax revenues foregone due to tax preferences for farmland owners. These tax preferences are usually arranged through tax levies on farm use rather than full market property values; the legislative intent is to reduce property tax expenses and encourage mainte-nance of farmland in its current use (Tremblay *et al.* 1987). Reliable, compre-hensive estimates of tax expenditures for agri-environmental measures in the United States are not available (Bills 2007), but previous work comparing outlays for agri-environmental programs in New York State and England showed that tax expenditures can dramatically alter comparative AEM relationships in sections of the United States where local governments are heavily dependent on local property tax levies to fund public services (Bills and Gross 2005). However, recent economic research and literature in the United States almost uniformly fails to acknowledge the influence tax expenditures wield on AEM funding (see, for example, Batie 2003; Blandford and Boisvert 2002; Dobbs 2002; Dobbs and Pretty 2001 and 2004; Hellerstein *et al.* 2002; Hollis and Fulton 2002; Libby 2000).

Calculations for aggregate New York State federal and state subsidy, inclu-sive of tax expenditure estimates, are presented in Figure 4.3. This estimate includes federal support for both AEM and direct payments for all other farm programs. State funds for both water quality and farmland protection measures

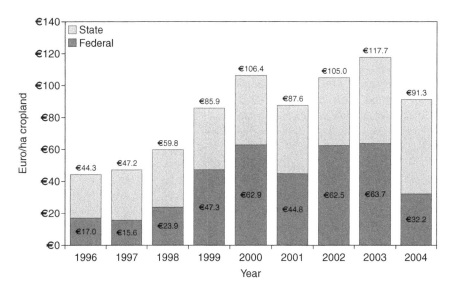

Figure 4.3 Estimated federal and state payments/tax expenditures for farming, New York State, 1996–2004 (source: US Department of Agriculture 2008 and Bills *et al.* 2005).

are also included in the estimate. While state and local program support is some-times ignored in debates over international trade relationships and in WTO nego-tiations, results presented here for New York State suggest that state and local efforts can be an instrumental component of the agri-environmental management regime in the United States. Consideration of state contributions in New York State boosted average public subsidy from €32.4 to €91.3 per hectare of crop-land in 2004 (Figure 4.3). Time-series calculations show that state contributions are increasing systematically in current terms, with support nearly doubling over the nine-year interval from 1996 through 2004. The increase is attributable both to higher state appropriations and to steady increases in the value of benefits generated through foregone property tax revenues.

Expenditures for AEM in the EU and Germany in the context of overall direct farm payments

Turning to the EU and Germany, the design of the programs of Pillar II is only one indicator of the effectiveness and efficiency of pursuing environmental objectives by the EU and its member states. At least as important for judging the priority policy gives to environmental goals are AEM expenditures in compari-son to the market and production subsidies received by farmers in the EU under Pillar I. The CAP budget has been rising steadily over the years but has been capped as a consequence of the EU enlargement from 15 to 27 member states. For the budget period, 2007–2013, the fixed budget amount is €369.8 billion. For 2007, €52 billion has been spent on natural resources with the biggest part reserved for agriculture.

The task here is to put these expected outlays in perspective for the EU and for Germany using the best available data. Unfortunately, data available are at this time confined to values for EU-27. This broadens the discussion to include nations just now ascending to EU membership and detracts from comments made above using the EU-15 as a reference point. These reservations have to be kept in mind when interpreting the 2007 EU outlays for the CAP (Figure 4.4). Total 2007 subsidy is expected to approach €52 billion with 70 percent and 19 percent, respectively, allocated to the newly crafted single farm payment (SFP) and to rural development.

Within the broad rural development category is an understory of programs, some of which focus on agri-environmental management. At present there are no data about the area which is under AEM contracts. Data are only available for the previous funding period. The average premium was €89/ha, varying between approximately €240/ha in Greece and about €38/ha in France; Germany paid slightly less than the average at about €79/ha (European Commission, DG Agri-culture 2003). A further distinction is made between expected outlays for AEM and other categories of rural development assistance.

To illustrate, we weight these expected outlays by total utilized agricultural area (UAA) as shown in Figure 4.5. Results show that the single farm payment is, on average, €228.2/ha UAA for all EU-27 member countries. In contrast,

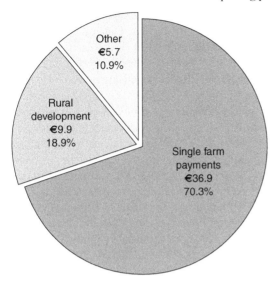

Figure 4.4 Common agricultural policy (CAP) budget for the EU-27, 2007 (source: von Haaren and von Ruschkowski (in preparation); data: European Commission, 2007a).

AEM payments are pegged at €14.1/ha UAA while other rural development support is estimated at €47/ha UAA. This brings total support to €289, on average, for every utilized agricultural hectare.

Figure 4.5 also displays companion data for Germany. Single farm payments are pegged at €336.1/ha of utilized agricultural area, an amount well above the EU-27 average of €228.2. Support payments from the EU to German farmers for

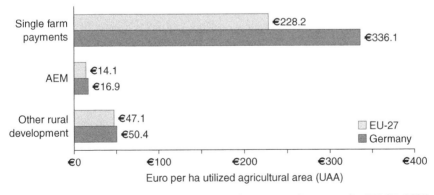

Figure 4.5 Agricultural payments by purpose, Germany and average for EU-27, 2007 (source: von Ruschkowski and von Haaren (2008); data: EU Commission 2006; Eurostat 2007; BMELV 2007).

Note
*Other rural development includes Axes 1, 3 and 4 plus all non-214-code measures in Axis 2; AEM and Other rural development data only represent the EU funding share.

AEM are more in line with the EU average at €16.7/ha. Other rural development payments from the EU to Germany amount to €53/ha. Federal and state co-financing included, about €35/ha are available for AEM (von Ruschkowski and von Haaren 2008) and another €62 for other rural development supporting farms (rest of axis two including payments in disadvantaged areas and axis one; excluded are axis three payments of Pillar 2, of which farms do not benefit directly). This brings available total assistance to German farmers to an estimated average of €433 for every hectare of cropland, pasture and grassland.

The emphasis placed on AEM measures in Germany come up to the average of the EU member states. Pillar I (single farm payments) receive much greater emphasis than Pillar II measures (Osterburg *et al.* 2007). Like farmers in France, the UK, Denmark and the Netherlands, German farmers receive, by far, most of their support payments from Pillar I. In contrast, programs in Austria, Portugal and Finland feature a distinct emphasis on Pillar II compared to the share of payments farmers receive from Pillar I. This picture will change slightly as member states increase shares for Pillar II by modulation after 2008, which moves Pillar II above the compulsory share of 5 percent. Funding available for Pillar II also varies substantially in absolute terms. For example, in Austria about €160/ha UAA is available while in the UK less than €20 can be paid per ha UAA. The EU average is at about €61/ha UAA. Finally, an increasingly critical source of country-to-country variation stems from the growing presence of national and regional contributions to top off EU funding.

Discussion

Our assessment is that, in general, only a small and recently reduced share of CAP payments in the EU is dedicated to agri-environmental objectives, but there is much variation among member nations. Most of this variability can be explained by differences in the ability and willingness of member states to co-finance the EU payments. Rising world market prices for food and dedicated energy crops aggravate the problem of arranging sufficient AEM financing (European Commission 2007b). Farmers will opt out of AEM contracts in Germany because opportunity costs of participation are increasing. The amount of money necessary to finance common conservation objectives and obligations of the member states will likely exceed the budget share these states have earmarked for that purpose up to now. Either a more robust modulation or a rearrangement of budget between the first and second pillars of the CAP will be needed to solve this problem.

In addition, targeting these payments to environmentally sensitive or especially valuable sites is left to the discretion of the member states. A direct consequence is that funding is very diverse and, in many member states like Germany, only to a small degree the result of exacting requirements for environmental protection. As a consequence, only sites with low opportunity costs of compliance are enrolled in AEM programs. Such funding for environmental goods and services is a major thrust of this chapter, but the comparisons we are able to make are far from satisfying. Clearly, more can be done to smooth and rectify the comparative data. We suggest that such steps are probably worth taking as the international discussion over improved environmental management for farm and food production widens and deepens. To date, too little of that discussion is data driven and, as a result, policy-makers cannot benefit from the insights that can come from both qualitative and quantitative assessments of program direction in various nations. This issue will likely become more attenuated over time as more responsibility for AEM programs is devolved to EU member states.

The overall paradigm for farm support is moving in the same general direction in the EU and in the United States, with more emphasis on environmental goods and services and a greater inclination to target priority natural resource issues. However, in the United States, federal commodity support is still tied to production of a handful of program crops. Steps to uncouple that support and materially reorder assistance to farmers and landowners are debated but commodity interests are deeply entrenched. There is little evidence that the US Congress will initiate any major changes in federal policy direction. In the EU, in sharp contrast, decoupled farm or area-based payments were implemented in 2003.

Our analysis graphically illustrates that, on average, total US federal farm subsidies are lower on an area basis than those of the EU. The picture is far less clear, however, when comparisons move to AEM and a more nuanced view of public support that acknowledges layered efforts by different units of government. Along with federal outlays, some state and local governments also assist farmers and landowners with AEM measures to control pollution and improve water quality. Even greater sums are spent by state and local governments on farmland protection measures. These investments are sometimes swept into the discussion of AEM financing in the United States and sometimes are not.

Environmental concerns were integrated into US farm policy several generations before such changes took place in the EU, but the range of environmental issues addressed by the United States has been narrow. Emphasis has centered on soil erosion and land retirement. Today, US programs have a broader focus but do not directly address landscape amenities and biodiversity, while a large fraction of AEMs in the EU aim at improving or maintaining nature and landscape. Another striking difference between EU and US programs is the amount of effort put into targeting/directing conservation support to resources with relatively large conservation problems. Targeting efforts by the USDA are a hallmark of American AEM programs, along with the implementation of bidding systems in some cases to help guide allocation of public funds. In contrast, evaluations of the EU and German programs show that most contracts and (substantiated for Germany) finances go to spatially untargeted measures. We estimate that about 20 percent of the AEM expenditures in Germany are targeted to priority sites using appropriate environmental information from landscape planning. However, even in the case of spatially targeted programs, the uptake and efficiency is hampered by flat-rate payments, which are too low for some difficult sites and too high for others.

In the United States, as well as in the EU and the German federal system, a considerable and growing amount of discretion over agri-environmental programs is given to the states. However, in the United States, this diversity largely expresses itself in additional financial contribution by the states to a federal core which is designed and promulgated at the federal level. A noteworthy exception is state initiatives to afford farmers and farmland owners relief from the local property tax. Property tax considerations are far less important in the EU. Additionally, the AEM framework supplied by the EU is interpreted differently by the member states. One obvious effect of this policy is the lack of transparent, easily accessible, comparable data in the EU, while in the United States, at least at national and state levels, concise data on direct federal support are now readily available. Another effect, exemplified by the situation in Germany, is the disconnect between expenditure on AEM on one hand and environmental problem density/priorities on the other. This disconnect will take on considerable importance if EU priority areas cannot be safeguarded and managed properly in member states that are relatively poor or do not emphasize the environment in their rural development programs.

AEM payments have to be ultimately judged in the context of the complete toolbox used to solve agri-environmental problems, because the different tools may substitute for each other in some cases. A distinct difference between the United States and the EU in this respect is that good farming practices and other legal obligations arguably address a much broader range of environmental issues in the EU compared to cross-compliance measures now in play in the United States. The EU obligations refer to almost all utilized agricultural areas (UAA), and in general the enforcement mechanism is centered on conservation compliance with the good farming practice rules. The scope of conservation compliance, instituted in the United States more than 20 years ago, is more problematic. Farm legislation in the mid-1980s mandated conservation compliance on actively cropped land designated as being highly susceptible to soil erosion from rain or wind. Acceptable levels of erosion control, however, are not mandated but instead represent a precondition for receiving federal program support. Crop area falling under conservation compliance is only a fraction of the total because much US cropland erodes at or below accepted erosion tolerances under current management. And because not all farmers and all farmland owners have substantial access to federal program support, it is far from clear that denial of such benefits is always a sufficient incentive to deter less-than-satisfactory land stewardship. Conservation compliance provisions extend to fragile grasslands conversion and wetlands conversion, but again, compliance is voluntary.

Notes

1 Major program crops under federal farm legislation are wheat, corn, barley, oats, cotton, rice, soybeans, tobacco, peanuts and sugar. An additional 13 commodities receive limited federal support, largely through nonrecourse commodity loans.
2 Where US conservation program expenditures are reported in euros, the exchange rate is assumed to be US$1.30 per euro.

References

American Farmland Trust, AFT (2007a) "Status of Selected Local PACE Programs: Fact Sheet," American Farmland Trust, Washington, DC. Online, available at: www.farmlandinfo.org/documents/27749/PACE_Local_8–04.pdf.

American Farmland Trust, AFT (2007b) "Status of State PACE Programs: Fact Sheet," American Farmland Trust, Washington, DC. Online, available at: www.farmlandinfo.org/documents/30980/Pace_State_6–06.pdf.

Batie, S. (2003) "The Multifunctional Attributes of Northeastern Agriculture: a Research Agenda," *Agricultural and Resource Economics Review*, 32(1): 1–8.

Batie, S. and R. Horan (2002) "Green Payments Policy," in J. Outlaw and E. Smith (eds.) *The 2002 Farm Bill: Policy Options and Consequences*, Chicago: The Farm Foundation.

Bills, N. (2007) "Fifty Years of Farmland Protection Legislation in the Northeast: Persistent Issues and Emergent Research Opportunities," *Agricultural and Resource Economics Review*, 36(2): 165–173.

Bills, N. and D. Gross (2005) "Sustaining Multifunctional Agricultural Landscapes: Comparing Stakeholder Perspectives in New York (US) and England (UK)," *Land Use Policy*, 22(2): 313–321.

Bills, N., M. Kondo, G. Poe and L. Telega (2005) "Agriculture and the Environment," Chapter 11, *New York Economic Handbook* 2006, Department of Applied Economics and Management, Cornell University, 20pp.

Blandford, D. and R. Boisvert (2002) "Multifunctional Agriculture and Domestic/International Policy Choice," *The Estey Centre Journal of International Law and Trade Policy*, 3(1): 106–118.

Blandford, D. and R. Boisvert (2004) "Multifunctional Agriculture – A View from the United States," paper presented at the 90th symposium of the European Association of Agricultural Economists entitled "Multifunctional Agriculture, Policies and Markets: Understanding the Critical Linkages," Rennes, France.

BMELV (Bundesministerium für Ernährung Landwirtschaft und Verbraucherschutz) (2007) Agrarpolitischer Bericht der Bundesregierung. S. 96ff. Online, available at: www.bmelv.de/cln_044/nn_752130/DE/13-Service/Publikationen/Agrarbericht/AgrarpolitischerBericht2007.html__nnn=true.

Cattaneo, A., R. Claassen, R. Johansson and M. Weinberg (2005) "Flexible Conservation Measures on Working Land: What Challenges Lie Ahead?" *Economics Research Report* (No. 5), Washington, DC: United States Department of Agriculture.

Claassen, R. (2003) "Emphasis Shifts in US Agri-Environmental Policy," USDA-ERS, *Amber Waves*, Washington, DC. Online, available at: www.ers.usda.gov/AmberWaves/November03.

Claassen, R., V. Breneman, S. Bucholtz, A. Cattaneo, R. Johanasson and M. Morehart (2004) "Environmental Compliance in US Agricultural Policy: Past Performance and Future Potential," *Agricultural Economic Report* (No. 832), Washington, DC: Economic Research Service, US Department of Agriculture.

Claassen, Roger, Leroy Hansen, Mark Peters, Vince Breneman, Marca Weinberg, Andrea Cattaneo, Peter Feather, Dwight Gadsby, Daniel Hellerstein, Jeff Hopkins, Paul Johnston, Mitch Morehart and Mark Smith (2001) "Agri-Environmental Policy at the Crossroads: Guideposts on a Changing Landscape," *Agricultural Economic Report* (No. 794), Washington, DC: Economic Research Service, United States Department of Agriculture.

Dobbs, T. (2002) "Resource and Ecological Economics with a 'Multifunctionality' Perspective," *Economics Staff Paper* 2002–3, Economics Department, South Dakota State University, Brookings, South Dakota.

Dobbs, T. and J. Pretty (2001) "Future Directions for Joint Agricultural-environmental Polices: Implications of the United Kingdom Experience for Europe and the United States," South Dakota State University Economics Research Report 2001–1 and University of Essex Centre for Environment and Society Occasional Paper.

Dobbs, T. and J. Pretty (2004) "Agri-Environmental Stewardship Schemes and 'Mutifunctionality'," *Review of Agricultural Economics*, 26(2): 220–237.

European Commission (2005) COUNCIL REGULATION No 1698/2005 of 20 September 2005 on support for rural development by the European Agricultural Fund for Rural Development.

European Commission (2007a) "50 Budgets. Final Adoption of the General Budget of the European Union for the Financial Year 2007," *Official Journal of the European Union*, Volume 50, L 77, March 16, 2007. Section III: Commission Title 05: Agriculture and Rural Development Chapter 05 04: Rural Development. Online, available at: http://eur-lex.europa.eu/JOHtml.do?uri=OJ:L:2007:077:SOM:EN:HTML.

European Commission (2007b) "The 2007 Outlook for Worlds Agricultural Commodity Markets," *Monitoring Agri-trade Policy* (*MAP*) (No 01–07), May 2007. Online, available at: http://ec.europa.eu/agriculture/publi/map/index_en.htm.

European Commission (2007c) "Health Check of the Common Agricultural Policy – Fit for New Opportunities." Online, available at: http://ec.europa.eu/agriculture/health-check/index_en.htm.

European Commission, DG Agriculture (2003) Fact Sheet: Überblick über die Umsetzung der Politik zur Entwicklung des ländlichen Raums im Programmplanungszeitraum 2000–2006. Luxemburg: Amt für amtliche Veröffentlichungen der EU.

Eurostat (2007) "Pocketbooks Agriculture," *Main Statistics 2005–2006*. Online, available at: http://epp.eurostat.ec.europa.eu/portal/page?_pageid=1073,46587259&_dad=portal&_schema=PORTAL&p_product_code=KS-ED-07-002.

Freedgood, J. (1997) "Saving American Farmland: What Works," Northampton, MA: American Farmland Trust, p. 334.

German Advisory Council on the Environment (GACE) (2002) "Towards Strengthening and Reorienting Nature and Landscape Conservation," Special report, English summary and conclusions. Online, available at: www.umweltrat.de.

Gunderson, C., B. Kuhn, S. Offutt and M. Morehart (2004) "A Consideration of the Devolution of Federal Agricultural Policy," *Agricultural Economic Report* (No. 836). Washington, DC: Economic Research Service, US Department of Agriculture.

Hellerstein, D., C. Nickerson, J. Cooper, P. Feather, D. Gadsby, D. Mullarkey, A. Tegene and C. Barnard (2002) "Farmland Protection: The Role of Public Preferences for Rural Amenities," *Agricultural Economic Report* (No. 815). Washington, DC: Economic Research Service, USDA.

Hollis, L. and W. Fulton (2002) "Open Space Protection: Conservation Meets Growth Management," Solimar Research Group, Inc. A discussion paper prepared for the Brookings Institution Center on Urban and Metropolitan Policy, Brookings Institution, Washington, DC.

Libby, L. (2000) "Farmland as a Multi-service Resource: Policy Trends and International Comparisons. Paper prepared for the International Symposium on Agricultural Policies Under the New Round of WTO Agricultural Negotiations," Taipei, Taiwan, December 5–8.

Lubowski, R., S. Vesterby, A. Bucholtz, A. Baez and M. Roberts (2006) "Major Uses of Land in the United States," 2002. EIB-14 (May), Washington, DC: Economic Research Service, US Department of Agriculture.

New York State Department of Environmental Conservation (2004) "State Pollutant Discharge Elimination System (SPDES) General Permit For Concentrated Animal Feeding Operations (CAFOs)," Albany, New York. Online, available at: www.dec.ny.gov/docs/water_pdf/gp0402permit.pdf.

Osterburg, B., H. Nitsch, S. Wagner and A. Laggner (2007) "Analysis of Policy Instruments for Greenhouse Gas Abatement and Compliance with the Convention on Biodiversity, Impact of Environmental Agreements on the CAP," document number: MEACAP WP6 D16a. Online, available at: www.ieep.eu/projectminisites/meacap/index.php.

Société Oréade-Brèche (2005) "Évaluation des Mesures Agro-Environnementales EU," Rapport final financée par la Commission Européenne. Online, available at: http://ec.europa.eu/agriculture/eval/reports/measures/index_fr.htm.

Tremblay, R., J. Foster, J. MacKenzie, D. Derr, B. Lessley, G. Cole and N. Bills (1987) "Use Value Assessment of Agricultural Land in the Northeast," *NE Regional Research Publication*, Burlington: Vermont Agr. Exp. Station Bulletin 694, University of Vermont.

US Department of Agriculture (1984) "History of Agricultural Price-Support and Adjustment Programs 1933–84," Agriculture Information Bulletin No. 485, Washington, DC: Economic Research Service.

US Department of Agriculture (2007–2008) Office of Budget and Program Analysis, *Budget Summary and Performance Plan*, Washington, DC. Online, available at: www.obpa.usda.gov/budsum/fy08budsum.pdf.

US Department of Agriculture (2008) Economic Research Service, "Government Payments by State and Program," download data sets available at: www.ers.usda.gov/data/FarmIncome/finfidmuxls.htm.

von Ruschkowski, E. and C. von Haaren (2008) "Agrarumweltmaßnahmen in Deutschland im europäischen Vergleich," *Eine Bewertung und Optimierungsansätze für den Natur- und Klimaschutz. – Naturschutz und Landschaftsplanung*, 40(10): 329–335.

5   Evaluation of agricultural land preservation programs[1]

Lori Lynch, Wayne Gray and
Jacqueline Geoghegan

Introduction

Farmland preservation programs form part of the suite of agri-environmental policies used by state and local governments to maximize society's welfare. They are justified on a variety of agricultural and environmental grounds: to preserve a productive land base for the agricultural economy, to preserve the amenity values of open space and rural character, to slow suburban sprawl, to provide wildlife habitat, and to provide groundwater recharge in areas where suburban development is occurring (Gardner 1977; Nelson 1992; Hellerstein *et al.* 2002; Duke and Ilvento 2004). Since the late 1970s, state and local preservation programs have taken two basic forms, either purchase of development rights/purchase of agricultural conservation easements (PDR/PACE) or transfer of development rights (TDR) under which landowners may voluntarily choose to enroll. Most programs attach an easement to the preserved land that restricts the right to use the land for residential, commercial or industrial purposes. Participating landowners are provided with an incentive payment or tax benefit to compensate them for the restrictions imposed. As the government enters the land market for these rights, they incur a high cost for each parcel enrolled. The high cost and the limited budgetary resources may result in ineffective programs because few farms can be preserved. Therefore analysis examining the actual opportunity costs of participating landowners may provide needed information to adjust the programs and stretch farmland preservation dollars further.

More than 124 governmental entities in the United States have implemented farmland preservation programs; over 1.67 million acres (0.676 million hectares) are now in preserved status at a cost of almost $4 billion (American Farmland Trust 2005a, 2005b). Citizens continue to pass ballot initiatives generating funds for these types of programs: in 2000, $7.5 billion in conservation funding was authorized; in 2001, $1.7 billion; in 2002, $5.7 billion; and most recently in 2006, $5.73 billion. In addition, the Land Trust Alliance reports that US land trusts have doubled their conservation acres from six million to 11.9 million acres (2.43 to 4.82 million hectares) since 2000. The state of Maryland, the focus of the research in this chapter, has had a variety of state and county agricultural land preservation programs, preserving approximately 343,000 acres (139,000 hectares) since the late 1970s.

There is a growing body of research evaluating farmland preservation programs. Research has asked a broad range of questions related to the programs. Are enough acres enrolled? What types of farms are enrolled – hobby or productive? Does contiguity matter and is it achieved? Do certain programs work better than others (PDR versus TDR)? Do programs impact farmland loss or development patterns? Do preserved lands provide the amenity benefits people desire? Do the programs have spillover impacts? (Brabec and Smith 2002; Lynch and Lovell 2003; Duke and Ilvento 2004; Liu and Lynch 2006; Lynch and Carpenter 2003; Duncan 1984; Pfeffer and Lapping 1994; Feather and Barnard 2003; McConnell *et al.* 2006; Zollinger and Krannich 2001; Rilla and Sokolow 2000; Nelson 1992; Feitshans 2003). In Maryland's recent Smart Growth legislation, the Rural Legacy program set out to prioritize preserving contiguous farms to make orderly and fiscally responsible development more achievable and to create large agricultural zones (Lynch and Liu 2007). These papers provide some sense of how agricultural land preservation programs may be altered or formulated to improve social welfare.

Yet these papers and others continue to suggest that too much farmland is being lost[2] in part because PDR programs can be very expensive. To further complicate matters, preservation efforts can generate positive amenities for adjacent homeowners and may increase demand for housing near preserved parcels, which makes achieving the goals of preservation even more costly and thus more difficult (Geoghegan *et al.* 2003; Ready and Abdalla 2005; Irwin 2002).

One of the underlying motivations for farmland preservation programs is that the programs keep agricultural land affordable, because farms with conservation easements attached should sell at a discount. The lower-priced land should be more easily purchased by new and expanding farmers and thus help retain a viable agricultural sector (Gale 1993). Evaluating whether farmland preservation programs are facilitating the purchase of land for agricultural producers therefore requires an analysis of how much the easement restrictions decrease the selling price of preserved farms, compared to similar properties without easements.

Determining the optimal budget for a farmland preservation program is a related policy challenge. A recent Maryland report suggests that to achieve the current preservation goal (686,000 more acres/278,000 more hectares), the state would need to allocate as much as $4.58 billion to obtain the least expensive eligible acres (Lynch *et al.* 2007b). Addressing both the opportunity cost of enrollment and the size of the budget requires a better understanding of the "right" price farmers should be paid for their enrollment in the program. Conceptually, this is quite straightforward: the attachment of the easement reduces the value of the agricultural property because of the lost opportunity to develop. If the development rights have no value, i.e. the highest and best use for the land is an agricultural use, then no compensation should be paid. If the development rights are the full market value of the land, i.e. there is no profitable agricultural use, then a fee simple purchase by the public sector might be most appropriate.

An alternative approach to this issue is to ask if these programs are over-paying for the properties they enroll. For example, if agricultural lands that are enrolled are not selling for a reduced price with the restrictions attached, the preservation programs are not making land more affordable to farmers. Are these programs simply providing privately owned inaccessible open space at a large cost to the taxpayers?

Previous results

Capital Asset Price theory predicts that the restrictions imposed on further development with agricultural easements will reduce the sales price of a farm and thus farmland owners should be compensated.[3] Surprisingly, Nickerson and Lynch, using sales data for 223 farms (20 with easements) in Maryland during 1994–1997, found little evidence that easement restrictions affect sales prices. Using both hedonic pricing models and propensity score models, Lynch *et al.* (2007a) re-examined the impact of agricultural easements on sales prices using a substantially expanded dataset of 3,554 observations in 22 Maryland counties, including 249 preserved properties over 1997–2003. Results from the hedonic analysis suggest statistically significant reductions in price due to preservation, ranging from 11.4 percent to 16.9 percent. However, the results of a propensity score approach were quite different, taking advantage of a very strong predictor of program participation: the distance to the closest preserved parcel. With this distance variable in the model, the estimated impact of preservation on price became small and statistically insignificant. This means that unrestricted land located near preserved parcels tends to sell for the same low price as the preserved land. Anderson and Weinhold (2005) also find a statistically insignificant impact on the land value from the easement restrictions. They find a significant decrease only when limiting their analysis to vacant parcels and eliminating county binary variables, sales-year binary variables, and two of the minimum zoning variables from the analysis. They estimate a decrease in land value of between 35 percent and 50 percent for vacant land. A 47 percent reduction is found using eight of the 19 vacant easement parcels' sales with the most stringent easement restrictions. A 50 percent reduction is found when comparing the price of 36 vacant agricultural parcels that have not been preserved to that of the 11 vacant agricultural parcels with easements. Michaels (2007) also finds that preserved parcels in Baltimore County do not sell for less than unpreserved parcels, all else equal.

We found these results to be quite puzzling. If these results are true, then the agricultural preservation programs are paying much more than the opportunity costs of the landowners. In this chapter, we re-investigate the question once again, using a new measure to capture the influence of nearby preserved parcels, i.e. trying to further incorporate the spatial aspects of preservation and land markets. Instead of the distance to the nearest preserved parcel, we use GIS techniques to calculate the percent of preserved agricultural land within a 1 km and a 5 km buffer surrounding each agricultural sales parcel. We then analyze the impact of agricultural easements on sales prices, using both hedonic regression and propensity score approaches, including this new variable. To eliminate the potentially confounding effect of the residential services provided by structures on agricultural parcels, we also investigate a sample that contains only agricultural parcels without structures, as these parcels are strictly for agricultural use.

Maryland background

Maryland has been a leader among states in land preservation efforts, with several programs to retain land in forest and agricultural use. These programs began in part because the state lost almost 50 percent of its agricultural land, 1.9 million acres (0.769 million hectares), between 1949 and 1997 (USDA 1999), while its population increased by almost 120 percent (US Census Bureau 1999). While the losses have been large, Maryland still contains a fair amount of natural and working lands on its 6.2 million acres (2.51 hectares). In December 2002, developed lands represented only 20 percent of Maryland's total land area, and protected lands[4] accounted for another 19 percent. Much of the remaining 3.8 million acres (1.54 hectares) was privately owned undeveloped land, one-half in agriculture and one-half in forest or natural cover. Maryland recently set a goal of tripling the amount of land currently in preservation status to over one million acres by the year 2022.

In the 25 years that agricultural and other preservation programs have existed in Maryland, the state and county programs have preserved approximately 343,000 acres (139,000 hectares). If the programs have managed to purchase easements on the "easiest to enroll" parcels or those with the lowest cost (Horowitz *et al.* 2007), preserving twice this much land in just 20 years will require very efficient programs. Maryland's population is also projected to grow 11.5 percent to six million people by 2020, likely requiring ongoing conversion of agricultural and forest land to housing and commercial development. In addition, preservation is becoming more costly as the value of land continues to increase: between 2002 and 2006, average agricultural land values doubled in Maryland to $8,900 per acre (almost $22,000 per hectare).

Maryland began one of the first statewide purchase-of-development-rights (PDR) programs in the late 1970s with the creation of the Maryland Agricultural Land Preservation Foundation (MALPF). As of 2004, MALPF has preserved almost 233,000 acres at a cost of $329 million (MALPF Task Force 2005). MALPF uses appraisals and an "auction" to set the easement value. It uses the lower of:

1   a calculated easement value equal to an appraisal value minus the agricultural value; or
2   a bid made by the landowner.

Farms are accepted in order of highest value per dollar bid until the budget is expended.[5] MALPF has determined that the savings due to landowners being willing to take a lower value than the calculated easement value has been almost $102 million out of the total easement value of $398.9 million for the 217,460 acres (109,856 hectares) it had preserved through 2002. This computes to about a 25 percent discount in the easement values. Recent analysis suggests that the level of discounting has been decreasing with time (Horowitz *et al.* 2007). Minimum eligibility criteria were recently changed; now each farm must have 50 contiguous acres or contiguity to another preserved farm and at least 50 percent of its soil classified as USDA Class I, II or III, or Woodland Group I or II.

In addition to statewide efforts, individual counties have introduced their own agricultural preservation programs using both transfer-of-development-rights (TDR) and PDR formats. Calvert County and Montgomery County are considered leaders in the use of TDR programs. Howard County's use of installment purchase agreements is studied throughout the country. The Rural Legacy program, begun in 1997 as part of the state's Smart Growth program, seeks to preserve large contiguous blocks of natural and working landscapes. Statewide, the Rural Legacy program has encumbered $156 million worth of land through 2006 and preserved almost 52,000 acres (21,000 hectares). In addition, federal and state tax benefits provide incentives to landowners to enroll their property in preservation programs and with the Maryland Environmental Trust (MET).

MALPF and some of the local preservation programs are funded in part by the continued conversion of farmland to other uses. An agricultural transfer tax is collected when farmland leaves an agricultural use for a residential, commercial or industrial use. Through simple calculations, one can determine the cost of preserving one acre of land at the average 2002 MALPF easement price per county when the agricultural transfer tax is the sole funding mechanism. Carroll County would require the conversion of $60,051 worth of farmland, Baltimore County the conversion of $76,352, St. Mary's County the conversion of $49,607, and Talbot County the conversion of $40,722. In terms of acres, the preservation of just one acre of land in Carroll County would require the loss of 11.65 acres (4.7 hectares) elsewhere in the county, in Baltimore County the loss of 9.6 acres (3.9 hectares), in St. Mary's County the loss of 12.75 acres (5.16 hectares) and in Talbot County the loss of nine acres (3.64 hectares) (Lynch *et al.* 2007b). Recent legislation proposed an increase in the agricultural transfer tax to provide more funding for preservation (Environmental Law Institute 2008).

Theoretical framework

In a competitive land market, land is assumed to yield a stream of net returns. Ricardian theory states that the profitability of agricultural land is based on fertility or soil characteristics and that this fertility determines the land rent an agricultural producer would pay. Von Thunen, Mills and others proposed that the stream of benefits of living or farming at a particular location relative to the town center determines the rent an individual would be willing to pay. Hardie *et al.* (2001) combined the Ricardian and Von Thunen models to find that the market values of parcels in suburban counties are the sum of the Ricardian rent and the location or accessibility rent. Capozza and Helsley (1989) and later Plantinga and Miller (2001) and Plantinga *et al.* (2002) added an expectation component (possible capital gains) when valuing land at the urban fringe. This expected stream of rents and potential gains determines the market price per acre P_i of the parcel *i*. The market value is thus the expected sum of agricultural rents, A_i, from time $t = 0$ up to an optimal conversion date t^*, at which time the land is converted into a residential use with expected net returns of R_i as shown in equation 5.1.[6]

Agricultural and residential rents are a function of X_i, the characteristics and location of the land, and *s*, time.

$$P_i = E_t\left[\int_{t=0}^{t^*} A_i(X_i, s)e^{-r(s-t)}ds + \int_{t^*}^{\infty} R_i(X_i, s)e^{-r(s-t)}ds\right] \qquad (5.1)$$

Land ownership may be thought of as a bundle of rights, one of which is the right to develop the land up to the allowable zoning density, which a landowner can sell without relinquishing ownership of the land. An agricultural landowner can extract the value of these development rights by selling the rights to a preservation program and receiving a net easement payment, EV_i. The new market price would be the expected sum of agricultural rents forever as shown here.

$$P_i = E_t\left[\int_{t=0}^{\infty} A_i(X_i, s)e^{-r(s-t)}ds\right]$$

Landowners will enroll their parcel in an agricultural preservation program if

$$E\left[\int_0^{t^*} A_i(X_i, s)e^{-r(s)}ds + \int_{t^*}^{\infty} R_i(X_i, s)e^{-r(s)}ds\right] < E\left[\int_0^{\infty} A_i(X_i, s)e^{-r(s)}ds\right] + EV_i$$

or

$$E\left[\int_{t^*}^{\infty} R_i(X_i, s)e^{-r(s)}ds\right] < E\left[\int_{t^*}^{\infty} A_i(X_i, s)e^{-r(s)}ds\right] + EV_i.[7]$$

However, whether or not the restrictions are fully capitalized into the land value is an empirical question. In a Washington State PDR program, Blakely (1991) found that while the permanent easement restrictions did lower the prices of preserved farms relative to unpreserved farms, the resulting prices were much higher than the agricultural use value based on the stream of agricultural rents. Nickerson and Lynch (2001) found lower prices for restricted parcels but only weak statistical evidence that the easement restrictions were the explanation. Lynch *et al.* (2007a) found limited evidence of price impacts using propensity score methods. Anderson and Weinhold (2005) and Michaels (2007) also found very limited evidence of significant effects on land price due to the restrictions.

Method

The hedonic model is the traditional approach for estimating a capitalization effect, and we begin our analysis using this approach. Hedonic modeling has a long tradition in agricultural economics and has been used in innumerable applications. Unfortunately, simply including a dummy variable for the existence of an agricultural easement in the regression is problematic, since landowners may have (not) entered farmland preservation programs specifically because their parcel's market value was lower (higher) than other parcels. Nickerson and Lynch (2001) used a Heckman model to control for sample selection as did Anderson and Weinhold (2005), but neither found a significant selection effect.

In addition to a hedonic model, we also used a non-parametric approach: the propensity score method. This method has multiple benefits. First, the matching protocol ensures that the preserved parcels will be matched to those non-preserved parcels that are most similar in terms of characteristics, so dissimilar parcels and outliers will have little or no influence in the analysis. Second, the method does not assume that preservation status is exogenous, i.e. the decision to participate could depend on the parcel's expected sale price and the expected PDR payment. Finally, unlike the hedonic model, this approach does not assume a specific functional form for the price equation.

The propensity score matching method was developed by Rosenbaum and Rubin (1983). This method has been used in related economic studies to evaluate the plant birth effects of environmental regulations (List *et al.* 2003); the land market effects of zoning (McMillen and McDonald 2002); the effect of designated preservation areas on preservation and conversion rates (Lynch and Liu 2007); the impact of preservation programs on farmland loss (Liu and Lynch 2006); in addition to earlier work on agricultural easements (Lynch *et al.* 2007a).

Assessing the impacts of easement restrictions is difficult because of incomplete information. While one can identify whether a parcel is preserved (treated) or not (not treated or control) and the outcome (market price) conditional on its treatment, one cannot observe the counterfactual, i.e. what would have happened if the parcel had not been enrolled in a farmland preservation program. Thus, the fundamental problem in identifying the treatment effect is constructing the unobservable counterfactuals for the treated observations.

Let Y_1 denote the outcome in the group of observations if treatment has occurred ($D=1$), and Y_0 denote the outcome for the group of control observations ($D=0$). If one could observe the treated and the control states, the average treatment effect, τ, would equal $\bar{Y}_1 - \bar{Y}_0$ where $\bar{Y}_1$ equals the mean outcome of the treatment group and $\bar{Y}_0$ that of the control group. Unfortunately, only $\bar{Y}_1$ or $\bar{Y}_0$ are observed for each parcel. In a laboratory experiment, researchers solve this problem by randomly assigning subjects to be treated or not treated and then construct the counterfactual. Outside of the laboratory, however, $\tau \neq \bar{Y}_1 - \bar{Y}_0$ unless the treatment condition was randomly assigned. The propensity score matching (PSM) method proposed by Rosenbaum and Rubin (1983) demonstrates that if the data justify matching on some observable vector of covariates, X, then matching pairs on the estimated probability of selection into treatment or control groups based on X is also justified. We assume a Conditional Independence Assumption (CIA) condition that:

$$E[Y_0|D = 1, X] = E[Y_0|D = 0, X] = E[Y_0|X], P(D = 1|X) \in (0, 1)$$

to estimate the average treatment effect.

The average treatment effect on the treated equals the expected difference in outcome Y between the treated observations and their corresponding counterfactuals, which are constructed from the matched controls.

$$\Delta^{TT} = E(Y_1|D = 1) - E(Y_0|D = 1) = E(Y_1|D = 1) - E(Y_0|D = 0, P(X))$$

For the weaker condition to hold, the conditioning set of X needs to include all of the variables that affect both selection and outcome. Finding parcels that have identical values for all covariates in X is not possible since the set of X is usually multidimensional. However, Rosenbaum and Rubin (1983) demonstrate that if one calculates a propensity score such that $P(X) = P(D = 1|X)$, this is equivalent to conditioning on $P(X)$. So, in our example, all factors that may affect the land price and the existence of an easement on a parcel except the treatment state are included to estimate $P(X)$. By assuming that the X's are equivalent for the matched treatment and control observations, we are controlling for the effects of these factors that may impact the market price.

Data[8]

Our main data source is the GIS-based MDPropertyView 2002 Database (from the Maryland Department of Planning), consisting of all arm's-length agricultural land parcels greater than ten acres (4.5 hectares) that were sold between 1997 and 2003.[9] In order to calculate the per-acre land value, we subtracted the assessed value of any improvements to the parcel (such as structures) from the market price, and then divided by parcel size to get PRICE per acre. We included both parcels with and without homes. We did, however, drop parcels deemed either unrepresentative of those a preservation policy would target or those which appeared to have data errors. Thus we dropped all parcels that had improvement values of more than $1 million and those with residential structures that had no improvement value listed. Parcels with per-acre land value less than $300 were also dropped as this was the minimum assessed agricultural use value. Due to Critical Area regulations, which might interact with preservation development restrictions, we dropped all parcels with waterfront area. This resulted in 3,359 observations, of which 245 had easement restrictions. We also dropped observations from Montgomery County as we could not determine the exact number of TDR rights individual parcels within Montgomery County had sold or retained and thus the level of restrictions on these properties.

The dataset creation relies on the ArcView 3.2 and ArcGIS 8.2 Geographic Information Systems (GIS) software programs to extract and combine data for geographically referenced parcels. The compiled dataset contains one record for each parcel in the state of Maryland at least ten acres (4.5 hectares) in area, with geocoded parcel-level attribute data for each parcel.

The MdPropertyView 2002 Database (MDPVD) includes data updated through October 2002 from the state's Department of Assessments and Taxation. For each parcel, data were collected from MDPVD on the most current transfer date; price paid for the entire parcel at last transfer date; how the parcel was conveyed (arm's-length or non-arm's-length); whether it was part of a multi-parcel sale; number of acres in the parcel; waterfront area for those counties near the Atlantic Ocean, Chesapeake Bay or major tributaries; the assessed value of the land; the assessed value of all improvements; and the total assessed value. The parcels are also spatially referenced by the x and y coordinates, allowing the use of GIS techniques to extract parcel-level information. Each parcel is identified by a unique account number that allows parcel-level links between the various MdPropertyView 2002 data files and parcel-level datasets created by other state agencies.

A wealth of data characterizing Maryland lands is linked to the MDPVD land parcels spatially through GIS techniques. For example, the Maryland Department of Planning has detailed land-use data from satellite and aerial photography taken as recently as 2002. Land uses are categorized into Urban Areas, Agriculture and Forest. Urban Areas includes the sub-categories low-density residential, medium-density residential and high-density residential. Agriculture includes cropland, orchards, vineyards and agricultural buildings and storage (CROP). PASTURE was treated as a separate land use. Forest (FOREST) includes deciduous, evergreen and mixed forests as well as brush. ArcView is used to extract the land-use data for each buffer parcel as the percent of the parcel in each land-use category.

Soil data are extracted from the US Department of Agriculture Soil Conservation Service and Maryland Department of State Planning's 1973 maps which classify all Maryland soils. The Natural Soil Groups Technical Report (Maryland Department of State Planning 1973) provides estimated chemical and physical properties for each soil group. Soils are grouped by productivity, erosion potential, permeability, stoniness and rockiness, depth to bedrock, depth to water table, slope, stability and susceptibility to flooding. We followed the Maryland classification system in defining prime soils (PRIME) as agriculturally productive, permeable, having limited erosion potential and having minimal slope (Maryland Department of State Planning 1973). GIS techniques were also used to add distance to the nearest metropolitan area (Washington, DC or Baltimore) based on Euclidean distance. These distances were transformed to logged variables to allow for nonlinear impacts (LDDC, LDBALT).

Maryland Department of Planning has also developed a generalized zoning map based on the individualized zoning within each county. ArcView was used to extract a generalized zoning code for each parcel within the database to create comparability between counties. ZONE1 (most protective), ZONE2 (moderately protective) and ZONE3 (less protective) describe the generalized zoning codes for the rural areas of each county, while ZONE4 includes all other less-restrictive zoning categories combined (residential, commercial and industrial). ZONE1 is the most restrictive with a density of one dwelling unit for each 20 acres (8.09 hectares) or more. ZONE2 is less restrictive with a density of one dwelling unit for each ten to 20 acres (4.05 to 8.09 hectares). ZONE3 is the least restrictive rural and residential zoning, with a density of one dwelling unit for each one to ten acres (0.40 to 4.05 hectares).

Data was obtained on existing agricultural easements from the Maryland Agricultural Land Preservation Foundation (MALPF) published in 2004.[10] Additional easements and preservation acquisitions made by state, local and private organizations were compiled from several datasets.[11] Maryland Environmental Trust easements are also perpetual restrictions on development. Private conservation groups' parcels, such as land trusts, were only included when easement restrictions could be ensured; otherwise these parcels were deleted from the database. Subsequently, the amount of easement area surrounding each agricultural sales parcel at a 1 km (EASE1K) and 5 km (EASE5K) radius was calculated using all preserved properties, not only those that sold during the study period.

In some cases, multiple parcels were purchased by the same person on the same date and the recorded sales price was not divided between parcels. Instead, the total price for the entire transaction was recorded, making it necessary to aggregate these parcels into one transaction. These parcels were aggregated to the "farm-level" where properties were adjacent, defined as being within one-quarter mile of each other, using the edges of the circular parcel buffer as the measurement points. The parcel-level data were aggregated to the farm level by weighting each parcel's characteristics by the number of acres in that parcel. This applied to the size of the parcel in acres, the number of acres in easements, the percentage of prime soil, and the percentage of the parcel in various land uses. The farm-level transaction price and the assessed values for land, improvements and total value were obtained by summing over prices and assessed values per parcel in that farm. If more than one parcel was purchased on the same date by the same person, but parcels were further apart than 0.25 miles, they were considered separate parcels. In this case, we divided the total sale price weighted by the number of acres in each parcel bought.

Table 5.1 presents descriptive statistics for the full sample, as well as the sub-samples of preserved and unpreserved parcels and parcels without structures. Preserved parcels have a lower per-acre land price on average: $3,293 compared to $5,677 ($8,137 compared to $14,007 per hectare). Preserved parcels have a greater amount of preserved land in their vicinity: approximately two and a half times as much for the smaller 1 km area, and almost half again as much for the larger 5 km area. Preserved parcels are (not surprisingly) more likely to qualify for the MALPF program; they are larger, with a higher percent of prime soils and cropland. Only a small fraction of these agricultural parcels are located in residential, commercial or industrial zones, although this is more common for the non-preserved parcels. The land price per acre is lower for parcels without structures, even after subtracting the assessed value of the structure for those parcels with structures.

Table 5.1 Descriptive statistics and variable definitions

	Preserved				
	3,152 – full sample n = 3,152 Mean	Standard Dev.	Yes n = 255 Mean	No n = 2897 Mean	
price	5,484	8,732	3,293	5,677	Price ($/acre, adjusted)
hprice	13,551		8,137	14,003	Hprice ($/hectare)
logpr	8.076	0.987	7.820	8.099	Log (Price)
agprot	0.081	0.273	1.000	0.000	Preserved parcel (0/1)
ease1k	0.082	0.141	0.181	0.073	Fraction preserved within 1 kilometer
ease5k	0.074	0.074	0.116	0.070	Fraction preserved within 5 kilometers
elig	0.397	0.489	0.773	0.364	Meets eligibility criteria for
prime	0.427	0.423	0.583	0.413	Fraction of prime quality soil in parcel
crop	0.504	0.349	0.678	0.489	Fraction of cropland in parcel
struct	0.548	0.498	0.620	0.542	Structure present (0/1)
lacres	3.742	0.911	4.455	3.679	Log (Acres)
ldbalt	11.136	0.697	11.006	11.148	Log (distance to Baltimore, MD)
lddc	11.368	0.475	11.284	11.376	Log (distance to Washington, DC)
popg78	0.236	0.179	0.245	0.236	Census Tract population growth 70–80
popg89	0.155	0.129	0.160	0.155	Census Tract population growth 80–90
popg90	0.109	0.116	0.115	0.108	Census Tract population growth 90–00
zone1	0.184	0.388	0.106	0.191	Most restrictive rural zoning
zone2	0.260	0.439	0.447	0.244	Less restrictive zoning
zone3	0.488	0.500	0.435	0.493	Least restrictive zoning
zone4	0.067	0.251	0.012	0.072	All other zoning (residential, commercial, industrial)

Results

In order to test our hypothesis concerning the capitalization of easements into agricultural sales prices, we developed a suite of econometric specifications. We performed a side-by-side comparison of a traditional hedonic model and a propensity score-matching approach, using the same set of covariates in each modeling approach. In our initial analysis, the results suggested that agricultural properties without structures were potentially a separate market from parcels with structures, so the models were also estimated for the sub-sample of parcels without structures.

Table 5.2 presents the results of an OLS hedonic model of parcel prices for the entire sample for three different specifications. Model 2a is a base case that includes no variables relating to nearby easements; models 2b and 2c include the fraction of preserved lands in 1 km and 5 km buffers, respectively, plus an interaction term between these variables and the existence of a structure.[12] That is, EASE1K is the effect of protected land within one kilometer for parcels without structures, and EASE1K + EASE1K_S is the effect for parcels with structures (EASE1K_S is the marginal impact of EASE1K for parcels with structures).

Estimated per-acre land prices for preserved parcels in the hedonic models are about 11 percent lower than prices for non-preserved parcels, and this effect is statistically significant across model specification. There may be a neighborhood effect of preservation, although the evidence here is weak. For parcels without structures, increasing the fraction of the buffer land enrolled in preservation programs by ten percentage points would decrease the selling price of the parcel by 0.9 percent for the 1 km buffer and by 2.8 percent for the 5 km buffer. For parcels with structures, the estimated effect is opposite: for the 1 km buffer, prices would increase by 1.5 percent, while for increases in the 5 km buffer, prices would increase by 0.7 percent.

The control variables generally have the expected effects: higher prices per acre for properties with prime agricultural soils, with higher levels of crop rather than pasture or forest, and with structures present; lower prices per acre for parcels farther from cities or with more acres. One of the zoning variables did not behave as expected. With the excluded category of ZONE3 (the least restrictive rural zoning), the estimated coefficient on ZONE4 (all other residential and commercial zoning) is positive and statistically significant, as expected, and the estimated coefficient on ZONE2 is negative and statistically significant (as fewer houses are permitted per acre, i.e. zoning density decreases, the market value of the land decreases). However, the estimated coefficient on ZONE1 is counter-intuitively positive and statistically significant.

The population growth rates in the 1970s and 1980s did not have a statistically significant impact on the selling price of agricultural property, but the population growth rate between 1990 and 2000 did have a positive and statistically significant impact on the market value, suggesting that only recent population growth has affected sales prices.

Moving from the hedonic approach to the propensity score approach, the first stage of the propensity score analysis involved estimating a probit model of the propensity for a property to be preserved. Table 5.3 presents these results. Similar to the hedonic approach, we estimated three different specifications: a

Table 5.2 Hedonic results: full sample ($n = 3,152$)

Depvar:	logprice		
Model:	2a	2b	2c
Intcpt	16.377	16.387	16.411
	(25.64)	(25.66)	(25.59)
Agprot	−0.114	−0.119	−0.113
	(−2.33)	(−2.40)	(−2.30)
Struct	0.159	0.140	0.133
	(6.06)	(4.64)	(3.64)
Lacres	−0.401	−0.401	−0.401
	(−27.20)	(−27.18)	(−27.15)
Prime	0.168	0.169	0.170
	(4.57)	(4.58)	(4.60)
Ldbalt	−0.40	−0.40	−0.401
	(−10.65)	(−10.64)	(−10.63)
Lddc	−0.220	−0.220	−0.220
	(−3.59)	(−3.58)	(−3.59)
Crop	0.272	0.274	0.274
	(6.92)	(6.94)	(6.95)
zone1	0.135	0.132	0.137
	(3.55)	(3.43)	(3.56)
zone2	−0.245	−0.250	−0.244
	(−6.76)	(−6.79)	(−6.52)
zone4	0.172	0.172	0.172
	(3.25)	(3.24)	(3.23)
popg78	0.084	0.087	0.087
	(0.96)	(0.99)	(0.99)
popg89	−0.166	−0.169	−0.164
	(−1.37)	(−1.40)	(−1.36)
popg90	0.635	0.628	0.628
	(5.21)	(5.15)	(5.15)
ease1k		−0.092	
		(−0.66)	
ease1k_s		0.238	
		(1.31)	
ease5k			−0.283
			(−0.93)
ease5k_s			0.348
			(0.99)
R-sq	0.484	0.485	0.484

base, with EASE1K, and with EASE5K. We found a greater probability of easements on properties that are larger, with more cropland and prime agricultural soils, and (not surprisingly) properties indicated to be eligible for the program. Interestingly, having a structure on the property, distance to cities and population growth rates have no statistically significant impact on the probability of enrollment. The individual easement buffer variables (EASE1K and EASE5K) significantly increase the probability of enrollment – the more neighboring land is enrolled, the greater the probability of a parcel being enrolled, all else being equal. In addition, the inclusion of the EASE1K or EASE5K increases the value of the pseudo-R-squared. The same pattern of results on the zoning variables from the hedonic models hold for these models as well: relative to ZONE3, ZONE4 decreases and ZONE2 increases the probability of enrollment, as expected, but ZONE1 unexpectedly decreases the probability of enrollment.

Table 5.4 presents the final results of the propensity score analysis for the full sample and the two sub-samples: those parcels with and those without structures. The "average effect of treatment on the treated" (ATT) values were calculated as the difference between the sales price of each easement property (the treatment group) and the average sales price for a comparison (control) group of non-easement properties with similar estimated probabilities of participating in a preservation program. We considered two approaches for forming the control groups: nearest-neighbor (based on the single closest control observation to the treatment observation) and kernel (based on a distance-weighted average of all observations "reasonably close" to the treatment observation).

For the full sample, using propensity scores calculated for the base model, the nearest-neighbor matching method estimated the market price of preserved parcels to be 6.2 to 9.1 percent lower than comparable non-preserved parcels, although the bootstrapped t-statistics are somewhat weak. The kernel method substantially increased the estimated effect of preservation, with 13.6 to 14.7 percent lower prices for preserved parcels, while allowing nearly all of the non-preserved parcels to serve in one or more of the comparison groups. Including the EASE1K and EASE5K variables, respectively, changed the coefficients and t-statistics only slightly. Thus the impact of the easement restrictions is robust to the measures of the degree of preservation of lands near the parcel (unlike the results of the Lynch *et al.* (2007a) paper where the "distance to nearest preserved parcel" variable was used).

The results for the no-structure dataset demonstrated a greater estimated effect of easements on sales price. The kernel model approach generated statistically significant results: market land values per acre decreased from 18.2 percent to 22.6 percent. Parcels with no structures and with limited ability to build structures in the future are the ones we would most expect to demonstrate a price decrease due to easement restrictions.

The results for the structure sub-sample were similar although almost 50 percent smaller overall. The kernel model approach generated statistically significant results while the nearest neighbor method did not. The decrease in market land values per acre for preserved parcels, relative to similar non-preserved parcels, ranged from 10.4 percent to 13.3 percent due to the easement restrictions.

Table 5.3 Probit model of easement participation: full sample ($n = 3,152$)

Probability of being preserved			
Model:	3a	3b	3c
Intcpt	−3.864	−4.252	−5.421
	(−2.06)	(−2.16)	(−2.75)
Elig	0.471	0.519	0.522
	(3.52)	(3.72)	(3.81)
Struct	0.109	0.089	0.015
	(1.42)	(0.91)	(0.12)
Lacres	0.290	0.271	0.265
	(4.00)	(3.62)	(3.58)
Prime	0.327	0.337	0.369
	(3.08)	(3.04)	(3.36)
Ldbalt	0.026	0.058	0.089
	(0.23)	(0.49)	(0.74)
Lddc	−0.011	−0.010	0.052
	(−0.06)	(−0.05)	(0.27)
Crop	0.771	0.746	0.746
	(6.04)	(5.66)	(5.72)
zone1	−0.342	−0.471	−0.443
	(−2.83)	(−3.66)	(−3.50)
zone2	0.262	0.133	0.108
	(2.65)	(1.29)	(1.04)
zone4	0.706	−0.690	−0.685
	(−2.58)	(−2.41)	(−2.45)
popg78	0.327	0.510	0.537
	(1.25)	(1.84)	(1.93)
popg89	−0.223	−0.617	−0.457
	(−0.58)	(−1.45)	(−1.08)
popg90	0.385	0.254	0.284
	(1.02)	(0.63)	(0.71)
ease1k		1.737	
		(5.26)	
ease1k_s		0.403	
		(0.95)	
ease5k			2.926
			(3.43)
ease5k_s			1.098
			(1.13)
R-sq	0.181	0.224	0.206

Table 5.4 Average effect of treatment on the treated (ATT) models

	ATT – nearest neighbor			*ATT – kernel*		
Full sample (3,152 obs)						
BASE	255/218[a]	−0.088[b]	−1.0255[c]	255/2768[a]	−0.147 [b]	−2.7[c]
EASE1K	255/206	−0.062	−0.7	255/2582	−0.136	−2.7
EASE5K	255/207	−0.091	−1.2	255/2681	−0.146	−2.5
No Structure sub-sample (1,424 obs)						
	ATT – nearest neighbor			*ATT – kernel*		
BASE	97/86[a]	−0.149[b]	−1.0 [c]	97/1243[a]	−0.226[b]	−2.9[c]
EASE1K	97/78	−0.149	−1.2	97/1139	−0.191	−2.4
EASE5K	97/82	−0.152	−1.3	97/1205	−0.182	−2.4
Structure sub-sample (1,728 obs)						
	ATT – nearest neighbor			*ATT – kernel*		
BASE	158/141[a]	+0.016[b]	+0.1[c]	158/1416[a]	−0.104[b]	−1.9[c]
EASE1K	158/125	+0.001	+0.0	158/1319	−0.109	−1.7
EASE5K	158/126	+0.067	+0.7	158/1338	−0.133	−2.3

Notes
a Number of treated observation/number of matched controls.
b Average treatment effect on the treated.
c t-test statistic.

Conclusions

Hedonic models of land price per acre suggested statistically significant reductions in price due to preservation, ranging from 11.4 percent to 16.8 percent and the propensity score-matching approach (using the kernel method) showed a similar, and statistically significant, range of 10.4 percent to 22.6 percent. We found that results differed between the sub-samples for parcels with and without structures – these latter parcels sold at a greater discount, suggesting a much different market between parcels with structures (which might be purchased as "hobby farms" or benefit from the amenity value of the open space) and parcels without structures (where the land value may be more related to agricultural production). As a bottom line, we did see a price decrease in the parcels that have sold with an easement.

In addition, we found that preserved parcels have a greater amount of preserved land in their vicinity: approximately two and a half times as much for the smaller 1 km area, and almost half again as much for the larger 5 km area. This suggests that some degree of contiguity is being achieved although the mean values are quite small (18 percent for the preserved area within 1 km and 12 percent for that within 5 km). Preserved parcels are also larger than non-preserved parcels (on average 86 acres compared to 39 acres – 34.8 to 15.8 hectares). They also have a higher average quality of soil (58 percent prime soils compared to 41 percent for the unpreserved parcels) and higher average cropland per parcels (68 percent compared to 49 percent). Fewer than 1 percent of preserved parcels are located in residential, commercial or industrial zones, with over 55 percent in the two most restrictive zoning areas. In comparison, only 44 percent of the unpreserved parcels are located in the most restrictive zones.

However, the population growth in the block groups surrounding the pre-served parcels was surprisingly similar to those of the unpreserved parcels, although only the recent population growth was statistically significant in the models explaining sale prices. While these variables were included to control for growth pressures, perhaps other measures, such as population density, are required to capture this effect. Somewhat surprisingly, preserved parcels were slightly closer to Baltimore, MD, or Washington, DC, than unpreserved parcels. These attributes of preserved parcels, albeit only the ones that have sold since their preservation, suggest that the programs are retaining the types of farms desired, that they are achieving some degree of continuity, and that they may be preserving threatened agricultural parcels.

Even though this set of preserved parcels appeared to have desirable charac-teristics given the goals of the programs relative to non-preserved parcels, the impact on land values for the degree of easement restriction was surprisingly small (approximately 10–20 percent). This suggests that MALPF and other pres-ervation programs may be paying too much or offering tax benefits that are too large. Landowners receive payments from MALPF for their development value but the market does not appear to decrease their land value by a commensurate degree. For this sample, the predicted decrease in value averaged only $660 per acre ($1,631 per hectare), whereas the average easement payment in 2002 was $2,717 per acre ($6,714 per hectare). Hypothetically, then, landowners could sell their land after enrolling it in a preservation program and make an "extra" $2,000 per acre ($4,942 per hectare). Of course, an issue with any voluntary program is the need to pay sufficiently to induce participation. Waiting lists and low dis-counting on some bids suggest that some landowners have realized they are better off enrolling prior to any sale. Clearly, landowners do not gain this extra benefit until they actually sell the land.

One interpretation of our results is that landowners do not enroll in preserva-tion programs in those areas where land values are high (or likely to become high in the near future). We tried to control for this using distance-to-metropolitan-area measures as well as population growth rates over the past 30 years, but including these variables had little impact. Because high land values are likely to be linked to local development pressures, we may be missing this effect by including the entire state of Maryland in a single analysis. Similarly, the zoning categories may be acting as proxies for some county-level attributes other than development density for those counties that have very protective zoning. Therefore, we plan to treat different sub-regions of Maryland as sepa-rate markets and re-estimate these models to test the extent of regional differences.

Many people suggest PDR programs are not effective because they cost too much money and thus cannot enroll enough acres. Our results suggest that they may not be efficient because they pay more for the development rights than the landowners' opportunity costs to the landowners of foregoing them. It is possible that programs may be able to pay less and still induce individuals to participate. In this manner, the budget will stretch further and more acres may be enrolled. Given the voluntary nature of this type of agri-environmental program, achieving sufficient enrollment is crucial to fulfilling society's goals.

Notes

1 Support for this project was provided by the Harry R. Hughes Maryland Center for Agro-Ecology, Inc., and the National Center for Smart Growth Education and Research. We would like to thank Karen Palm, Sabrina Lovell, Jay Harvard and Sam Dworkin for their assistance.
2 No real analysis of what is the "optimal" amount of farmland to retain is provided. Some authors propose that too much farmland preservation may be occurring (McConnell 1989).
3 This assumes that the development restrictions are binding.
4 Protected lands include lands publicly owned at the federal, state and local levels, as well as private preserves and privately owned lands with conservation easements.
5 This has recently been changed to allow individual counties to set alternative ranking schemes. However, the change does not impact our analysis.
6 To simplify the model only two land uses are employed. However, in some cases the landowner will maximize present value by shifting the land use to commercial, industrial or other alternative land uses.
7 Lynch and Lovell (2003) argue that participation is actually based on the utility of the farmland owner under the preserved and non-preserved states and thus may include non-market values beyond those mentioned here.
8 The data description is derived from that of Lynch *et al.* (2007b).
9 Using the Index of Prices Received by Farmers (USDA), prices were adjusted to a base year of 2003 to account for any inflation or deflation that may have occurred during this time period.
10 For Howard, Calvert, Carroll and Montgomery Counties, we also had information on easement acquired through the county programs that might not have been included in the state-level data. We thank Virginia McConnell, Elizabeth Kopits and Margaret Walls for assistance with updating the Calvert's TDR database. For other counties, we were unable to locate a source of this information. Therefore, if the county had not transmitted information on county-level easements to the state, the analysis would not include them.
11 Parcels with certain types of easements were excluded from the analysis. For example, parcels with easements labeled as "exclusion, inholding, and road" or with easements which did not have identifiable boundaries, tax identification numbers or geocoded centroids were not included.
12 Including this interaction term was necessary in order for the PSM model to pass balancing tests. The hedonic model had qualitatively similar results without the interaction term, but the results presented here include the interaction terms to facilitate direct comparisons between the two modeling approaches.

References

American Farmland Trust (AFT) (2005a) "Status of Selected Local PACE Programs: Fact Sheet," Washington, DC.
American Farmland Trust (AFT) (2005b) "Status of State PACE Programs: Fact Sheet," Washington, DC.

Anderson, K. and Weinhold, D. (2005) "Do Conservation Easements Reduce Land Prices? The Case of South Central Wisconsin," London School of Economics, draft.

Blakely, M. (1991) "An Economic Analysis of the Effects of Development Rights Purchases on Land Values in King County, Washington," unpublished MS thesis, Washington State University.

Brabec, E. and Smith, C. (2002) "Agricultural Land Fragmentation: The Spatial Effects of Three Land Protection Strategies in the Eastern United States," *Landscape and Urban Planning*, 58: 255–268.

Capozza, D. and Helsley, R. (1989) "The Fundamentals of Land Prices and Urban Growth," *Journal of Urban Economics*, 26(3): 295–306.

Duke, J.M. and Ilvento, T.W. (2004) "A Conjoint Analysis of Public Preferences for Agricultural Land Preservation," *Agricultural and Resource Economics Review*, 33(2): 209–219.

Duncan, M.L. (1984) "Towards a Theory of Broad-based Planning for the Preservation of Agricultural Land," *Natural Resources Journal*, 24(1): 61–135.

Environmental Law Institute Research Report (2008) *Maryland Farmland Conservation: Supporting Sustainable Use of Land through Tax Policy*, contributors: Rebecca Gruby, James McElfish, Lori Lynch and Qing Li, Washington, DC: Harry R. Hughes Center for Agroecology, University of Maryland, Wye Mills, MD.

Feather, P. and Barnard, C.H. (2003) "Retaining Open Space with Purchasable Development Rights Programs," *Review of Agricultural Economics*, 25(2): 369–384.

Feitshans, T.A. (2003) "Meshing Compensatory and Regulatory Approaches in the Preservation of Farmland," in N. De Cuir, A.D. Sokolow and J. Woled (eds.), *Compensating Landowners for Conserving Agricultural Land*, Davis: University of California, Davis.

Gale, H.F. (1993) "Why Did the Number of Young Farm Entrants Decline?" *American Journal of Agricultural Economics*, 75(1): 138–146.

Gardner, B.D. (1977) "The Economics of Agricultural Land Preservation," *American Journal of Agricultural Economics*, 59(Dec.): 1027–1036.

Geoghegan, J., Lynch, L. and Bucholtz, S. (2003) "Capitalization of Open Spaces into Housing Values and the Residential Property Tax Revenue Impacts of Agricultural Easement Programs," *Agricultural and Resource Economics Review*, 32(April): 33–45.

Hardie, I.W., Narayan, T.A. and Gardner, B.L. (2001) "The Joint Influence of Agricultural and Nonfarm Factors on Real Estate Values: An Application to the Mid-Atlantic Region," *American Journal of Agricultural Economics*, 83(1): 120–132.

Hellerstein, D., Nickerson, C., Cooper, J., Feather, P., Gadsby, D., Mullarkey, D., Tegene, A. and Barnard, C. (2002) "Farmland Protection: The Role of Public Preferences for Rural Amenities," Washington, DC: US Department of Agriculture, ERS Agr. Econ. Rep. 815, October.

Horowitz, John K., Lynch, Lori and Stocking, Andrew (2007) "Competition-Based Environmental Policy: An Analysis of Farmland Preservation in Maryland," *Land Economics*, November 2009.

Irwin, E.G. (2002) "The Effects of Open Space on Residential Property Values," *Land Economics*, 78(4): 465–480.

List, J., Millimet, D.L., Fredriksson, P.G. and McHone, W.W. (2003) "Effects of Environmental Regulation on Manufacturing Plant Births: Evidence From a Propensity Score Matching Estimator," *The Review of Economics and Statistics*, 85(4): 944–952.

Liu, X. and Lynch, L. (2006) "Do Agricultural Preservation Programs Affect Farmland Conversion? Evidence From a Propensity Score Matching Estimator," working paper 06–08, College Park, MD: Department of Agricultural and Resource Economics.

Online, available at: www.arec.umd.edu/Publications/Papers/Working-Papers-PDF-files/06–08.pdf.

Lynch, L. and Carpenter, J.E. (2003) "Is There Evidence of a Critical Mass in the Mid-Atlantic Agricultural Sector Between 1949 and 1997?" *Agricultural and Resource Economics Review*, 32(1): 116–128.

Lynch, L. and Liu, X. (2007) "Impact of a Designated Preservation Area: Preliminary Evidence," *American Journal of Agricultural Economics*, 89(5): 1205–1210.

Lynch, L. and Lovell, S.J. (2003) "Combining Spatial and Survey Data to Explain Participation in Agricultural Land Preservation Programs," *Land Economics*, 79(2): 259–276.

Lynch, L., Gray, W. and Geoghegan, J. (2007a) "Are Farmland Preservation Programs Easement Restriction Capitalized into Farmland Prices? What Can a Propensity Score Matching Analysis Tell Us?" *Review of Agricultural Economics*, 29(3): 502–509.

Lynch, L., Palm K., Lovell, S. and Harvard, J. (2007b) "Using Agricultural and Forest Land Values to Estimate the Budgetary Resources Needed to Triple Maryland's Preserved Acres," Harry R. Hughes Center for Agroecology, Wye Mills, MD: University of Maryland. Online, available at: http://agroecol.umd.edu/files/Lynch%20Full%20 Report%20HRHCAE%20Pub%202007–04.pdf.

McConnell, K.E. (1989) "The Optimal Quantity of Land in Agriculture," *Northeastern Journal of Agricultural and Resource Economics*, 18: 63–72.

McConnell, V., Kopits, E. and Walls, M. (2006) "Using Markets for Land Preservation: Results of a TDR Program," *Journal of Environmental Planning and Management*, 49: 631–651.

McMillen, D.P. and McDonald, J.F. (2002) "Land Values in a Newly Zoned City," *The Review of Economics and Statistics*, 84(1): 62–72.

Maryland Agricultural Land Preservation Foundation (MALPF Task Force) (2005) Task Force to Study the Maryland Agricultural Land Preservation Final Report. Online, available at: www.malpf.info/reports/TFFinalReport2005.pdf.

Maryland Department of State Planning (1973) *Natural Soil Groups of Maryland*. Tech. Serv. Publ.

Michaels, J. (2007) "Impact of Easement Restrictions on Land Values in Baltimore County, Maryland," working paper, Towson, MD: Towson University.

Nelson, A.C. (1992) "Preserving Prime Farmland in the Face of Urbanization: Lessons from Oregon," *Journal of American Planning Association*, 58(4): 467–488.

Nickerson, C.J. and Lynch, L. (2001) "The Effect of Farmland Preservation Programs on Farmland Prices," *American Journal of Agricultural Economics*, 83(2): 341–351.

Pfeffer, M.J. and Lapping, M.B. (1994) "Farmland Preservation, Development Rights and the Theory of the Growth Matching: The Views of Planners," *Journal of Rural Studies*, 10(3): 233–248.

Plantinga, A.J. and Miller, D. (2001) "Agricultural Land Values and Future Development," *Land Economics*, 77(1): 56–67.

Plantinga, A.J., Lubowski, R.N. and Stavins, R.N. (2002) "The Effects of Potential Land Development on Agricultural Land Prices," *Journal of Urban Economics*, 52(3): 561–581.

Ready, R. and Abdalla, C. (2005) "The Amenity and Disamenity Impacts of Agriculture: Estimates from a Hedonic Price Model," *American Journal of Agricultural Economics*, 87(2): 314–326.

Rilla, E. and Sokolow, A.D. (2000) "California Farmers and Conservation Easements: Motivations, Experiences, and Perceptions in Three Counties," Research Paper No. 4, University of California, Agricultural Issues Center (December).

Rosenbaum, P. and Rubin, D. (1983) "The Central Role of the Propensity Score in Observational Studies for Causal Effects," *Biometrika*, 70: 41–55.

US Census Bureau (1999) Statistical Abstract of the United States.

US Department of Agriculture (USDA), National Agricultural Statistics Service (1999) 1997 Census of Agriculture, 1A, 1B, 1C (CD-ROM set), Washington, DC: USDA/ NASS.

Zollinger, B. and Krannich, R.S. (2001) "Utah Agricultural Operators' Attitudes Toward Commonly Used Agricultural Land Preservation Initiatives," *Journal of the Community Development Society*, 32(1): 35–64.

6 Modeling the economic impacts of critical habitat designation

Thomas Foulke, David T. Taylor and Roger H. Coupal

All animals are created equal but some animals are more equal than others.
George Orwell, *Animal Farm*

Background

After 35 years, the ramifications of the Endangered Species Act (ESA) are still being felt, sometimes in ways more subtle than the original legislators may have foreseen. For while the public focuses on high-profile species such as bears, wolves and eagles, government regulators are required, under the law, to try to preserve *all* threatened and endangered species. Billions of dollars have been spent on habitat development, captive breeding and litigation. Many of these processes involve limiting human interaction with the species in order to allow its population to stabilize. Often overlooked in the equation are local landowners whose actions to disturb or preserve a species (knowingly or not) are trumped by government bureaucracy and political agendas. This is partly because many threatened and endangered species are found primarily on large tracts of public land whose periphery is often populated by private landowners.

More recently, the focus in environmental thinking has shifted to species that had not been in the spotlight before, species considered by some to be "indicators" for the health of ecosystems. Others have viewed the listing of these species as an attempt by environmental organizations to push a political agenda. One such species is the Preble's Meadow Jumping Mouse. This case furnishes an example of how agriculture has been affected by ESA-spurred land-use change (in this case away from rural residential development), as well as how the use of the ESA as a political tool has had unintended consequences.

In May 1998 the Preble's Meadow Jumping Mouse (PMJM), *Zapus Hudsonius Preblei*, was listed as a threatened species by the US Fish and Wildlife Service (USFWS) under the Endangered Species Act. The PMJM is a small rodent about nine inches in length, 60 percent of which is tail. The PMJM occupies shrub habitat adjacent to streams and along irrigation ditches of the Front Range of the Rocky Mountains in Colorado and southeastern Wyoming. At the time of listing, the species' range in Wyoming was thought by the USFWS to be confined to portions of five counties (Albany, Converse, Goshen, Laramie and Platte).

The listing of the PMJM was almost immediately controversial due to the location of its habitat along the Front Range in Colorado, where suburban and rural residential development is occurring at a rapid pace. Developers and agriculturalists were quick to claim that environmental groups had been searching for a species which they could use, under the guise of the Endangered Species Act, to slow development in the region. The area of mouse habitat in Wyoming, for the most part, does not have the development pressures of Colorado. Rather, it is primarily rural ranch land.

In July 2002, the USFWS proposed designating critical habitat in Wyoming and Colorado. The proposed critical habitat in Wyoming included about 237 miles (379 km) of rivers and streams and over 20,000 acres (8,097 ha) of land. Approximately 77 percent of this land was privately owned, and approximately 94 percent was currently used for agricultural production. In June 2003, the USFWS made the final designation of critical habitat for PMJM (USFWS 2003). It included about one-half of what was originally proposed for Wyoming: 125 miles (200 km) of rivers and streams and 10,540 acres (4,267 ha) of critical habitat. Much of the private land is hay meadows which produce critical winter feed for ranches in the region. Under sections 7, 9 and 10 of the ESA, some or all of this production would have been affected. Eighty-eight percent of the final designation lands are privately held.

The state of Wyoming holds the position that the PMJM is not a separate species and therefore should not be protected under the ESA. A DNA analysis was conducted by Ramey *et al.* in 2004. Their findings rocked the endangered species community at the time, showing that the PMJM is not a distinct species at all, but in fact the more common *Zapus Hudsonius Campestri*, the Bear Lodge Jumping Mouse. Naturally, these findings were immediately disputed and the USFWS commissioned a review of the methods that Ramey *et al.* used. Another series of tests were conducted by King *et al.* from the US Geological Survey. King *et al.* (2006) found that the PMJM was a distinct *sub*-species (the argument has been over whether or not the PMJM is a distinct *sub*-species of *Zapus Hudsonius*. "Sub-species" can be listed under the ESA. In the interest of brevity, the authors will hereafter dispense with the "*sub-*" prefix). Faced with conflicting studies, the USFWS resorted to a panel of experts to resolve the issue. The report issued by the Sustainable Ecosystems Institute (SEI) in July 2006 confirmed the findings of King *et al.*, supporting the contention that the PMJM is a distinct species.

The USFWS proposed delisting the mouse after the first DNA study showed that the PMJM was not a distinct species. However, with the King study ongoing and the SEI panel at work, the delisting process was essentially put on hold. In the meantime, pressure was growing for the USFWS to make a decision: the state of Wyoming sued the USFWS, and the suit was eventually settled out of court. The resulting settlement agreement between the USFWS and the state of Wyoming stated that a decision would be made by October 2007; the USFWS issued its decision on October 31 of that year.

Previous work

The authors' involvement with the PMJM came at the request of the Office of the Governor of the State of Wyoming, which was interested in what critical habitat would mean for the economy of the southeastern part of the state. A year-long economic study was completed in September 2004 that used a three-step approach to estimate the potential economic impact of critical habitat designation on the five-county region. The basis of the approach was to determine the impacts at the firm level and scale them up to the regional level.

As a first step, listening sessions were held in each of the five counties in the region. This was an opportunity for local landowners, businessmen and county officials to indicate their concerns regarding the efforts to protect the PMJM and for the researchers to collect production information. The University of Wyoming Cooperative Extension Service in each county coordinated these listening sessions. Information obtained during these sessions served as the starting point for the analysis.

The results of the listening sessions were startling. Anger, frustration, confusion and distrust were some of the sentiments expressed. Landowners and community leaders present unanimously felt that what was happening with the mouse bypassed some of the fundamental tenets of the American way of life. Many of the participants felt that the ESA and the process used to implement it threatened their property rights. At times the sessions became emotionally charged. One County Commissioner was so incensed that she suggested Wyoming should secede from the Union if the ESA were allowed to continue this assault on private property owners. Another producer commented that "this takes the heart right out of your operation," referring to the potential loss of hay meadows. The researchers also gathered information on which production practices would continue, which would be curtailed, and how profitability might be affected by loss of land to critical habitat designation.

One issue that aroused heated emotions among the producers was that of a "federal nexus": the regulatory effects of critical habitat designation under section 7 of the ESA, triggered by activities conducted, authorized or funded by a federal agency. Section 7 of the ESA requires federal agencies to confer with the USFWS on any action that is likely to result in the destruction or adverse modification of proposed critical habitat, regardless of whether the action is physically located on public or private land. Activities that require consultation include:

Any activity that results in development or alteration of the landscape of a unit.
Any activity that results in changes in the hydrology of the unit.
Any sale, exchange, or lease of Federal land that is likely to affect habitat.
Any activity that detrimentally alters natural processes in a unit.
Any activity that leads to the introduction, expansion, or increased density of exotic plants or animal species.

(USFWS 2001)

A federal nexus, or "connection," has particularly onerous connotations among area producers because it could allow federal officials legal access to their private lands (some producers claimed that they had already ejected trespassing USWFS personnel from their properties). Because of the interconnectedness of federal regulations and the resulting far reach of the federal government, landowners are particularly distrustful of the ESA, the USFWS and the federal government in general. For this reason, and the fear of triggering a federal nexus, a number of area producers told the listening sessions that they had not accepted the free cattle feed offered during the drought of 2002.

After the listening sessions, the second step was to evaluate the potential impact of the PMJM on agricultural operations in the region. The Draft Economic Analysis (Industrial 2003) and some of the language in the USFWS's Critical Habitat Designation left open the possibility of extending protective measures for species protection to a larger land area (see Taylor *et al.* 2004). Because the ESA protects the species wherever it is found, regardless of critical habitat designation, it was impossible to know the boundaries of the species or what the eventual area of protection would be. But since the PMJM lives close to water, it seemed logical that the largest impact would be on agricultural operations that use irrigated and sub-irrigated land in the region (sub-irrigated is the more technical term for "creek bottom" land that is naturally wetter than the surrounding land due to its proximity to a stream). Beauvais (2003) estimated there to be 832,825 acres (337,176 ha) of suitable habitat for the PMJM in the five-county region, 77 percent (or 677,422 acres (274,260 ha)) of which was private land. So while the USFWS designated only 10,540 acres (4,267 ha) as critical habitat, the potential for an expanded range and thus expanded economic impact was clear.

The authors adapted a linear programming model developed for the W-192 (now W-1192) USDA regional research project to southeastern Wyoming to estimate the economic impact on profitability of a typical ranch in the region. Other factors considered in this part of the analysis included effects on economic viability of agricultural operations and the potential for a federal nexus among producers in the region. Analysis of economic viability was based on USDA Economic Research Service's Commodity Cost and Returns Estimates for cow-calf operations in the northern Great Plains. Information on the potential for a federal nexus among agricultural producers in southeastern Wyoming was obtained from various federal government reports and agencies.

In order to adapt the model, an appropriate measure had to be found to evaluate the effect initiated by a policy change. The USFWS designated critical habitat for PMJM as 110 meters from the edge of either side of a stream (for stream orders 1 and 2; larger streams were given a 120-meter boundary). This measure is rather difficult to use as a meaningful value from an economic perspective. Therefore, the researchers translated the 110-meter measurement into an area to assess what the value of habitat per linear mile of stream would be and how its withdrawal from the ranchstead would affect profitability. Figure 6.1 shows a schematic of a hypothetical one-mile section of a typical stream or ditch in southeastern Wyoming.

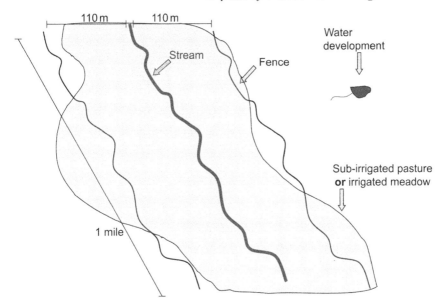

Figure 6.1 Southeastern Wyoming stream section schematic.

Figure 6.1 also illustrates an important point: the shape of hay meadows in this region. Due to the geographic location of the ranches (adjacent to the Laramie Range), many of the creek bottoms are narrow. These ranches were homesteaded in the late nineteenth century, and the construction of some of the irrigation ditches (and their accompanying water rights) date from this period. The technology of the time meant that ditches had to very nearly follow the contours of the land. Consequently, many of the hay meadows in the region are also long and narrow, following the creek bottom (Figure 6.2). This means that often most of an operation's hay meadow is located within 110 meters of a stream and that these operations would be significantly impacted by the PMJM protection policies.

The results show that one mile of sub-irrigated pasture would have an estimated cost of $2,271 ($25.96 per acre or $64.12 per hectare) per year, and that the per-mile costs increase with each additional mile of sub-irrigated pasture on the ranch. On average, one mile of sub-irrigated critical habitat would reduce ranch profitability by about 6 percent per year.

When hay meadow was considered, the estimated cost per mile was significantly higher. The model shows that a mile of irrigated hay meadow reduced ranch profits by $7,163 ($81.90 per acre or $202.29 per hectare) per year. This would reduce ranch profitability by nearly 20 percent per year. Again, these per-unit costs increase with each additional mile on the ranch. With three miles of irrigated hay meadow critical habitat withdrawn from the ranch, the income for the ranch would fall below the US Census Bureau's definition of poverty for a family of four.

98 T. Foulke et al.

Unidentified hayfield in relation to
suitable habitat

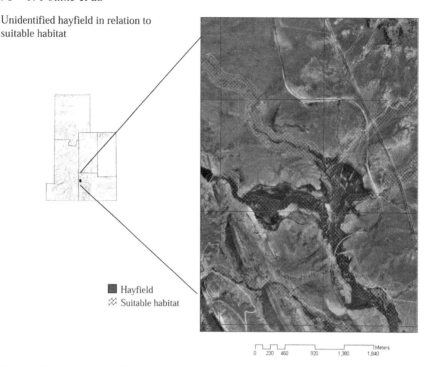

Figure 6.2 Aerial photo of a typical southeastern Wyoming stream section.

The cost differences between sub-irrigated pasture and irrigated hay meadow
are a direct result of the difference in productivity between the two types of land.
Sub-irrigated pasture productivity in the region ranges from essentially dry land
pasture quality of 0.52 animal unit months (AUMs) per acre to 1.34 AUMs/acre.
Irrigated hay meadow produces an average of 1.5 tons/acre of hay for winter
feed or sale (Taylor *et al.* 2004).

Table 6.1 shows how profitability is affected on the model ranch. For each
mile of the selected class of land, ranch profits, herd size (brood cows) and purchased alfalfa hay are shown. If only sub-irrigated pastures are affected by the
withdrawals, alfalfa hay purchases decline with herd size because the producer is
still able to winter the herd on grass hay produced on the ranch and is only reducing herd size in response to a decrease in available summer grazing land.

However, if irrigated hay meadow land is affected, the results are more dra-
matic. The producer is trying to stay in business (the model assumes that the
producer wants to continue to raise cattle and will try to find a way to do so)
even though the critical winter feed base has been reduced. The producer will
therefore purchase additional alfalfa hay even as herd size and profitability are
decreasing with each mile of land withdrawn to protect PMJM.

The third step in the analysis was to evaluate the economic impact of the
changes in agricultural production on the economy of communities in southeastern Wyoming. An IMPLAN model of the five-county region was developed to

Table 6.1 Linear programming model results

	Base	1 mile	2 miles	3 miles	4 miles	5 miles	6 miles
Sub-irrigated pasture							
Ranch profits	$39,423	$37,152	$34,754	$32,170	$29,443	$25,898	$22,328
Cows (head)	430	424	417	408	398	382	366
Alfalfa purchased (tons)	94.5	85.7	79.7	78	76	73	70
Irrigated pasture							
Ranch profits	$39,423	$32,260	$24,978	$17,673	$10,071	$2,056	−$6,253
Cows (head)	430	413	404	395	384	367	349
Alfalfa purchased (tons)	94.5	174	287	395	502	596	690

estimate the economic impacts of PMJM on total (direct and secondary) jobs and income in the region. Because the number of agricultural operations and the actual amount of affected production were unknown, the researchers estimated the impact of irrigated agriculture on the region. This provided an indication of the economic importance of the sector that would be most impacted by conservation of the PMJM. It also provided an upper limit on the potential economic impacts of the PMJM on agriculture in the region.

Table 6.2 summarizes the economic impact of irrigated agriculture in southeastern Wyoming. The value of production for agriculture is estimated to decrease by $177.2 million per year, from $220.5 million with irrigation to $43.3 million without. The $177.2 million loss represents more than 21 percent of the value of production for all agricultural commodities in Wyoming in 2000 (USDA-NASS, Wyoming Field Office 2002). Nearly 50 percent of this loss was due to the decrease in hay production ($85.4 million).

Employment (both direct and secondary) is estimated to decrease from approximately 4,000 jobs (Table 6.3) with irrigation to approximately 1,000 jobs without. Approximately 70 percent of the total jobs lost would be in agriculture, with the rest coming from other sectors of the region's economy. Nearly 64 percent of the job losses would be due to the decrease in hay production. Total

Table 6.2 Value of agricultural production in southeastern Wyoming

	Value of production w/ irrigation	*Value of production w/o irrigation*	*Change*	*Percent change*
Hay production	$122,516,662	$37,144,458	−$85,372,204	−69.7
Corn production	$57,709,019	$4,208,579	−$53,500,440	−92.7
Sugar beet production	$34,721,982	$899,798	−$33,822,184	−97.4
Dry bean production	$5,594,749	$1,035,635	−$4,559,114	−81.3
Total	$220,542,412	$43,288,470	−$177,253,942	−80.4

Table 6.3 Agricultural employment in southeastern Wyoming

	Employment w/irrigation	Employment w/o irrigation	Change	Percent change
Hay production	2,778.8	870.7	−1,908.1	−68.7
Corn production	767.8	67.2	−700.6	−91.3
Sugar beet production	319.5	14.4	−305.1	−95.5
Dry bean production	101.6	16.5	−85.1	−83.8
Total	3,967.7	968.8	−2,998.9	−90.1

employment in the agricultural sector would decline by 75 percent under these conditions.

Table 6.4 estimates that labor earnings (both direct and secondary) could decrease by $75.7 million per year from $84.1 million with irrigation to $8.4 million without. Approximately 60 percent of the total labor earnings lost would be in agriculture with the rest coming from other sectors of the region's economy. Nearly 72 percent of the labor earnings loss would be due to the decrease in hay production. Labor earnings in the agricultural sector would decline by 95 percent under this scenario. Average earnings per job for all sectors would decline from $21,190 with irrigation to $8,624 without.

Policy implications

The PMJM has policy implications on several levels and is a watershed species in regard to national environmental policy. It is the first species where DNA analysis is playing a major role in determining whether or not a species should have protection under the ESA.[1] The PMJM is the first species that has a significant percentage of its critical habitat on private land, which has increased calls for ESA reform from property rights activists and others. So the issues of habitat, taxonomy and policy (interpretation of the Act) have combined to put the PMJM in the limelight.

The DNA issues are largely beyond the scope of this chapter, but they grabbed the majority of the headlines. Indeed, reading only mainstream media reports would have given the impression that the entire issue was focused on the

Table 6.4 Agricultural labor earnings in southeastern Wyoming

Labor income	Labor income w/ irrigation	Percent w/o irrigation	Change	Percent change
Hay production	$61,605,412	$7,183,970	−$54,421,442	−88.3
Corn production	$13,262,850	$801,962	−$12,460,888	−94.0
Sugar beet production	$8,033,204	$171,460	−$7,861,744	−97.9
Dry bean production	$1,175,414	$197,345	−$978,069	−83.2
Total	$84,076,880	$8,354,737	−$75,722,143	−90.1

taxonomy of the species. And yet beyond the legal challenges, the repercussions were already being felt in the biological sciences. The Sustainable Ecosystem Institute report (2006) stated that:

> All readers should recognize that taxonomy is a field undergoing evolutionary change of its own. The integration of genetic data into "classical" taxonomy is far from complete, and there are as yet no clear guidelines on, for instance, which characters are more or less "important". There will be cases where expert opinion will be divided.
>
> (SEI 2006: ii)

This means that the relatively new science of DNA analysis is changing our perception of what we call a species, and that naming conventions have not yet been developed to match. How this process plays out, and whether it plays out on campuses or in the courts, may have further repercussions for the ESA.

In the long run, questions of geography and economics may have overshadowed the taxonomic issues. Eighty-eight percent of the land designated as critical habitat for the PMJM in Wyoming is private land, most of which is within 110 meters of a stream or irrigation ditch (due to the policy constraint set by the USFWS and the location of the PMJM habitat). These lands are either sub-irrigated meadow or hay meadow. Hay meadow is the "heart" of the ranch from a productivity standpoint. If hay meadow acreage is reduced, the overall carrying capacity of the ranch is reduced because the ability to feed cattle during the winter is impaired. Reducing the carrying capacity of the ranch reduces producer income, which in turn impacts the local economy. Taylor *et al.* (2004) have shown the level of the region's dependency on agriculture and how this might affect the regional economy.

With critical habitat for the PMJM already designated, landowners knew they could be told that they were no longer allowed to hay or graze their land. If landowners had to give up land for the habitat of the PMJM, and had to pay for fencing to keep their cattle out of mouse habitat on their own land, legal as well economic consequences would have been likely. Landowners may well have felt that this qualified as a "taking" under section 7 of the ESA and sought compensation from the federal government. It is estimated that the fencing alone for the 125 miles of critical habitat would cost approximately $2.4 million (not including annual maintenance). Additionally, landowners would have wanted compensation for the lost use of their land. This cost could have ranged from $200,000 to $1.5 million per year, depending on the land use and quality. Administration and enforcement costs would have accrued as well. All other costs would be annual and continue in perpetuity.

The above costs were estimated for what was designated as critical habitat in Wyoming. However, there was the potential for a much wider scope, had the USFWS determined that PMJM in Wyoming qualified for continued protection under the ESA. The Draft Economic Analysis notes "Section 9 and 10 of the Act [ESA] apply to all landowners with PMJM on their property regardless of whether a Federal nexus exists or whether their property is located with critical habitat" (page B-1). The Draft Analysis further notes, "Because the PMJM inhabits riparian areas in or surrounding irrigation ditches and hay fields, some incidental take of individual mice is inevitable during normal farming and ranching operations in the mouse's range" (ibid.). As a result, the effects of protecting the PMJM could have been much more widespread and significant than just the designation of habitat under section 7 of the ESA (Industrial Economics 2003). Figure 6.3 shows suitable habitat as developed from trappings and modeling of the PMJM's environment by Beauvais (2003). The amount of (in this case, proposed) critical habitat is relatively small compared to where the mouse could possibly be found, adding weight to the argument of potentially much larger impacts.

This also shows that uncertainty regarding future regulation for the protection of the PMJM created mixed signals, at the very least, for landowners in the region. The effects on agriculture from PMJM remain unclear. In the final critical habitat designation USFWS noted: "While some aspects of irrigated hayfields are undoubtedly beneficial to the Preble's, overall effects on Preble's populations are likely complex and have not yet been studied" (2004: 54). In addition, it observed:

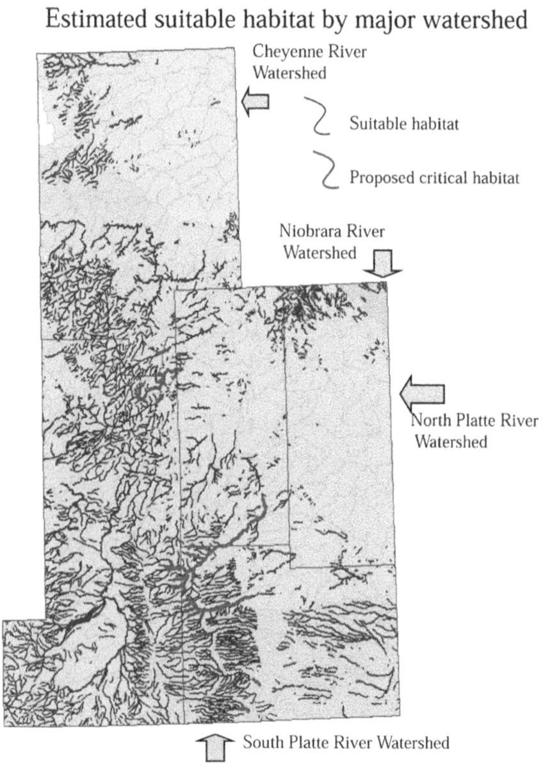

Estimated suitable habitat by major watershed

Figure 6.3   Suitable and proposed critical PMJM habitat in southeastern Wyoming.

The Service has adjusted the discussion of grazing and water management to indicate that these activities, under certain management scenarios, may be consistent with Preble's conservation. However, the Service still views both grazing and water management as threats to the Preble's.

(USFWS 2004: 89)

In essence, then, the argument comes down to a political one (with economic and legal implications, of course) regarding what value society places on the PMJM, how much it is willing to spend, and who will bear the costs. The ESA is primarily concerned with species protection, not economics in general. Species protection was an important focus when the Act was passed 35 years ago. At that time, there were a number of high-profile species, such as the Bald Eagle, that were on the verge of extinction and that society, in general, was willing to pay a high price to conserve. Today, the USFWS is moving forward with delisting the Bald Eagle and the Grizzly Bear (while still protecting them), and delisted the Grey Wolf in March 2008. The country's environmental consciousness is more focused today on global warming and greenhouse gases. It may be difficult to invoke the same amount of sympathy for a mouse that was formerly felt for high-profile species. And yet the PMJM has all the same protections under the law, and the USFWS is required to protect it in the same way. This can only change if the law is changed, which does not seem likely any time soon. So while scientists argue about whether or not the PMJM is a separate species, the real argument is whether or not society is willing to make available the resources needed to conserve the animal.

In November 2007, the USFWS did something Solomon-esque: it cut the geographic range of the mouse in half. The Service's press release (USFWS 2007) announced the proposed removal of the PMJM from threatened status in Wyoming. However, the PMJM would remain on the list across the state line in Colorado. The press release stated, in part, that:

Land use across Preble's habitat in Wyoming is dominated by agriculture, mostly haying and grazing. Continuation of these long-standing activities does not appear to pose a threat to existing Preble's populations. In addition, there is also no indication that these agricultural practices are likely to change in the foreseeable future in ways that would affect Preble's populations. A low projected human population growth rate is predicted for the four Wyoming counties (Albany, Laramie, Platte, and Converse) that support Preble's populations. Consequently, few of the development-related impacts occurring in Colorado's portion of the Front Range urban corridor will impact Preble's populations in Wyoming.

(USFWS 2007)

The press release continues on to state that "The best commercial and scientific information currently available demonstrates that the Preble's meadow jumping mouse is a valid subspecies and should not be removed from the Federal List of Threatened and Endangered Species based upon taxonomic revision" (ibid.).

This language, though somewhat contradictory to statements found in earlier USFWS documents, appears to recognize the importance of agriculture to Wyoming and its role in sustaining the PMJM population over the last 130 years while reiterating the findings of King *et al.* (2006) and the SEI panel (2006) that the PMJM is a valid sub-species. Keeping the PMJM on the list of threatened species in Colorado ensures that the controversy will continue. For while the issue is now somewhat stabilized in Wyoming, confining the threatened status to a geographic location separated by an imaginary line (the Wyoming–Colorado state line) may be courting litigation. Agricultural activities that are now permitted in Wyoming are still regulated in Colorado to aid the mouse, leaving all the questions of ranch profitability and property rights still valid in that state.

An important point is that the costs imposed by the ESA will have to be borne by someone in order to comply with the provisions of the law. Because the USFWS has decided that the PMJM is a distinct species and qualifies for protection, it can simply impose these costs on Colorado landowners through regulation. Landowners could mount a legal challenge to this as a taking. Furthermore, there could be some longer-term effects due to preservation costs. When this land changes hands, the new owners will know that profitability was impacted for the previous owner and that a portion of the land that they are purchasing is effectively out of their control. With the exception of a neighbor buying to consolidate, new owners would likely have to look for a new land use beyond agriculture. With the rapid rural residential development occurring along Colorado's Front Range, development is one option for some of these parcels. Of course, the area of critical habitat could not be developed, but contiguous lands outside of the critical habitat designation would not be affected. So in a twist of irony, efforts to preserve the mouse could end up fueling the very activity that it was enlisted to stop.

This is where the implications for national environmental policy become important and where the political aspect of the issue comes to the fore. The question of who pays for species protection on private land if the landowner's livelihood is significantly impacted is a complicated legal one. Because most species protection has been concentrated on public lands, individual landowners have been impacted, but not on a region-wide basis. When a large group of citizens face potential impact, implementing a decision becomes politically difficult. The USFWS decision to delist the PMJM in Wyoming but not Colorado appears to avoid this situation and the potential for any precedent-setting legal rulings. The final rule amending the listing for PMJM was issued in July 2008 (USFWS 2008). As of this writing (November 2008), the authors know of no legal challenges to the delisting of the PMJM in Wyoming.

Conclusions

This chapter recasts the authors' previous work on the economic impact of critical habitat designation for the PMJM in a different light. The impact analysis is framed in a discussion of how the PMJM controversy has affected Wyoming landowners and the implications for national environmental policy.

The authors' earlier work has been summarized to familiarize the reader with the situation and place it in context. This work was driven by the need to understand the impact on local landowners and the regional economy at a time when large areas of southeastern Wyoming riparian area could have been designated as critical habitat for the PMJM. Since that time, the regulatory picture has changed due to a decision by the USFWS regarding the threatened status of the PMJM in Wyoming.

What appeared to be the main controversy over the PMJM seems to be resolved with USFWS's November 2007 decision to delist the PMJM in Wyoming but retain its threatened species status in Colorado. The affirmation that the PMJM is a distinct sub-species by the service lends additional credibility to the call for continued protection. However, this same decision calls into question the need for protection while in an adjacent area the PMJM is deemed as not threatened "for the foreseeable future" (USFWS 2007).

And yet there are larger questions and larger implications for science, policy and the regional economy of southeastern Wyoming and the Colorado Front Range. The science of taxonomy is grappling with what the precise definition of a species is, given new information by DNA analysis. Policy questions arise as to who will bear the cost of species conservation when there are significant amounts of critical habitat on private land. Landowners in the region are angry and confused.

It is too early to say that the controversy is over. Time and again over the last decade it has appeared that a resolution is at hand and each time one or the other side has driven the issue back into the courts. That there is no pending litigation at the moment is a positive sign, but by no means suggests the end.

The PMJM is a small rodent about nine inches in length, 60 percent of which is tail. Its activities have been unnoticed until recently, but these small feet are leaving very big tracks indeed.

Note

1   The PMJM was the first species proposed for removal under the ESA, but this decision was later reversed by the USFWS. The Bliss Rapids snail, *Taylorconcha Serpenticola* [Idaho, USA] has also been proposed for removal from threatened status (June 2007) after genetic testing revealed that it was not a separate species.

References

Beauvais, Gary P. (2003) "Preble's Meadow Jumping Mouse in Wyoming, Status Report: July, 2003," Appendix K in "The Potential Economic Impact on the Economy of South-eastern Wyoming from Designation of Critical Habitat for Preble's Meadow Jumping Mouse," University of Wyoming, Department of Agricultural & Applied Economics (2004). Unpublished report to the Governor of the State of Wyoming. Online, available at: http://agecon.uwyo.edu/EconDev/PMJM1.htm. (accessed November 18, 2007).

Industrial Economics, Incorporated (2003) "Draft Economic Analysis of Critical Habitat Designation for the Preble's Meadow Jumping Mouse," prepared for US Fish and Wildlife Service by Industrial Economics Incorporated Cambridge, MA. Online, available at: www.fws.gov/mountain-prairie/species/mammals/preble/peer/peerindex.htm (accessed November 18, 2007).

King, T.L., Switzer, J.F., Morrison, C.L., Eackles, M.S., Young, C.C., Lubinski, B.A. and Cryan, P. (2006) "Comprehensive Genetic Analyses of Molecular Phylogeographic Structure Among Meadow Jumping Mice (Zapus hudsonius) Reveals Evolutionary Distinct Subspecies," a report submitted to the US Fish and Wildlife Service, US Geological Survey-Biological Resources Division, Kearneysville, WV. January 2006. Online, available at: www.fws.gov/mountain-prairie/species/mammals/preble/peer/peerindex.htm (accessed November 18, 2007).

Ramey, R., Hsiu-Ping, L. and Carpenter, L. (2004) "Testing the Taxonomic Validity of Preble's Meadow Jumping Mouse," Report to the Governor of Wyoming and the US Fish and Wildlife Service (Revised), Denver Museum of Nature and Science, Denver, CO, March 2004. Online, available at: www.fws.gov/mountain-prairie/species/mammals/preble/peer/peerindex.htm (accessed November 18, 2007).

Sustainable Ecosystems Institute (2006) "The Evaluation of Scientific Information Regarding Preble's Meadow Jumping Mouse," The Sustainable Ecosystems Institute, P.O. Box 80605, Portland, OR 97280, Report to US Fish and Wildlife Service. Online, available at: www.fws.gov/mountain-prairie/species/mammals/preble/peer/peerindex. htm (accessed November 18, 2007).

Taylor, David T., Coupal, Roger H., Foulke, Thomas and Feeney, Dennis (2004) "The Potential Economic Impact on the Economy of Southeastern Wyoming from Designation of Critical Habitat for Preble's Meadow Jumping Mouse," University of Wyoming, Department of Agricultural & Applied Economics, unpublished report to the Governor of the State of Wyoming. Online, available at: http://agecon.uwyo.edu/EconDev/PMJM1.htm (accessed November 18, 2007).

United States Department of Agriculture, National Agricultural Statistical Service (USDA-NASS), Wyoming Field Office (2002) *Wyoming Agricultural Statistics 2002*. Wyoming Agricultural Statistics Service, P.O. Box 1148, Cheyenne, Wyoming 82003.

United States Department of Interior, Fish and Wildlife Service (USFWS) (2001) *Designation of Critical Habitat for the Preble's Meadow Jumping Mouse*, 50 CFR Part 17, Vol. 66, No. 169, pp. 45829–45833. Online, available at: http://ecos.fws.gov/speciesProfile/SpeciesReport.do?spcode=A0C2 (accessed November 19, 2007).

United States Department of Interior, Fish and Wildlife Service (2003) *Designation of Critical Habitat for the Preble's Meadow Jumping Mouse*, 50 CFR Part 17, Vol. 68, No. 120, pp. 37275–37332. Online, available at: http://ecos.fws.gov/speciesProfile/SpeciesReport.do?spcode=A0C2 (accessed November 19, 2007).

United States Department of Interior, Fish and Wildlife Service (2004) *Designation of Critical Habitat for the Preble's Meadow Jumping Mouse*, 50 CFR Part 17, Vol. 67, No. 137. Online, available at: www.fws.gov/mountain-prairie/species/mammals/preble/Index.htm (accessed November 18, 2007).

United States Department of Interior, Fish and Wildlife Service (2007) News Release: US Fish and Wildlife Service Proposes to Revise the Endangered Species Act Listing for Preble's Meadow Jumping Mouse, November 1, 2007. Online, available at: www.fws.gov/mountain-prairie/species/mammals/preble/Index.htm (accessed November 18, 2007).

United States Department of Interior, Fish and Wildlife Service (2008) Final Rule to Amend the Listing for the Preble's Meadow Jumping Mouse (Zapus Hudsonius Preblei) To Specify Over What Portion of Its Range the Subspecies is Threatened, 50 CFR Part 17, Vol. 73, No. 133. Online, available at: www.fws.gov/mountain-prairie/species/mammals/preble/73FR39790.htm (accessed November 5, 2008).

Part II

New perspectives on modeling agri-environmental relations

7 Multi-scale and integrated modeling of landscape functionality

Louise Willemen, Peter H. Verburg,
Koen P. Overmars and Martha M. Bakker

Introduction

Human-induced land use changes can have major effects on landscape patterns and the functioning of the landscape, either through a complete change in land cover or through changes in the spatial configuration of the landscape. Land use changes are caused by a change in the demand for land-based commodities. Demand for land depends on market dynamics driven by anthropogenic or environmental processes, or can be induced by policy. Current research on land use change aims at predicting land-cover change in response to land use change, driven by global demographic and economical processes. Because land use and land cover are presumed to be related, we refer to this type of research as land use/cover modeling. Investigating land use/cover dynamics is of great potential interest to policy-makers because they can use the outcomes to design and fine-tune policies that aim at best uses of landscape resources. Specific tools to explore future scenarios of land use/cover change are used to assess impacts of this change and evaluate possible results of land use policies (Uran and Janssen 2003; Geertman and Stillwell 2004; McIntosh *et al.* 2007). Because land use changes are a result of different processes at different scales (Verburg and Chen 2000; Walsh *et al.* 2001; Bürgi *et al.* 2004), these land use/cover change tools should ideally be able to capture all important land use related processes at multiple scales.

Changes in land cover and its composition and pattern can influence the functionality of the landscape (Metzger *et al.* 2006). With landscape functions, we refer to the capacity of the landscape to provide goods and services to society. These include goods such as harvested crops or timber, and services such as landscape aesthetics, provision of habitat or regulation of water systems. The capacity of a landscape to provide goods and services depends on socioeconomic and biophysical processes and components of the landscape, which include, among others, land cover (de Groot 1992). Landscape functions do not necessarily relate directly to land cover. Landscape functionality is defined by a number of characteristics, including a range of land cover types and their spatial configurations (Willemen *et al.* 2008). In many rural regions of Europe, landscapes provide more than one good or service at the same time, resulting in multifunctional landscapes. A landscape could, for instance, facilitate recreational activities, be used for agricultural production, and provide habitat for meadow birds at the same time. Within such multifunctional landscapes, interactions like conflicts or synergies may occur between landscape functions. For example, intensive agriculture conflicts with suitability of land for habitat provision.

Policy-makers are confronted with a demand for a broad range of landscape goods and services by society, but landscape function is currently not included in policy tools (Pinto-Correia *et al.* 2006; Vejre *et al.* 2007). Information on current landscape functions, the potential pressure on these functions, and the potential capacity of landscapes to function could all support land use planning. Current land use/cover models relate primarily to the classic spatial policy focus on agriculture and urban development. Because landscape functionality depends on land cover, results of large-scale land use/cover models could be used to explore the dynamics in landscape functionality. By using land use/cover model outputs, multi-scale processes can be taken into account when analyzing functionality on a landscape scale.

The objective of this chapter is to illustrate how analyses of land use/cover and landscape functionality can be complementary. We argue that analysis on multiple scales is necessary to adequately address the complex structure of the land use system and illustrate how land use/cover changes can translate into impacts on landscape functionality. This chapter contains two sections. First, we identify possibilities and limitations to current land use/cover model outputs based on projected future changes in Europe. Second, a more detailed study in the Netherlands is presented to identify landscape functionality and to address possible effects of land use/cover changes on landscape functionality.

Land use/cover change modeling

Large-scale land use/cover models are available to simulate land use/cover change in response to demography, economy and trade (Heistermann *et al.* 2006; Verburg *et al.* 2006, 2008). In this section we focus on land use/cover models currently being used in Europe to assess the effects of global developments on Europe's rural areas (e.g. EURURALIS (WUR and MNP 2007; Verburg *et al.* 2008) and SENSOR (Helming *et al.* 2008)). Currently, the most prominent land use change processes happening in Europe are urbanization, intensification of agriculture, subsequent abandonment of agricultural lands and increasing protection of nature. Such land use change processes are very region-specific. Because the exact location of the projected land use/cover changes is important for identifying the potential implications of these changes, models are used to describe land use/cover dynamics.

No single model is able to capture all key processes related to driving forces and impacts of land use/cover change; therefore, multiple models, addressing different processes and different scales, are often linked or integrated. The major economic processes leading to land use/cover change on the scale of individual countries are captured by macroeconomic models (e.g. GTAP model (Van Meijl *et al.* 2006) or NEMESIS (Brécard *et al.* 2006)). Sometimes these macroeconomic models are combined with an environmental model (e.g. IMAGE (Alcamo *et al.* 1998)) and thereby incorporate climate change, or with specific sector models allowing a more detailed analysis of transport, forestry, agriculture and tourism. Such macroeconomic models are not able to make an assessment beyond the resolution of individual countries. The spatial variability of land use/cover within a country is determined by local variability in social and biophysical conditions. Furthermore, the driving factors of land use/cover change are often region-specific as a consequence of different contextual conditions, specific variation in the socioeconomic and biophysical conditions, and the influence of land use history and culture (Iverson Nassauer 1995; Naveh 2001). Results of macro-models are downscaled from country-level data to landscape level using spatially explicit land use/cover change models (e.g. Dyna-CLUE (Verburg *et al.* 2006, 2008)).

The uncertainty in the development of external drivers of models, such as demography, economy and trade, are generally described and quantified by means of scenarios. Such scenarios may represent different future developments (e.g. enhanced global cooperation to regionalization or strong to weak government intervention (Westhoek *et al.* 2006)), or a likely baseline scenario serving as a reference to assess policy impacts. The results of the modeled land use/cover changes in Europe are intended primarily to support discussions on the future of rural areas and to identify hotspots of landscape change that need special consideration.

Figure 7.1 illustrates the findings of the EURURALIS study under the scenario of strong globalization with weak government intervention at a spatial resolution of 1 km^2. These model results indicate hotspots of two dominant processes of land use/cover change that directly relate to the development of rural regions in Europe: urbanization and a decrease of agricultural land. On the left, Figure 7.1 shows future expansion of urban areas. This urbanization mainly occurs in peri-urban areas, resulting in a declining agricultural sector in these regions (Verburg *et al.* 2006). However, the figure shows decreasing influence of agricultural functions not only in the regions indicated on the urbanization map; in many regions with less favorable conditions for intensive agriculture, especially the mountainous regions across Europe, the model simulations also indicate a decrease of agricultural land. In these regions, agricultural land abandonment takes place, eventually leading to an increase in forest and semi-natural areas.

Landscape functionality

The large-scale model results show where land use/cover is likely to change and therefore how patterns in the landscape will change. The results of this land use/cover study, however, do not explicitly indicate change in landscape functionality. This limitation can be illustrated by an example in the central region of the Netherlands (Figure 7.2). According to the large-scale land use/cover projections,

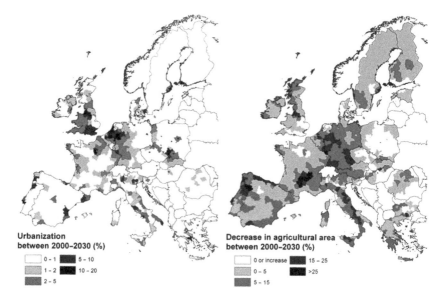

Figure 7.1 Urbanization and decrease in agricultural land between 2000–2030 as pre-
          dicted by the EURURALIS model chain under the scenario of strong globali-
          zation with weak government intervention.

we expect strong urbanization here. We may also expect that such changes will
directly or indirectly change landscape functionality; for instance, more land in
peri-urban areas will be used for outdoor recreation. However, from the large-
scale model results we cannot observe how these land use/cover changes affect
functioning of the rural landscape (Figure 7.2). In the model simulations, the
agricultural land use/cover classes only show changes in the agricultural function, determined by changes in area under agriculture. However, according to
Dutch farm census data, between 1999 and 2005 average growth of 8.3 percent
occurred in the number of farms that incorporated recreational activities into
their operations. In the same period an extra 11.3 percent of farms per year were
participating in a type of landscape conservation program (nature and cultural
heritage). Therefore, although the land use/cover model results do not show a
change in functionality of agricultural land, changes in landscape functionality
in this strongly urbanizing region are likely.

There are several reasons why functionality cannot be displayed in the land
use/cover change model results. First, the land use modeling approach relates the
spatial allocation of land use to land cover while landscape functioning extends,
as mentioned before, beyond land cover. Additionally, the macroeconomic
models of the presented modeling approach focus solely on the dynamics of
agricultural production, without taking into account other commodity and non-
commodity goods for which demands are difficult to simulate with existing
approaches. Furthermore, in many locations with a rural land cover, multiple

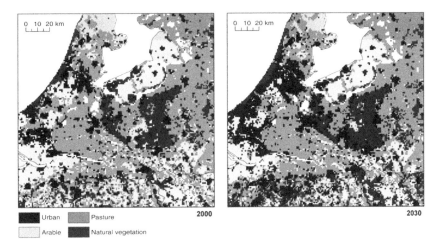

Figure 7.2 Land use/cover changes from 2000 to 2010 and 2030 in the central region of the Netherlands as predicted by the EURURALIS model chain under the scenario of strong globalization with weak government intervention.

activities are combined at one location. These multifunctional areas play an important role in landscape management and policy-making but cannot be taken into account in the presented land use/cover modeling approach as the spatial allocation procedure assigns only a single land-use type per location.

Within the central region of the Netherlands we analyzed landscape functionality and the possible influences of peri-urban development in respect to landscape functioning. Landscape functions are studied at a detailed spatial resolution of 100 meters. Spatial indicators related to land cover and social and biophysical characteristics of the landscape were developed to assess the location of landscape functions and their capacity to provide goods and services. The resulting landscape function maps provide information on where and how many goods and services are supplied.

For this rural region in the Netherlands six landscape functions were analyzed, namely, the capacity of the landscape to provide:

1   areas for residential use;
2   locations for intensive livestock husbandry;
3   information on cultural heritage;
4   zones for drinking-water extraction;
5   an attractive landscape for overnight tourism; and
6   an attractive landscape for leisure cycling.

These landscape functions are all strongly related to land cover. The actual landscape functionality was quantified by the current supplied measurable goods and services.

Function mapping methodology

The basis of the overall mapping methodology is the link between landscape functions and land cover or policy delineations. Using the direct information on the location of the functions, three different groups could be distinguished (Willemen *et al.* 2008):

1   landscape functions that are directly observable from the land cover or those which are spatially defined by policy regulations;
2   landscape functions that are not directly observable from the land cover but whose locations were partly known based on sample point data; and
3   landscape functions that are not directly observable from the land cover and lack any spatially referenced information on their location.

Different methods were used for each group to define the capacity and extent of the landscape functions (Figure 7.3).

The first group consists of landscape functions that directly relate to land cover *(residential* areas and *intensive livestock* farm locations) or those directly defined by policy *(cultural heritage* areas and *drinking water* extraction zones). The location of each of these functions is exactly known. Spatially referenced data were used to quantify the capacity of the function at that location. This resulted in quantitative function maps.

The second group consists of landscape functions that do not relate directly to a single land cover, such as the capacity to provide an attractive landscape for *tourism*. It is assumed that land-cover patterns and composition, together with

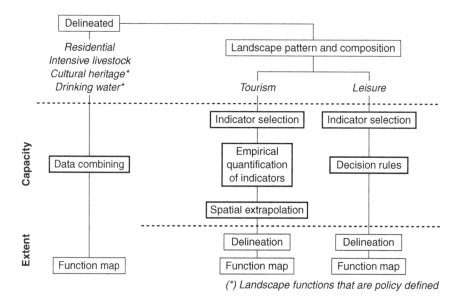

Figure 7.3 Overview of the landscape function mapping approach.

biophysical and socioeconomic landscape components, can be used to describe the location and capacity of these landscape functions. All of these landscape components can be translated into spatial indicators. Using sample data, multi-variate regression techniques are then used to empirically quantify the influence of these spatial indicators on function variability. Using the empirically derived relations, the landscape function is extrapolated to a quantitative landscape function map covering the whole study area. After defining the function capacity, a threshold is introduced to delineate the assumed presence for human use or policy-making of the specific landscape function.

The third group consists of landscape functions that are also influenced by land-cover patterns and composition, but for which any data on function location and extent are lacking. In this case spatial indicators and expert-based decision rules are used to develop quantitative landscape function maps. Here again a threshold value is determined and used to delineate the area in which the function was considered to be present. The capacity of the landscape to provide an attractive landscape for *leisure cycling* falls into this function group.

Function maps

Each of the four land-cover or policy delineated functions of this study area were combined with quantitative spatial data to determine the function capacity. The *residential* function was delineated by the location of residential neighborhoods and quantified by population per neighborhood. The *intensive livestock* husbandry function was delineated by the location of intensive livestock farms and quantified by the economic farm size. The landscape function providing information on *cultural heritage* was delineated using the location of high-value historical landscapes as defined by the provincial government. Because authenticity of the landscape is considered an important aspect of this landscape function (Daugstad *et al.* 2006), the percentage of unchanged land use between the years 1900 and 2000 within 250 meters of each grid cell was used to quantify the function. Another policy-delineated function in our study area was the *drinking-water* extraction zones function. Here we used policy-defined groundwater protection zones for function delineation. Within these protected areas, water remains in the underground aquifer for approximately 25 years before it is extracted. The permitted quantity of drinking water that companies may extract (in m^3/yr) at these locations was used to quantify this function. The landscape functions maps are presented in Figures 7.4 a through d.

The attractiveness of the landscape for *tourism* was estimated via regression analysis by using spatial landscape indicators and sample data on tourist accommodation locations. All predictive variables ($p < 0.01$) together with their beta estimates for the tourist function are presented in Table 7.1. Locations with abundant and accessible natural areas, and that are situated away from highways and in neighborhoods with many small local roads that could facilitate recreational cycling, have a higher probability to act as tourism destinations. The variables that showed a negative relation with tourist accommodation locations were

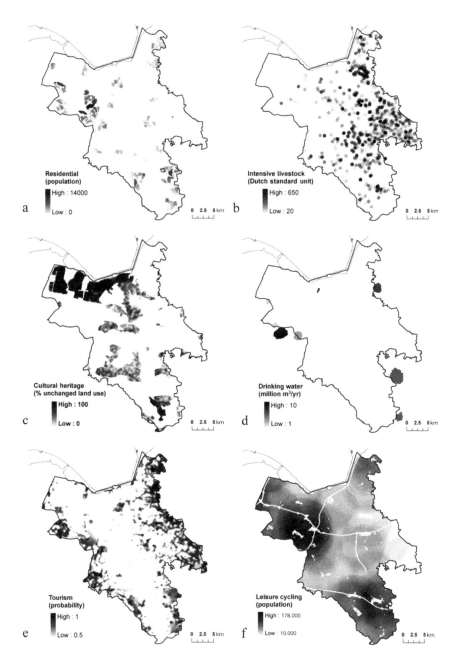

Figure 7.4 Landscape function maps for the central Netherlands: a) Residential function; b) Intensive livestock function; c) Cultural heritage function; d) Drinking-water function; e) Tourism suitability function; f) Cycling leisure function.

Table 7.1 Regression results ($p > 0.01$) for the tourism suitability function ($n = 794$)

Variable	Beta estimate
Intercept	1.3576
Agricultural land cover within 500 m (%)	−0.0195
Natural land cover within 500 m (%)	−0.0578
Clustered natural area within 5 km (%)	0.0247
Openness (m)	−0.0004
Distance to highway (m)	0.0001
Industrial elements within 500 m (%)	−0.0343
Distance to natural area >1 km^2 (m)	−0.0002
Distance to swimming location (m)	−0.0001
Accessible nature within 500 m (%)	0.0242
Local roads within 500 m (%)	0.0388
AUC	0.84

openness of the landscape, distance to natural areas larger than 1 km^2, high percentage of industrial elements, and homogeneous natural and agricultural surroundings. The performance of the regression model was assessed by the area under the curve (AUC) of the relative operating characteristic (Swets 1988). The tourism model showed an AUC of 0.84, which in land use studies is interpreted as "very good" (Hosmer and Lemeshow 2000; Lesschen *et al.* 2005). All areas with an estimated tourism probability greater than 0.5 were considered to have the capacity to provide an attractive landscape for tourist accommodations. Interpreting the tourism suitability map (Figure 7.4e), tourism areas are mainly located on the border of our study area where a mix of natural and agricultural areas are found.

The *leisure cycling* function was spatially characterized using landscape indicators together with expert-based decision rules. Indicators to assess the attractiveness of the landscape for leisure cycling activities were selected based on a literature review. Most leisure cycling takes place in the direct neighborhood of residential areas (Goossen *et al.* 1997; CBS 2000). As leisure cycling requires cycling facilities, all areas with paved local roads within a distance of 5 km around each residential neighborhood were included as leisure areas. Locations with highways, industry, business parks and waste dumps were excluded from the suitable leisure-cycling areas (Goossen and Langers 2000; Gimona and van der Horst 2007). The leisure function was quantified based on the population that could reach the suitable cycling area. The leisure area was delineated by excluding all areas with a potential leisure population of less than 10,000 (Figure 7.4f). Leisure population is especially concentrated around and between the main residential areas. The quantitative landscape function maps show in detail which goods and services are supplied in this region.

Landscape functionality relates, among other factors, to land cover and its spatial configuration. Table 7.2 summarizes the relations between landscape functionality and land cover indicators resulting from our analyses for the rural study area in the Netherlands. Changes in land cover will be reflected in the

Table 7.2 Relationship between landscape functions and land cover-based landscape indicators

Landscape function	Land cover indicator	Influence
Residential	Residential areas	+
Intensive livestock	Intensive livestock farms	+
Cultural heritage	Change in land use/cover	−
Drinking-water extraction	None	
Tourism	Distance to highway	−
	Amount of small roads	+
	Homogeneous agricultural area	−
	Homogeneous natural area	−
	Distance to a large accessible natural area	+
	Presence of business park/industry	−
Leisure cycling	Distance to residential areas	+
	Presence of highway	
	Amount of small roads	+
	Presence of business park/industry	−

listed landscape functions, provided that these are causal relations. Dynamics of landscape functions related to a single land cover are straightforward (e.g. more houses mean more residential functions). Other functions will be affected by changes in landscape composition; the tourism function is one example of this.

Many locations with multiple landscape functions are present in our regional study area (Figure 7.4). In regions with high pressure on land, as is the case in the Netherlands, the use of multifunctional landscapes could be a solution for reducing land demand to comply with all societal needs for goods and services. However, not all functions can be combined without influencing the overall capacity of the landscape to provide goods and services. For example, the presence of intensive livestock husbandry conflicts in many cases with other functions; its presence can decrease the attractiveness of landscape for tourism or the possibility of drinking-water extraction. By combining landscape function maps, areas can be identified in which conflicting combinations of functions can lead to reduced functionality. Figure 7.5a shows, for example, spatial overlap between the intensive livestock and tourism function locations for a portion of the study area. At these multifunctional locations, a loss of landscape functionality may occur. For example, the attractiveness for tourism of a location near intensive livestock farms is diminished because of increased emissions of ammonia. On the other hand, Figure 7.5b shows that two conflicting functions, drinking-water extraction and intensive livestock farming, are spatially separated, so that potential conflicts do not exist. This example shows that spatial policy can mitigate possible function conflicts; drinking-water extraction zones are strictly protected by numerous rules concerning land use. Suitable tourism areas, on the other hand, are not specifically included in Dutch spatial planning.

Policy-makers can use spatially explicit information on landscape functions to design spatial policies and (*ex ante*) evaluate the effect of their land use strategies.

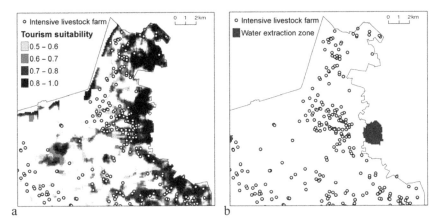

Figure 7.5 Multifunctional areas in a part of the study area: a) intensive livestock
husbandry and suitable tourism areas; b) intensive livestock husbandry and
drinking-water extraction.

Regional qualities in terms of functionality can be interpreted from landscape
function maps, and spatial indicators can be used to understand the relationship
between landscape characteristics and landscape functionality. Additionally, locations with potentially conflicting landscape functions can be identified. Especially
for areas with high pressure on land resources, good management of interacting
functions within a multifunctional landscape promotes sustainable land use.

Integrated analysis of land use/cover and function dynamics

The continental-scale land use/cover and regional function model approaches
presented in this chapter were treated as complementary; both models described
different land change aspects but were not directly coupled. In an attempt to
make an integrated assessment of land change, modeled land use/cover dynamics could serve as an input to allow assessment of future changes in landscape
functions. By linking the two modeling approaches, changes in landscape functionality at a regional scale could be explored to reflect European-level and
global processes of change, which could then account for the multi-scale dimensions of rural change (Figure 7.6). For example, changes in demand for agricultural products at the EU level can have an impact at the regional scale on
landscape functionality and quality, in terms of tourism suitability or cultural
heritage. By relating landscape functionality to land use/cover changes, hotspots
of change in landscape functionality can be identified. Additionally, detailed
analyses of threats and new possibilities for landscape functions can be defined
and explored.

The approach presented in Figure 7.6 is driven by a demand for land related
to a certain land use/cover. This demand primarily relates to either urban or

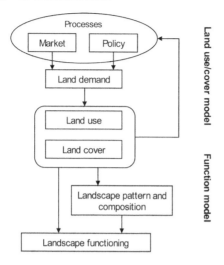

Figure 7.6 Coupling land use/cover and landscape function modeling.

agricultural uses. However, there is also a strong demand for the use of services that emerge from the landscape, such as the demand for attractive areas for recreation or tourism. This is especially true in peri-urban areas. Policy-makers are currently trying to incorporate this multitude of demands for goods and services by society into their spatial planning (e.g. the Common Agricultural Policy of the EU (EC 2004) or the Dutch spatial planning act (VROM 2006)). A fully integrated land-use modeling framework should therefore be able to account for all demands on land resources from society. Figure 7.7 shows a conceptual

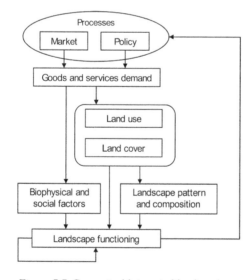

Figure 7.7 Conceptual integrated land use/cover model framework.

integrated land use/cover modeling approach in which the demand for goods and services that need to be provided by landscape functions is the driving factor of land change. Landscape functioning does not only depend on land cover; many biophysical factors (such as groundwater level) or social factors (such as policies or population pressure) play a role in the capacity of the landscape to provide goods and services. The provision of drinking water is an example of a function highly dependent on biophysical and social factors rather than on land cover directly. In this chapter we showed that interactions between landscape functions can take place at multifunctional locations. As these biophysical and social factors, together with function interactions, influence the overall capacity of the landscape to provide goods and services, these factors must also be simulated within the integrated modeling framework.

Conclusions

In this chapter, two spatial approaches for analyzing the dynamics of rural areas in Europe were presented. The first section of this chapter focused on land use/ cover changes within Europe. Based on scenarios related to future land demand, this approach included multi-scale interactions resulting in a land use/cover map. The second part focused on landscape functioning at a regional scale. The capacity of the landscape to provide goods and services was made spatially explicit using landscape indicators including land cover. Both modeling approaches deal with different aspects of land change and can therefore be seen as complementary.

However, to move toward an integrated land dynamic approach, the two modeling approaches could be linked. In this way changes at global and European levels, reflected in regional landscape functionality, can be explored. We presented a conceptual model framework in which multi-scale integrated land use/ cover modeling contributes to a better understanding and management of land resources, including the provided goods and services. The analysis on multiple scales is shown to be necessary in order to adequately address the complex structure of the land use system. Integrating this multi-scale analysis with landscape functionality analyses is of high importance to account for societal demand for a wide spectrum of different goods and services from the land.

References

Alcamo, J., Leemans, R. and Kreileman, E. (eds.) (1998) "Global Change Scenarios of the 21st Century: Results from the IMAGE 2.1 Model," London: Pergamon and Elsevier Science, 1–296.

Brécard, D., Fougeyrollas, A., Le Mouël, P., Lemiale, L. and Zagame, P. (2006) "Macroeconomic Consequences of European Research Policy: Prospects of the Nemesis Model in the Year 2030," *Research Policy*, 35: 910–924.

Bürgi, M., Hersperger, A.M. and Schneeberger, N. (2004) "Driving Forces of Landscape Change – Current and New Directions," *Landscape Ecology*: 857–868.

CBS (2000) *Statline*, Centraal Bureau voor de Statistiek, Voorburg/Heerlen.

Daugstad, K., Ronningen, K. and Skar, B. (2006) "Agriculture as an Upholder of Cultural Heritage? Conceptualizations and Value Judgements – A Norwegian Perspective in International Context," *Journal of Rural Studies*, 22: 67–81.

de Groot, R.S. (1992) "Functions of Nature, Evaluation of Nature in Environmental Planning, Management and Decision Making," Groningen: Wolters-Noordhoff.

EC (2004) "The Common Agricultural Policy Explained," European Commission Directorate General for Agriculture, p. 33.

Geertman, S. and Stillwell, J. (2004) "Planning Support Systems: an Inventory of Current Practice," *Computers, Environment and Urban Systems*, 28: 291–310.

Gimona, A. and van der Horst, D. (2007) "Mapping Hotspots of Multiple Landscape Functions: A Case Study on Farmland Afforestation in Scotland," *Landscape Ecology*, 22: 1255–1264.

Goossen, M. and Langers, F. (2000) "Assessing Quality of Rural Areas in the Netherlands: Finding the Most Important Indicators for Recreation," *Landscape and Urban Planning*, 46: 241–251.

Goossen, C.M., Langers, F. and Lous, J.F.A. (1997) "Indicatoren Voor Recreatieve Kwaliteiten in het Landelijk gebied," Rep. No. *Rapport 584*, DLO-Staring Centrum, Wageningen.

Heistermann, M., Müller, C. and Ronneberger, K. (2006) "Land in Sight? Achievements, Deficits and Potentials of Continental to Global Scale Land-use Modeling," *Agriculture, Ecosystems and Environment*, 114: 141–158.

Helming, K., Tscherning, K., Koning, B., Sieber, S., Wiggering, H., Kuhlman, T., Wascher, D., Perez-Soba, M., Smeets, P., Tabbush, P., Dilly, O., Huttl, R. and Bach, H. (2008) "Ex Ante Impact Assessment of Land Use Changes in European Regions – the SENSOR Approach," in Helming, K., Perez-Soba, M. and Tabbush, P. (eds.), *Sustainability Impact Assessment of Land Use Changes*, Berlin Heidelberg: Springer-Verlag, p. 507.

Hosmer, D.W. and Lemeshow, S. (2000) "Applied Logistic Regression," New York: Wiley and Sons.

Iverson Nassauer, J. (1995) "Culture and Changing Landscape Structure," *Landscape Ecology*, 10: 229–237.

Lesschen, J.P., Verburg, P.H. and Staal, S.J. (2005) "Statistical Methods for Analysing the Spatial Dimension of Changes in Land Use and Farming Systems," Nairobi, Kenya and Wageningen, the Netherlands: ILRI & LUCC Focus 3 Office.

McIntosh, B.S., Seaton, R.A.F. and Jeffrey, P. (2007) "Tools to Think With? Towards Understanding the Use of Computer-based Support Tools in Policy Relevant Research," *Environmental Modelling and Software*, 22: 620–648.

Metzger, M.J., Rounsevell, M.D.A., Acosta-Michlik, L., Leemans, R. and Schroter, D. (2006) "The Vulnerability of Ecosystem Services to Land Use Change," *Agriculture, Ecosystems and Environment*, 114: 69–85.

Naveh, Z. (2001) "Ten Major Premises for a Holistic Conception of Multifunctional Landscapes," *Landscape and Urban Planning*, 57: 269–284.

Pinto-Correia, T., Gustavsson, R. and Pirnat, J. (2006) "Bridging the Gap between Centrally Defined Policies and Local Decisions – Towards more Sensitive and Creative Rural Landscape Management," *Landscape Ecology*, 21: 333–346.

Swets, J. (1988) "Measuring the Accuracy of Diagnostic Systems," *Science*, 240: 1285–1293.

Uran, O. and Janssen, R. (2003) "Why are Spatial Decision Support Systems Not Used? Some Experiences from the Netherlands," *Computers, Environment and Urban Systems*, 27: 511–526.

Van Meijl, H., Van Rheenen, T., Tabeau, A. and Eickhout, B. (2006) "The Impact of Different Policy Environments on Agricultural Land Use in Europe," *Agriculture, Ecosystems and Environment*, 114: 21–38.

Vejre, H., Abildtrup, J., Andersen, E., Andersen, P., Brandt, J., Busck, A., Dalgaard, T., Hasler, B., Huusom, H., Kristensen, L., Kristensen, S. and Præstholm, S. (2007) "Multifunctional Agriculture and Multifunctional Landscapes – Land Use as an Interface," in Mander, Ü., Helming, K. and Wiggering, H. (eds.), *Multifunctional Land Use: Meeting Future Demands for Landscape Goods and Services*, Heidelberg and Berlin: Springer, pp. 93–104.

Verburg, P.H. and Chen, Y.Q. (2000) "Multi-scale Characterization of Land-use Patterns in China," *Ecosystems*, 3: 369–385.

Verburg, P.H., Eickhout, B. and van Meijl, H. (2008) "A Multi-scale, Multi-model Approach for Analyzing the Future Dynamics of European Land Use," *The Annals of Regional Science*, 42: 57–77.

Verburg, P.H., Rounsevell, M.D.A. and Veldkamp, A. (2006) "Scenario-based Studies of Future Land Use in Europe," *Agriculture, Ecosystems and Environment*, 114: 1–6.

VROM (2006) "Nota Ruimte; Ruimte Voor Ontwikkeling," Deel 4: tekst na parlementaire instemming, p. 200.

Walsh, S.J., Crawford, T.W., Crews-Meyer, K.A. and Welsh, W.F. (2001) "A Multi scale Analysis of Land Use Land Cover Change and NDVI Variation in Nang Rong District, Northeast Thailand," *Agriculture, Ecosystems and Environment*, 85: 47–64.

Westhoek, H.J., van den Berg, M. and Bakkes, J.A. (2006) "Scenario Development to Explore the Future of Europe's Rural Areas," *Agriculture, Ecosystems and Environment*, 114: 7–20.

Willemen, L., Verburg, P.H., Hein, L. and van Mensvoort, M.E. (2008) "Spatial Characterization of Landscape Functions," *Landscape and Urban Planning*, 88: 34–43.

WUR and MNP (2007) *Eururalis 2.0 CDrom*, Alterra Wageningen UR, Wageningen, the Netherlands.

8 Nonmarket valuation of multifunctional farm and forest preservation

Joshua M. Duke and Robert J. Johnston

Introduction

Although the term "multifunctionality" is more familiar in Europe (Batie 2003), residents on both sides of the Atlantic recognize and appreciate non-production, or multifunctional, outputs from agricultural land. Public policies increasingly seek to supply these often nonmarket outputs, especially through the creation of new and more innovative policies or by better aligning existing policies to promote stewardship (Dobbs and Pretty 2004). This chapter focuses on policies that help achieve an important goal of stewardship – the provision and preservation of landscape and open-space amenity benefits (Abler 2004).

Many policies affect the provision of such amenity benefits (Duke and Lynch 2006), but land preservation policies represent the principal interventions affecting their allocation by land markets. The most common types of land preservation policies include:

1   regulatory methods, including conservation-oriented zoning;
2   purchase of agricultural conservation easements (PACE); and
3   acquisitive or fee-simple purchase.

At the risk of considerable oversimplification, it is generally presumed that European policy places greater emphasis on regulatory programs, while US policy is more likely to promote policies that favor market incentives. Nevertheless, both approaches would benefit from more systematic evidence concerning nonmarket amenity benefits derived from various types of policy intervention. Europe could then better balance the social value of competing land uses, and the United States could gain greater recognition of the value of nonmarket amenity benefits resulting from market incentive programs.

Economists have been estimating the value of agricultural amenity benefits for over two decades. In a comprehensive review of the literature, Bergstrom and Ready (2009) find that these values can be significant. Benefits vary with location, land use and public access. Johnston and Duke (2007) show that values also vary with the policy selected to achieve preservation outcomes. Such results naturally lead to efficiency calculations on the margin, i.e. exploring whether preserving a specific parcel produces benefits that exceed costs. This chapter discusses the conceptual role of economics in prioritization strategies for the preservation of farmland and associated amenity benefits, as well as the use of empirical results to inform such strategies.

Given recent progress in estimating benefits associated with farmland preservation, it is surprising how little impact valuation research has made on the associated policy processes. Research on benefits is mainly disseminated through academic journals and not in a policy-relevant form, i.e. one in which benefit estimates allow policy-makers to better understand relative marginal values for a wide class of preserved land attributes (Johnston and Swallow 2006). As a result, land use policy rarely reflects the amenity values held by the broader public.

This shortcoming goes beyond considerations of efficiency; it is a broader limitation of the land use policy process that preservation decisions are made without systematic consideration of public values or even preferences. Consider the example of selection criteria used in PACE programs to prioritize parcels for preservation. Such programs, like Land Evaluation and Site Assessment (LESA), use criteria that focus largely on attributes of parcels associated with profitable agricultural production (soil quality, size, proximity to other agricultural operations, etc.) and very little on amenity provision or public preferences. In effect, PACE creates a market in which the public buys amenities but has little say in the type of parcels preserved – in what other market would buyers pay for a good but not require that their preferences affect the choice among goods? The policy process would likely improve simply by enhancing its recognition of public preferences, and by better incorporating such information into prioritization strategies. Although this argument has been made repeatedly over the past two decades (e.g. Kline and Wichelns 1994), and is relatively uncontroversial among economists, there are few if any examples where public preferences for farmland amenities have been explicitly and completely incorporated into parcel selection criteria within the policy process.

Many economists would further argue that the process would also become more effective if parcels selected for preservation were valued more highly by the public than those not selected. This, in part, would be due to the resultant increase in public support for the actions of public and private preservation entities, thereby potentially reducing conflict resolution costs (e.g. costs of legal challenges, hearings, public correspondence or coalition building) associated with more controversial or less highly valued preservation options. Hence, greater attention to public preferences would not only increase the benefits of land preservation directly (by engaging in those preservation options that generate the greatest social welfare), but also indirectly through the potential to render the policy process itself more procedurally efficient.

Notwithstanding the benefits of greater integration of valuation research into the policy process, policy makers remain almost universally unaware of the existence of such information. There is a clear need for a bridge between valuation research and a user-friendly understanding of the public values for farm and forest preservation. To this end, this chapter offers a detailed application of valuation research to preservation in Delaware. Using parametric results of community and statewide surveys for the preservation of farm and forest parcels, this chapter presents results on the benefits of preservation in a fast-growing community in Delaware. The model explicitly allows for benefits to vary as a function of multifunctional attributes and clarifies trade-offs involved in policies designed to promote multifunctionality.

Model results illustrate the benefits of using different types of policies to preserve different types of farms. These results support several conclusions. First, preservation benefits can be substantial, but can also vary greatly, and may *sometimes* be lower than the costs of preservation. Second, preservation benefits vary according to many attributes of preserved acreage but, surprisingly, not by land use (in this study). Third, public access has a large, positive impact on preservation benefits. These and other conclusions imply that economic research can help guide policy-makers in their preservation decisions, and that common prioritization strategies based primarily on factors related to agricultural productivity may not lead to the most socially beneficial outcomes.

Not only do the results have clear implications for parcel prioritization, but they also suggest that some parcels should not be preserved at all. The benefits of prioritizing preservation activities based on associated multifunctional benefits would be numerous. Effective prioritization would target parcels that generate the maximum total net benefits from collective preservation efforts. We also suggest, however, that prioritization would help align expectations among stakeholders in the policy process. This would help to avoid conflict and associated conflict resolution costs. Rather than preservationists and developers arguing for all-or-nothing solutions, more effective prioritization would allow both sides to be accommodated in a more systematic and efficient manner.

Conceptual framework

The economic theory of land preservation (Gardner 1977) and the role of stated preference analysis in estimating land preservation values (Bergstrom and Ready 2009) are mature and, though not entirely settled, available in numerous other papers. Therefore, they will only be briefly summarized here. Some utility associated with agricultural land use decisions accrues to people who are not involved in decision-making on the farm parcel and who do not compensate the decision-maker for the utility gained. These positive externalities are realized outside existing markets and, to the extent that they are nonrival in consumption, take on the character of a public good. These benefits will be provided at an inefficiently low level by markets and require some form of collective action to increase their supply. From an economic perspective, this is the primary justification for government action to preserve farmland parcels (Gardner 1977).

Common policies for land preservation include conservation zoning or similar regulatory methods, PACE, and fee-simple purchase. Duke and Lynch (2006) argue that institutional issues complicate the comparison of the social efficiency of regulatory policies, which establish markets, and governmental-participatory policies, which enhance demand for certain land uses. For this reason, this chapter will not treat preservation as a means to provide the socially efficient amount of agricultural land use, i.e. q^*. Rather, efficiency refers to enhancements *at the margin* – where benefits of preservation exceed the costs.

This chapter also discusses prioritization and targeting of preservation actions; this discussion extends marginal efficiency calculations beyond simple one-parcel efficiency decisions to include options for selecting among multiple parcels. Operationally, this means that parcels with the greatest total net benefits should be selected for preservation; alternatively, parcels with the highest benefit-to-cost ratios should be preserved in a sequential process until the budget is expended. This prioritization strategy may be readily implemented when benefit measures are available. Nevertheless, when implementation constraints are also important, a binary linear programming model has been shown to produce the same or superior prioritization (Messer 2006).

Framing preservation policy considerations in this way is standard practice in environmental economics, though it is acknowledged that answers to these questions may not necessarily be associated with ecological sustainability because they do not recognize feedback from biological processes (Bromley 2007). Hence, results of research into public preferences may provide the most useful insight when viewed within the context of realistic policy sets defined by models of natural biological processes. Examples of models that coordinate economic and ecological research to prioritize environmental policies are provided by Johnston *et al.* (2002a, 2002b), among others.

Valuation research is driven by the assumption that if people gain utility from preservation, then the maximum amount they would be willing to pay (WTP) for that preservation measures the benefits they receive. Caveats and debates have been expressed regarding this assumption (Bromley 2007), but these issues are well documented in existing literature. Stated preference methods are used to elicit this WTP measure. Since land preservation is a multi-attribute good, this study uses a choice experiment (CE) to estimate associated willingness to pay. This capitalizes on the ability of CEs to explicitly estimate trade-offs and WTP associated with multi-attribute policy options (Adamowicz *et al.* 1998). Individual demands for preservation are aggregated vertically because preservation is assumed to be nonrival in consumption, following the public goods argument presented above. This also reflects standard practice in the literature. This chapter builds an economic model of choice in the standard manner, using a random utility model (Hanemann 1984).

In this model, household h may gain utility from various preservation attributes. Preserved parcels vary in terms of the specific levels of amenities provided and thus are modeled as multi-attribute goods. A key attribute of parcels is their relative proximity to household h, and so the jurisdictional policy scale k is modeled separately – preservation either occurs somewhere within the household's community or simply within the state.[1] As discussed by Johnston and Duke (2009), this choice context of land preservation mimics referenda, which typically provide funds for particular types of preservation within specified political jurisdictions. Thus, preservation occurring via a program i that will preserve a hypothetical parcel at jurisdictional scale k is given by

$$U_{ihk}(X_{ik}, W_{ik}, Y_h - Fee_{ihk}) = v_{ihk}(X_{ik}, W_{ik}, Y_h - Fee_{ihk}) + \varepsilon_{ihk}$$

Where X_{ik} = vector of variables characterizing attributes of preservation program i at jurisdictional scale k; W_{ik} = a vector of variables characterizing the policy process of preservation program i at jurisdictional scale k: Fee_{ihk} = cost to household h of preservation plan i at jurisdictional scale k through a mandatory payment vehicle; Y_h = disposable income of household type h; $v_{ihk}(\cdot)$ = function representing the empirically measurable component of utility; and ε_{ihk} = unobservable component of utility, modeled as econometric error. The jurisdictional scales reflect community preservation $(k = C)$ and statewide preservation $(k = S)$. The policy process attributes allow the model to reflect preferences for preservation secured through alternative strategies, such as PACE and zoning.

Following standard methods for CEs, the household is assumed to choose among three preservation plans, $(j = A, B, N)$. It may choose option A, option B, or may reject both options and choose the status quo (neither plan, $j = N$). A choice of neither plan would result in zero preservation $(X_{ik} = 0)$ and household cost $(Fee_{ihk} = 0)$. The household assesses utility resulting from available options and chooses that which offers the greatest utility. For example, the household will choose option A if:

$$v_{Ahk}(X_{Ahk}, W_{Ahk}, Y_h - Fee_{Ahk}) + \varepsilon_{Ahk} \geq v_{zhk}(X_{zhk}, W_{zhk}, Y_h - Fee_{zhk}) + \varepsilon_{zhk}$$

for $z = \{B, N\}$. Model estimates for jurisdictional scales $k = C$, S provide two unique estimates of observable utility $v_{ihk}(\cdot)$. Econometric approaches depend on assumptions regarding ε_{ihk}, and include conditional (CL) or mixed logit (ML) models (Maddala 1983; Greene 2003).

Data

The data are derived from two parallel CEs conducted in Delaware – one at the community jurisdiction (or policy scale) and one at the state jurisdiction. Details of the survey procedures and measurement are provided in Johnston and Duke (2007) and will only be summarized here. Community jurisdiction results are drawn from the Smyrna/Clayton and Georgetown Land Preservation surveys, which were functionally identical instruments designed to target two similar, growing Delaware communities. Random samples of 750 residents in each community were contacted. The state jurisdiction data are drawn from responses from 1,000 residential contacts for the Delaware Land Preservation Survey, which was a parallel survey targeted at statewide preservation and which was implemented over a random statewide sample. Survey development required more than 18 months, and included 14 focus groups, a large number of individual pretests, and interviews with land preservation practitioners and other experts.

The CE questions in the survey provided respondents with two preservation options that would each preserve land with varying attributes and using different policies, "Option A" and "Option B," as well as two status quo options. The key difference between the community and statewide surveys was the size of the jurisdiction within which land preservation would occur. That is, respondents in the community CE were told that land would be preserved somewhere in their home community, while respondents in the state CE were told that land would be preserved somewhere in their home state. This mimics the context of farmland preservation policy decisions such as voting on preservation bond referenda, in which specific parcel locations are unknown when voting choices are made, but individuals are aware of the political jurisdiction within which preservation will occur.

Other attributes that were varied within the CE included: the type of land preserved, the number of acres, the provision of public access, the risk of development of unpreserved parcels and the cost of preservation to the respondent's household. Choice questions also specified the technique that would be used to preserve the land in question, as well as the agent who would be responsible for implementing preservation techniques. Table 8.1 describes the attributes that distinguished hypothetical preservation options, including summary statistics for both the community and state survey versions. Additional details are provided by Johnston and Duke (2009).

To prevent protests and the potential for respondent confusion, it is critical that policies described in survey scenarios are "perceived as realistic and feasible" (Bateman *et al.* 2002: 116). Following guidance from focus groups and policy experts, this led to a small number of differences between the community and state CE. Principal differences between the survey instruments at the two jurisdictional scales involved the levels of the acres, cost and access attributes. Acres and cost were both higher in state survey versions, which reflected focus group respondents' expectations about the relative size and cost of community versus statewide programs. Focus groups for the community surveys also revealed that scenarios were viewed as most realistic when allowing for specific types of access (e.g. hunting, walking/biking) on preserved parcels. At the state scale, in contrast, it was perceived as unrealistic that the state could mandate access for any specific activity on all preserved acres. Hence, the statewide survey characterized public access as the percentage of preserved acres for which access would be permitted (e.g. 100 percent, 50 percent, 0 percent). While these differences do not influence model validity (as state and community results are not pooled), they should be considered when interpreting model results. Of 1,385 deliverable community surveys, 491 were returned, for an average response rate of 35.5 percent. Of the 919 deliverable statewide surveys, 334 were returned, for a response rate of 36.3 percent. The reader is referred to Johnston and Duke (2009) for further details.

Table 8.1 Variables and descriptive statistics

Variable	Description	Mean value[a] (std. dev)	
		Delaware community	Delaware state
Neither	Alternative specific constant (dummy) identifying the status quo option.	0.33 (0.47)	0.33 (0.47)
Acres	Number of acres preserved by preservation plan.	63.10 (70.78)	4007.79 (3956.68)
Acres*Nursery	Multiplicative interaction between *Acres* and a Binary (dummy) variable indicating that the parcel is an active nursery (omitted default is a food or dairy farm).	11.98 (39.52)	846.88 (2464.72)
Acres*Forest	Multiplicative interaction between *Acres* and a binary (dummy) variable indicating that the parcel is forest (omitted default is a food or dairy farm).	12.80 (41.22)	777.10 (2347.00)
Acres*Idle	Multiplicative interaction between *Acres* and a binary (dummy) variable indicating that the parcel is idle farmland (omitted default is a food or dairy farm).	13.35 (41.37)	793.02 (2355.59)
Acres*Trust Easement	Multiplicative interaction between *Acres* and a binary (dummy) variable indicating that preservation is accomplished through conservation easements, implemented by land trusts, using block grant funds from the state (omitted default is preservation by conservation zoning).	6.73 (30.43)	468.16 (1889.80)
Acres*State Purchase	Multiplicative interaction between *Acres* and a binary (dummy) variable indicating that preservation is accomplished through fee-simple purchase of the parcel, implemented by the state (omitted default is preservation by conservation zoning).	20.85 (50.44)	1291.67 (2914.34)

Variable	Description		
Acres*Trust Purchase	Multiplicative interaction between *Acres* and a binary (dummy) variable indicating that preservation is accomplished through fee-simple purchase of the parcel, implemented by the land trusts, using block grant funds from the state (omitted default is preservation conservation zoning).	21.31 (50.77)	1326.22 (2951.25)
Acres*State Easement	Multiplicative interaction between *Acres* and a binary (dummy) variable indicating that preservation is accomplished through conservation easements, implemented by the state (omitted default is preservation by conservation zoning).	6.95 (30.53)	450.20 (1847.70)
Acres*Moderate Access	Multiplicative interaction between *Acres* and a binary (dummy) variable indicating that the preserved parcel would offer moderate levels of public access. This is defined as access for walking and biking in the locality survey, and access on 50% of preserved parcels in the state survey (omitted default is no public access).	14.56 (43.00)	832.32 (2430.74)
Acres*High Access	Multiplicative interaction between *Acres* and a binary (dummy) variable indicating that the preserved parcel would offer high levels of public access. This is defined as access for hunting in the locality survey, and access on 100% of preserved parcels in the state survey (omitted default is no public access).	12.91 (40.57)	916.67 (2529.63)
Acres*No Development 30 Years	Multiplicative interaction between *Acres* and a binary (dummy) variable indicating that the land, if not preserved, would likely remain undeveloped for at least 30 years (omitted default is development likely in less than ten years).	22.00 (52.40)	1357.05 (2991.33)
Acres*Development 10–30 Years	Multiplicative interaction between *Acres* and a binary (dummy) variable indicating that the land, if not preserved, would likely be developed in ten to 30 years (omitted default is development likely in less than ten years).	19.79 (47.95)	1290.99 (2911.03)
Fee	Unavoidable household cost of preservation (state/town taxes and fees), with sign reversal.	−43.53 (61.79)	−77.49 (102.24)

Note
a Includes zeros for the "neither" option.

The econometric model

Besides acreage, all preservation attributes reflect the outcome or policy features of preserved land. Hence, the influence of these attributes on utility should depend on the acreage preserved. This is modeled econometrically by entering land type, pres-ervation method, public access and development risk as multiplicative interactions with the number of preserved acres. Linear variables are limited to preserved acres, program cost and an alternative specific constant (ASC) for "neither plan."

Using this specification, household utility from policy option k is given by:

$$v_{ik} = \beta_{i0}(Neither) + \beta_{i1}Acres_k + \sum_{n=2}^{M} \beta_{in}(Acres_k)(X_{kn}) + \sum_{n=M+1}^{N} \beta_{in}(Acres_k)(W_{kn}) + \beta_{i(N+1)}(Fee_k)$$

where *Neither* is the alternative specific constant (ASC), $Acres_k$ is the number of acres preserved by option k, X_{kn} are attributes of preserved acres, Fee_k is the una-voidable household cost of the plan, and the betas (β) are coefficients to be esti-mated. The subscript i reflects the fact that coefficients may differ across jurisdictional scale $k=\{C, S\}$.

Mixed logit (ML) is used for estimation with random coefficients on two varia-bles (ASC and *Fee*). A normal distribution is assumed for the coefficient on *Neither*; a lognormal distribution is assumed for the coefficient on *Fee*, with sign-reversal used to adjust the cost variable prior to estimation (cf. Hensher and Greene 2003). These conventions follow standard approaches for variables of these types (Hensher and Greene 2003; Hu *et al.* 2005).[2] Two ML models are estimated – one at the statewide jurisdictional level and one from pooled Delaware community data. Log-likelihood tests (Mazzotta and Opaluch 1995) fail to reject the appropri-ateness of pooling individual community data ($p=0.38$). Specifications are identi-cal for all models, subject to caveats noted in the previous section concerning the differences in variable definitions between state and community surveys. All models are estimated using maximum likelihood with Halton draws applied in the simulation. The statistical fit of ML models is superior to parallel conditional logit (CL) models at $p < 0.01$ in both cases, so only ML results are illustrated below.

Results

Table 8.2 presents model results. Both models are statistically significant at $p < 0.01$, with statistically significant coefficients conforming to prior expecations, where expectations exist. In addition, coefficient estimates imply that per-acre welfare effects associated with community-scale preservation exceed those associ-ated with state-scale preservation, *ceteris paribus*. One might expect lower per-acre WTP measures at the state scale both because of the lesser degree of expected proximity to preserved land, and also due to diminishing marginal utility; the statewide survey incorporated much larger acreages, such that the marginal utility per acre would be expected to decline relative to the community-scale analysis. Table 8.3, discussed below, shows that household WTP per acre for preservation in the community is between one and two orders of magnitude above the value of preservation at the statewide level. In addition, community and state coefficient estimates vary in significance, which may reflect different preference patterns and scarcities at the local level relative to the statewide level.

The primary focus of the analysis, however, is on WTP rather than raw coefficient estimates. To calculate WTP from random coefficients, we follow

Table 8.2 Mixed logit results

	Delaware community	Delaware state
Neither (ASC)	−0.93298	−0.720424
	(0.20365)***	(0.293863)***
Fee (lognormal, sign reverse)	−3.72041	−4.520530
Acres	(0.24206)***	(0.323230)***
	−0.00237	−0.000009
	(0.00207)	(0.000043)
Acres*Nursery	−0.00106	−0.000027
	(0.00123)	(0.000026)
Acres*Forest	0.00008	−0.000006
	(0.00124)	(0.000029)
Acres*Idle	0.00066	−0.000011
	(0.00126)	(0.000027)
Acres*Trust Easement	0.00171	0.000098
	(0.00226)	(0.000047)**
Acres*State Purchase	0.00421	0.000089
	(0.00189)**	(0.000041)**
Acres*Trust Purchase	0.00096	0.000091
	(0.00197)	(0.000042)**
	0.00573	0.000091
Acres*State Easement	(0.00209)***	(0.000050)*
	0.00803	0.000086
Acres*Moderate Access	(0.00156)***	(0.000030)***
	0.00609	0.000072
Acres*High Access	(0.00151)***	(0.000029)***
Acres*No Development	−0.00061	−0.000106
30 Years	(0.00097)	(0.000023)***
Acres*Development	−0.00149	−0.000019
10–30 Years	(0.00116)	(0.000022)
	1.53389	1.784680
std NE	(0.39456)***	(0.493429)***
	2.56899	2.677350
std Cost	(0.30388)***	(0.443947)***
Log-Likelihood Chi-Square	630.01***	444.83***
Pseudo-R^2	0.20	0.21
N	4,308	2,952

Note
Single (*), double (**) and triple (***) asterisks denote p-values of 0.10, 0.05 and 0.01, respectively.

Hu *et al.* (2005) and Johnston and Duke (2009) and present welfare estimates as the mean over the parameter simulation (1,000 draws over all parameters, following the parametric bootstrap of Krinsky and Robb (1986)) of median WTP calculated over the coefficient simulation (1,000 draws over random coefficients). This approach (using median rather than mean WTP over the distribution of random coefficients) prevents unrealistic mean WTP estimates, which are otherwise unduly influenced by the lognormal distribution (long right-hand tail) of the program cost coefficient (Hensher and Greene 2003). As discussed by Hu *et al.* (2005), there is no theoretical justification for choosing between mean or median welfare measures. Nevertheless, it is important to note that when aggregating WTP across households, this method using the mean-of-medians will not necessarily match aggregation over a set of means. Since the medians used are smaller than the means for the welfare simulations (as one would expect given the lognormal distribution of the cost parameter), the resulting aggregate WTP estimates provide conservative welfare estimates.

The experimental design that resulted from this welfare simulation procedure included four attributes used to distinguish per-acre WTP:

1   land type at four levels;
2   preservation policy at five levels;
3   development risk at three levels; and
4   access at three levels.

Thus, there are $4 \times 5 \times 3 \times 3 = 180$ possible combinations of amenity attributes that characterize a hypothetical acre to be preserved.

For the present analysis, WTP for all 180 options was estimated for both the community and state scale analyses and then aggregated to a total value. In order to render associated numbers more easily interpretable for policy purposes, it was necessary to transform the per-acre, per-household, per-year welfare measures derived from simulation results to capitalized, per-jurisdiction values. This involved two steps. First, the present value of per-year WTP estimates was calculated as the perpetuity of yearly estimates (derived directly from welfare simulations), assuming a discount rate of 6 percent. The resulting per-household present values were then aggregated to the jurisdictional scale by multiplying by the number of households in the jurisdiction (community or state). These two present values were then added together; however, it should be noted that this is a somewhat conservative assumption because it assumes that households right outside the community are more similar to the state itself than the community. In actuality, there is more likely a benefit gradient. Our model cannot capture this gradient, so our assumptions remain conservative.

Willingness to pay for the preservation of multifunctional amenities

Over all 180 combinations, the mean present value of aggregated (i.e. state and community) WTP per acre was $49,954. The range was from –$87,063 to

$134,436. One-half of the combinations have estimated WTP of $52,136 or more. These benefit measures are substantively significant. Given that past preservation costs in Delaware have not typically exceeded $20,000 and the historical average cost is $1,611 (Delaware Department of Agriculture 2009), results imply that many parcels preserved will have high net benefits (i.e. preservation benefits minus costs).

Nevertheless, these results suggest that some parcels may not pass a benefit-cost test or may be low priority for preservation. Thirty-two of 180 WTP estimates were negative, and six more estimates were less than $10,000. Most (18 of 32) of the negative WTP estimates were associated with preservation achieved through conservation zoning – an unsurprising result given focus group evidence suggesting negative public preferences associated with such regulatory policies. To illustrate policy implications of these results, consider that the per-acre cost of non-regulatory preservation typically exceeds $10,000 in Delaware (this is a fairly typical per-acre cost for PACE and fee simple policies). If costs exceed $10,000, model results suggest that approximately 21 percent of parcel types would not pass a benefit-cost test. Preservation costs are likely to be somewhat heterogeneous, varying with development potential, preservation policy, and land characteristics. Nevertheless, the results suggest that the net benefits of preservation vary widely. Effective preservation policy would require that parcels be prioritized so that those with the maximum benefit-to-cost ratios are selected first. Model results indicate that certain preservation options will provide markedly greater benefits, suggesting that such prioritization can have substantial implications for public welfare and support for preservation policy.

Ideally, prioritization would proceed through a sequential series of marginal decisions, where the amenity values of all parcels are known. Actual policy processes, however, are more likely to establish less precise selection criteria. For this reason, it is important to understand how the attributes of preserved land tend to affect WTP in a broader sense. A truly effective program will use these demand-side tendencies in designing a prioritization strategy. A subset of the 180 combinations (Tables 8.3 and 8.4) are selected to illustrate key patterns in how these attributes affect WTP for preservation.

Development risk

Table 8.3 shows how development risk may affect WTP for the preservation of cropland or livestock acreage. Results show that the highest WTP tends to be associated with the preservation of high-risk acreage at both the community and statewide jurisdictions. For example, when no access is provided, aggregate WTP for a high-risk acre is $54,691 and WTP for an identical acre at low risk is only $2,233. As development risk lessens, this relationship can vary in a surprising, asymmetric manner. At the statewide level, WTP tends to fall as development risk declines; however, at the community level, the lowest values are associated with the intermediate development risk category. In other words, communities appear to prefer high-risk over low-risk acreage, and low-risk over intermediate-risk. Although this result may appear counterintuitive, it was also found in a previous Delaware conjoint study by Duke and Ilvento (2004) who rationalized that residents may want to focus their preservation efforts on relatively undeveloped areas where agriculture has a critical mass (low-risk) before preserving the areas that are at the suburban–rural fringe (moderate-risk).

Public access

Table 8.3 shows the clear, positive impact that access has on WTP for preservation. The highest benefit estimates, however, are associated with *moderate* levels of access. For the community, this implies walking, biking or similar passive recreational access to preserved parcels. At the state level, this implies that the preservation program would provide access on 50 percent of the parcels preserved. The point-estimate WTP values for high access levels are slightly below

Table 8.3 Effect of development risk and access on per-acre willingness to pay for preservation

Risk of development[a] (in years)	Estimated WTP per household in Smyrna/Clayton[b]	Estimated per household in Delaware[b]	Aggregate WTP[c]
	No access provided		
Under 10	$2.41	$0.13	$54,691
10 to 30	$1.36	$0.10	$38,662
Over 30	$1.99	$(0.04)	$2,233[e]
	Moderate access[d]		
Under 10	$8.10	$0.27	$134,436
10 to 30	$7.05	$0.24	$118,407
Over 30	$7.67	$0.10	$81,979
	High access[d]		
Under 10	$6.74	$0.24	$117,590
10 to 30	$5.69	$0.21	$101,561
Over 30	$6.31	$0.07	$65,132

Notes

All values assume a crop or livestock farm and that preservation is conducted via a state-level PACE program. WTP for forest preservation is not reported, but is no more than 7.1 percent different than values reported for crop or livestock farms.

a For community level survey, these values represented the timeframe during which the parcel being considered was likely to be developed. For the statewide survey, respondents were told that preservation policies emphasized selection of parcels from areas at three levels of development risk.

b These values are the mean of medians from ML simulation. The values have been capitalized, using a discount rate of 6 percent.

c Aggregate WTP is calculated as the summation of two numbers: (1) estimated mean WTP from Smyrna/Clayton times the number of housing units in the community; and (2) estimated mean WTP from Delaware times the number of households in Delaware, not including Smyrna/Clayton. The US Census (2000) estimates 6,901 housing units in the Smyrna and Clayton zip codes – the same zip codes used to draw the sample – and 291,835 other households in Delaware.

d The community and statewide surveys differed in terms of the definition of access (see this chapter's data section for details).

e If statewide value WTP per household is assumed to be zero, then aggregate WTP is $13,725.

Table 8.4 Effect of preservation policy on per-acre willingness to pay for preservation (by land-use type)

Preservation policy used	Estimated aggregate WTP (% of PACE by state)			
	Crop or livestock land use	Forest land use	Nursery land use	Average estimated aggregate WTP
Zoning	$61,978 46.1%	$59,423 45.1%	$45,140 38.4%	$56,754 43.9%
Fee-simple by state	$125,828 93.6%	$108,490 82.3%	$94,207 80.1%	$109,516 84.8%
Fee-simple by land trust	$111,045 82.6%	$115,179 87.3%	$100,896 85.8%	$110,838 85.8%
PACE by land trust	$117,735 87.6%	$123,272 93.5%	$108,989 92.7%	$118,580 91.8%
PACE by state	$134,436	$131,881	$117,598	$129,212

Notes
All values assume a crop or livestock farm, the highest development risk level, and that the middle-level of access is provided. WTP for idle farmland preservation is not reported, but is no more than 1.7 percent different than values reported for forest for all five policies.

moderate access, but both exceed the no-access level by substantial (and statistically significant) amounts. A large component of the highest WTP estimates is due to access. Of the 180 combinations, the highest WTP for a no-access parcel was $54,691 – at the fifty-second percentile.

These results suggest that the public recognizes that access can potentially provide an additional set of preserved land amenities, i.e. multifunctional agriculture has an additional output. However, there seems to be a subtle recognition that too much access can degrade resources. This suggests that the public would be willing to pay for access on some parcels, but may want others preserved in a more traditional state. Several caveats are in order. First, access to preserved parcels in Delaware is not common, except when purchased fee-simple. Hence, the WTP estimates for access represent a marginal level of provision that is on the highest part of the demand curve. These values should be high, but it is unknown how elastic this demand may be. Second, the costs of providing access are likely to be high. As a result, the benefit-to-cost ratio of providing access with a preserved parcel may be far lower than the benefit-to-cost ratio of simply preserving the parcel without access.

Land-use type

Table 8.4 shows the impact of land use on WTP. The principal result here is that land use has a small and generally statistically insignificant impact on benefits. The public seems to simply demand preservation services but does not have strong preferences for the type of land preserved. This result accords with Duke and Ilvento (2004), who found that preferences for preserving forest and crop-land in Delaware were statistically indistinguishable. It, however, contradicts findings of some prior stated preference research demonstrating statistically significant public preferences associated with agricultural productivity and/or type of farmland (Kline and Wichelns 1996; Ozdemir *et al.* 2004).

The main implication of this result is that effective preservation may also pri-oritize the preservation of forest and idle land because the costs of preservation may be less. Delaware's PACE program currently uses criteria that emphasize prime agricultural land and the most financially viable farms. These parcels tend to have high agricultural use values but also high development values. The results suggest that a low-production forest parcel may provide approximately the same benefits, *ceteris paribus*, but may cost less to preserve. Irwin *et al.* (2003: 22) drew a similar conclusion in a review of the preservation valuation literature: "The most efficient approach may be to target marginal, cheaper farm-land that generates substantial rural amenities." Intuitively, any preservation strategy that prioritizes parcels based on demand-side characteristics will likely diverge from current programs and their supply-oriented selection.

Preservation policy

The most significant finding here is that the choice of preservation policy has a substantive impact on WTP. Table 8.4 shows that, when one holds all the attributes of preserved acreage constant, WTP can be reduced by up to 62 percent if a less-preferred preservation policy is chosen. In all cases presented, preserva-tion benefits secured through conservation zoning are substantively lower than other forms of preservation, *ceteris paribus*. Fee-simple preservation by a state agency or a land trust is preferred to the same preservation achieved through zoning by a factor of approximately two. PACE preservation is the most pre-ferred, with state preservation slightly preferred over that of land trusts. The impact of these results on stated-preference research is discussed in Johnston and Duke (2007).

These results again suggest that residents may have subtle, sophisticated pref-erences for preserved-land attributes. Although fee-simple preservation provides a more complete set of legal rights to land, the public tends to prefer preserva-tion through PACE, even when all else is held constant. This suggests that the public's interest in preserved-land amenities truly accords with the concept of multifunctionality; the public wants to preserve land that will continue to be owned and operated by a private owner. The public seems to value those owner-ship and autonomy amenities more than having the same lands owned by the state or a nonprofit group. Since fee-simple purchase should be costlier than PACE, this result suggests that the total net benefits of preservation via PACE will tend to dominate those of fee-simple under a variety of land uses. As such, marginal efficiency criteria suggest that the public should emphasize preserva-tion through PACE relative to fee-simple purchase.

This general conclusion must be taken in context, however, especially given the significant role of public access in determining public WTP. Although it is in theory possible for public access to be provided using PACE, it is more commonly provided only on parcels obtained through fee-simple purchase. Therefore, a balance must be struck not only between the cost differentials associated with PACE versus fee-simple acquisition, as discussed above, but also the potential difference in benefits that might result from the provision of access on land fully owned by the preserving agency. Such trade-offs illustrate the importance of model results such as these that can quantify specific trade-offs in preservation costs and benefits.

Caution should be exercised when interpreting the WTP results on zoning. Duke and Lynch (2006) argue that the efficiency of a large preservation plan through zoning cannot be compared to that of PACE and fee-simple purchase. And even though the WTP estimates here represent preservation of a small number of acres *on the margin*, zoning does not typically operate in that manner. Instead, zoning tends to change the permitted uses on land over a large *non-marginal* area. Some hybrid preservation techniques, such as agricultural preservation districting, have many of the characteristics of zoning and can be adopted on a parcel-by-parcel basis. WTP estimates apply in these cases. However, the WTP estimates do not necessarily imply that PACE should be prioritized over zoning. Although the benefits of preservation through zoning are relatively low, the costs are likely to be low, too. The results suggest that researchers and planners should undertake the difficult task of developing estimates of the social costs of rezoning parcels, including the opportunity costs of complex incentives – agricultural preservation districts may offer protection from nuisance suits and the ability to avoid real estate transfer taxes. Only with these cost estimates can the net benefits of marginal preservation via conservation zoning be compared to those of PACE.

Policy trade-offs and multifunctionality

Taken together, model results suggest the many trade-offs involved in the preservation of multifunctional agriculture. For example, some of the most valued attributes such as public access are typically available only at high cost, while preservation methods with perhaps the lowest direct cost (e.g. conservation zoning) are typically associated with much lower preservation values. Moreover, attributes such as soil and/or crop type, which are often given the most attention by current preservation programs, seldom have much impact on broader public support or WTP. Given the complexity of these trade-offs, and the extent to which they vary depending on jurisdiction (e.g. preservation at the state versus community scale), it seems unlikely that existing programs are optimizing the net social benefits that could otherwise be associated with the preservation of multifunctional amenities. Through results such as those presented above, however, one could easily envision prioritization algorithms that could increase the net social benefits associated with ongoing preservation programs.

Conclusions

This chapter described the results of a Choice Experiment (CE) on the WTP for agricultural land preservation at two different jurisdictional scales. A set of attributes allowed the CE to control for a large set of land and open-space amenities, including preservation policy attributes. These amenities represent an important part of the nonmarket outputs of agricultural land and thereby constitute an important component of multifunctional agriculture. Policies to reward multifunctionality can be improved by better understanding the relative importance of these preserved land amenities. This study focused on WTP in order to provide the most direct, quantitative measure of these amenities for use in policy.

Empirical results suggest definitive relationships and general tendencies in the WTP for preservation amenities. WTP is highest for high-risk acreage and for moderate access. Low-risk acreage is preferred to moderate-risk, and high access is preferred to none. Land use is found to have very little impact on WTP. Moreover, in many cases PACE is found to be preferable to preservation via fee-simple purchase. Overall, the results suggest that WTP for preservation can be substantial, but it varies widely and may be low or negative for some acreage. One of the more complicated relationships discovered is that between preservation via PACE and zoning. WTP for PACE exceeds WTP zoning dramatically, but one may find that in practice zoning is much less expensive to implement. Hence, this chapter suggests that additional research on the costs of zoning is needed. Other complex trade-offs involve the role of public access, which is typically provided only using more expensive fee-simple purchase mechanisms but also provides substantial amenity benefits.

The results may also provide useful economic guidance for policy. In terms of efficiency on the margin, the results suggest that many parcels will have positive net benefits from a preservation intervention. However, these net benefit estimates vary widely, are significantly affected by heterogeneous cost patterns, and may be negative in a significant number of cases. Thus, an efficient program will prioritize parcels so that preservation does not occur when net benefits are negative. WTP estimates can be used to derive a systematic prioritization plan. With high-quality cost data – which tend to be available for PACE preservation – the WTP estimates can be used to rank parcels so that limited preservation budgets can target those parcels with the highest total net benefits. In practice, it may be too costly to estimate benefits and costs on each parcel, so the general relationships described above can help guide the design of prioritization strategies that emphasize demand-side criteria.

Acknowledgment

This research was funded by the Coastal Community Enhancement Initiative at the University of Delaware and by the National Research Initiative of the Cooperative State Research, Education and Extension Service, USDA, Grant #

2003–35400–13875. The experimental design was completed by Lidia Rejto and Diccon Bancroft at the University of Delaware STATLAB. Any remaining errors are those of the authors. Opinions belong solely to the authors and do not imply endorsement by the funding agencies.

Notes

1 Such issues are discussed in greater detail by Johnston and Duke (2009).
2 Preliminary models were also estimated in which the coefficient on preserved acres (*Acres*) was randomized; many of these models showed no statistically significant improvement over specifications in which a fixed (non-random) coefficient was specified. Hence, a fixed coefficient is specified for this variable. In addition, to simplify subsequent welfare simulations (see below) and prevent convergence difficulties, coefficients on multiplicative interactions were also specified as fixed.

References

Abler, D. (2004) "Multifunctionality, Agricultural Policy, and Environmental Policy," *Agricultural and Resource Economics Review*, 33(1): 8–17.

Adamowicz, W., Boxall, P., Williams, M. and Louviere, J. (1998) "Stated Preference Approaches for Measuring Passive Use Values: Choice Experiments and Contingent Valuation," *American Journal of Agricultural Economics*, 80(1): 64–75.

Bateman, I.J., Carson, R.T., Day, B., Hanemann, M., Hanley, N., Hett, T., Jones-Lee, M., Loomes, G., Mourato, S., Ozdemiroglu, E., Pierce, D.W., Sugden, R. and Swanson, J. (2002) *Economic Valuation with Stated Preference Techniques: A Manual*, Northampton, MA: Edward Elgar.

Batie, S.S. (2003) "The Multifunctional Attributes of Northeastern Agriculture: A Research Agenda," *Agricultural and Resource Economics Review*, 32(1): 1–8.

Bergstrom, J.C. and Ready, R.C. (2009) "What Have We Learned from over 20 Years of Farmland Amenity Valuation Research in *North America Review of Agricultural Economics*, 31(1): 21–49?".

Bromley, D.W. (2007) "Environmental Regulations and the Problem of Sustainability: Moving Beyond 'Market Failure,'" *Ecological Economics*, 63(4): 676–683.

Delaware Department of Agriculture (2009) Delaware Agricultural Lands Preservation Foundation Round 14 Selections (May 2009). Online, available at: http://dda.delaware.gov/aglands/forms/2009/051209_CSR.pdf (last accessed May 31, 2009).

Dobbs, T.L. and Pretty, J.N. (2004) "Agri-environmental Stewardship Schemes and 'Multifunctionality,'" *Review of Agricultural Economics*, 26(2): 220–237.

Duke, Joshua M. and Ilvento, Thomas W. (2004) "A Conjoint Analysis of Public Preferences for Agricultural Land Preservation," *Agricultural and Resource Economics Review*, 33(2): 209–219.

Duke, J.M. and Lynch, L. (2006) "Four Classes of Farmland Retention Techniques: Comparative Evaluation and Property Rights Implications," *Land Economics*, 82(2): 189–213.

Gardner, B.D. (1977) "The Economics of Agricultural Land Preservation," *American Journal of Agricultural Economics*, 59(5): 1027–1036.

Greene, W.H. (2003) *Econometric Analysis*, 5th edn, Upper Saddle River: Prentice Hall.

Hanemann, W.M. (1984) "Welfare Evaluations in Contingent Valuation Experiments with Discrete Responses," *American Journal of Agricultural Economics*, 66(3): 332–341.

Hensher, D.A. and Greene, W.H. (2003) "The Mixed Logit Model: The State of Practice," *Transportation*, 30: 133–176.

Hu, W., Veeman, M.M. and Adamowicz, W.L. (2005) "Labeling Genetically Modified Food: Heterogeneous Consumer Preferences and the Value of Information," *Canadian Journal of Agricultural Economics*, 53(1): 83–102.

Irwin, E.G., Nickerson, C.J. and Libby, L. (2003) "What are Farmland Amenities Worth?" *Choices* (Third Quarter): 21–24.

Johnston, R.J. and Duke, J.M. (2007) "Willingness to Pay for Agricultural Land Preservation and Policy Process Attributes: Does the Method Matter?" *American Journal of Agricultural Economics*, 89(4): 1098–1115.

Johnston, R.J. and Duke, J.M. (2009) "Willingness to Pay for Land Preservation Across States and Jurisdictional Scale: Implications for Benefit Transfer," *Land Economics*, 85(2): 217–237.

Johnston, R.J. and Swallow, S.K. (2006) "Introduction – Economics and Contemporary Land Use Policy," in R.J. Johnston and S.K. Swallow (eds.), *Economics and Contemporary Land Use Policy: Development and Conservation at the Rural–Urban Fringe*, Washington, DC: RFF Press.

Johnston, R.J., Grigalunas, T.A., Opaluch, J.J., Diamantedes, J. and Mazzotta, M. (2002a) "Valuing Estuarine Resource Services Using Economic and Ecological Models: the Peconic Estuary System Study," *Coastal Management*, 30(1): 47–66.

Johnston, R.J., Magnusson, G., Mazzotta, M. and Opaluch, J.J. (2002b) "Combining Economic and Ecological Indicators to Prioritize Salt Marsh Restoration Actions," *American Journal of Agricultural Economics*, 84(5): 1362–1370.

Kline, J. and Wichelns, D. (1994) "Using Referendum Data to Characterize Public Support for Purchasing Development Rights to Farmland," *Land Economics*, 70(2): 223–233.

Kline, J. and Wichelns, D. (1996) "Public Preferences Regarding the Goals of Farmland Preservation Programs," *Land Economics*, 72(4): 538–549.

Krinsky, I. and Robb, A.L. (1986) "On Approximating the Statistical Properties of Elasticities," *Review of Economics and Statistics*, 68(4): 715–719.

Maddala, G.S. (1983) *Limited Dependent and Qualitative Variables in Econometrics*, Cambridge: Cambridge University Press.

Mazzotta, M.J. and Opaluch, J.J. (1995) "Decision Making When Choices Are Complex: A Test of Heiner's Hypothesis," *Land Economics*, 71(4): 500–515.

Messer, K.D. (2006) "The Conservation Benefits of Cost-effective Land Acquisition: a Case Study of Maryland," *Journal of Environmental Management*, 79: 305–315.

Ozdemir, S., Boyle, K.J., Ahearn, M., Alberini, A., Bergstrom, J., Libby, L. and Welsh, M.P. (2004) *Preliminary Report: Farmland Conservation Easement Study for the United States, Georgia, Ohio and Maine Samples*, Working Paper, Department of Resource Economics and Policy, University of Maine, Orono.

9 Agent-based land use models for collaborative learning about agri-environmental policies

Thomas Berger and Pepijn Schreinemachers

Introduction

Multi-agent systems (MAS) are increasingly used as a tool to disentangle and explore the complex relationships between land use and land cover change (LUCC), policy interventions and human adaptation. The development and application of these tools has been made possible by the rapid increase in computational power available at modest cost. The strength of agent-based land-use models (MAS/LUCC) lies in their ability to combine spatial modeling techniques, such as cellular automata or GIS, with biophysical and socioeconomic models at a fine resolution.

Multi-agent systems are flexible in their representation of human land-use decisions and therefore appeal to scholars from diverse backgrounds such as sociology, geography and economics (Schreinemachers and Berger 2006). The behavior of individual actors can be modeled one-to-one with computational agents, which allows for direct observation and interpretation of simulation results. A large part of their fascination – especially to scholars who are otherwise skeptical of any attempt to quantify and model human behavior – rests on this intuitive and potentially interactive feature. Scholars from CIRAD (French Agricultural Research Center for International Development), for example, combine MAS/LUCC with role-playing games in which a group of resource users, typically farmers using some common-pool resource, specify the decision rules of computational agents and observe how these rules might affect both people's well-being and their natural resource base (Bousquet *et al.* 2001; D'Aquino *et al.* 2003; Becu *et al.* 2003).

In this chapter we reflect on the interactive use of multi-agent models not only for participatory simulation of land-use changes but also for teaching, extension and collaborative learning in general. At Hohenheim University, we have used our Mathematical Programming-based Multi-agent Systems (MP-MAS) software for teaching at the MSc and PhD levels, taught training courses for water resource managers in Chile and parameterized the MP-MAS model for empirical applications in Thailand, Uganda, Chile and Ghana (Berger 2001; Berger *et al.* 2006; Schreinemachers *et al.* 2007, 2009). MP-MAS distinguishes itself clearly from most other agent-based land-use models in its use of a constrained optimization routine, based on mathematical programming (MP), for simulating agent decision-making. Apart from describing the rationale behind this modeling approach, this chapter reports on various case-study applications, and the use of the model for collaborative learning and research.

Multi-agent systems of land-use/cover change

Multi-agent systems models of land-use/cover change (MAS/LUCC) couple a cellular component that represents a landscape with an agent-based component that represents human decision-making (Parker *et al.* 2002). MAS/LUCC models have been applied in a wide variety of settings (for overviews see Janssen 2002; Parker *et al.* 2003) yet have in common that agents are autonomous decision-makers who interact and communicate and make decisions that can alter their environment. Most MAS applications have been implemented with software packages such as Cormas, NetLogo, RePast and Swarm (Railsback *et al.* 2006).

Decision-making of agents

The philosophy of agent-based modeling has always been to replicate the complexity of human behavior with relatively simple rules of action and interaction. In empirical applications to the complexity of land-use changes, the question arises of how simple these rules need to be, especially when it comes to representing the economic decision-making of agents. Most agent-based applications have used relatively simple heuristics – also called condition-action rules, stimulus-response rules, or if-then rules. One simple example would be a rule that agents must grow maize to meet their subsistence needs, but if subsistence needs are met then agents grow fruit trees on the remaining plots. The heuristic approach works particularly well in abstract and experimental applications or in empirical applications where the objective is not to quantify change but, for instance, to support collective decision-making processes (Becu *et al.* 2008). If the objective, however, is to quantitatively support policy intervention and to get detailed knowledge about the agricultural land-use systems then a decision-making model including detailed production and consumption functions is perhaps the more suitable method. Schreinemachers and Berger (2006) argued that "heuristic" agents in such applications may have too limited heterogeneity and rather low adaptive capacity and therefore recommended implementing agents with goal-driven behavior based on mathematical programming.

Mathematical programming models

The use of mathematical programming has a long tradition in agricultural economics, especially in cases where only limited statistical data but sufficient a priori "engineering" information is available (Hazell and Norton 1986). The mathematical programming approach, however, has its limits when the empirical research involves high degrees of heterogeneity and multiple spatial interactions.

Conventional aggregate mathematical programming models that maximize a common (sectoral) objective function can account for heterogeneity in the constraints, but not in the objective function. Dynamic interactions can be represented through equations of motion, but these models are difficult to implement from a programming perspective and are also difficult to solve. Yet, conventional aggregate programming models perform well when representing relatively homogeneous farm economies characterized by perfect, competitive market environments. Otherwise, they are often plagued by aggregation errors and corner solutions that might then be alleviated by adding additional information to the objective function (Howitt 1995). Such positive mathematical programming models have favorable features when it comes to model calibration, but great care has to be taken that the model structure is still acceptable in terms of underlying economic theory.

Another solution to mitigating the aggregation error is the representative farm programming approach that has been extensively applied in recent years in the field of bio-economic modeling (see, for example, Ruben *et al.* 2000). Instead of one model with an objective function aggregated over all farms, a sample of representative farm models with independent objective functions is taken whose outputs are then aggregated using appropriate sampling weights. Clearly, the representative farm model approach can capture higher degrees of heterogeneity, which makes this model specification a preferred one when rural economies are to be modeled whose actors deviate from pure profit-maximizing behavior. The major limitations of independent representative farm models, however, are their difficulties in capturing interactions between farms; the classical examples are markets for intermediate goods such as forage for ruminants or piglets in pig fattening. The required model iterations for achieving market clearance between separate MP models are tedious and time-consuming, in particular, when the intermediate goods face high transport costs and therefore the spatial context of farm interactions has to be taken into account. Further complications arise when interactions occur in space but no equilibrium mechanism is in place, such as is the case of irrigation return flows and soil or pollutant transport (Berger 2001).

Discrete and connected MAS

Because multi-agent systems can be built from disaggregated independent farm models, they have clear advantages for modeling interactions among farms as well as between farms and their biophysical environment. As explained in more detail in Berger *et al.* (2007), multi-agent systems provide a spatial framework for connecting, for example, standard biophysical model components of crop growth and nutrient leaching with model components of agricultural markets and technology diffusion. Such connected MAS may therefore help to identify sustainable development paths and impacts of policy interventions.

This is not meant as a plea for substituting the well-established mathematical programming approaches used in agricultural economics for connected MAS.

As long as interactions between farms and their spatial context can reasonably be neglected bio-economic farm sample models (or discrete MAS) will yield good results. Moreover, in complex applications, it is convenient to apply a sequence of simulation experiments, starting with discrete MAS and then step-by-step adding more heterogeneity and interactions until fully connected MAS are specified (Berger *et al.* 2006). But there are certain applications, which we will discuss in the next section, where connected MAS clearly have the potential for greater explanatory power as existing mathematical programming models.

The MP-MAS approach

Examples of agent-based land-use models using mathematical programming are Balmann (1997) and Happe *et al.* (2006) who analyzed structural change in German agriculture using the software AgriPoliS. In applications to Chile and Uganda, Berger (2001) and Schreinemachers *et al.* (2007) applied the Mathematical Programming-based Multi-agent Systems (MP-MAS) modeling framework, which we present here. For details about the model components, parameters and equations, the reader is referred to these two papers and Berger *et al.* (2007). MP-MAS shares many characteristics with bio-economic farm household models mentioned above; however, three important additional features distinguish MP-MAS from the independent, representative farm modeling approach.

1   Number of farm models: each real-world farm household is individually represented by a single agent in the model; that is, there is a one-to-one correspondence between real-world households and modeled agents. Monte Carlo techniques have been developed to generate alternative agent populations from random sample surveys (Berger and Schreinemachers 2006).
2   Spatial dimension: the MP-MAS model is spatially explicit and employs a grid cell-based data representation where each grid cell corresponds to one farm plot held by a single landowner. Sub-models of water runoff and crop growth are linked to this cell-based spatial framework.
3   Direct interactions: MP-MAS explicitly implements several types of interactions among agents and their environments, such as the communication of information, the market exchange of land rights and water resources, the return flows of irrigation water, the irrigation of crops, soil nutrient management and crop growth.

This one-to-one MAS representation is able to capture biophysical and socio-economic constraints and interactions at a very fine spatial resolution. Including this heterogeneity of constraints and interactions of farm agents and their biophysical environment broadens the scope of land-use modeling significantly. Phenomena that conventional models cannot easily address – such as local resource degradation, technology diffusion, heterogeneous policy responses and land-use adaptations – can now be explicitly modeled.

Outline of the model

MP-MAS is a freeware software application developed at Hohenheim University and can be downloaded from www.uni-hohenheim.de/igm. A detailed user manual is available from the same website. MP-MAS was written in C++ programming language and is available for both Unix and Windows operating systems. MP-MAS works with a set of input files that are organized in Microsoft Excel workbooks. These workbooks have a modular structure shown in Table 9.1. The structure of the mathematical programming matrix is defined in *Matrix.xls* and is generic for all farm agents and all simulation periods. Parameters in this matrix are, however, continuously updated to capture each agent's decision problem.

Three files define the initial conditions of the agent population: *Population.xls* defines the agents' resource endowments and household composition, *Map.xls* defines all spatial information (location of farmsteads, plots, soils, water-sheds, etc.), and *Network.xls* defines the characteristics of agriculture-related technologies. Four subsequent input files define the dynamics over time: *Demography.xls* defines the labor supply, fertility rates, mortality rates and food requirements. *Perennials.xls* defines the growth rates of perennials (e.g. fruit orchards, and timber) and the input requirements over the age of the orchard. *Market.xls* defines farm-gate selling and buying prices for inputs and outputs such as fertilizer, seed, credit interest rates and food cash crops. In the standard model set-up, market prices for variable inputs, farm outputs and consumption goods are exogenous while market prices for land and water are endogenous. Finally, *Livestock.xls* defines for different types of livestock (e.g. cattle, pigs, goats) their weight gains, food and pasture requirements and offspring.

The number of input files can vary between applications depending on what biophysical components (water, soils or crops) are included. For example, select-ing *Soils.xls* makes soil nutrients endogenous in the model and adjusts crop yields depending on the plant nutrient supply. *Routing.xls* defines levels of water inflow and precipitation in the watershed and allocates water rights to agents as a proportion of the inflow that each agent is allowed to divert from the main stream. *CropWat.xls* contains parameters of FAO's CropWat model (Allen *et al.* 1998), which translates the difference between water supply and agents' water demands into a crop yield reduction.

The policy relevance of the model comes from the use of scenarios (Berger *et al.* 2006). First a baseline scenario is set up that best reflects the current situation and current drivers of change. Then alternative scenarios are set up that alter some of the basic assumptions, for example, by assuming that soil fertility will not decline. The alternative scenario is then compared to the baseline scenario and the difference in outcomes between both scenarios can be attributed to the assump-tion that was relaxed. Scenarios are set up in *ScenarioManager.xls* by defining the name of the input file, the name of the parameter, and its alternative value.

Figure 9.1 shows the interface and the Visual Basic macros (included as an Excel add-in) that allow the user to convert the Excel input files and run the model.

Table 9.1 The input file structure of MP-MAS

Nr.	Input file	Explanation	Function	
1	ScenarioManager	Contains VBA macros that covert Excel workbooks to ASCII format and manages simulation experiments	To set up scenarios and run the model	
2	BasicData	Contains basic parameter values applicable for multiple modules		Non-optional
3	Matrix	The programming matrix (Mixed Integer Linear Program or MILP)	Simulates agent decision-making	
4	Population	Used to generate agent populations		
5	Map	All spatial information including the location of agents and plots	Define initial agent characteristics	
6	Network	Connects agents by an innovation network and gives details about each innovation		
7	Demography	Specifies the life span of agents, fertility, mortality and available labor hours		
8	Market	Market prices (exogenous price information)	Define the changes over time (e.g. human aging, tree and livestock growth, price changes)	
9	Perennials	Specifies the time-related attributes of perennial crops		
10	Livestock	Livestock attributes		
11	Soils	Crop yields and soil dynamics		Optional
12	Routing	Water distribution	Endogenous biophysics (soils, water, crop yields)	
13	CropWat	Crop yields as a function of crop water supply		

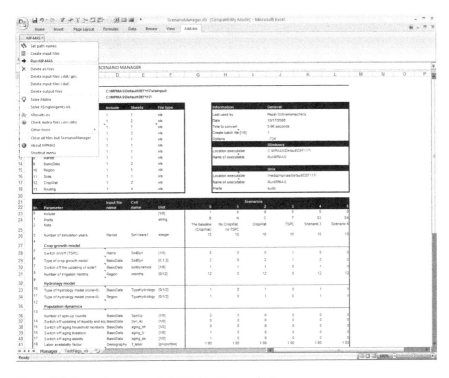

Figure 9.1 Scenario manager in MP-MAS (screenshot).

Applications

MP-MAS has been applied to a variety of case studies in Chile (Berger 2001), Uganda (Schreinemachers *et al.* 2007), Ghana and Thailand. Applications to Uganda and Thailand have been small-scale applications at a village or small watershed level including 520 and 1,309 agents, respectively. Applications to Chile and Ghana have been large-scale applications at the level of larger watershed areas and have included thousands of agents (Table 9.2).

In all case studies, the research questions related to the interaction between the economic and biophysical sub-systems at the farm household level (Table 9.3). The objective of the Uganda application, for example, was to assess the effect of high-yielding maize varieties on soil-nutrient dynamics and economic well-being (Schreinemachers *et al.* 2007). The agent-based approach gave a detailed assessment of distributional consequences and led to the conclusion that although poverty could be substantially reduced, the incidence ratio of households below the poverty line would still be 20 percent. In Chile and Thailand, MP-MAS was applied for the *ex ante* analysis of technology diffusion and policy interventions. The simulation experiments helped to identify the most constraining factors to adoption and the likely speed of diffusion for specific technology packages – water-saving irrigation

Table 9.2 Applications using MP-MAS

Application	No. of farm agents	Spatial dimension		Temporal dimension		Type of agriculture
		extent [km²]	resolution [m]	duration [years]	time step [days]	
1 Chile, Maule Basin	3,592	5,300	100	20	30	Market-oriented and commercial
2 Ghana, White Volta Basin	34,691	3,779	100	15	30–365*	Semi-subsistence rice, millet, maize, onion and tomato
3 Uganda, Southeastern	520	12	71	16	30–365*	Semi-subsistence; maize, cassava, bean and plantain
4 Thailand, Northern Uplands	1,229	140	40	15	30–365*	Commercial vegetable and fruit production

Note
*Components of the model have different time steps. The decision-making follows an annual sequence while land, labor, crop water requirements, irrigation water supply and rainfall are specified on a monthly base.

techniques in Chile (Berger 2001) and greenhouse cultivation in Thailand (Schrein-emachers *et al.* 2009). In both case studies, the environmental impacts of technology diffusion could be quantified and corrective policy interventions could be tested.

Empirical parameterization

Robinson *et al.* (2007) compared five empirical methods for building agent-based models in land-use science: sample surveys, participant observation, field and labo-ratory experiments, companion modeling and GIS and remotely sensed spatial data. The empirical base of MP-MAS is typically random sample surveys of farm house-holds and GIS data. Both of these are used to define the initial conditions of the model (Berger and Schreinemachers 2006). Additional parameters, mostly related to the dynamics of the model, are based on secondary data, qualitative data from field observation and feedback from stakeholders. For instance, fertility and mortal-ity levels are obtained from statistical agencies, crop yield responses from field experiments, while agent interactions can be based on qualitative field observation.

Collaborative research and learning

As argued above, one of the key advantages of agent-based modeling is the one-to-one correspondence of real-world and computational agents, which facilitates participatory simulation and model-enhanced learning (e.g. Becu *et al.* 2008).

Table 9.3 Model features of each application

Application	Objective	Economic component	Biophysical component
1 Chile	To provide information to water resource managers (small and large-scale infrastructure projects).	Detailed production functions especially on irrigation methods (MP with 1,119 activities, 224 constraints).	Crop growth under water deficits. Spatial distribution of surface water flows.
2 Ghana	To test the profitability of irrigated agriculture. Land and water use mostly under rainfed conditions.	MP contains 752 activities and 250 constraints. Includes a detailed expenditure system.	Model simulates the water supply and water distribution with a feedback to crop yields.
3 Uganda	To disentangle the relationship between technology adoption, soil nutrients, and poverty levels.	Detailed production functions; 2,350 activities, 560 constraints. Includes a detailed expenditure system.	Soil nutrients (N, P, K) and organic matter are endogenous and affect crop yields.
4 Thailand	The *ex ante* assessment of technology adoption and sustainability strategies.	Based on gross-margin analysis; 1,819 activities and 812 constraints.	Model simulates the water supply and water distribution with a feedback to crop yields.

Using agent-based land use models effectively – so that model users receive early warnings, share their system understanding and improve the outcomes of their land-use decisions (Hazell *et al.* 2001) – poses a number of challenges that have not yet been fully resolved yet (for example, see von Paassen (2004) who reported mixed success for applications of MP models in developing countries). Based on our practical knowledge of using MAS/LUCC models, the authors reflect on the following critical issues:

1   participatory techniques for model validation;
2   building trust in model results;
3   using MP-MAS for agricultural extension; and

Participatory techniques for model validation

Recent experiences in the CGIAR Challenge Program on Water and Food (see project website www.igm.uni-hohenheim.de) have shown that MP-MAS has a clear advantage over other integrated modeling approaches previously applied, such as aggregate regional land-use models. In MP-MAS, single-agent models for representative farm households can be constructed and validated jointly with stakeholders in interactive model validation rounds. Farm-specific data were first collected on factor endowments such as labor, land and water, and then processed for a stand-alone version of MP-MAS. The Excel workbook *Matrix. xls* was used to calibrate each single-agent model to replicate current land-use decisions and perform sensitivity tests together with stakeholders. Through what-if scenarios (for example: "how do you adjust your land use if you receive less irrigation water?"), additional constraints farmers faced and that were originally not included in *Matrix.xls* could be elucidated. The single-agent models were then gradually improved until sufficient model fit for each of the representative farm households was reached. In a second step, the full-agent model for the study area was calibrated and validated, using the Monte Carlo approach as described in Berger and Schreinemachers (2006). The use of stand-ardized questionnaires seems to be an efficient way of collecting basic agent data on agricultural land use. The alternative of stakeholder group interviews, as used by other scholars (see Robinson *et al.* 2007) is much more time-consuming.

Building trust in model results

The interactive modeling rounds for parameter testing and model validation can help to build trust in the simulation results of MP-MAS. Because farmers and water managers are directly involved in compiling the model database and performing the sensitivity analyses, they become familiar with the model and its interfaces. Results from special model computations, for example, of individual water shadow prices, can be compared with local data and experience and create confidence in the model if the results are plausible. Typically, testing and calibrating of MP-MAS requires more than one modeling round. The authors' impression from applying MAS models with many feedback rounds is that stakeholders and potential model users are prone to lose interest if these rounds consume much of their time. The interactive modeling rounds should therefore generate information that is perceived as immediately useful by stakeholders. In the case of market-oriented farm households, such information typically involves estimates of crop yields, farm profitability and household income; in the case of water managers it involves minimum river flows, average water uptake and water use efficiency per irrigation section.

Using MP-MAS for agricultural extension

Mathematical programming is one of the planning methods taught in farm management schools and is used in agricultural extension. Standard farm decision problems such as partial budgeting, investment and income analysis can be directly addressed by the tools incorporated in MP-MAS, making use of the database that has to be built up for the model application. Workers in farm extension programs can therefore be convinced with relative ease of using the single-farm features of MP-MAS. The practical challenge, however, is the maintenance and adaptation of the MP-MAS input files, which requires some minimum knowledge in database management and about mathematical programming. To address this challenge, this project used the ubiquitous MS-Excel for input/output operations and formed a team of advanced users of MP-MAS.

Conclusion

MP-MAS is a software application for agent-based modeling that through the use of mathematical programming represents goal-driven behavior of farm agents. Biophysical models simulating soil fertility dynamics, water supply or crop yields have been spatially integrated with agent decision-making through the use of GIS layers. The method is suitable for research questions related to the interaction of economic and biophysical sub-systems and assessing distributional consequences of policy and environmental change. MP-MAS has been applied to case studies in Chile, Uganda, Ghana and Thailand, and valuable experiences have been gained from using MP-MAS in participatory settings. Research is ongoing; the evaluation of the effectiveness of the MP-MAS approach in improving land-use decisions is still not completed. The initial results from using MP-MAS in interactive settings are promising, but more research on methods is needed to fine-tune and include MP-MAS as an effective tool into land-use planning and farm extension programs.

Acknowledgments

The authors gratefully acknowledge the financial support of the Deutsche Forschungsgemeinschaft (DFG) under SFB-564 and the CGIAR Challenge Program Water and Food.

References

Allen, R.G., Pereira, L.S., Raes, D. and Smith, M. (1998) "Crop Evapotranspiration – Guidelines for Computing Crop Water Requirements," FAO Irrigation and drainage paper 56. Online, available at: www.fao.org/docrep/X0490E/X0490E00.htm.

Balmann, A. (1997) "Farm-based Modelling of Regional Structural Change: a Cellular Automata Approach," *European Review of Agricultural Economics*, 24: 85–108.

Becu, N., Neef, A., Schreinemachers, P. and Sangkapitux, C. (2008) "Participatory Computer Simulation to Support Collective Decision-making: Potential and Limits of Stakeholder Involvement," *Land Use Policy*, 25(4): 498–509.

Becu, N., Perez, P., Walker, B., Barreteau, O. and Le Page, C. (2003) "Agent-based Simulation of a Small Catchment Water Management in Northern Thailand: Description of the CATCHSCAPE Model," *Ecological Modelling*, 170: 319–331.

Berger, T. (2001) "Agent-based Models Applied to Agriculture: A Simulation Tool for Technology Diffusion, Resource Use Changes and Policy Analysis," *Agricultural Economics*, 25: 245–260.

Berger, T. and Schreinemachers, P. (2006) "Creating Agents and Landscapes for Multi-agent Systems from Random Samples," *Ecology and Society*, 11(2): 19. Online, available at: www.ecologyandsociety.org/vol.11/iss2/art19.

Berger, T., Birner, R., Díaz, J., McCarthy, N. and Wittmer, H. (2007) "Capturing the Complexity of Water Uses and Water Users within a Multi-Agent Framework," *Water Resources Management*, 21(1): 129–148.

Berger, T., Schreinemachers, P. and Woelcke, J. (2006) "Multi-Agent Simulation for Development of Less-Favored Areas," *Agricultural Systems*, 88: 28–43.

Bousquet, F., Lifran, R., Tidball, M., Thoyer, S. and Antona, M. (2001) "Agent-based Modelling, Game Theory and Natural Resource Management Issues," *Journal of Artificial Societies and Social Simulation*, 4(2). Online, available at: www.soc.surrey.ac.uk/JASSS/4/2/0.html.

D'Aquino, P., Le Page, C., Bousquet, F. and Bah, A. (2003) "Using Self-designed Role-playing Games and a Multi-agent System to Empower a Local Decision-making Process for Land Use Management: the SelfCormas Experiment in Senegal," *Journal of Artificial Societies and Social Simulation*, 6(3). Online, available at: http://jasss.soc.surrey.ac.uk/6/3/5.html.

Happe, K., Kellermann, K. and Balmann, A. (2006) "Agent-based Analysis of Agricultural Policies: an Illustration of the Agricultural Policy Simulator AgriPoliS, its Adaptation and Behavior," *Ecology and Society*, 11(1): 49. Online, available at: www.ecologyandsociety.org/vol.11/iss1/art49.

Hazell, P.B.R. and Norton, R. (1986) "Mathematical Programming for Economic Analysis in Agriculture," New York: Macmillan. Online, available at: www.ifpri.org/pubs/otherpubs/mathprog.htm.

Hazell, P.B.R., Chakravorty, U., Dixon, J. and Celis, R. (2001) "Monitoring Systems for Managing Natural Resources: Economics, Indicators and Environmental Externalities in a Costa Rican Watershed. EPTD," discussion paper no. 73, International Food Policy Research Institute. Online, available at: www.ifpri.org/divs/eptd/dp/papers/eptdp73.pdf.

Howitt, R.E. (1995) "Positive Mathematical Programming," *American Journal of Agricultural Economics*, 77: 329–342.

Janssen, M.A. (ed.) (2002) "Complexity and Ecosystem Management: the Theory and Practice of Multi-agent Systems," Cheltenham, UK and Northampton, MA: Edward Elgar.

Parker, D.C., Berger, T. and Manson, S.M. (eds.) (2002) Agent-based Models of Land Use/Land Cover Change. LUCC Report Series No. 6, Louvain-la-Neuve, 79–88. Online, available at: www.globallandproject.org/Documents/LUCC_No_6.pdf.

Parker, D.C., Manson, S.M., Janssen, M.A., Hoffmann, M.J. and Deadman, P. (2003) "Multi-agent Systems for the Simulation of Land-use and Land-cover Change: A Review," *Annals of the Association of American Geographers*, 93(2): 314–337.

Railsback, S., Lytinen, S. and Jackson, S. (2006) "Agent-based Simulation Platforms: Review and Development Recommendations," *Simulation*, 82(9): 609–623.

Robinson, D.T., Brown, D.G., Parker, D.C., Schreinemachers, P., Janssen, M., Huigen, M., Wittmer, H., Gotts, N., Promburom, P., Irwin, E., Berger, T., Gatzweiler, F. and Barnaud, C. (2007) "Comparison of Empirical Methods for Building Agent-based Models in Land Use Science," *Journal of Land Use Science*, 2(1): 31–55.

Ruben, R., Kuyvenhoven, A. and Kruseman, G. (2000) "Bioeconomic Models and Ecoregional Development: Policy Instruments for Sustainable Intensification," in D.R. Lee and C.B. Barrett (eds.), *Tradeoffs or Synergies? Agricultural Intensification, Economic Development and the Environment*, CABI Publishing, Wallingford, pp. 115–133.

Schreinemachers, P. and Berger, T. (2006) "Land-use Decisions in Developing Countries and Their Representation in Multi-agent Systems," *Journal of Land Use Science*, 1(1): 29–44.

Schreinemachers, P., Berger, T. and Aune, J.B. (2007) "Simulating Soil Fertility and Poverty Dynamics in Uganda: A Bio-economic Multi-agent Systems Approach," *Ecological Economics*, 64(2): 387–401.

Schreinemachers, P., Berger, T., Sirijinda, A. and Praneetvatakul, S. (2009) "The Diffusion of Greenhouse Agriculture in Northern Thailand: Combining Econometrics and Agent-based Modelling," *Canadian Journal of Agricultural Economics*, forthcoming.

van Paassen, J.M. (2004) "Bridging the Gap: Computer Model Enhanced Learning About Natural Resource Management in Burkina Faso," dissertation, Wageningen. Online, available at: www.gcw.nl/dissertations/3530/dis3530.pdf.

10 Castles or cattle?

A regional analysis of working lands policies

Andrew Seidl, Lindsey Ellingson and C.J. Mucklow

Introduction

Natural amenities are essential features of outdoor recreation, tourism, amenity migration and retirement drivers of local economic development (Bennett 1996; Frederick 1993; Jakus *et al.* 1995; Keith and Fawson 1995; Keith *et al.* 1996; Marcouiller 1997; Marcouiller and Clendenning 2005; McDonough *et al.* 1999). However, many valuable features of the landscape are not easily separable or captured by individual market transactions. Due to the public good features of these desirable attributes, non-rival and non-exclusive features of the rural landscape are underprovided by market-based resource allocations. In addition, features of the landscape are bundled, or jointly produced, with other locational attributes. This creates challenges in discerning the value of each attribute. Finally, they may be relatively location-specific, resulting in a more inelastic demand curve and more residual consumer surplus than for most freely tradable goods and services.

In rapidly growing, high natural-amenity communities, the market provides strong incentives to convert working landscapes into higher intensity rural, residential or commercial uses (Seidl 2005; Orens *et al.* 2006). The long-term effect of market transactions will not result in a socially optimal (welfare maximizing) allocation of land among its potential uses where significant public good attributes of the landscape are found. While the influence of most urban developments on economic returns to the region are quite easily understood through market signals, the potential benefit of *not* developing the open space may be substantially less easy to detect and analyze. As a result, the potential for crafting welfare-enhancing public policy to better capture the economic value of land use change is clear.

Ranch open space, or working landscapes, contributes to the vacation experience of tourists (Ellingson 2007; Rosenberger and Walsh 1997; Orens *et al.* 2006; Orens and Seidl 2009) and to the quality of life of residents (Magnan and Seidl 2004; Magnan *et al.* 2005; Rosenberger and Loomis 2001). These public good attributes of working landscapes are provided, without external compensation, through the stewardship of landowners, who also presumably benefit from these features. Tourists and residents, both landowning and non-landowning, can be viewed as consumers of working landscape attributes. In addition to producing cattle and hay, the landowners are also producers of those non-consumptive use values. The local government represents residents directly and is charged with maximizing their welfare; however, local government policy must also take into account the welfare of visitors. Effectively maximizing tourists' welfare and then capturing it locally enhances the welfare of the local residents as producers of tourism services.

Local government can affect the supply of working landscapes through public policy. The land use policy alternatives available to local governments to discourage land conversion, or encourage rural land stewardship, include regulatory options (e.g. zoning, animal density limits, set-back requirements, rural planned unit development standards), incentives (payment for ecosystem services (PES), purchase – agricultural-conservation-easements, purchase of development rights (PDR), right-to-farm legislation) and disincentives (nuisance laws, technology restrictions, production restrictions). Such public policies can be financed by taxing tourists (lodging tax), residents (property tax/mill levy), both (sales tax), or neither (agricultural zoning). Each policy option is costly in terms of direct costs to stakeholders, in addition to opportunity costs of foregone or restricted land use alternatives. From a social cost – benefit perspective, a policy is potentially justified so long as the total benefits exceed the total costs of the policy and the policy that creates the maximum net benefits is most desirable. However, it may be reasonable or desirable for local government to seek to redistribute the burden and benefits of rural land stewardship through policy such that the incentives to generate public values are more appropriately aligned. Private property rights are strong in the institutional and cultural context of the western United States. As a result, compensatory (incentive-based) programs are typically favored over regulatory programs, and voluntary compliance or participation is often sought over governmental mandates or restrictions.

In this chapter, we use the results of two recent surveys to simulate the welfare effects of four potential agricultural land-preservation policies. We define the relevant stakeholder groups as non-landowning residents, landowning residents and summer tourists. Local government is simply considered a conduit through which costs and benefits can be redistributed among the stakeholder groups. In our results section, we first discuss the total annual consumer surplus derived by residents (Magnan 2005) and summer tourists (Ellingson 2007) to Routt County, Colorado. Next, we estimate the total regional and distributional effects of a lodging tax, a mill levy and a sales tax to finance a purchase-of-agricultural-conservation-easement program. We also estimate the total regional and distributional effects of a non-compensatory zoning program.

Particular care must be taken in characterizing gains and losses in economic value relative to regional economic impact. Consumer surplus is value that has not been captured in the formal economy and may represent economic opportunity. Policy can capture this value and redistribute it. Total non-market value may remain the same, but economic activity may change due to direct, indirect and induced effects of the policy. Thus, the connections among non-market valuation, policy and economic development are highlighted. This policy-simulation exercise can inform local decision-making by illustrating the likely total and distributional implications of several classes of policy options local leaders can use to guide land use.

Study site: Routt County, Colorado

Steamboat Springs, the county seat of Routt County, Colorado, is a unique community and tourist destination, possessing a distinctive Rocky Mountain landscape, plentiful outdoor recreation, culinary and cultural opportunities, and a long tradition of the "Old West." Cattle ranching and its related industries have long been central features of Routt County's private land use and community culture. The combination of natural amenities and cultural traditions makes Routt County one of the fastest growing and wealthiest counties in the United States. However, economic growth is not without its challenges. One of the growth-related concerns of county residents is the conversion of privately held farms and ranches on large tracts of land into rural residential properties; in the local vernacular, such converted properties are commonly called "ranchettes" or "hobby farms" or, when the residences are particularly large, the more derisive "McMansions" or "starter castles" (Magnan *et al.* 2005).

Recognizing the contribution working landscapes make to the well-being of the community, Routt County implemented a voluntary PACE PDR program in order to help preserve this traditional lifestyle in the county's vast valleys. In 1995, Routt County residents passed a referendum to raise property taxes one mill for ten years to protect agricultural lands and natural areas. In 1996, that tax generated nearly $400,000 and by 1999 the one-mill levy was worth some $748,000 to the program. Over the ten-year life of the original program, the tax raised an estimated $6 million for the preservation of rural lands in the county (Magnan *et al.* 2005). In 2007, the PDR budget was $1.2 million per year with 3 percent allocated to cover administrative expenses.

Colorado has a highly decentralized tax revenue generation structure that allows local governments freedom to determine how they will collect taxes. Due to this structure, the combination of state and local taxes are among the lowest in the nation, while local taxes are among the highest (Greenwood and Brown undated; Magnan and Seidl 2004). Although the county government has a variety of tools at its disposal (e.g. fee-simple purchase, zoning), it has pursued a policy to purchase (or accept donation) of conservation easements or development rights from local landowners. The right to develop land can be separated from the right to own and use the land by placing such an easement against the property. In a parallel fashion, local, regional and national private non-profit organizations (often called land trusts or conservancies) have participated in the purchase of development rights or the outright purchase of properties and donation of the development rights of agricultural lands in the county. Currently, 55,000 acres of agricultural land are held under conservation easements in Routt County.

Research methodology

Our policy simulations depend upon the results of two recent surveys: a contingent behavior and contingent valuation survey of residents (Magnan 2005) and a parallel survey of summer tourists (Ellingson 2007) incorporating travel cost information. These surveys queried respondents regarding their preferences for Routt County working lands, motivations for these preferences, revealed preference information (in the case of tourists) and demographic information.

The visitors' survey represents summer tourists to Routt County, intercepted, via stratified random sample, throughout Routt County from early July through mid-September 2005. Survey collection areas were equally distributed among three main locations: the airport (32.3 percent), the visitor center at Steamboat Lake (28.8 percent) and locations around the town of Steamboat Springs (38.9 percent). The survey crew consisted of Colorado State University graduate students, who were visibly identifiable as such. A total of 420 tourist surveys were collected from a four-page survey instrument that took tourists approximately 15 minutes to complete. Respondents were asked about their trip activities, preferences about natural and man-made assets, reasons for maintaining open space, the length of their trip and other general demographic information (Ellingson 2007).

The parallel resident surveys were sent to 1,074 potential respondents from August to October 2004. A total of 459 surveys were returned after three mailings (survey, postcard, survey), resulting in a 44 percent response rate. The resident survey instrument precisely paralleled the tourist survey and was four pages and 23 questions in length (Magnan 2005).

Respondents were asked to rate how natural and man-made assets contributed to their enjoyment of living and vacationing in Steamboat Springs. The rating was based on a nine-point Likert scale where nine represented the asset strongly contributing to their enjoyment and one represented the asset strongly detracting from their enjoyment of Steamboat Springs. The natural environment was rated as the asset that most strongly added to both the tourists' and residents' experience in the Steamboat Springs area. Ranch open space was more highly rated by residents than by tourists; however, both felt that it added significantly to their experience. Tourists valued the local recreation amenities more than the residents, while the residents valued the community services more than the tourists. Logically, summer tourists were mainly attracted to Steamboat Springs due to its recreational opportunities, and did not utilize the local community services as much as the residents. Lastly, both tourists and residents indicated that local urban development was a relatively minor attractive feature of the Steamboat Springs area.

Respondents were asked to predict their spending and/or visitation behavior contingent upon reductions in the quantity of local ranch working landscapes. The contingent valuation questions were couched in terms of a willingness to pay to avoid the change. Responses from the valuation questions were used to derive a mean willingness to pay to maintain the current quantity and quality of ranch working landscapes. Total consumer surplus associated with the non-consumptive use value of each stakeholder group was also derived. Mean values were extrapolated to represent the total values of the summer tourist population and the resident population of Routt County.

Policy scenarios

Maintaining valuable rural landscapes attributes in a fast-growing, increasingly wealthy and naturally endowed community is a costly endeavor. Depending on the choice of policy tool, the costs and benefits can accrue to the general resident population, to particular sub-groups of the resident population (e.g. landowners, particular service users), or to visitors. These costs and benefits may enter into the formal economy or may remain as uncaptured economic value (consumer surplus). Standard economic policy research simulates and compares the effect of a "marginal" change across policies, typically defined as a 1 percent change, resulting in different total and distributional implications for the generation of tax revenue. Here, we are interested in illustrating the distributional implications of policy choice, so choose to control for the level of tax revenue (about $1.2 million per year) rather than the tax rate. We examine the total and distributional effects of a 3.5 percent lodging tax increase, an additional 1.5 mill property tax, a 0.5 percent sales tax increase, and agricultural zoning to maintain local working landscapes at their current levels. Our survey information would allow an analogous simulation that would illustrate the effect of less than the current supply of local landscapes. However, the pure effect of the policy instrument would potentially be masked due to estimated changes in expenditures and visitation behavior.

Lodging taxes

Lodging taxes are assessed as a proportion of the cost of a hotel or motel room. If people with more income tend to stay in more expensive hotels, lodging taxes can be considered progressive in nature. Lodging taxes are a commonly used fiscal management tool in county and municipal governments across Colorado. Funds generated through these taxes offset the additional government services demanded by the visitors to a region, provide funds for tourism promotion and lessen the relative tax burden on residents (Seidl *et al.* 2006). Seidl *et al.* (2006) consider it unlikely that potential visitors know whether or not a community has a lodging tax and would not base a decision to visit a community upon its lodging tax, especially because the tax is so commonplace. Weston (1983) demonstrates that lodging taxes are an effective public finance strategy for generating tax revenue almost entirely from tourists. Therefore, it is assumed that the burden of the lodging tax will be placed solely on the tourists to Routt County but will not affect their visitation levels.

In this scenario, we assume that because the tourists' lodging expenditures increase by 3.5 percent, their other expenditures decrease by the same amount; therefore, their total trip expenditures neither increase nor decrease. In turn, we redistribute this tax to landowners in order to encourage their tourism-enhancing land stewardship. Alternatively, we could assume that there is a net injection of economic activity equivalent to 3.5 percent of lodging expenditures derived from the substantial consumer surplus of summer tourists. This implies no change in other tourist expenditures and a transfer of funds to landowners. In either case, the effect on the general resident population is no change. That is, they still receive the benefits of rural land stewardship, but are not required to pay for its provision. Depending on our assumptions, the lodging tax could potentially have a dual effect on the regional economy. The tax could represent new money in the economy by capturing part of the tourists' consumer surplus and funneling it into the farm and ranch sector, or there could be no new money in the economy but a difference in local economic activity due to differences in the local multiplier effect of money in the lodging sector relative to the farm and ranch sector. Because such stewardship payments are fully fungible, we assume that landowning residents use the funds toward the betterment of the farm and ranch operation.

Mill levy

A mill levy is a proportional tax on the value of real estate. Because income is generally correlated with home value, property taxes are generally considered progressive. This tax falls to homeowners, not all of whom are residents. In addition to tourists, high amenity areas such as Steamboat Springs also attract retirees and non-resident homeowners (Machlis and Field 2000; Magnan and Seidl 2004). Routt County has a large percentage (30.4 percent) of non-resident homeowners. As a result, one can consider this broad set of homeowners to be subsidizing the smaller set of fewer full-time residents, and especially the independent set of visitors, because both groups benefit from the valuable goods and services provided by the tax (Magnan and Seidl 2004). It is unlikely that the preferences of non-resident homeowners are reflected in local policy formation through the democratic process because of their part-time residency status. This has the potential to result in local policies that could be construed as unfair to significant portions of the community (Magnan and Seidl 2004).

Routt County's current purchase of an agricultural conservation easement program is financially supported by a one-mill levy on property. Here, we examine the effect of a 1.5-mill levy on property. Property owners' consumer surplus will be reduced and tourists' consumer surplus will remain unchanged. Landowners are a subset of the property owners and must therefore provide a portion of the property tax. However, they will receive the entire benefit of the tax in rural land stewardship, resulting in a net injection of new money into the farm and ranch economy.

Sales tax

A sales tax is a levy proportional to the value of consumer purchases. Local sales taxes tend to be across all consumer purchases, unlike special "sin" sales taxes on items that are considered to have negative social externalities, such as tobacco and alcohol. Because a relatively large proportion of taxable purchases tend to be for necessities such as food, and because the proportion of income spent on food is inversely related to income, sales taxes are generally considered regressive. However, unlike the mill levy and lodging tax, sales taxes are paid by all classes of potential beneficiaries of the landscape: all residents and all tourists. Moreover, to the extent that the value of the services provided by working landscapes is time dependent (that is, two days of experience has greater value than one day), a sales tax may be considered to better reflect non-consumptive use value if the purchase of consumer goods also accumulates over time. Yet tourists can typically be counted on to spend on average more per day than residents, which potentially puts a greater daily tax burden on the tourists. Unfortunately, teasing out the proportion of total taxable sales made by the different stakeholder groups is not feasible with the data available.

Steamboat Springs attracts a significant number of tourists all year round and has a fairly small residential population. As a result, it can be assumed for ease of exposition that the tax burden will equally affect residents and tourists in Routt County on a per-person, per-year basis, therefore leading to a diminished consumer surplus for both parties. Steamboat Springs is one of many cities throughout the United States, particularly in tourist locations, that has a local sales tax collected by the local government and not the state. Here, we will examine the economic impacts to the local economy of a 0.5 percent sales tax increase, viewing as a net transfer of non-consumptive use value from tourists and non-landowning residents to resident landowners.

Agricultural zoning

Routt County could choose to zone all land currently in agriculture as ineligible for any higher intensity use. Such regulatory solutions are generally unpopular in Colorado and probably unenforceable, as a landowner always retains the right to petition for a change of zoning. However, it has been argued that agricultural zoning is pro-Right to Farm; facilitates the maintenance of a vibrant local agricultural economy; improves wildlife habitat and, thus, complementary non-agricultural economic activities on farms and ranches; and reduces the likelihood of nuisance suits and urban–agricultural conflicts. If only for this exercise, it is appropriate to explore the possibility that Routt County would switch their land-use protection policy to zoning regulations rather than voluntary development-rights purchase incentives. In this case, the (opportunity) costs of the policy fall exclusively to landowners and the benefits fall to all other stakeholder groups. Tourists and non-landowners maintain their consumer surplus. The landowners' economic activity is diminished by the amount that they would have received under the current program to protect their land, and the program funds are returned to the broader set of resident homeowners. This simulation can be implemented by taking $1.2 million in output away from the farm and ranch sector and re-inserting it across the broader economy in a manner proportional to the relative economic composition of the community.

Comparative regional analysis of policy alternatives

Following Kiker and Hodge's (2002) analysis in North Florida, we use IMPLAN to estimate the economic benefits of land conservation in Routt County. Indirect effects multipliers and induced effects multipliers are calculated in standard form to determine how a dollar of direct spending impacts indirect and induced sales (Stynes 1999). Direct sales represent the initial sales in a given industry. Indirect sales are the inter-industry transactions that arise as supplying industries respond to sales from the directly affected industries. Induced sales are the local spending that results from income changes in the directly or indirectly affected industries (Kiker and Hodges 2002). Industrial sectors are categorized by a three-digit NAICS code and are reported in 2004 dollars and structural matrices.

Results

Summer tourists' expenditures and benefits from working landscapes

A tourist spends an average of $177 per day to vacation in Routt County; approximately $153 of that amount is spent per day in Steamboat Springs' local economy (Ellingson 2007). On average, a tourist travels to Steamboat Springs for four days, which translates into an average of $708 spent per vacation to Routt County with $612 of that spent in Steamboat Springs' local economy. Tourists' expenditures are broken down as follows: 46.6 percent is spent on lodging, 35 percent on food and drinks, 9.7 percent on transportation and 8.7 percent on entertainment activities.

In order to extrapolate the per-person per-trip values to an annual impact value, the total number of summer tourists must be estimated. The Steamboat Springs Chamber of Commerce estimates that approximately 224,770 tourists stay in hotels during a summer tourist season (Evans Hall 2006). To arrive at the number of tourists who camp, we divided the total visitor days at Routt County State Parks (535,968) by the average length of a trip derived from our sample and found that 134,242 total visitors camped at the Steamboat Lake and Stagecoach State Parks located within Routt County (Colorado State Parks 2005a and 2005b). The actual percentage of tourist versus resident campers at these state parks is unknown. For simplicity, it is assumed that half of the visitors were Routt County residents, so 67,121 of the total camp visitors are considered non-resident tourists to Routt County. Combining this figure with the number of tourists who stay in hotels shows that approximately 291,891 tourists visit Routt County during the summer months.

Some 54.7 percent of the survey respondents stated they would reduce their trips to Steamboat if existing ranch lands were converted to urban uses. In other words, approximately 159,664 tourists per year can be expected to change their trip behavior if the lands were converted. To estimate the loss of summer tourist revenue, we multiply the mean value of reduction in spending ($227.82) by the total number of tourists changing their trip behavior (Kiker and Hodges 2002).

The estimated loss of summer tourist revenue if Routt County ranchlands were developed is $36,373,940 per year.

To estimate the current loss in consumer surplus, we multiply the mean willingness to pay by the total number of summer tourists to Routt County (291,891). The mean willingness to pay to retain the current amount of ranch working landscapes, based upon estimates of consumer surplus, is $122.57 per visitor, which represents $35,777,079 of additional value in a Routt County vacation and potential revenue not currently finding its way into local hands.

Residents' benefits from working landscapes

In the study of the value of ranchlands to residents in Routt County, Magnan *et al.* (2005) found a positive response (93.7 percent stated "yes") to preserving ranchland open space.

Respondents were asked about their willingness to pay to protect local ranch open space through the county government. Magnan *et al.* (2005) found that residents would be willing to pay an average of $220 per year to protect the existing ranchland in Routt County. The aggregate benefit of ranch open space conservation can be calculated by multiplying the number of households affected by the mean household willingness to pay (Magnan *et al.* 2005; Willis and Garrod 1993). The number of households in Routt County in 2004 was 9,890, which results in a total annual benefit of $2,175,800, or nearly three times the 2005 Routt County program budget of $748,000 (Magnan *et al.* 2005). Residents' benefit of ranchland open space is approximately 6 percent of the summer tourists' benefit considering the number of residents relative to visitors.

Total annual benefits of working landscape stewardship

The non-consumptive use value of ranchland open space in Routt County to summer tourists and residents is $38.5 million per year. Approximately 94.4 percent of the total non-consumptive use value can be translated as the tourists' consumer surplus, while the remaining 5.6 percent represents residents' consumer surplus. This demonstrates a relatively large opportunity for the local people to capture some of the value they are creating for visitors. Such redistributive opportunities are potentially realized through a variety of public policy alternatives.

Policy simulations

Industry output for hotels and motels (NAICS = 479) is examined to estimate the effect of a lodging tax on the local economy. The industry output for hotels and motels is $29,450,000; therefore, a 3.5 percent increase in the lodging tax rate would result in total lodging tax revenue of $1,030,750. Total lodging tax revenue is injected back into the economy through the cattle ranching and farming sector (NAICS = 11), which can be analyzed in IMPLAN as two models. The first model will demonstrate a negative shock to industries related to the tourists' other trip expenditures, proportional to their contribution to the tourists' trip budgets. The total direct negative impact equates to the lodging tax revenue and is distributed among the following industries: food services and drinking places (–$675,141), gasoline stations (–$187,597) and gambling and recreational industries (–$168,012). The second model is an equivalent positive shock to the cattle ranching and farming sector.

Table 10.1 illustrates how increasing the lodging tax rate by 3.5 percent impacts regional employment and output for the top ten affected industries. The top three industries experiencing an economic loss in sales or output are food service and drinking places, gasoline stations and gambling and recreational industries. Routt County's regional economy would experience a negative economic impact totaling $1,496,148 and a positive economic impact totaling $1,841,170, for a net positive impact of $345,023.

The cattle ranching and farming sector is the industry most positively affected by an increase in the lodging tax, gaining 12 jobs, while the food services and drinking places industry faces the largest negative impact, an equivalent loss of approximately 15 jobs. The net employment impact is a total loss of approximately five jobs to Routt County.

The indirect effects and induced effects multipliers can be calculated from the industry output impacts. The indirect and induced multipliers, as a result of the direct loss to the food and drink, transportation and recreation-related industries, are 1.2 and 1.5, respectively. This implies that each dollar lost due to the tax increase results in a $0.50 loss in indirect and induced sales. The indirect and induced multipliers as a result of a direct gain to the cattle ranching and farming industry are 1.7 and 1.8, respectively. Therefore, a dollar gained in the cattle industry due to the tax increase results in an additional $0.80 gain in indirect and induced sales. Imposing an increase in the lodging tax to support the voluntary purchase-of-development-rights program generates a net gain of $0.30 of economic activity in Routt County for each dollar of tax revenue.

It is also possible that tourists will not change their visitation behavior in the face of a lodging tax increase. That is, their lodging expenditures go up by 3.5 percent, but their other expenditures do not change; new money is captured in the local economy through the consumer surplus of tourists. This result is easier to simulate because there will be no negative impacts on the general tourist expenditures, only positive effects on the cattle ranching and farming sectors. Note that this tax revenue is collected from non-residents who have a larger total, but smaller individual, consumer surplus relative to the residents in regards to ranch open space surrounding Steamboat Springs.

The total assessed value of Routt County's land is required to estimate what would occur in the local economy with an additional one-mill increase in property taxes. According to Routt County's Assessor (2007), the total assessed valuation of land within Routt County is $812,913,220. A 1.5-mill levy increase would generate a total of $1,219,369 in tax revenue for one year. The total mill-levy tax revenue will be collected from residents (owner-occupied dwellings, NAICS = 509) and injected back into the economy through the cattle ranching

Table 10.1 Economic impacts of a 3.5 percent lodging tax increase

Employment impacts (in number of jobs)

Top ten impacted industries	Direct	Indirect	Induced	Total
481 Food services and drinking places	-14.51	-0.12	-0.22	-14.85
11 Cattle ranching and farming	9.82	2.38	0.00	12.20
478 Gambling and recreation industries	-1.46	0.00	-0.03	-1.50
407 Gasoline stations	-1.10	0.00	-0.01	-1.12
10 All other crop farming	0.00	0.84	0.00	0.84
18 Agriculture and forestry support activities	0.00	0.62	0.00	0.62
449 Veterinary services	0.00	0.52	0.00	0.52
467 Hospitals	0.00	0.00	-0.18	-0.18
465 Offices of phys., dentists and other health	0.00	0.00	-0.16	-0.16
412 Nonstore retailers	0.00	-0.06	-0.09	-0.15
TOTAL NEGATIVE EMPLOYMENT IMPACT	-17.07	-1.93	-2.54	-21.54
TOTAL POSITIVE EMPLOYMENT IMPACT	9.82	5.80	1.06	16.69
NET EMPLOYMENT IMPACT	**-7.25**	**3.87**	**-1.48**	**-4.86**

Output impacts (in 2004 dollars)

	Direct	Indirect	Induced	Total
11 Cattle ranching and farming	1,030,750	249,720	22	1,280,492
481 Food services and drinking places	-675,141	-5,478	-10,462	-691,081
407 Gasoline stations	-187,597	-754	-2,334	-190,684
10 All other crop farming	0	189,711	22	189,734
478 Gambling and recreation industries	-168,012	-55	-3,484	-171,551
449 Veterinary services	0	31,941	266	32,207
509 Owner-occupied dwellings	0	0	-24,479	-24,479
431 Real estate	0	28,648	-8,329	20,319
18 Agriculture and forestry support activities	0	18,681	17	18,698
467 Hospitals	0	0	-17,820	-17,820
TOTAL NEGATIVE OUTPUT IMPACT	-1,030,750	-211,517	-253,880	-1,496,148
TOTAL POSITIVE OUTPUT IMPACT	1,030,750	704,044	106,376	1,841,170
NET OUTPUT IMPACT	**0**	**492,527**	**-147,504**	**345,023**

and farming industry (NAICS=11), which can be analyzed in IMPLAN as a negative shock to all landowners and a positive net shock to cattle ranchers and farmers. Table 10.2 highlights the employment and output regional impacts for the top ten affected industries, respectively, due to the mill-levy increase.

In this scenario, agricultural-related industries are the top three beneficiaries of a 1.5 mill increase in the property tax, generating a total of 20 jobs. The parallel negative employment impact is about two jobs, resulting in a net employment gain of 18 jobs for Routt County. The cattle ranching and farming industry receives the largest economic gain from a 1.5-mill increase, equating to a total positive impact of more than $1.5 million. The tax revenue comes from residents who experience a total economic loss of $1.2 million. However, accounting for the additional money generated through indirect and induced sales, the total net gain is $792,035.

Each dollar lost due to a property tax increase results in a $0.14 loss in indirect and induced sales. Each dollar injected into the cattle industry results in an additional $0.80 in indirect and induced sales. Therefore, a property tax that benefits agricultural landowners creates an additional $0.66 of economic activity in Routt County's economy. Unlike the lodging tax, which generates its revenue from tourists and adds $0.30 to the economic activity, the mill levy generates two times the amount of economic activity but collects the taxes from residents, who have a much smaller total consumer surplus relating to ranch open space than the tourists do.

In order to estimate with the impact of a 0.5 percent sales tax increase on the local economy, a great variety of industries need to be examined. If we assume consumers will adjust their purchases to reflect the tax rate change, each of the affected industries will experience a direct loss equivalent to the sales tax revenue, modeled as negative shocks to each respective industry. The total sales tax revenue of $962,000 will be injected back into the economy through the cattle ranching and farming industry (NAICS=11), which can be analyzed in IMPLAN as a positive shock.

The cattle ranching and farming industry is most positively affected by a 0.5 percent increase in the sales tax, gaining 11 jobs, while the food services and drinking places industry experiences the most negative impact, losing ten jobs. The net employment impact of the sales tax increase is a loss of approximately four local, typically low-paying jobs. The cattle ranching and farming industry demonstrates the largest positive output impact, gaining an annual total of $1.2 million. Food services and drinking places experience the largest negative impact (−$476,951). Including indirect and induced effects, Routt County's economy would experience a negative economic impact totaling $1.4 million and a countervailing positive economic impact of $1.7 million, resulting in a $300,384 net positive impact.

Each dollar lost due to the sales tax increase results in a $0.50 loss in indirect and induced sales in the retail sector. Each dollar injected into the cattle industry results in an additional $0.80 in indirect and induced sales. Therefore, a 0.5 percent sales tax increase creates an additional $0.30 of economic activity in

Table 10.2 Economic impacts of a 1.5 mill increase

Employment impacts (in number of jobs)

Top ten impacted industries	Direct	Indirect	Induced	Total
11 Cattle ranching and farming	11.62	2.82	0.00	14.44
10 All other crop farming	0.00	0.99	0.00	0.99
18 Agriculture and forestry support activities	0.00	0.73	0.00	0.73
449 Veterinary services	0.00	0.61	0.01	0.62
431 Real estate	0.00	0.32	0.03	0.35
390 Wholesale trade	0.00	0.21	0.03	0.24
458 Services to buildings and dwellings	0.00	-0.22	0.00	-0.22
493 Civic, social, prof. and similar orgs	0.00	-0.21	0.02	-0.19
481 Food services and drinking places	0.00	0.02	0.14	0.17
412 Nonstore retailers	0.00	-0.12	-0.01	-0.13
TOTAL NEGATIVE EMPLOYMENT IMPACT	0.00	-1.55	-0.32	-1.87
TOTAL POSITIVE EMPLOYMENT IMPACT	11.62	6.86	1.26	19.74
NET EMPLOYMENT IMPACT	**11.62**	**5.31**	**0.94**	**17.87**

Output impacts (in 2004 dollars)

	Direct	Indirect	Induced	Total
11 Cattle ranching and farming	1,219,369	295,417	26	1,514,812
509 Owner-occupied dwellings	-1,219,369	0	15,606	-1,203,763
10 All other crop farming	0	224,427	27	224,454
431 Real estate	0	55,441	5,310	60,751
449 Veterinary services	0	37,786	315	38,101
390 Wholesale trade	0	31,858	3,988	35,847
30 Power generation and supply	0	23,319	3,803	27,122
18 Agriculture and forestry support activities	0	22,100	20	22,120
42 Maint./repair of farm and nonfarm resid.	0	-16,814	-85	-16,900
430 Monetary author. & deposit. credit inter.	0	9,226	3,206	12,431
TOTAL NEGATIVE OUTPUT IMPACT	-1,219,369	-134,880	-31,805	-1,386,054
TOTAL POSITIVE OUTPUT IMPACT	1,219,369	832,878	125,843	2,178,090
NET OUTPUT IMPACT	**0**	**697,998**	**94,037**	**792,035**

Table 10.3 Economic impacts of a 0.5 percent sales tax increase

Employment impacts (in number of jobs)

Top ten impacted industries	Direct	Indirect	Induced	Total
11 Cattle ranching and farming	9.17	2.22	0.00	11.39
481 Food services and drinking places	-9.91	-0.11	-0.23	-10.25
405 Food and beverage stores	-1.82	-0.02	-0.09	-1.93
479 Hotels and motels – including casino hotels	-1.72	-0.02	-0.03	-1.76
404 Building material and garden supply stores	-1.06	-0.01	-0.04	-1.11
10 All other crop farming	0.00	0.78	0.00	0.78
407 Gasoline stations	-0.81	0.00	-0.01	-0.83
18 Agriculture and forestry support activities	0.00	0.57	0.00	0.58
449 Veterinary services	0.00	0.48	0.00	0.49
465 Offices of phys., dentists and other health	0.00	0.00	-0.16	-0.16
TOTAL NEGATIVE EMPLOYMENT IMPACT	-15.32	-1.80	-2.52	-19.64
TOTAL POSITIVE EMPLOYMENT IMPACT	9.17	5.41	0.99	15.57
NET EMPLOYMENT IMPACT	**-6.15**	**3.61**	**-1.53**	**-4.07**

Output impacts (in 2004 dollars)

	Direct	Indirect	Induced	Total
11 Cattle ranching and farming	962,000	233,064	21	1,195,085
481 Food services and drinking places	-461,150	-4,989	-10,812	-476,951
10 All other crop farming	0	177,058	21	177,079
479 Hotels and motels – including casino hotels	-147,250	-1,362	-2,304	-150,916
407 Gasoline stations	-138,100	-795	-2,314	-141,209
405 Food and beverage stores	-120,250	-1,467	-5,619	-127,337
404 Building material and garden supply stores	-95,250	-1,179	-3,547	-99,976
449 Veterinary services	0	29,811	248	30,059
509 Owner-occupied dwellings	0	0	-25,299	-25,299
431 Real estate	0	26,603	-8,607	17,996
TOTAL NEGATIVE OUTPUT IMPACT	-962,000	-204,258	-251,723	-1,417,982
TOTAL POSITIVE OUTPUT IMPACT	962,000	657,085	99,281	1,718,366
NET OUTPUT IMPACT	**0**	**452,827**	**-152,442**	**300,384**

Table 10.4 Economic impacts of a zoning regulation

Employment impacts (in number of jobs)

Top ten impacted industries	Direct	Indirect	Induced	Total
11 Cattle ranching and farming	-11.44	-2.77	0.00	-14.21
10 All other crop farming	0.00	-0.97	0.00	-0.97
33 New residential 1-unit structures – all	0.92	0.00	0.00	0.92
431 Real estate	1.02	-0.26	0.06	0.81
18 Agriculture and forestry support activities	0.00	-0.72	0.00	-0.72
38 Commercial and institutional buildings	0.63	0.00	0.00	0.63
20 Coal mining	0.51	0.04	0.00	0.55
439 Architectural and engineering services	0.29	0.21	0.01	0.51
390 Wholesale trade	0.00	-0.21	-0.03	-0.24
430 Monetary author. & deposit. credit inter.	0.00	-0.06	-0.02	-0.08
TOTAL NEGATIVE EMPLOYMENT IMPACT	-11.44	-6.75	-1.24	-19.42
TOTAL POSITIVE EMPLOYMENT IMPACT	10.20	2.42	2.99	15.61
NET EMPLOYMENT IMPACT	**-1.23**	**-4.33**	**1.75**	**-3.82**

Output impacts (in 2004 dollars)

	Direct	Indirect	Induced	Total
11 Cattle ranching and farming	-1,200,000	-290,724	-26	-1,490,750
10 All other crop farming	0	-220,862	-26	-220,888
20 Coal mining	165,828	13,221	430	179,479
431 Real estate	177,582	-45,958	9,870	141,494
33 New residential 1-unit structures – all	133,937	0	0	133,937
481 Food services and drinking places	73,134	4,521	21,181	98,836
509 Owner-occupied dwellings	61,312	0	29,009	90,321
481 Food services and drinking places	73,134	2,849	12,398	88,381
38 Commercial and institutional buildings	66,554	0	0	66,554
467 Hospitals	36,966	0	20,962	57,928
TOTAL NEGATIVE OUTPUT IMPACT	-1,200,000	-819,648	-123,844	-2,143,492
TOTAL POSITIVE OUTPUT IMPACT	1,200,000	260,252	298,644	1,758,897
NET OUTPUT IMPACT	**0**	**-559,396**	**174,800**	**-384,595**

Routt County's economy, which is similar to the lodging tax. While both the lodging tax and the sales tax generate the same level of economic activity, the lodging tax is collected mainly from non-residents, while the sales tax is collected from residents and non-residents. Like the lodging tax, we could alternatively assume that consumers are not sensitive to changes in the sales tax rate and that new taxes dip into the consumers' surplus rather than into their current expenditures. This would eliminate the negative cross-economy effects and result in only positive effects in the farm and ranch sectors.

A great variety of industries also need to be examined in order to estimate what would occur in the local economy if Routt County were to zone all land currently in agriculture as ineligible for any higher intensity use. Each of the industries would experience a gain equivalent to the positive rezoning impact, modeled as positive shocks to each respective industry. The total purchase-of-development-rights budget of $1.2 million would be taken from the cattle ranching and farming industry (NAICS = 11) because the zoning would lead to the extinction of the PDR program. The loss to the cattle ranching and farming industry can be analyzed in IMPLAN as a negative shock.

The cattle ranching and farming industry is most negatively affected due to the rezoning policy, losing 14 jobs, while there is no industry with a positive employment impact greater than one job. The net employment impact due to rezoning policy is a loss of approximately four jobs. The cattle ranching and farming industry demonstrates the largest negative output impact, losing a total of $1.5 million annually. The coal-mining industry experiences the largest positive impact ($179,479). Including indirect and induced effects, Routt County's economy would experience a negative economic impact totaling $2.1 million and a positive economic impact of $1.8 million, resulting in a $384,595 net loss.

Each dollar lost due to rezoning results in a $0.80 loss in indirect and induced sales. Each dollar injected into the cattle industry results in an additional $0.50 in indirect and induced sales. Therefore, rezoning creates a $0.30 loss of activity in Routt County's economy, resulting in economic *in*activity. That is, a regulatory approach is not costless relative to a compensatory approach. This is an interesting artifact of the analysis that assumes the PDR program is, essentially, a property right. The elimination of a taxpayer-funded compensation program results in a lower level of economic activity when the taxpayers' money is returned to them. This is due to lower relative multipliers in the broader economy relative to the agricultural sub-sector of the local economy.

Conclusion

This chapter evaluated the welfare (total and distributional) implications associated with the policy options available to Routt County, Colorado, to manage its ranch open space. The policy options analyzed were a lodging tax, a mill-levy tax, a sales tax and zoning. IMPLAN was used to quantify the regional economic impacts (fiscal, total and distributional) and run the policy simulations. Throughout the chapter we explored the implications of assuming:

1   that policies are simply redistributive of existing expenditures; or
2   that they instead result in capturing heretofore unrealized economic oppor-
    tunity found within the consumer surpluses of the relevant stakeholder
    groups.

In this way we highlighted some of the important distinctions between economic value and economic activity in addressing economic development issues in communities highly endowed with natural amenities.

We sought to isolate the distributional implications of policy alternatives by controlling for the revenue stream rather than the rate of assessment. We found that the net effect of a lodging tax is to transfer income from tourists to agricultural producers in order to encourage their stewardship of working landscape characteristics of public value. Such a transfer results in a net multiplier effect of five jobs and $0.30 of additional economic activity for every dollar of tax revenue collected. We found that the net effect of a mill levy is to transfer income from local property owners to rural landowners, creating a net increase of 18 jobs and a return of $0.66 in economic activity for each dollar in property tax collected. We found that a general sales tax results in a transfer of funds from local businesses, residents and visitors, to local landowners, and a net return on investment of about $0.30 per dollar of tax revenue collected, but a net loss of four local jobs. Finally, zoning results in a transfer from local landowning farmers and ranchers to the top 25 active industries in Routt County, causing a net loss of $384,595 and four jobs.

In general, the increase in the sales tax generates the most revenue and jobs for Routt County while the zoning policy generates a loss of revenue and jobs. The most important aspect of the analysis is the question of who generates the revenue, non-residents or residents? Because non-residents revealed that they hold a significantly larger value of ranch open space, it would seem logical to capture their consumer surplus via the tax increases. While both the lodging tax and sales tax scenarios target tourists to Routt County, it is uncertain what proportion of the sales tax is generated from tourists versus residents. Therefore, further research needs to be conducted in order to determine what percentage of retail-type industry sales comes from tourists versus residents in order to make a sound policy decision for generating additional revenue for the voluntary purchase-of-development-rights program in Routt County.

References

Bennett, D.G. (1996) "Implication of Retirement Development in High-Amenity Non-metropolitan Coastal Areas," *Journal of Applied Gerontology*, 15: 345–360.
Colorado State Parks (2005a) Stagecoach State Park FY04–05 Park Facts. Online, available at: www.parks.state.co.us/home/publications/Fact_Sheets/0405_Fact_Sheet/Stagecoach_06.pdf (accessed May 22, 2006).
Colorado State Parks (2005b) Steamboat Lake State Park FY04–05 Park Facts. Online, available at: www.parks.state.co.us/home/publications/Fact_Sheets/0405_Fact_Sheet/Steamboat_06.pdf (accessed May 22, 2006).

Ellingson, L.J. (2007) "Comparing Methodologies to Estimate Tourists' Nonconsumptive Use Values of Recreation, Roadways and Ranches: International and Domestic Applications," dissertation, Colorado State University.

Evans Hall, S. (2006) "Summer Hotel Occupancy Estimates," Steamboat Springs Chamber of Commerce (Phone Conversation) (May 22, 2006).

Frederick, M. (1993) "Rural Tourism and Economic Development," *Economic Development Quarterly*, 7: 215–224.

Greenwood, D. and Brown, T. (undated) "An Overview of Colorado's State and Local Tax Structures," Center for Colorado Policy Studies. Online, available at: http://web.uccs.edu/ccps/pdf/Tax%20Overview%20Article.PDF (accessed November 2003).

Jakus, P.M., Siegel, P.B. and White, R.L. (1995) "Tourism as Rural Development Strategy: Finding Consensus in Residents' Attitudes," *Tennessee Agricultural Science*, Fall: 22–29.

Keith, J. and Fawson, K. (1995) "Economic Development in Rural Utah: is Wilderness Recreation the Answer?" *Annals of Regional Science*, 29: 303–313.

Keith, J., Fawson, K. and Chang, T. (1996) "Recreation as an Economic Development Strategy: Some Evidence from Utah," *Journal of Leisure Research*, 28: 96–107.

Kiker, C. and Hodges, A.W. (2002) "Economic Benefits of Natural Land Conservation: Case Study of Northeast Florida," final report submitted to Defenders of Wildlife in Fulfillment of Sponsored Project Agreement.

McDonough, M., Fried, J., Potter-Witter, K., Stevens, J. and Stynes, D. (1999) "The Role of Natural Resources in Community and Regional Economic Stability in the Eastern Upper Peninsula," Research Report 568, Michigan Agricultural Experiment Station, Michigan State University.

Machlis, G. and Field, D. (2000) "Introduction," in G. Machlis and D. Field (eds.) *National Parks and Rural Development*, Washington, DC: Island Press, pp. 1–11.

Magnan, N. (2005) "The Economic Value of Ranch Open Space to Residents: a Contingent Valuation Study of Changes Over the Past Decade," thesis, Colorado State University.

Magnan, N. and Seidl, A. (2004) "Community Economic Considerations of Tourism Development," Department of Agricultural and Resource Economics, Cooperative Extension, Colorado State University. June 2004-EDR 04–06.

Magnan, N., Seidl, A., Mucklow, C.J. and Alpe, D. (2005) "The Societal Value of Ranchlands to Routt County Residents, 1995–2005," Department of Agricultural and Resource Economics, Cooperative Extension, Colorado State University. October 2005-EDR 05–01.

Marcouiller, D.W. (1997) "Toward Integrative Tourism Planning in Rural America," *Journal of Planning Literature*, 11: 337–357.

Marcouiller, D.W. and Clendenning, G. (2005) "The Supply of Natural Amenities: Moving from Empirical Anecdotes to a Theoretical Basis," in G.P. Green, S.C. Deller and D.W. Marcouiller (eds.) *Amenities and Rural Development: Theory, Methods and Public Policy*, Northampton, MA: Edward Elgar, pp. 6–33.

Orens, A. and Seidl, A. (2009) "Working Lands and Winter Tourists in the Rocky Mountain West: A Contingent Behavior, Revealed Preference and Input–output Analysis," *Tourism Economics*, 15: 215–242.

Orens, A., Seidl, A. and Weiler, S. (2006) "Winter Tourism and Land Development in Gunnison County, Colorado," in T. Clark, A. Gill and R. Hartmann (eds.) *Mountain Resort Planning and Development in an Era of Globalization*, Cognizant Communications Corporation, pp. 91–107.

Rosenberger, R.S. and Loomis, J.B. (2001) "Benefit Transfer of Outdoor Recreation Use Values: A Technical Document Supporting the Forest Service Strategic Plan" (2000 Revision), General Technical Report RMRS-GTR-72, Fort Collins: USDA Forest Service, Rocky Mountain Research Station.

Rosenberger, S.R. and Walsh, G.R. (1997) "Nonmarket Value of Western Valley Ranchland Using Contingent Valuation," *Journal of Agricultural and Resource Economics*, 22(2): 296–309.

Routt County Assessor (2007) "Routt County Assessed Valuation – Abstract Totals." Online, available at: www.co.routt.co.us/assessor.html (accessed August 23, 2007).

Seidl, A. (2005) "Failing Markets and Fragile Institutions in Land Use: Colorado's Experience," in S.J. Goetz, J.S. Shortle and J.C. Bergstrom (eds.) *Land Use Problems and Conflicts: Causes, Consequences and Solutions*, London: Routledge, pp. 50–63.

Seidl, A., Sullins, M. and Cline, S. (2006) "A Lodging Tax for Custer County? Issues and Answers," Department of Agricultural and Resource Economics, Cooperative Extension, Colorado State University. May 2006-EDR 06–05.

Stynes, D. (1999) "Economic Impacts of Tourism," working paper, Michigan State University.

Weston, R. (1983) "The Ubiquity of Room Taxes," *Tourism Management*, 4: 194–198.

Willis, K.G. and Garrod, G.D. (1993) "Valuing Landscape: A Contingent Valuation Approach," *Journal of Environmental Management*, 37: 1–22.

Part III

The scope for emerging policies

11 Compliance with agri-environmental standards in Europe and the United States

Roel Jongeneel and Floor Brouwer[1]

Introduction[2]

Farmers in many countries today face regulatory landscapes that cover an ever-increasing array of topics, including environment, biodiversity, food safety, animal identification and animal welfare. Agriculture is less and less seen as an isolated business, but is now viewed as an industry that by its nature has a complex interaction with ecology, nature and landscape services (multifunctionality). The need for sustainability is therefore emphasized more in agriculture than in any other sector. Increasingly, it is recognized that the still-wide public support given to agriculture should enhance rather than hinder sustainability. In the EU a recent Common Agricultural Policy (CAP) reform (Luxembourg Agreement 2003) introduced obligatory cross-compliance, an enforcement mechanism emphasizing the importance attached to farmers' compliance with regulations. Farmers eligible for direct payments of the CAP who are detected to be non-compliant are, depending on the degree of violation, punished with a partial or complete reduction of these payments. Where the EU relies on the stick, other countries are more reliant on the carrot, i.e. using voluntary approaches that might be combined with positive financial incentives.

Farmers not only face regulatory constraints, but at the same time are increasingly involved in voluntary certification schemes or standards in order to provide assurances about the quality and the safety of their products and the environmental sustainability of their production techniques. These voluntary certification schemes might interact with the obligatory regulatory requirements, which also specify certain minimum standards on often related areas (Farmer *et al.* 2007). Under some conditions, voluntary schemes driven by the private sector (self-regulation), or as facilitated and encouraged by the public authorities, might even be thought of as an alternative strategy to achieve the same policy goals.

This chapter focuses on regulatory standards rather than voluntary standards and certification regimes. The first aim is to describe and analyze the impacts of the main regulations as included in the EU's obligatory cross-compliance package, introduced with the 2003 CAP reform (Luxembourg Agreement). A second aim is to provide a brief comparative analysis with respect to the EU's key competitors, notably the United States, Canada and New Zealand. This analysis explores the extent to which these competitors regulate the same issues as the EU and, as far as possible, compares differences in approaches and impacts.

Analyzing the impact of regulations and standards is difficult for various reasons. Data on degree of compliance and costs of compliance with regulations are in most cases only scarcely available or are fragmented. Moreover, there exist intricate relationships between various regulations and standards. For example, while one regulation imposes a cost, complying with a related voluntary standard might bring an associated cost-offset (e.g. the interaction between the Birds and Habitat Directive and Agri-Environmental Schemes). In addition, the costs associated with a combined set of regulations or standards might differ from the aggregate sum of costs associated with the single standards. Synergies between standards may reduce the accumulation of costs. This lack of information and abundance of complexities is the reason that analyses often have a qualitative or case-specific character. This chapter attempts to combine both qualitative and quantitative analyses of a broad set of regulations and standards, emphasizing the general overview and orders of magnitude, rather than exploring tiny detail. With regard to impacts, the main focus is on the economic impacts, and less on the benefits achieved (such as increased sustainability). Particular attention is paid to impacts on the EU's (external) competitiveness with respect to three key trading-partners: the United States, Canada and New Zealand.

This chapter is organized as follows. The next section discusses several issues of regulation, notably the theory of enforcement based on the responsive regulation approach, a summary of results from the economic theory explaining compliance behavior and the potential impact of regulation on competitiveness. The third section discusses indicative best estimates of compliance and costs of compliance for the EU's cross-compliance measures and regulations. It also includes information on the estimated order of magnitude of impacts on competitiveness. The fourth section provides further details about comparative regulation by the EU's key competitors. The fifth section focuses on differences in regulatory approaches implemented by these countries. The final section provides concluding remarks.

Issues of regulation

A regulator perspective: regulatory strategies and styles of enforcement

Several issues can be raised with respect to regulation and standards, such as the reasons to regulate, the selection of a certain regulatory strategy, explanations for the chosen type of regulation, the setting of standards, regulatory enforcement and risk issues (see Baldwin and Cave (1999) for a general overview). In this case our aim is more limited and mainly focuses on issues of enforcement and compliance. Regulation generally comprises three stages:

1 the enactment and enabling of legislation;
2 the creation of regulatory administrations and rules; and
3 the bringing to bear of those rules on the persons or institutions sought to be influenced or controlled (Hutter 1997).

The third stage, enforcement, is far from trivial and is as vital to the success of the regulation as the first two.[3] Poor enforcement can undermine the most sophisticated regulatory design. Failure to identify and deal with breaches of rules may reduce regulatory statutes to mere paperwork.

Regulatory officials may seek compliance with laws or standards not merely by resorting to formal enforcement and prosecution (which is often very time-consuming and costly), but also by using a host of informal techniques, including persuasion, education, advice, technical assistance, negotiation and incentives. The theory of regulation provides relevant frameworks for our examination. As part of their responsive regulation approach, Ayres and Braithwaite (1992) developed a "pyramid of enforcement strategies" and a "pyramid of sanctions." These pyramids are discussed first in order to create a general framework for analyzing and understanding different approaches to regulation in agriculture.

As shown in Figure 11.1, the pyramid of enforcement strategies distinguishes between styles of enforcement: the degree of enforcement increases when moving upward, beginning at the base with a "light touch" style of enforced self-regulation and ending with strict command and control at the pinnacle. The pyramid of sanctions illustrates that regulators may seek gains in compliance not merely by formal enforcement and prosecution, but by using a host of other

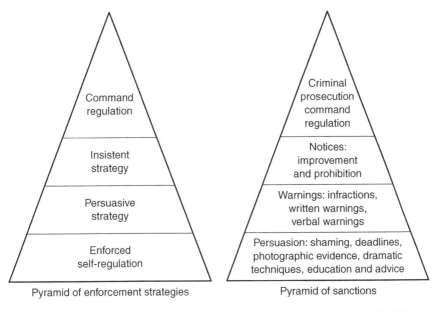

Figure 11.1 Pyramids of responsive regulation (source: Baldwin and Cave 1999: 100).

informal techniques, such as education, advice, persuasion and negotiation. In this respect sometimes the distinction is made between compliance and deterrence approaches to enforcement. In order to seek compliance with regulations, the compliance approach emphasizes the use of measures falling short of prosecution. The deterrence approach emphasizes penalties and prosecution as mechanisms to deter future infractions (Baldwin and Cave 1999: 97). Within the compliance strategy, Hutter (1997) has added two sub-strategies, labeled respectively as the persuasive and insistent strategies (see Figure 11.1, left panel). Both aim to secure compliance, but the first is more accommodating than the second.

The so-called responsive regulation approach sees enforcement as involving a progression through different compliance-seeking strategies and sanctions. In the model of "responsive regulation," those regulated are subjected to increasingly interventionist regulatory responses as they continue to infringe and to less interventionist actions as they come to comply (Baldwin and Cave 1999: 99). These authors further comment that rejecting punitive regulation is naïve, but to be totally committed to it is "to lead a charge of the light brigade." The trick of successful regulation is to create a balance and synergy between punishment and persuasion.[4]

Rather than relying on obligatory regulation, governments might also try to improve environmental quality by offering voluntary schemes with or without technical assistance and financial incentives to farmers. In the latter case these voluntary schemes might operate as a direct substitute for the obligatory regulation approach chosen by the EU and strengthened by the recently added cross-compliance mechanism. It is even possible that the government might use the voluntary standard approach as a first step, transforming such schemes at a later stage into regulatory constraints, thereby then imposing obligatory compliance on all participants. Indeed some non-EU countries seem to follow just this voluntary approach. On the other hand, voluntary standards or certification might also originate from the private sector or have a hybrid public–private character. In that case they usually are complementary, specifying performance levels that go beyond the minimum requirements as imposed by the regulatory authorities and addressing particular commercial and marketing interests (see Farmer *et al.* 2007).

Compliance behavior: understanding the response of the regulated

Regulations and standards are aimed at adjusting the farmer's or supply chain's behavior in such a way that an increased performance level is achieved. Whether this will actually be realized depends on the conformity to standards. As compliance to standards might impose costs and benefits, the individual actor's degree of compliance is likely to be a function of these costs and benefits. When non-compliance is considered, the costs of punishment also play a role. In general, these costs of punishment depend on the magnitude of the fine associated with (various degrees) of non-compliance as well as on the probability of detection. The latter in turn depends on the intensity of the monitoring and inspection regime associated with the standards.

In the case of voluntary standards, there will be no direct punishment in the case of non-participation, but rather exclusion from the benefits related to participation. The decision to participate will thus depend on the net benefits (e.g. price premium less additional costs of production associated with the voluntary standard) that can be realized from participating as compared to those of not participating. If farmers participate, however, they are obliged to follow the requirements of the standard and will be punished for non-compliance. In extreme cases, farmers might even be excluded from the voluntary scheme and lose the net benefits it generates. In the case of regulatory constraints, participation is obligatory, and the choice not to participate is illegal.

From the economic theory of regulation (Sutinen and Kuperan (1999) offer a general discussion of the economic theory of regulation, which is also open to account for certain non-economic factors, and OECD (2004b) and Herzfeld and Jongeneel (2008) offer a discussion of environmental compliance), it can be summarized that the degree of compliance will be higher or increase (relative to an initial situation and/or relative to other standards and regulations):

1 the higher the net benefits of participation;
2 the lower the costs of compliance;
3 the less restrictive the requirements following from regulations or standards;
4 if the probability of detection increases (for example, due to a more intensive inspection and monitoring regime);
5 if the penalty is increased (for example, by increasing the marginal penalty or by increasing the fixed penalty); and
6 when farm support payments received are made conditional on the degree of compliance (additional enforcement mechanism).

Economic impacts: assessing competitiveness

Although often used in business and policy language, the notion of competitiveness surprisingly has no single definition or clearly established link to economic theory. In itself, competition is a complex economic phenomenon, which alongside the notion of classical price competition includes a multitude of other dimensions. The competitiveness concept has been used in a broad set of contexts and levels of aggregation (country, industry and firm levels) and is often defined relative to its use.

From a producer's perspective competitiveness could be described as the ability to supply goods and services in the location, form and place sought by buyers, at prices that are as good as or better than those of other potential suppliers, while earning at least the opportunity costs of the return on resources employed. Alternatively, competitiveness at the national sector level refers to the ability of a country to produce goods and services that meet the test of foreign or world market competition, while simultaneously maintaining and expanding domestic real income.

Regulations and standards might affect competitiveness in various ways. As regulations will often have a cost-increasing impact on production, they are likely to weaken the competitive position relative to those not faced with these regulations or those faced with less strict regulations. Voluntary standards are likely to be viable only if they in one way or another improve the competitive position of a product or production process. One could think of quality assurance schemes as creating a price premium in the market, which more than compensates for the additional costs that have to be made. Another possibility could be that a quality assurance game preserves or restores consumer trust in the concerned product, and as such creates market access. Although not creating a premium in the market, consumer trust and access can also be seen as benefits. Whereas in the case of voluntary standards the market "cares" (the impacts on competitiveness are balanced with costs), with regulatory standards this is likely to be different. Because regulations impose obligatory standards aimed not primarily at achieving a market premium but rather at other policy goals, they are more likely to negatively affect competitiveness.

Although one should be careful about drawing conclusions regarding competitiveness from simple cost-of-production comparisons, knowledge of the components of costs are useful for better understanding competitiveness. Moreover, cost components may be used to approximate shifts in supply curves (Sharples 1990). For example, suppose we are interested in evaluating the impact on EU competitiveness of a 25 percent increase in pesticide costs in cereal production (resulting from one of the requirements associated with cross-compliance). By knowing the ratio of pesticide costs to total variable costs and fixed costs of production and marketing of cereals, and assuming that there would be no significant change in the input mix, one can approximate how much the EU's supply curve would shift upwards (see Jongeneel *et al.* 2006 for further details). Combining cost changes with elasticity information or a trade model allows for the assessment of competitiveness impacts (Larson 2002; Jongeneel *et al.* 2006).

The EU's cross-compliance

Regulatory approach

A regulator's perspective

This section addresses how the EU's cross-compliance regime can be positioned within the theoretical regulatory enforcement framework presented in the previous section. The EU's obligatory cross-compliance package consists of two types of standards: the Statutory Management Requirements (SMRs) and the conditions for Good Agricultural and Environmental Practices (GAECs). They cover a broad range of fields, although the selection of standards has a certain degree of arbitrariness (based on political consensus). There are SMRs that address biodiversity (Birds and Habitat Directives), environment (Sewage Sludge Directive, Nitrate Directive, Groundwater Protection Directive), public, animal and plant health (including regulations of food safety, identification and registration of animals, restrictions on the use of plant protection products and growth promoters in the animal sector), animal welfare, notification of contagious diseases (foot and mouth, BSE, blue tongue) and good agricultural and environmental practice conditions (including soil erosion standards, soil organic matter content, maintenance and preservation of permanent pasture).

In a strict sense all SMRs and GAECs can be characterized as command measures. The EU's introduction of cross-compliance (beyond the already-legal sanctioning system) is part of an insistent strategy of compliance (see Figure 11.1, left panel). By using the direct payments associated with the CAP to create leverage, the European Commission increases the enforcement pressure and signals its insistence on compliance with the concerned regulations both to member states and farmers. The threat of a reduction of direct payments in the case of non-compliance could be added as an additional type of sanction (see Figure 11.1, right panel). Although not explicitly mentioned, the requirements regarding sampling (based on risk assessment, inspecting each year at least 1 percent of farmers receiving direct payments) and additional reporting and record keeping by farmers could be added as further instruments to enforce compliance or prove the farmer's state of compliance.[5]

By introducing the cross-compliance instrument, the Commission not only gave farmers eligible for direct payments a further incentive to comply with EU regulations (micro level), it also encouraged compliance (i.e. the proper implementation of EU legislation at the member-state level) at the macro level. Note that along with opening an infringement procedure, the EU can now withdraw payments if a member state is non-compliant.[6] Moreover, it could be argued that with cross-compliance the Commission introduces a harmonized EU-wide incentive system, which makes it less dependent on national legal sanctioning systems that vary across member states. Finally, the cross-compliance instruments can be argued to have an attractive proportionality property: big farms receiving relatively large direct payments, but also having large shares in production, in absolute terms face the threat of a relatively large reduction in payments received. By following a so-called whole-farm approach, some pressure is indirectly exerted on branches of production in mixed operations that are not in themselves eligible for direct payments.

Costs and benefits of (non-)compliance

The introduction of obligatory cross-compliance together with a system of (increased) partially decoupled payments which compensated for the announced intervention price declines for a number of products (Luxembourg Agreement 2003) implied a strengthening of the enforcement system. Before the arrival of cross-compliance, farmers already faced unconditional binding obligations (the pre-existing SMR legislation). However, cross-compliance added to this the single-farm payment to be made conditional on compliance with these regulations, thereby adding to the leverage exerted on farmers.[7] When violating the regulations, farmers could not only face legal punishment, but could also lose (part) of their single-farm payments. Moreover, a more strict monitoring and inspection regime was imposed (1 percent of the farms should be inspected each year, with sample selection based on risk profiles of farmers).

With cross-compliance, the effectiveness of the EU's sanctioning system and the probability of being detected are both increased relative to the initial situation. Because the direct payments became part of the sanctioning mechanism, they increased its leverage and thereby its effectiveness.[8] The theoretical framework developed so far should provide farmers with an incentive to improve their degree of compliance to the regulations. The increased compliance might induce further costs for the EU's agricultural sector, which in turn might affect competitiveness, which is the next issue to consider.

Competitiveness

With regard to competitiveness, it is important to realize that since most of the standards concerned (all SMRs and often also parts of the GAECs) already existed before EU (or national) legislation, in principle cross-compliance cannot be said to introduce additional costs (see also next section). The costs are primarily related to standards rather than to the enforcement mechanism. However, to the extent that cross-compliance improves the degree of compliance with standards, it may lead to increased costs, at least to the extent that these standards were previously ignored. From this perspective, more information about both the initial degree of compliance as well as the (additional) costs of compliance becomes crucial for a competitiveness impact assessment. An attempt to recover this information is provided in the next section. This information will also be used for a preliminary quantitative analysis.

Degrees and costs of compliance in the EU

The estimated degree of compliance for all SMRs, as well as for the GAECs for old and new member states, is summarized in Table 11.1. The new member states are those that joined the EU since 2004. Although they had to adopt the Acquis Communautaire (i.e. all EU regulations) they were temporarily exempted from cross-compliance. Initially, only non-compliance with the GAEC requirements could lead to payment sanctions, whereas from 2009 onwards non-compliance with the SMRs also can lead to a reduction in direct payments received.

Table 11.1 summarizes the information gathered in detailed country reports about cross-compliance with respect to a selection of EU member states (Farmer *et al.* 2006; Fox and Ramlal 2006; Jongeneel *et al.* 2006; Karaczun 2006; Meister 2006; Müssner and Leipprand 2006; Ortega and Simó 2006; Poux 2006, Roest 2006; Winsten 2006) as well as information from other sources (see Jongeneel *et al.* (2007) and Elbersen and Jongeneel (2008) for further details). Because of the uncertainties and problems with exact measurement, general classifications are reported in place of specific numbers. The following indicative legend was used.

Table 11.1 Cross-compliance in the EU: best estimates of degree and costs of compliance

Theme	EU legislation	Degree of compliance		Costs of compliance	
		Old member states (EU-15)	New member states (EU-12)	Cost to comply with standard	Additional compliance costs due to CC
Environment	Birds and Habitat Directives	high (management plans not yet in place in most areas)	n.a.	low	zero
	Groundwater Protection Directive	high–very high	n.a.	low	zero
	Sewage Sludge Directive	very high	n.a.	low	zero
	Nitrate Directive	low–very high	n.a.	low–significant	very low
Identification and Registration of Animals	Identification and Registration of bovine animals Regulation	moderate–high	low	low	very low
	Identification and Registration of ovine and caprine animals Regulation	low–high	low	low	very low
Public, animal and plant health	Plant protection products Directive	high	n.a.	low	very low
	Food Traceability and Food Safety Directive	n.a.	n.a.	n.a.	n.a.
	Hormones and beta-antagonists Directive	n.a.	n.a.	low	zero
	Notification of diseases Directives	high, no precise estimate available	n.a.	low	zero
Animal Welfare	Housing of calves Directive	expected to be high	n.a.	low–moderate	zero
	Housing of pigs Directive	expected to be high	n.a.	low–moderate	zero
Good Agricultural and Environmental Condition	Soil erosion control	high	high	low	low
	Maintain Soil Organic Matter	moderate–high	high	low	low
	Soil Structure	moderate–high	high	low	low
	Minimum Level of Maintenance	high	high	low	low

Source: own estimates based on information from Cross Compliance project (Jongeneel et al. 2007) and CCAT project (Elbersen and Jongeneel 2008).

1   Compliance is labeled as "very high" if the degree of compliance is esti-
    mated to be greater than 95 percent (more than 95 percent of the farmers are
    fully compliant).
2   Compliance is labeled as "high" if the degree of compliance is estimated to
    be in the interval 90–95 percent.
3   Compliance is labeled as "moderate" if the degree of compliance is esti-
    mated to be in the interval 80–90 percent.
4   Compliance is labeled as "low" if the degree of compliance is estimated to
    be in the interval 70–80 percent.

The general impression offered by Table 11.1 is that compliance is rather high
for the groundwater protection and sewage sludge requirements. With respect to
the Nitrate Directive and the identification and registration of bovine, ovine and
caprine animals, compliance rates are significantly below the level of full
compliance.

In a number of cases the rates of compliance were difficult to establish. In the
case of the Birds and Habitat Directives, for example, the relevant Natura 2000
areas are now properly selected for most countries, but most management plans
have yet to be defined and implemented, so this prevents detection of non-
compliance. A second example is the requirement to report diseases such as Foot
and Mouth, BSE, swine vesicular disease and blue tongue. Whether notification
is properly done can only be observed in cases of outbreaks. Although this complicated the empirical measurement of compliance, it is still estimated that compliance will be very high.

Animal welfare requirements only became part of cross-compliance in 2007,
which may explain why no systematic information about compliance was yet
available. In principle, however, this does not preclude the measurement of compliance, since the legislation already exists, independent of cross-compliance.

A lack of compliance could reflect different situations. For example, a farmer
who does not come close to meeting the requirements does not comply, but
neither does a farmer who only fails to comply in a minor respect. With the
current information available, it turned out to be infeasible to obtain a refined
understanding of the extent of compliance with all the standards.[9]

In two important cases, the Identification and Registration of Animals and the
Nitrate Directive, significant levels of non-compliance were found. There have
been infringement procedures with the Netherlands, Germany and Italy for the
Nitrate Directive case, which illustrates that compliance is not only an issue at
the level of the farmers, but also sometimes at the member-state level. As shown
in Table 11.1, there may be a significant degree of non-compliance with the
Identification and Registration of Animals Directive, with up to 30 percent non-
compliance at the member-state level. A large part of the lack of compliance
seems to be due to the loss of eartags, which are inherent to the EU's current
system. Loss rates of 4 percent are normal, but sometimes peak rates of about 20
percent also were recorded. Loss rates in general depend on farming practice and
systems. In general, non-compliance with the ovine and caprine animal identifi-

cation and registration requirements is much higher than for ovine animals (based on information from France, Germany and the Netherlands).

Rather than identifying the level of compliance in a certain year (as is estimated here for the year 2005), one would like to assess whether the introduction of cross-compliance is likely to lead to an improved rate of compliance. In principle this would require a comparison of the rate of improvement in compliance without cross-compliance introduced (reference rate of improvement or deterioration in compliance) with the rate of improvement in compliance as observed under cross-compliance.[10] In general it was not possible to conduct such an analysis, which would require a time-series of rates of compliance.[11] However, even without such an analysis, it is possible to combine rates of compliance with expected improvements in compliance. If the current rate of compliance is already very high, the rate of improvement due to cross-compliance is likely to be limited. On the other hand, where current rates of compliance are low, cross-compliance could potentially contribute to improvement in compliance.

Regarding the costs of compliance, a clear distinction has to be made between costs associated with cross-compliance, which mainly operates as an additional enforcement mechanism, and costs associated with the underlying SMRs. Because the SMRs all existed prior to legislation, cross-compliance in this domain has not led to new requirements on farmers. To the extent that the induced improvements in compliance will lead to additional costs, these costs are primarily related to those standards rather than to cross-compliance. With respect to the SMRs, cross-compliance may only lead to a marginal increase in costs due to some added administrative and record-keeping procedures (see Table 11.1, far right column). The field where cross-compliance could be linked to new requirements is the newly imposed GAEC conditions. Although this is newly introduced legislation, it is estimated that about 40 percent of the GAEC measures consist of pre-existing national legislation. In this respect, the costs that can be attributed to cross-compliance are likely to be low because the new legislation introduced in this field is also limited.[12]

To estimate the potential impacts increased compliance may have on the costs of production and competitiveness, two pieces of information are crucial: the change in the degree of compliance and the costs of compliance. Note that the change in compliance is not available from the previous sections (see Table 11.1), which only report levels of compliance, not changes in compliance. Because information on the policy-induced improvement of compliance is lacking currently only hypothetical scenarios can be analyzed, which evaluate the impact of an assumed increase of compliance. Table 11.1 indicates the specific maximum improvements (gap closure) that might be achieved under idealized conditions (assuming full compliance). The cost of an improvement in compliance is likely to be a function of the gap in compliance and dependent on the type of measure. In general, costs are estimated to be rather limited (a few hundred euros per farm), except in the case of the Nitrate Directive and animal welfare requirements, which are estimated to amount to several thousands of euros per farm (see Table 11.1 and Jongeneel *et al.* (2006) for more details).

The EU's key competitors: the United States, Canada and New Zealand

In this section and the next, a brief comparative analysis is made of the EU's cross-compliance regime with the regulatory frameworks and approaches of three of its key competitors: the United States, Canada and New Zealand.

The United States

The major US federal policies related to agriculture and issues of environmental quality, animal identification, food system health, and animal welfare that were reviewed differ significantly from the standards applied in the EU. US policies are usually less restrictive and rely more on voluntary than obligatory participation. The inventory of federal policies did not generally provide information on the specific constraints imposed by the regulations at the farm level. The specific regulations that apply to US farms of various types are highly dependent on the products and states in which the farming and marketing operations occur. One of the main results drawn from the federal policy inventory is the large variation of regulations and implementation levels across policy areas in the United States. For example, several comprehensive laws that address environmental quality have been in existence for decades. However, in recent years some of the environmental laws have only been implemented and enforced at the farm level. Good examples of this are the Concentrated Animal Feeding Operations (CAFO) regulations enacted in 2002 under the Clean Water Act of 1972.

Canada

Canadian farmers have to comply with numerous federal and provincial environmental regulations that govern agricultural production practices. Additionally, many programs do require that environmental standards be applied in primary agriculture in Canada. Farmers also participate in voluntary, industry-led standards that aim to mitigate the negative impacts of agricultural production practices on the environment. These voluntary standards are embodied in voluntary programs, often in partnership with governments, which may be certified by a government agency or otherwise. These Codes of Practice are usually initially described as voluntary, but are used as the basis for payments in government agri-environmental programs. This is the way in which environmental cross-compliance is applicable in Canada. Farmers can, if they so desire, receive a payment under a government program, if they comply with an environmental standard that is often embodied in a voluntary Code of Practice.

New Zealand

New Zealand's situation is special in that farming has played and still plays an influential role and is still part of the backbone of New Zealand's economy. The country has a specialized natural advantage for agriculture, in particular for pastoral farming, horticulture, forestry and seafood. About 85 percent of New Zealand's production is currently exported, with agricultural, horticultural and forestry products earning over 60 percent of its total export income. The large agricultural sector is operating with almost no government support.

Although farming is in general less intensive than in the EU, New Zealand faces significant soil erosion problems in some areas, resulting from the removal of natural forest cover for pastoral farming. The resulting sediment along with nutrient runoff and discharge of agricultural wastes have contributed to an increasing concern about water quality. With respect to the management of issues of eutrophication and nitrates, and reduced water clarity, New Zealand's current system, which mainly relies on consents, voluntary approaches and non-regulatory rules, does not seem to satisfactorily achieve full compliance of all dairy farmers with the environmental management requirements.

The main tool for managing natural resources and safeguarding the life-carrying capacity of air, water, soil and eco-systems is the 1991 Resource Management Act (RMA). This RMA involves several key concepts, including the development of comprehensive effects-based legislation, the desirability of intervening only where required and clearly justified, the requirement of clearly focused outcomes (targets) where intervention is justified, and the need to use appropriate policy instruments in order to achieve cost-effective solutions. The standards set by the RMA authorities can differ from region to region depending on differences in environmental issues and situations.

Comparative analysis

Table 11.2 provides an indicative overview of the five main areas of regulation (biodiversity, environment, health, animal identification registration and welfare, and good farming practices) covered by the EU's cross-compliance and how these are addressed by the EU's competitors.

As can be seen in Table 11.2, the main issue concerning biodiversity is the preservation of habitats and their protection from degradation. In the United States, the Endangered Species Act and some EPA programs aimed at addressing the detrimental effects of pesticides on listed wildlife species should be mentioned. In Canada, several biodiversity initiatives, often including economic incentives, aim to address such issues as agricultural practices (conservation tillage, rotational and delayed grazing, buffer zones around pastures) and habitat conversion and fragmentation. New Zealand's landscape has dramatically changed, with approximately 63 percent of its area being converted from native forest, wetland and tussock land to farm, exotic forests, settlements and roads. The subsequent decline in indigenous biodiversity has since the 1980s induced a government response, including the adoption of a biodiversity strategy in the 1990s. However, so far the policies seem to be insufficient to turn the tide.

In preserving the environment as a whole, the preservation of water quality is central. The US Clean Water Act, a law originally focused on point sources of

Table 11.2 Main problem areas addressed with regulation

Theme	US	Canada	New Zealand	EU
Biodiversity	No specifics	Protection of habitats	Decline in indigenous biodiversity; habitat preservation	Protection and preservation of habitats
Environment	Water quality; environmental pressure from Concentrated Animal Feeding Operations (CAFO)	Pesticide use, water (safe drinking wells, increasing importance of nitrate contamination, and air quality (odor)	Degrading water quality; increasing importance of nitrate contamination	Nitrate, heavy metals, water quality
Health	Food safety	Food safety; hormone growth promoter products use; animal disease surveillance	Food safety; hormone growth promoter products use	Food safety; hormone growth promoter products use; registration and traceability of animals; contagious animal diseases; use of plant protection products
Animal identification, registration and welfare	Voluntary scheme is transformed in mandatory one; long-distance transportation	Industry-led national scheme for cattle and bison	No public system	Identification and registration of bovine, ovine and caprine animals
		Minimum housing requirements; intensive livestock farming practices; humane transportation and slaughter	Minimum requirements, dry sow stall	Minimum space, and minimum requirements regarding other animal "needs"
Good agricultural and environmental practice	Mainly erosion	Erosion and soil quality (has improved already)	Erosion and sustainable land use (vegetation clearance and soil disturbance)	Erosion, organic matter content, soil structure

pollution, was expanded to non-point pollution sources, with agriculture being a prime case. However, specific rules governing large-scale intensive farm operations were not addressed until 2002. In Canada environmental concerns are addressed through a combination of policy measures at several levels of government: federal and provincial legislation and regulation; municipal and zoning permit processes; common law litigation and liability with respect to nuisance, public nuisance and riparian rights; national and provincial voluntary stewardship initiatives such as Codes of Practices, Environmental Farm Plans and Best Management Practices; and economic instruments such as payments. In New Zealand discharges to water and the management of water quality is usually delegated to Regional Councils, whereas the RMA empowers local authorities to control land use in order to achieve a number of sustainable management objectives (restricting expansion of potentially damaging activities to vulnerable land and amenity concerns such as dust and odor). Nitrate contamination of groundwater is a key issue in the EU and is of growing importance in Canada and New Zealand. For example, in Canada the water quality guideline for nitrate–nitrogen concentration is ten milligrams per liter. A survey study showed that in several provinces a significant number of wells (10 percent or more) exceed this concentration (Fox and Ramlal 2006). It is likely that more restrictive application requirements will follow in the future.

Food safety is a primary goal of public health programmes. The food safety regulation includes measures about the use of hormone growth promoters at the farm level. This is a particular issue for the EU, but it also indirectly affects the EU's trading partners (e.g. the beef hormone dispute between the EU and the United States). Another key issue is the monitoring and surveillance of contagious animal diseases, where New Zealand has a special position since it is still free from some major animal diseases (partly related to its relatively isolated location).

For the EU's competitors, animal identification and registration and animal welfare issues are currently mainly consumer or market-driven. In the United States long-distance transportation receives specific attention.[13]

The main subject covered by regulations on good farming practices is erosion, although the scope in the EU is somewhat broader. The majority of government interventions with respect to land management in US agriculture take the form of voluntary programs that use technical assistance and cost-sharing to establish best management practices. There are a host of such programs, mainly administered by the USDA, the five most important being the Conservation Reserve Program, the Environmental Quality Incentives Program, the Wetland Reserve Program, the Conservation Security Program and the Grassland Reserve Program.

In Canada each province has its own soil conservation programs and regulations. In the east these programs mainly deal with drainage, soil fertility and reforestation; in the west the focus is more on land rehabilitation, erosion control, drainage, irrigation and tillage. Just as in the United States, many of these voluntary programs include provisions for technical and financial assistance to farmers for implementing appropriate management practices as well as for purchasing equipment or building erosion structures. Soil health also receives attention (e.g. National Soil Conservation Program, established in 1989).

In New Zealand the Regional Councils have regulatory power and have specified different rules that vary with regional circumstances. Many operate extension services on resource management issues and may provide financial assistance for farm erosion-prevention schemes. Most of the management of erosion-prone land is through control of vegetation clearance and soil disturbance. In the Eastern Region rather strict requirements are formulated, which are expected to raise the cost of farming.

Varying regulatory approaches

As shown in the previous section, the regulations in the United States, Canada and New Zealand differ substantially from those in the EU, although most regulations address the same issues. Table 11.3 summarizes the primary differences in regulatory approaches and associated choice of instrument. Whereas the EU is tending toward unification in legislation, particularly in terms of minimum requirements, the structure of legislative responsibilities in other countries allows for more differentiation over the national territory. Although this might reduce general transparency, it has the potential advantage of better addressing local issues.

Referring back to the theoretical framework about enforcement of regulations (discussed in the second section), it is clear that the United States, Canada and New Zealand follow different approaches from the EU. In general these three countries operate more on the lower layers of the pyramids of sanctions and enforcement strategies. Elements such as incentives (e.g. voluntary cross-compliance in Canada), education, advice and technical assistance (e.g. erosion-combating schemes in Canada and New Zealand) as well as persuasion play a relatively important role. In terms of the pyramid of enforcement strategies, it can be argued that the EU's competitors generally follow a persuasive regulatory approach, strongly appealing to voluntary actions. In particular, New Zealand's Resource Management Act appears to be a good example of responsive, well-targeted and proportional regulation contributing to cost-effective solutions.

A responsive regulatory approach that starts by facilitating and stimulating voluntary participation with standards might end by transforming private standards into obligatory regulations that all must comply with. For example, in regulating modern agriculture's nitrate problems, light-touch approaches may ultimately not be sufficient to address the problems. There further increases in enforcement strategies and sanctioning instruments (i.e. climbing the pyramids) could be expected in the future for the EU's competitors, whereas the EU itself may have to fall back to stricter standards. So far the issue of setting appropriate standards has not been discussed. The setting of standards needs a good evaluation of the intended benefits and the degree to which these are realized. Such an assessment, although very relevant, is beyond the scope of this chapter, and generally not easy (e.g. Baldwin and Cave 1999: 118–124).[14]

Table 11.3 Regulatory policy approaches chosen

Policy instrument	US	Canada	New Zealand	EU
Direct regulation	In particular applied for regulation food safety, plant protection products	In particular applied for regulation food safety, plant protection products	In particular applied for regulation food safety, plant protection products	Dominant kind or regulation applied
Cross-compliance	Compliance only required for cost-sharing assistance with best management practices	Farmers can receive payments if they comply with standards embodied in a voluntary code of practice	Instrument not used	Obligatory cross-compliance since Luxembourg agreement (2003) covering biodiversity, environment, health and animal welfare
Taxes and subsidies	Financial incentives linked to voluntary conservation programs	Financial incentives linked to specific good agricultural practices	Some financial assistance for farm erosion schemes	Selectively used to encourage collection of used transmission oil, a.o.; implicit subsidization of farm assistance
Technical assistance	Plays an important role, in particular regarding environment and good farming practices	Plays an important role, in particular regarding environment and good farming practices	Plays an important role, in particular regarding environment and good farming practices	Farm advisory service complementary to cross-compliance, will be in place in 2007
Contracts and voluntary schemes	Play an important role, in particular regarding environment, animal welfare, registration of animals	Play an important role, in particular regarding environment, animal welfare, registration of animals	Play an important role, in particular regarding environment, animal welfare, registration of animals	No use of voluntary schemes for achieving minimum standards as in the CC package, instrument only used for achieving "services" going beyond minimum standards

Concluding remarks

Regarding the responsive theory of regulation enforcement and the economic theory of compliance, the EU arguably follows a relatively heavy regulatory regime, whereas its main competitors rely more on light-touch approaches, with strong reliance on persuasion, advice, education, voluntary participation and positive incentives (voluntary cross-compliance, technical assistance). With the introduction of cross-compliance, the EU introduced an additional enforcement mechanism, signaling the Commission's insistence on farming practices and land use that preserve the environment, take care of biodiversity, save the physical capital of the soil, ensure food safety, deal in a proper way with health aspects of animals and plants, and ensure that commercial interests are balanced with animal welfare considerations.

Cross-compliance introduced an added enforcement incentive, harmonized over EU member nations, aimed at improving sustainability both at the member-nation and farm levels. As such, it goes beyond the national legal sanctioning systems, which are still intact. The added enforcement mechanism might reduce the variation in application and implementation associated with the national approaches and as such make achieved compliance levels less dependent on national discretion and variations in monitoring and inspection systems over member states (including variation in macro-compliance). According to the economic theory of compliance this additional incentive structure (threat to lose direct payments in case of non-compliance and the increased probability of being detected) should improve the sector's compliance with regulations. Anecdotal empirical information confirmed this, although it appeared impossible with the currently accessible and available data to quantitatively assess the increases in compliance.

Compliance with regulations in the EU was estimated to be generally high. This holds for the SMRs as well as for the GAECs, with the two main exceptions being the Nitrate Directive and the Identification and Registration of Animals requirements. Compliance with the Identification and Registration requirements was hampered by a significant loss of eartags, which need replacement over time. The experience with electronic systems outside the EU (e.g. New Zealand) suggests that cheaper and more robust identification systems are available.

Except for the marginal costs associated with additional record keeping and administrative procedures associated with the SMRs and the additional costs resulting from newly introduced GAECs, cross-compliance has no (additional) costs. Since the SMRs that are part of cross-compliance are all pre-existing legislation, the costs associated with compliance should be primarily attributed to this legislation (the standards) and not to cross-compliance. As such, the benefits of cross-compliance (improved compliance) are likely to easily outweigh its costs. A counter-argument to this claim could be that the increased monitoring and inspection costs have to be taken into consideration. The (additional) costs of cross-compliance associated with the GAECs are found to be rather low. Ordinary costs of compliance with the SMR standards can be significant. In particular, the costs associated with the Nitrate Directive and Animal Welfare requirements could have serious impacts.

Regarding the EU's key competitors, the comparative analysis covering all the themes addressed in the SMRs and GAECs showed that in general the intensity of regulation is lower in these countries than in the EU. Lower regulation intensity, however, does not necessarily imply a higher level of environmental degradation, biodiversity loss or harm to animal welfare. All three non-EU countries have a similar approach toward measures to control the environment, which relies to a relatively large extent on voluntary action. This action is facilitated and encouraged by financial incentive and assistance schemes. The financial incentives include (voluntary) cross-compliance mechanisms (e.g. Canada, where participating in voluntary schemes is sometimes a side condition for receiving specific direct payments).

This chapter focused more on the impact that regulation has on costs and competitiveness rather than on its benefits. A benefits assessment was clearly beyond the scope of this chapter. However, for a proper and integrated evaluation of regulatory systems and regulatory requirements, an evaluation of the achieved benefits is required. This will then also introduce issues such as the appropriate setting of standards (i.e. in such a way that the policy objectives aimed at with the various regulations can feasibly be realized). There are some signals both from outside and inside the EU that improvements can and need to be made here (e.g. OECD 2004a; ECA 2008). Further research in this direction is needed.

Notes

1 This chapter is one result of the Cross-Compliance 6th Framework Project.
2 The authors gratefully acknowledge the contributions made by various partners of the Cross-Compliance 6th Framework Project (see the reference list for the specific country reports (Deliverable 5) produced within this project, from which material is synthesized (see website http://leidh040s/cross-compliance)). For a synthesis report see Jongeneel *et al.* (2008).
3 One might argue that the provision of positive financial incentives to obey the law provides a wrong signal (by eroding internal intrinsic motivation) to the regulated. However, given that economic actors generally behave selfishly and opportunistically, automatic full compliance cannot be taken for granted. As such, complementary financial incentives, whether structured as fines or subsidies, can be justified as rational.
4 The theory of regulation further elaborates on the linkages between enforcement strategies and regulatory policy design (i.e. the relationships between the pyramids), an issue that will not be further discussed here since the focus is not primarily on the specific content and specification of individual regulations. However, for a more elaborate analysis of compliance this issue deserves additional attention (e.g. OECD 2004b). Note that regulations need not only to be enforced, but also to be enforceable.
5 Note that this chapter does not try to explain the introduction of the cross-compliance measure based on the theory of regulation, but rather to position it within a broader context of possibilities. With regard to the introduction of cross-compliance, it is recognized that political motives such as legitimizing the introduced de-coupled direct payments (payments "for nothing") by linking them to "proper" and responsible farmer behavior, as well as avoiding land abandonment, also played a role (e.g. IEEP 2006).

6 Formally there is a distinction between regulation following from an EU Regulation, which is directly applicable in all member states and therefore needs no implementation in national law, and regulation following from EU Directives, which relies on implementation in national law. However, in the case of EU Regulations the Commission depends on member states for private enforcement. EU Directives leave more room for member-state influence and adaptation to specific situations, since they are generally binding with respect to the end to be achieved but less so as regards the means to achieve this.

7 Some might argue that the EU is using a degenerate form of cross-compliance and by making legal requirements the subject of cross-compliance creates a redundancy. However, this presupposes that the legal sanction system is adequate and proper in inducing a full compliance with the regulations and that the monitoring and inspection intensity remains the same. With cross-compliance a systematic inspection regime is usually imposed, whereas under normal legal requirements this is not always the case. Moreover, in practice the legal sanction systems are often not sufficient to banish all non-compliance behavior. So cross-compliance can also be relevant for already-existing binding statutory management requirements. From the first evidence it becomes clear that the actual fines imposed on farmers have still been rather limited (see Brand and Jongeneel 2008).

8 This underscores the need, when assessing the impacts of regulatory policies, to put them in a proper context and not in isolation. Market and price support policies, modulation of direct payments, cross-compliance and regulations interact.

9 More detailed information is available within government circles but was not (yet) accessible for this research. A survey of Dutch farmers gave the impression that in most cases the non-compliance was not a serious issue. This means that when there is no full compliance often it is only a limited number of issues with which the farmer is not complying (see remark about eartag loss below).

10 One should consider that without the introduction of cross-compliance, the degree of compliance might also improve over time. One reason why the degree of compliance might improve over time is because satisfying the requirements is likely to be at least partly linked with (replacement) investments, i.e. the ongoing upgrading of farm technology and equipment.

11 In the case of the Netherlands, where a detailed survey was completed, it was found that for Dutch dairy farmers degrees of compliance have been improved, in particular with respect to the Identification and Registration of Animals. Also anecdotal evidence from Germany suggests that degrees of compliance have been improved.

12 This is even more so because member states are not obliged to come up with a regulatory measure for each possible entry, but have a certain freedom in the exact specification of measures.

13 The EU also has a regulation regarding long-distance transport of live animals, but this is not part of the cross-compliance package.

14 In their 2008 evaluation the European Court of Auditors criticized the EU's cross-compliance policy because of its weakness with respect to the policy aims and the assessment of needs (ECA 2008).

References

Ayres, I. and Braithwaite, J. (1992) *Responsive Regulation: Transcending the Regulation Debate*, Oxford: Oxford University Press.

Baldwin, R. and Cave, M. (1999) *Understanding Regulation: Theory, Strategy and Practice*, Oxford: Oxford University Press.

Brand, H. and Jongeneel, R. (2008) "Cross compliance," in H. Silvis, A. Oskam and G. Meester (eds.) *EU-beleid voor landbouw, voedsel en groen; Van politiek naar praktijk*, Wageningen: Wageningen Academic Publishers, pp. 157–171.

ECA (2008) "Is cross compliance an effective policy?" Special Report No 8/2008 (pursuant to Article 248(4), second subparagraph, EC) Luxembourg, European Court of Auditors.

Elbersen, B.S. and Jongeneel, R. (2008) "Compliance and costs of compliance: a procedure to obtain estimates at a disaggregated level," unpublished note presented at CCAT research meeting, October 9, 2008, Alterra, Wageningen.

Farmer, M., Bartley, J. and Swales, V. (2006) "Deliverable 5: mandatory standards in 7 EU countries and 3 non-EU countries," Country Report, London, United Kingdom: IEEP.

Farmer, M., Swales, V., Jongeneel, R., Karaczun, Z., Müssner, R., Leipprand, A., Schlegel, S., Poux, X., Ramain, B., de Roest, K., Varela Ortega, C. and Simó, A. (2007) "Exploring the synergies between cross compliance and certification schemes" (LEI). Report 6.07.20. The Hague.

Fox, G. and Ramlal, E. (2006) "Deliverable 5: mandatory standards in 7 EU countries and 3 non-EU countries," Country Report, Guelph, Canada: University of Guelph, Department of Food, Agricultural and Resource Economics.

Herzfeld, T. and Jongeneel, R. (2008) "Economics of compliance: a review of theories and application to agriculture," paper presented at IAMO Forum Conference, IAMO, Halle an der Saale, 2008.

Hutter, B.M. (1997) *Compliance: Regulation and Environment*, Oxford: Oxford University Press.

IEEP (2006) Background paper for the Cross-Compliance Seminar held in Paris, July 3, 2006, London, IEEP.

Jongeneel, R. (2006) "Deliverable 5: mandatory standards in 7 EU countries and 3 non-EU countries," Country Report, Netherlands: The Hague, Agricultural Economics Institute.

Jongeneel, R., Bezlepkina, I. and Farmer, M. (eds.) (2008) "Cross compliance," FINAL REPORT, (LEI) Project no. SSPE-CT-2005-006489. The Hague.

Jongeneel, R., Brouwer, F., Farmer, M., Müssner, R., de Roest, K., Poux, G.F.X., Meister, A., Karaczun, Z., Winsten, J. and Ortéga, C.V. (2007) "Compliance with mandatory standards in agriculture; a comparative approach of the EU vis-à-vis the United States, Canada and New Zealand" (LEI), Rapport 6.07.21, Den Haag.

Jongeneel, R., Demont, M. and Mathijs, E. (2006) "Developing a framework to analyze the relationship between compliance to standards and the external competitiveness of European agriculture," paper presented at the USDA and AIEA2 International Meeting, "Competitiveness in Agriculture and the Food Industry: US and EU Perspectives," June, 15-16, 2006, Bologna, Italy.

Karaczun, Z.M. (2006) "Deliverable 5: mandatory standards in 7 EU countries and 3 non-EU countries," Country Report, Warsaw, Poland: University of Warsaw, Department of Environmental Protection SGGW.

Larson, B.A. (2002) "European Union environmental policies and imports of agricultural products from the United States," paper presented at the 2002 AAEA Summer Meetings, Long Beach, CA (working draft).

Meister, A.D. (2006) "Deliverable 5: mandatory standards in 7 EU countries and 3 non-EU countries," Country Report, Massey, New Zealand: Massey University, Department of Applied and International Economics.

Müssner, R. and Leipprand, A. (2006) "Deliverable 5: mandatory standards in 7 EU countries and 3 non-EU countries," Country Report, Berlin, Germany: Ecologic.

OECD (2004a) *Agriculture and the Environment: Lessons Learned from a Decade of OECD Work*, Paris: OECD.

198   *R. Jongeneel and F. Brouwer*

OECD (2004b) *Economic Aspects of Environmental Compliance Assurance*, Paris, OECD (Proceedings from the OECD Global Forum on Sustainable Development, December 2-3, 2004, Paris, France), OECD Headquarters.

OECD (forthcoming) *Environmental Cross Compliance: Concept, Design and Implementation*, Paris: OECD.

Ortéga, C.V. and Simó, A. (2006) "Deliverable 5: mandatory standards in 7 EU countries and 3 non-EU countries," Country Report, Madrid, Spain: Departamento de Econmía y Ciencias Sociales Agrarias, Universidad Politécnica de Madrid.

Poux, X. (2006) "Deliverable 5: mandatory standards in 7 EU countries and 3 non-EU countries," Country Report, Paris, France: Application des Sciences de l'Actions.

Roest, K. de (2006) "Deliverable 5: mandatory standards in 7 EU countries and 3 non-EU countries," Country Report, Italy: Centro Richerche Produzioni Animali, Reggio Emilia.

Roest, K. de, Corradini, E. and Brouwer, F. (2006a) "Deliverable D7: framework for analysis of the cost of compliance," Centro Richerche Produzioni Animali, Reggio Emilia.

Sharples, J.A. (1990) "Costs of Production and Productivity in Analyzing Trade and Competitiveness," *American Journal of Agricultural Economics*, 72(5): 1278–1282.

Sutinen, J.G. and Kuperan, K. (1999) "A Socio-economic Theory of Regulatory Compliance," *International Journal of Social Economics*, 26 (1/2/3): 174–194.

Winsten, J.R. (2006) "Deliverable 5: mandatory standards in 7 EU countries and 3 non-EU countries," Country Report, Burlington, Vermont, United States: Winrock University of Vermont.

12 Public preferences for protecting working landscapes

Kathleen P. Bell

Introduction

Throughout the world, in parallel discussions, communities are reflecting on the relative value of different characteristics of landscapes and pondering alternative future landscapes. Central to these discussions is recognizing various externalities related to land use and management and designing policies to internalize these forces. Various programs designed to protect working landscapes, such as subsidies, direct payments, land acquisition and property tax relief, are justified as a means to compensate private, working landowners for public services they provide but are not compensated for by the market, such as biodiversity, habitat and scenic views. In addition to these programs focused on positive externalities, a suite of policies exists to diminish the negative externalities of working lands, such as odors and pollution. This latter set of programs encourages private, "working" landowners to recognize the full costs of their actions. An improved comprehension of public preferences for protecting working landscapes is arguably central to understanding and managing these external effects.

This chapter begins with a brief transatlantic comparison of agri-environmental programs in the European Union and the United States. The objective of this comparison is to identify similarities and distinctions as well as to consider potential drivers of variation in these programs. The remainder of the chapter summarizes an empirical case study of public preferences for protecting working landscapes using data from Maine, giving emphasis to variation in preferences on the local scale. This study contrasts recent voting results on two ballot initiatives related to landscape protection in Maine. A set of reduced-form discrete-choice models of the voting outcomes is estimated using community-scale data, where the proportion of voter support for an initiative is explained as a function of demographic, landscape, location, employment and political characteristics.

Transatlantic comparison

Discussion of preferences for protecting working landscapes is complicated somewhat by uncertain terminology. For example, it is not evident what is meant by the term "working." For whom (residents or tourists) are the lands working, and how (commodity production or recreation) are they working? In land use planning and land economics literature, working lands are often synonymous with lands used for productive resource-extraction activities. While this definition of working lands is adopted in this analysis, we recognize the potential for different interpretations of this term. An exhaustive review of policies and programs designed to protect working lands in the United States and the European Union is beyond the scope of this chapter. Because agri-environmental programs are a prominent means by which governments strive to protect working landscapes, a comparison of these programs is informative.

Cooper *et al.* (2005) offer an excellent overview of agri-environmental programs in the European Union and the United States. Several key findings emerge from this overview. First, increasing emphasis is being given to non-agricultural commodity services provided by agricultural and forest lands in both the European Union and United States. This concomitantly includes recognition of positive and negative externalities associated with agricultural production. Both the European Union and the United States have modified requirements for traditional, direct producer-support programs to address some of these external effects. In addition, increased funding is being devoted to the protection of working lands in both the European Union and the United States, and much of this funding is dedicated to incentive-based policies.

Second, policy objectives to lessen the negative environmental impacts of agricultural production differ markedly in the European Union and United States. The United States programs tend to center on reducing soil erosion and nutrient runoff and have promoted retirement of active land. In contrast, the European Union programs have much broader ecological targets, strive to prevent land abandonment, and view agriculture as an important component of natural environments.

Third, the European Union promotes protection of rural landscape attributes in its agri-environmental policies. United States agricultural policy has no parallel program. European Union programs more directly acknowledge the broad spectrum of services provided by working lands. A strong link between rural economic development and agri-environmental objectives is reflected in the 2003 reforms of the European Union's Common Agricultural Policy.

Finally, considerable variation exists within regions of the United States and Europe in terms of implementation and participation in these programs. From an economics perspective, much of this variation makes sense, as the participation of entities in such programs varies with the costs of participation, including the opportunity costs of changing production practices, and the demands for non-commodity services, such as open space and environmental quality.

The Council of Europe's 2000 European Landscape Convention offers further evidence of the broader recognition of working lands and the services they provide in European countries relative to the national and state policies of the United States. Text from the preamble underscores these differences:

> The landscape has an important public interest role in the cultural, ecological, environmental and social fields, and constitutes a resource favourable to eco-

nomic activity and whose protection, management and planning can contribute to job creation; contributes to the formation of local cultures and is a basic component of the European natural and cultural heritage, contributing to human well-being and consolidation of the European identity; is an important part of the quality of life for people everywhere: in urban areas and in the countryside, in degraded areas as well as in areas of high quality, in areas recognised as being of outstanding beauty as well as everyday areas; is a key element of individual and social well-being and its protection, management and planning entail rights and responsibilities for everyone (Council of Europe 2000).

(Preamble to the European Landscape Convention, Florence, October 20, 2000; www.coe.int/t/e/Cultural_Cooperation/Environment/Landscape)

The assumption of a complementary relationship between economic growth and landscape protection and the deep recognition of the public aspects of landscape services are notable. An intriguing report prepared for the Council of Europe (Depoorter 2003) compares landscape policies in its member states. Although the report reveals differences within European countries, it also speaks to commonalities among these countries and the appreciation of and infrastructure for landscape protection. Additional research examines the authenticity of these landscape protection and multifunctionality interests, noting the challenges of designing policies to achieve such goals, uncertainties regarding restructuring of the agricultural sector, and concerns over protectionism (Potter and Burney 2002; Potter and Lobley 1998).

As noted previously, variations in programs and public preferences for the services provided by working lands are expected within regions of the United States and Europe. Potential drivers of variation include attributes of an area's landscape as well as its dependence on resource-extraction activities and public preferences for non-commodity landscape services. Baylis *et al.* (2006) and Brouwer and Godeschalk (2004) examine European Union member-state variation related to agri-environmental programs. Both studies analyze the motivations for past policies and speak to future trends, highlighting differences across member states. Baylis *et al.* (2006) note that the catalyst for environmental reforms arises from northern member states (Denmark, Germany, the Netherlands, the UK and northern Italy), whereas, southern member states (France, Spain, Portugal, southern Italy and the Alpine countries) are driven by concerns over rural depopulation and land abandonment. Brouwer and Godeschalk (2004) contrast policies to pursue nature and biodiversity objectives in the Netherlands, Denmark, Germany and England. They find a common goal of protecting water quality through agri-environmental programs in Denmark and Germany, agri-environmental programs reflecting broad goals related to nature and landscape in the Netherlands, and agri-environmental programs integrated with Pillars 1 and 2 of the Common Agricultural Policy in England.

Results from a poll of European Union residents (European Commission 2007) reflect the variation in demand for agri-environmental services across member-state populations. Interestingly, the Eurobarometer survey conducted in 2006 demonstrates widespread acknowledgment that agriculture and rural areas are key to the European Union's future (88 percent) and reductions in direct payments to farmers that fail to respect environmental standards are justified (83 percent). Thirty-three percent ranked promoting respect for the environment as a priority for agricultural policy, ranking fourth in priorities after healthy and safe food products (41 percent), fair standard of living for farmers (37 percent), and reasonable food prices for consumers (35 percent). Opinions vary across respondents from different member states, with some of this variation correlated with educational attainment, age and population density of residence. Overall, respondents from the original member states gave higher rankings to environmental and animal welfare priorities than did respondents from new member states.

Hellerstein *et al.* (2002) offer a thoughtful summary of farmland protection programs in the United States, comparing state programs by type and amenities intended to be provided. Their careful review of programs reveals regional variation in farmland protection programs. For example, northeastern, Great Lakes and Pacific northwest states strive to maintain all classes of amenities whereas states of other regions focus on a smaller set of amenities associated with maintaining productive farm lands. The researchers suggest that variation in state programs is related to variations in stocks of agricultural land as well as other conservation lands, such as forest lands and parks. Hellerstein *et al.* (2002) also provide a review of stated-preference studies examining public preferences for amenities provided by these programs. Johansson (2006) focuses on federal working-land conservation programs, noting the potential value of flexible, incentive-based programs in the United States, such as the Environmental Quality Incentives Program and the Conservation Security Program, to complement conventional approaches, such as land retirement. Daniels (2001) provides an overview of state and local efforts targeting working lands in the United States. His research emphasizes the tendency of these efforts to rely on voluntary programs and novel public–private partnerships and stresses the different objectives of federal (maintenance of soil and water quality) and local (prevention of development) efforts.

Programs designed to maintain working lands are becoming more common throughout the world. In turn, there is considerable variation across the communities of the globe in terms of what they perceive as working landscapes and how they value the services generated from these lands. Further research on the potential drivers of this variation may inform the development of future policies. While some research has compared public preferences within member states of the European Union and individual states of the United States, little transatlantic comparative work of public preferences has been completed. Future research in this area may offer valuable insights.

Case study – Maine, United States

The previous discussion emphasized the variation in programs and policies aimed to protect working landscape features in the United States and the

European Union as well as within individual states of the United States and member states of the European Union. This empirical analysis adopts a more local perspective, examining variation in support for working-lands protection programs throughout communities in Maine, a rural, forested state located in the New England region that has a large base of working lands.

This case study compares recent voting on two referenda related to landscape protection:

1   a constitutional amendment to protect working waterfront lands via current-use property taxation and
2   a bond measure to support broader public land acquisition and land conservation, including the protection of working lands.

The empirical analysis examines variation in support for these initiatives across 495 communities in Maine. A set of reduced-form discrete-choice models of voting outcomes is estimated, where the proportion of supporting votes by community is explained as a function of numerous community attributes that are intended to capture the variation in the perceived net benefits of the land protection programs.

Relevant literature

Building on the approaches adopted by similar studies (e.g. Deacon and Shapiro 1975; Kline and Wichelns 1994; Rothstein 1994; Kahn and Matsusaka 1997; Kotchen and Powers 2006; Schlapfer and Hanley 2006), this chapter combines voting data with demographic, economic, political and environmental data to explore public support for land protection programs. Early work by Deacon and Shapiro (1975) continues to provide the economic foundation of studies of aggregate voting behavior and offers the basic economic intuition of this case study. In short, voting represents perceptions of net returns of these public programs, where greater support corresponds with greater net returns.

In completing their analysis of two California referenda that respectively authorized a coastal zone conservation program and a rapid transit program (BART), Deacon and Shapiro (1975) employ city-level data to explain voting outcomes as a function of demographic characteristics, regional economic characteristics and community attributes. Voter participation and response are both modeled explicitly. Several explanatory variables are used to capture variation in tastes and preferences. They find that voters with higher levels of education, income and more liberal political beliefs were more likely to support coastal zone conservation and rapid transit (BART). Employment in industries presumed to be negatively impacted by the public programs is used to approximate income and employment effects. Lower levels of support for coastal conservation are found in areas with higher employment of laborers. Similarly, lower levels of support for rapid transit are found in areas with higher employment levels in the transport sector. Community attributes, such as location, area and population density, are employed to distinguish access to or level of the collective good provided by the two programs. Higher support for the coastal conservation program is found in southern areas with lower initial levels of environmental quality. Higher support for the rapid transit program is found in larger, more densely populated areas, where transit could be more efficient. The trade-offs addressed in their analysis of the coastal conservation program closely relate to the working lands protection programs, stressing the potential variation in net benefits from public landscape conservation programs across individuals and communities.

Kahn and Matsusaka (1997) explore voter support for 16 environmental ballot propositions in California between 1970 and 1994. Employing county-scale data, these authors stress the importance of controlling for price and income effects when analyzing voting data related to public programs. A subset of the propositions examined in their research relates to land management and includes measures addressing parks, coastal conservation and forest preservation. They find lower levels of support for environmental initiatives in counties with employment in industries affected by the proposed programs. In contrast, higher levels of support for these same initiatives are found in more urban counties. Their empirical results raise questions about the extent to which counties with the highest per capita incomes support programs devoted to maintaining public spaces such as parks, noting the possibility of private substitution and disapproval of public provision of these services.

Kline and Armstrong (2001) examine voter support for an Oregon ballot initiative designed to promote sustainable forestry practices and conserve forest ecosystems. Restrictions on clearcut logging and herbicide and pesticide use are linked with the championed sustainable forestry practices. He employs county-level data to examine variation in voter support for this referendum and its associated forest management policies. The results are generally consistent with the previous findings of Deacon and Shapiro (1975) and Kahn and Matsusaka (1997), with higher support in areas with higher population densities, income and educational attainment, and lower support in areas with higher forest employment. This research is partially motivated as an investigation of changing values related to forestlands and addresses the role of in-migration in diversifying attitudes toward forest management as well as the demand for services provided by forestlands. Similar trends are surfacing in Maine, reminding land managers of the dynamic nature of markets and public preferences for services from forestlands. An important theme raised by this research is how demands for services from working lands evolve over time. These dynamics have strong implications for the design of public programs to protect working lands. In short, flexible programs may be more suitable.

Studies addressing voting responses to open space and farmland protection programs offer additional insights into public preferences for working landscapes. Kline and Wichelns (1994) examine voting responses to statewide farmland preservation referenda in Pennsylvania and Rhode Island. Using county-level data, the authors explain support for purchasable development-rights programs as a function of land use pattern (percent of county land in farmland; change in farmland acreage over last five years), agricultural profitability (reported change in market value of agricultural land over last five years), and growth pressures (percentage change in population over last ten years; percentage change in housing values). A reduced-form model estimated by ordinary least squares is utilized to examine voting responses. They determine that support for such programs is greater in areas with higher rates of population growth and housing value appreciation. Loss of farmland acreage drives support for such programs in Rhode Island but not in Pennsylvania. These results suggest voters living in higher growth areas with less farmland may be willing to pay more to protect farmland at the margin, *ceteris paribus*.

Schlapfer and Hanley (2003) extend the work of Kline and Wichelns (1994), giving emphasis to the potential importance of landscape characteristics in influencing voter response. Their research examines voter response to a referendum to increase public funding for local landscape amenities in Zurich, Switzerland. They find no support for a decreasing marginal utility effect related to open space, as municipalities with higher amounts of open space revealed higher levels of support for the increased funding. Municipalities with higher levels of landscape amenities on non-forest lands and historical heritage townscapes similarly expressed higher support. An insignificant correlation was found between voter support and the percentage change (reduction) in the level of these amenities over a 12-year period.

Kotchen and Powers (2006) employ a unique data set based on Trust for Public Land summaries of votes throughout the United States related to open-space conservation.[1] They conduct two types of empirical analysis: a national analysis, including state, county and local votes, and a local analysis of votes in New Jersey and Massachusetts. Unlike this chapter, which considers variation across communities in response to a single vote, Kotchen and Powers (2006) make use of data obtained from multiple votes, with voters in different areas voting on different programs. This national-scale pooled analysis reveals a preference for open-space protection programs funded by bonds rather than taxes and designed to preserve local farmlands. This latter finding suggests an interest in working lands protection. The preference for farmland preservation is also supported in their local analysis of votes in New Jersey. These authors strive to identify relationships between stock of open-space lands and rate of open-space loss and voter support for open-space protection. The results of their Massachusetts analysis suggest higher support for protection programs when stocks of open space are higher. Interestingly, both local studies show increasing support for open-space protection programs when modest open-space loss has recently occurred, but declining support once recent open-space loss becomes large. The empirical work featured in this paper shares a similar goal to this chapter in improving understanding of the relationship between current landscape characteristics and support for land protection programs.

A growing number of stated-preference studies address themes relevant to the protection of working lands (e.g. Kline and Wichelns 1994; Vossler *et al.* 2003;

Schlapfer *et al.* 2004; Schlapfer and Hanley 2006; Hellerstein *et al.* 2002). These studies often employ conjoint or contingent valuation methods to examine individual preferences for land protection programs. These studies collectively offer important insights into preferences for landscape features and speak to the variation in preferences across communities.

This research builds on the economic intuition and econometric methods of the aforementioned studies of elections data and stated preferences. The conceptual framework of this research and the details of the empirical analysis are presented in the subsequent sections.

Conceptual framework

The conceptual framework adopted in this case study draws from the utility maximization framework employed by Deacon and Shapiro (1975) and Schlapfer and Hanley (2006). For example, voting behavior on funding for a land protection program is cast as a comparison of utility with and without the increased funding. Intuitively, a supporting vote indicates a higher level of expected utility with the increased funding. Utility for individual *i* is presumed to be a function of consumption of private goods, z^i, and consumption of public goods, G. Consumption of public goods is divided into classes: the overall level of the collective good, G, and an accessible level of this collective good, G^i ($G^i \leq G$). This second term allows for explicit consideration of variation in access to the goods and services provided by the program. Distance measures are incorporated into the empirical analysis to capture some aspects of this variation. While these measures capture physical proximity, they do not address more abstract forms of access (Johnson *et al.* 2001).

Utility maximizing behavior is assumed and presumed constrained by income, I^i. Different landscape protection programs, k, provide different levels of public goods (G) and impose distinct income (I), tax liabilities (T) and prices of private goods (p). An individual's maximization problem may be written as follows:

$$\max_{z^i} U^i(z^i, G_k, G_k^i) + \lambda(I_k^i - T_k^i - p_k z^i) = V_k^i(G_k, G_k^i, p_k, I_k^i - T_k^i), \quad (12.1)$$

where *i* references the individual and *k* references the public program. Under this framework, an individual voter compares her utility with (V^i_1) and without (V^i_0) the landscape protection program and votes for the program only if a higher level utility is achieved ($V^i_1 > V^i_0$). An individual voter takes into account both the services received from the program and the cost of the program. Both of these attributes are expected to vary across individuals because of, among other factors, variations in perceived benefits and costs. This variation is reflected in the maximization problem shown in (12.1), as numerous variables change across individuals (*i*) under different programs (*k*). Central to this conceptualization of voting choices are representation of the changes in disposable income, the overall level of the public good, and the accessible level of the public good.

Lacking individual-scale data, we cannot directly model this utility maximization problem. Instead, this problem serves as the intuitive basis of an empirical model based on aggregate, community-scale voting data. While this research embraces the conceptual framework outlined in Deacon and Shapiro (1975), the empirical analysis of this chapter does not model voter turnout and is therefore a more basic representation of voting behavior. Voting data are aggregated to the community scale to allow for demographic characteristics to be linked with the voting data. The intuition of trade-offs driving voting choices extends to the community scale. The empirical model described in a subsequent section explains the level of support (proportion of YES votes) as a function of independent variables capturing variation in tastes and preferences that may influence evaluation of the benefits and costs of the public programs, income and tax liabilities, and the accessible level of the public goods conferred by the landscape protection program. The public goods relevant to this case study include those services derived from protecting working and non-working lands.

Empirical model

This research contrasts voting results from November 2005 on two ballot initiatives related to landscape management in Maine. Attributes of these two programs follow from the wording of the ballot questions:

> Do you favor amending the Constitution of Maine to permit the Legislature to authorize waterfront land used for commercial fishing activities to be assessed based on the land's current use in a manner similar to treatment now available for farms, open space and forestland?
>
> (2005 Working Waterfront Constitutional Amendment)

> Do you favor a $12,000,000 bond issue to purchase land and conservation easements statewide from willing sellers for conservation, water access, wildlife and fish habitat, outdoor recreation, including hunting and fishing, farmland preservation and working waterfront preservation to be matched by at least $7,000,000 in private and public contributions?
>
> (2005 Land for Maine's Future Bond Initiative)

These programs both impact attributes of Maine's landscape and the services it provides. In doing so, they alter the provision of services (private and public goods), influence the returns to land held in different uses, and modify production opportunities. The types of lands targeted by the programs are diverse, as are the means of implementing the programs. The Working Waterfront program relies on property tax relief to protect working lands, while the Land for Maine's Future program directly purchases lands and conservation easements. The Working Waterfront program is a more targeted public program, giving emphasis to the protection of working coastal lands. In contrast, the Land for Maine's Future program targets a broader set of lands, including both working and non-working lands. Voting patterns are expected to reflect these differences, as the perceived benefits and costs of the programs (e.g. the public goods; income and tax liabilities) will differ.

Election results data were obtained from the Maine Bureau of Corporations, Elections, and Commissions. Precinct data were aggregated to the county subdivision of the US Census Bureau geographic unit, referred to in this chapter as "community." Both ballot initiatives received high levels of support statewide, with 72 percent and 65 percent of voters approving the Working Waterfront and Land for Maine's Future programs, respectively.

Figures 12.1 and 12.2 display the spatial variation in support for these referenda by community. The left-side image shows the proportion of YES votes by community; the right-side image displays the absolute number of YES votes by community. The maps display the elections result data for 495 communities. Areas shown in white are not included in this analysis.[2] Figure 12.1 indicates high levels of support for the Working Waterfront program in coastal communities, with some evidence of distance decay moving away from the coast. Figure 12.2 reveals greater heterogeneity in proportional support for the Land for Maine's Future program relative to the Working Waterfront program. This finding is consistent with the broader targeting of lands (and services) by the Land for Maine's Future program. Both absolute images reflect the spatial distribution of population in Maine, with higher levels of population in the southern portion of the state. Southern and coastal areas of Maine have been experiencing higher rates of open space loss and land conversion, and generally have populations with higher income and educational attainment levels. Northern and downeast communities of Maine are more reliant on natural resource industries and therefore may have a greater proportion of working lands.

Tables 12.1 and 12.2 present descriptions and descriptive statistics of the independent and dependent variables employed in the empirical analysis. These statistics are based on community-scale data ($n=495$). PYES_WWF and PYES_LMF, the dependent variables, represent the proportions of supporting votes by community for the two landscape protection programs. Independent variables reflect community demographic, landscape, location, employment and political characteristics.

Measures of population density (LNPOPDEN), distance to Portland (LNPORT), Audubon membership (AUDUB), hunting and fishing licenses (HFISH), boating registrations (BOAT), and Republican political support (REPUB) strive to capture variation in tastes and preferences for the services provided by the public programs.

Following previous work that has identified variation in support in urban areas, LNPOPDEN and LNPORT distinguish communities by population density and proximity to Maine's largest and most urban center, Portland. Priors for the influence of these variables are unclear, as conflicting forces could support either sign. A positive influence may arise if more urban residents place higher values on the services offered by the programs. In contrast, a negative influence may reflect less accessibility to these services and hence lower perceived net benefits.

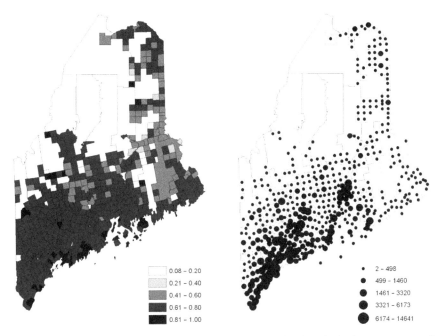

Figure 12.1 Working Waterfront voting results: proportional and absolute measures of voter support by community.

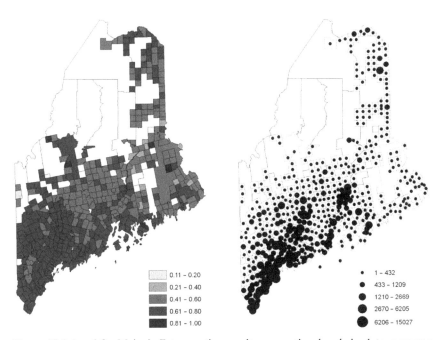

Figure 12.2 Land for Maine's Future voting results: proportional and absolute measures of voter support by community.

Table 12.1 Maine case study: variable descriptions

Variable	Description
PYES_WWF	Proportion of YES votes in support of the 2005 Working Waterfront ballot initiative
PYES_LMF	Proportion of YES votes in support of the 2005 Land for Maine's Future Ballot Initiative
LNPOPDEN	Natural logarithm of the population density (population per square mile; 2000 US Census of Population and Housing)
LNPORT	Natural logarithm of the distance to Portland (measured in meters)
AUDUB	Percentage of residents that are members of Maine Audubon (Maine Audubon)
HFISH	Percentage of residents with Maine Hunting and Fishing Licenses (InformME; Department of Inland Fisheries and Wildlife)
BOAT	Percentage of residents with Boat Licenses/Registrations (InformME; Department of Inland Fisheries and Wildlife)
REPUB	Percentage of residents that cast votes in support of President Bush in the 2004 Presidential Election
LNMEDINC	Natural logarithm of the 1999 median income (measured in $10,000; 2000 US Census of Population and Housing)
NREMP	Percentage of 2000 employment in agriculture, forest and fishing occupations (2000 US Census of Population and Housing)
CHNREMP	Percentage change (reduction) of employment in agriculture, forest and fishing occupations from 1990 to 2000 (2000 US Census of Population and Housing)
CMEDVAL	Median 1999 Housing Value of coastal communities; 0 otherwise (2000 US Census of Population and Housing)
LNCOAST	Natural logarithm of the distance to Maine's coast (measured in meters)
LNCLAND	Naturarl logarithm of the distance to the nearest conservation land (measured in meters)
AG_NC	Percentage of community with non-conserved agricultural land cover (2001 USGS NLCD data; Maine Office of GIS)
FOR_NC	Percentage of community with non-conserved forestland cover (2001 USGS NLCD data; Maine Office of GIS)
AG_C	Percentage of community with conserved agricultural land cover (2001 USGS NLCD data; Maine Office of GIS)
FOR_C	Percentage of community with conserved forestland cover (2001 USGS NLCD data; Maine Office of GIS)
CHAG	Percentage change (reduction) in agriculture cover from 1992 to 2001 (1992 USGS NLCD data; 2001 USGS NLCD data; Maine Office of GIS)
CHFOR	Percentage change (reduction) in forest cover from 1992 to 2001 (1992 USGS NLCD data; 2001 USGS NLCD data; Maine Office of GIS)

Table 12.2 Maine case study: descriptive statistics

Variable	Mean	Standard deviation
PYES_WWF	0.6764	0.0979
PYES_LMF	0.6074	0.0977
LNPOPDEN	3.3564	1.5431
LNPORT	11.6951	0.9997
AUDUB	0.4898	0.7703
HFISH	37.0113	25.8315
BOAT	12.7568	14.9438
REPUB	49.1961	10.5826
LNMEDINC	3.5148	0.2475
NREMP	6.7664	8.0994
CHNREMP	21.3740	71.4612
CMEDVAL	0.8180	1.8046
LNCOAST	7.6150	4.9480
LNCLAND	7.8070	1.6662
AG_NC	6.6293	7.9989
FOR_NC	65.0430	15.6229
AG_C	0.0360	0.1160
FOR_C	2.9955	7.2246
CHAG	1.4052	3.1584
CHFOR	6.0030	6.1721
NREMP*LNDCOAST	50.3483	75.1327
CHNREMP*LNDCOAST	133.4730	746.8076
AG_NC*NREMP	36.1153	77.9899
FOR_NC*NREMP	436.6333	531.4719

AUDUB, HFISH and BOAT are measures of participation in wildlife viewing, hunting and fishing, and boating across communities and are expected to have a positive influence on support for landscape protection programs. Working lands in Maine serve as key recreational assets in a largely privately owned (95 percent) landscape. Accordingly, these variables are expected to have a positive influence on voter support.

REPUB is included to address potential differences in support for public landscape protection programs across political parties. Because this variable may capture preferences for less government involvement and recognition of externalities, REPUB is expected to have a negative influence on support.

Because expectations that demand for landscape services are a normal good, communities with higher median income levels (LNMEDINC) may be expected to show greater support for both programs. Conversely, communities with higher incomes may also face higher tax liabilities to fund the programs. Accordingly, priors are mixed regarding the influence of median income (LNMEDINC).

Communities with higher levels of natural resource-based industry employment (NREMP) and higher reductions in employment in these industries (CHNREMP) are expected to show greater support for programs that enhance the "working" aspects of landscapes, though priors are also somewhat uncertain about the strength of this relationship. Communities with residents who rely on working lands are expected to support their protection. In particular, fishermen are expected to support the Working Waterfront program. It is not clear, however, how employees of the forest and agriculture industries will react to this waterfront current-use taxation program.[3] Interaction terms between NREMP and CHNREMP and distance to the coast are introduced as independent variables in the working waterfront empirical models to try to proxy for variation in fishing employment. The broader purview of the Land for Maine's Future program includes some actions that restrict natural resource extraction activities and may not necessarily protect working lands. As a result some communities with high natural-resource-based employment may view the Land for Maine's Future program as yielding negative net benefits due to the concentration of costs and income effects in these communities if and when lands are taken out of production to serve ecological or recreational interests.

Many of the independent variables discussed above address variation in the human aspects of landscapes. Additional sets of physical landscape attributes serve as independent variables to address variation in benefits, costs and "accessibility" of the public goods delivered by these two land protection programs. At the present time, we do not have access to a GIS coverage of existing working waterfront lands.[4] Accordingly, distance to the coast and fishing employment act as proxies for capturing the variation in working waterfront lands and hence the variation in where the public goods may originate on the landscape. Because proximity to the coast may relate to overall perceived and accessible benefits, distance from the coastline (LNDCOAST) is expected to have a negative influence on voter support for the Working Waterfront program. Coastal communities with higher median housing values (CMEDVAL) may face greater property tax shifts and hence tax liabilities under the current-use taxation plan of the Working Waterfront program. Accordingly, a negative influence is expected for CMEDVAL.

Anticipating where voters expect the public goods to be generated on the landscape is more troublesome in the case of the Land for Maine's Future program. At the time of the election, voters were not aware of where the increased funding would be applied to conserve land or for what purpose. For example, it was not clear how much, if any, of the funding would be spent on working lands protection. In this analysis, we test for relationships between the landscape of the voter's community and support for the program. One interpretation of these variables is that voters may believe the Land for Maine's Future dollars are likely to be spent in their community. Proximity to existing conservation lands is also incorporated as an independent variable.

Measures of the percentage of lands in agriculture and forest cover by community are based on analysis of the USGS National Land Cover Data (NLCD) for Maine from 1992 and 2001. By combining these data with spatial data on the location of conservation lands, variables measuring stocks of conserved (*C*) and non-conserved (*NC*) agricultural and forest lands are generated (AG_C; FOR_C; AG_NC; FOR_NC) for use in the analysis of the voting response to the Land for Maine's Future ballot initiative. These variables are proxies for undeveloped lands and may capture the variation across communities in terms of stocks of lands affected by the Land for Maine's Future program. A higher stock of non-conserved lands (AG_NC and FOR_NC) could generate higher support for the Land for Maine's Future program because of greater access to the benefits supported by this program. Alternatively, a higher stock of these lands could generate lower support because of concentrated income and employment effects due to changes in land use or land management that discourage resource extraction or require changes in practices. Interaction terms between these non-conserved land stocks and the percentage of natural resource employment are included in the Land for Maine's Future specification to allow for varied effects. Similar mixed expectations exist for the stocks of conserved agriculture and forest lands (AG_C and FOR_C). Decreasing marginal utility afforded by additional conservation may suggest a negative influence. In contrast, positive network externalities may support a positive influence, as additional conserved lands raise the value of existing lands in the conservation network. Communities experiencing a greater reduction in their stock of agriculture and forest lands (CHAG and CHFOR) may express higher support for the Land for Maine's Future program because of perceived scarcity as well as heightened awareness of landscape change.

Proximity to conservation land (LNDCLAND) serves as a proxy for familiarity and access to the public goods provided by the Land for Maine's Future program. If these information effects are significant, less support may be expected for the Land for Maine's Future program as distance to conservation land rises. Alternatively, one might expect higher support for the program as distance to conservation land rises because of scarcity of access to these lands.

Separate regression analyses are completed for the two different votes. A binary logit model with grouped data is estimated using maximum likelihood methods (Greene 2003: 686–689). The election data are grouped, having been reported at the precinct scale and aggregated to the community scale. The election results analyzed here take the form of proportions (PYES), and the number of voters (n_i) varies widely across communities. Weights of each observation are a function of the number of votes cast, and the errors are adjusted for heteroskedasticity. The log-likelihood function corresponding with the empirical model is as follows:

$$\ln L = \sum_{i=1}^{495} n_i \{PYES_i \ln F(x_i'\beta) + (1 - PYES_i)\ln[1 - F(x_i'\beta)]\},$$

where n_i represents the number of votes cast in community i, $PYES_i$ is the number of votes cast in support of the ballot initiative, F is the logistic cumulative density function, x_i contains the vector of independent variables for community i, and β is a vector of parameters to be estimated.

Empirical results

Tables 12.3 and 12.4 present the results of the regression analyses of voter response to the 2005 Working Waterfront and Land for Maine's Future ballot initiatives. Numerous specifications of these models were tested. Goodness-of-fit measures (shown at the bottom of the tables) guided the final selection of model specifications. All of the specifications shown in Tables 12.3 and 12.4 pass global tests of fit. The subsequent discussion of empirical results focuses on significant (at least 5 percent) parameter estimates.

Examination of the results shown in Table 12.3 reveals some interesting patterns in voter response to the Working Waterfront ballot initiative. Less support for the initiative is found in areas located farther from the coast (LNDCOAST), intimating that perceived accessible benefits from this program may decline with distance from the coast. Conversely, higher levels of support are found in communities located farther from Portland (LNPORT). A positive association is found between support for the ballot initiative and higher median incomes (LNMEDINC), suggesting that the services provided by working waterfront lands may be normal goods. Higher median housing values in coastal communities (CMEDVAL) has a positive influence on voter support. This unexpected result may suggest that the costs of the current-use taxation program are relatively small compared to the perceived benefits in these communities. Coastal communities with higher median housing values may have working waterfront lands under the greatest threat from development and stand to gain more from the protection program.

A negative association is found between reduced natural resource employment from 1990 to 2000 (CHNREMP) and voter support, implying communities that are losing employment in these industries are less likely to support working waterfront protections. This negative relationship weakens when moving away from the

Table 12.3 Maine case study: group logit regression analysis of the Working Waterfront ballot initiative

	Estimate	Pr > ChiSq	Estimate	Pr > ChiSq
Intercept	−0.6427	<0.0001	−0.5945	<0.0001
LNDCOAST	−0.0171	<0.0001	−0.0103	<0.0001
LNPOPDEN	0.00562	0.2525	−0.00754	0.1395
LNPORT	0.0136	<0.0001	0.0062	0.0016
LNMEDINC	0.5523	<0.0001	0.5707	<0.0001
CMEDVAL	0.0108	<0.0001	0.0130	<0.0001
NREMP	−0.0008	0.6020	0.0111	<0.0001
CHNREMP	−0.0003	0.0007	−0.0010	<0.0001
REPUB	−0.0128	<0.0001	−0.0120	<0.0001
BOAT	0.00351	<0.0001	0.0004	0.6443
AUDUB	0.0626	<0.0001	0.0681	<0.0001
LNDCOAST*CHNREMP			0.0007	<0.0001
LNDCOAST*NREMP			−0.0029	<0.0001
n = 495				
−2 LnL (intercept only)	459194.63		459194.63	
−2 LnL (covariates)	454403.80		454119.78	
AIC	454425.80		454145.78	
LR Global Null	4790.8278	<0.0001	5074.8489	<0.0001

Table 12.4 Maine case study: group logit regression analysis of the Land for Maine's Future ballot initiative

	Estimate	Pr > ChiSq	Estimate	Pr > ChiSq
Intercept	−0.1883	0.0289	−0.1805	0.0385
AG_NC	−0.0029	<0.0001	−0.0034	<0.0001
FOR_NC	−0.0002	0.6021	0.0006	0.1947
AG_C	−0.1241	0.0148	−0.1161	<0.0001
FOR_C	0.0080	<0.0001	0.0079	<0.0001
CHAG	0.0069	<0.0001	0.0061	<0.0001
CHFOR	0.0044	<0.0001	0.0037	<0.0001
LNDCLAND	−0.0082	0.0037	−0.0072	0.0114
LNPOPDEN	−0.0093	0.1156	−0.0064	0.2924
LNPORT	−0.0033	0.1039	−0.0054	0.0113
LNMEDINC	0.5182	<0.0001	0.5045	<0.0001
NREMP	0.0041	0.0036	0.0167	<0.0001
CHNREMP	0.0001	0.0811	0.0001	0.1735
REPUB	−0.0195	<0.0001	−0.0194	<0.0001
HFISH	−0.0044	<0.0001	−0.0043	<0.0001
AUDUB	0.0386	<0.0001	0.0389	<0.0001
AG_NC*NREMP			0.00007	0.5822
FOR_NC*NREMP			−0.0002	<0.0001
n = 495				
−2 LnL (intercept only)	517374.27		517374.27	
−2 LnL (covariates)	5121363.61		512117.43	
AIC	512165.61		512153.43	
LR Global Null (β = 0)	5240.658	<0.0001	5256.8393	<0.0001

coast (LNDCOAST*CHNREMP). The second specification in Table 12.3 shows a positive association between the extent of natural resource employment (NREMP) and voter support for the Working Waterfront program, and this positive relationship weakens when moving away from the coast (LNDCOAST*NREMP), perhaps suggesting limited support of protections designed for the fishing industry by communities dependent on agriculture and forestry.

A negative association is found between percentage of votes cast for President Bush in 2004 (REPUB) and voter support for the Working Waterfront program. In contrast, higher support is found in communities with higher rates of membership with Maine Audubon (AUDUB), suggesting individuals concerned about wildlife recognize potential gains from protecting working waterfront lands. A positive association between voter support and boat registrations (BOAT) was found in the first specification shown in Table 12.3.

Patterns in voter response to the Land for Maine's Future ballot are summarized in Table 12.4. Lower support for the initiative is found in areas with higher percentages of conserved and non-conserved agricultural land cover (AG_C and AG_NC), intimating fewer perceived benefits from the Land for Maine's Future program in agricultural communities. Percentage of conserved forest cover (FOR_C) has a positive influence on voter support of the program, giving some evidence of positive network externalities; communities with some conservation land prefer to have more conservation. A positive association is also found between greater reductions in agricultural (CHAG) and forest (CHFOR) land cover from 1992 to 2001 and voter support for the Land for Maine's Future program. These results may imply greater awareness of landscape change as well as perceptions of scarcity of specific landscape attributes.

Distance from conservation land (LNDCLAND) has a negative influence on voter support for the Land for Maine's Future program. This relationship may be capturing increased familiarity with and appreciation of specific landscape services in communities with proximity to conservation lands. Lower levels of support are found in communities located farther from Portland (LNPORT). This trend may be picking up differences in tastes and preferences for landscape attributes. A positive association is found between support for the ballot initiative and higher median incomes (LNMEDINC), suggesting the services provided by the Land for Maine's Future program are normal goods.

A positive association is found between the extent of natural resource employment (NREMP) and voter support for the Land for Maine's Future program. This suggests some form of broad support for land conservation by employees in these industries. The second specification in Table 12.4 indicates this positive relationship may decline with the extent of non-conserved forestlands in a community. The latter effect is sensible, as these communities may be targeted by the program and will experience both the benefits and costs of the program in a concentrated fashion.

As in the case with the Working Waterfront ballot initiative, a negative association is found between percentage of votes cast for President Bush in 2004 (REPUB) and voter support for the Land for Maine's Future ballot initiative. Higher rates of membership with Maine Audubon (AUDUB) are positively associated with support of the program, whereas higher rates of hunting and fishing licenses (HFISH) are negatively associated with support of the program. These results may reflect the relative magnitude of net benefits perceived by Maine Audubon members and hunters and fishers, offering some evidence that non-consumptive services may be greater than consumptive services on Land for Maine's Future lands.

Conclusions

At its outset, this chapter emphasized the global extent of community discussions regarding the relative value of different characteristics of landscapes and alternative future landscapes. A parsimonious review of United States and European Union agri-environmental policies suggests growing consideration of the multifunctionality of working lands and increasing funding of working lands protection programs. European Union policies are notably more encompassing, covering myriad aspects of working lands and their role in rural landscapes. Public programs to manage and understand preferences for working lands are heterogeneous at multiple scales, and future research examining the drivers of this variation has tremendous potential to inform future policies.

The results of the Maine case study illustrate the complexities of understanding preferences at a local scale. Drivers of variation in voter support for the two programs exhibit similarities and differences, as would be expected given the distinct nature of these two land protection programs. Future research is planned to extend the design and analysis of these empirical models, including modifying the empirical regression model to account for spatial dependence among the error terms and examining the potential implications of household sorting in response to landscape attributes.[5]

Notes

1 See the Trust for Public Land's website (www.tpl.org), and the Center for Conservation Finance's LandVote database and publications.
2 The majority of the communities (county subdivisions) omitted from this analysis are unorganized territories, with very limited populations and unreliable US Census of Population and Housing demographic data.
3 Employment data on these industries is aggregated into a single category.
4 A non-government organization is developing such data. When these data are complete, they will be incorporated into this analysis.
5 Schlapfer and Hanley (2003) present an excellent discussion of self-selection issues and raise potential concerns with using landscape attributes as independent variables if they are a driver of household sorting by preferences. The issue of sorting merits further attention in this empirical literature.

References

Baylis, K., Peplow, S., Rauser, G. and Simon, L. (2006) "Agri-environmental Policy in the European Union: Who's in Charge?" commissioned paper CP 2006–4, Canadian Agricultural Trade Policy Research Network.

Brouwer, F.M. and Godeschalk, F.E. (2004) "Nature Management, Landscape, and the CAP," The Hague Agricultural Economics Research Institute (LEI) Report 3.04.01, the Netherlands.

Cooper, J., Bernstein, J. and Claasen, R. (2005) "Overview of Agri-Environmental Programs in the European Union and the United States," *Farm Policy Journal*, 2(31): 31–41.

Council of Europe (2000) "European Landscape Convention." Online, available at: http://conventions.coe.int/Treaty/en/Treaties/Html/176.htm (accessed November 12, 2008).

Daniels, T.L. (2001) "State and Local Efforts in Conserving Privately-Owned Working Landscapes," background paper prepared for the National Governors' Association 2001 Conference, Private Lands, Public Benefits: A Policy Summit on Working Lands Conservation. Online, available at: www.nga.org/cda/files/LANDSSTATELOCAL.pdf.

Deacon, R. and Shapiro, P. (1975) "Private Preference for Collecting Goods Revealed Through Voting Referenda," *American Economic Review*, 65(5): 943–955.

Depoorter, M.F. (2003) "Synthesis of the Received Information Concerning Summary Descriptive Note on the Landscape Policies Pursued in the Council of Europe Member States," prepared for the Council of Europe T-FLOR 3(2003) 11 rev.

European Commission (2007) "Europeans, Agriculture, and the Common Agricultural Policy" (March 2007), Special European Union Barometer 276. Online, available at: http://ec.europa.eu/agriculture/survey/fullreport_en.pdf (accessed from the European Union website, August 2007).

218   *K.P. Bell*

Greene, W.H. (2003) *Econometric Analysis*, Upper Saddle River: Pearson Education.

Hellerstein, D., Nickerson, C., Cooper, J., Feather, P., Gadsby, D., Mullarkey, D., Tegene, A. and Barnard, C. (2002) "Farmland Protection: the Role of Public Preferences for Rural Amenities," Agricultural Economics Report No. 815, Washington, DC: USDA, ERS.

Johansson, R. (2006) "Working Lands Conservation Programs" (chapter 5.4), Agricultural and Resource Indicators, 2006 Edition/EIB-16, Washington, DC: USDA, Economic Research Service.

Johnson, F.R., Dunford, R.W., Desvousges, W.H. and Banzhaf, M.R. (2001) "Role of Knowledge in Assessing Nonuse Values for Natural Resource Damages," *Growth and Change*, 32: 43–68.

Kahn, M.E. and Matsusaka, J.J. (1997) "Demand for Environmental Goods: Evidence from Voting Patterns on California Initiatives," *Journal of Law and Economics*, 40(1): 137–173.

Kline, J. and Armstrong, C. (2001) "Autopsy of a Forestry Ballot Initiative: Characterizing Voter Support for Oregon's Measure 64," *Journal of Forestry*, 99(5): 20–27.

Kline, J. and Wichelns, D. (1994) "Using Referendum Data to Characterize Public Support for Purchasing Development Rights to Farmland," *Land Economics*, 70(2): 223–233.

Kotchen, M.J. and Powers, S.M. (2006) "Explaining the Appearance and Success of Voter Referenda for Open-space Conservation," *Journal of Environmental Economics and Management*, 52(1): 373–390.

Potter, C. and Burney, J. (2002) "Agricultural Multifunctionality in the WTO – Legitimate Non-trade Concern or Disguised Protectionism," *Journal of Rural Studies*, 18: 35–47.

Potter, C. and Lobley, M. (1998) "Landscapes and Livelihoods: Environmental Protection and Agricultural Support in the Wake of Agenda 2000," *Landscape Research*, 23(3): 223–236.

Rothstein, P. (1994) "Learning the Preferences of Governments and Voters from Proposed Spending and Aggregated Votes," *Journal of Public Economics*, 54: 361–389.

Schlapfer, F. and Hanley, N. (2003) "Do Local Landscape Patterns Affect Demand for Landscape Amenities Protection?" *Journal of Agricultural Economics*, 54(1): 21–35.

Schlapfer, F. and Hanley, N. (2006) "Contingent Valuation and Collection Choice," *Kyklos*, 59(1): 115–135.

Schlapfer, F., Roschewitz, A. and Hanley, N. (2004) "Validation of Stated Preferences for Public Goods: A Comparison of Contingent Valuation Survey Response and Voting Behaviour," *Ecological Economics*, 51(1–2): 1–16.

Vossler, C.A., Kerkvliet, J., Polasky, S. and Gainutdinova, O. (2003) "Externally Validating Contingent Valuation: An Open-space Survey and Referendum in Corvallis, Oregon," *Journal of Economic Behavior and Organization*, 51: 261–277.

13 Improving agri-environmental benefits within the CAP

Bettina Matzdorf, Klaus Müller,
Kurt Christian Kersebaum,
Joachim Kiesel and Thomas Kaiser

Introduction

Agri-environmental schemes are payments to farmers and other landholders to address environmental problems or promote the provision of environmental amenities (OECD 2003). Such payments may include implicit transfers such as tax and interest concessions. Agri-environmental measures are generally considered as belonging to the so-called "green box" of World Trade Organization (WTO) negotiation.

In this chapter, we examine area-based agri-environmental measures (AEM) as the most important part of payments for improving environmental objectives in agriculture. In the framework of the current European rural development policy under Council Regulation (EC) No. 1698/2005 and former Council Regulation (EC) No. 1257/1999, AEM summarized in agri-environmental programs (AEP) are the only mandatory parts of Rural Development Plans (RDP). AEP are implemented in all European member states at different spatial and administrative levels. Within the subsidiarity principle,[1] there is much room for the member states and regional authorities to design specific agri-environmental measures. During the last planning period (2000–2007) alone, 68 RDPs were implemented in the old EU member states ($n = 15$) (COM 2003). However, the number of agri-environmental programs was probably double (compare Buller (2000) for the planning period 1992–1999).

Currently, nearly all AEM are action-oriented as opposed to result-oriented. Payments of action-oriented AEM are based on farm practices such as the reduction of livestock density.

An important distinction has been made between "broad and shallow" and "deep and narrow" schemes (sometimes known also as "light green versus dark green" schemes). "Broad and shallow" schemes, also called "horizontal" schemes, tend to include a large number of farmers, cover a wide area, make relatively modest demands on farmers' practices, and pay correspondingly little for the environmental service provided. "Deep and narrow" or "dark green" schemes tend to target site-specific environmental issues and therefore include fewer farmers (COM 2005a). Horizontal measures, such as extensive grassland land management, represent the most important kind of AEM in terms of supported area. It is typical with this kind of AEM for environmental objectives to be quite general. Critics argue that "EU programs tend to be oriented towards multiple, sometimes nebulous goals" (Baylis *et al.* 2005: 268). Without clear goals, AEM are assessed as less effective, at least for specific environmental objectives (Primdahl *et al.* 2003; COM 2004; COM 2005b; Feehan *et al.* 2005; Knop *et al.* 2006; Kleijn *et al.* 2006). In particular, the lack of spatial equivalence for horizontal AEM is one of the main causes of effectiveness deficits (Piorr and Matzdorf 2004).

One way to improve spatial equivalence is to set up locally specific implementation areas. Such Environmentally Sensitive Areas (ESA) have been implemented in the United Kingdom since 1992. However, even in the United Kingdom, the biggest portion of AEM is not implemented site-specifically within horizontal schemes such as Countryside Stewardship Schemes (JNCC 2007).

An effective spatial management, based on ecologically defined regions and relationships, is "a challenging and radical departure from standard practice" (Scrase and Sheate 2002) and ultimately a question of transaction costs (Falconer *et al.* 2001; Rodgers and Bishop 1999) as well as equity considerations. Potential transaction costs as well as equity reasons could be seen as the main rationale for the resistance administrative bodies show toward these approaches. In addition to these constraints, centrally prescribed sensitive areas can also be ineffective, especially with regard to species and habitat diversity. With the issue of biodiversity, the entire range of site conditions, including historical use, has to be taken into account. Above all, the definition of inflexible management requirements is often less successful within the context of biodiversity. The impact assessment of AEM on biodiversity shows the specific issue (e.g. Kleijn *et al.* 2001; Swetnam *et al.* 2004; Herzog 2005).

Due to this fact, it is not surprising that first examples of result-oriented payments, as another opportunity to improve the effectiveness of AEM, are implemented to protect and to enhance biodiversity. Result-oriented, performance-based payments are directly linked to the desired ecological good or objective (Gerowitt *et al.* 2003; Matzdorf 2004a). For example, a farmer may receive payments for a "species-rich wet meadow." Action-oriented payments are linked to an adapted agricultural management practice that leads to the production of environmental goods. The farmer may receive payments for refraining from spreading manure in his meadow and for mowing it only once a year. The line between result-oriented and action-oriented approaches is blurred, but can be defined by the number of options for action.

In the case of incentives linked to specific environmental goals, farmers see environmental objectives as environmental goods and incorporate them into their economic calculation. Thus, farmers select the most appropriate (sensitive) areas in a decentralized way. They also enjoy greater flexibility in choosing methods for achieving the environmental objectives, and their choice is determined by their individual rational decision.

For these reasons, result-oriented remuneration is considered to have many advantages. Result-oriented remuneration prompts farmers to pursue environmental objectives for their own benefit, increases innovation potential, reduces information asymmetries, promotes cooperation between farmers and improves farmers' intrinsic motivation and interest in environmental objectives (Matzdorf 2004b).

There are first implementations of result-oriented agri-environmental measures (roAEM) in Switzerland and in the federal state of Baden-Württemberg (Germany) in the field of grassland biodiversity (Oppermann and Gujer 2003). Considering the political framework, the implementation of the regional AEP MEKA program[2] in Baden-Württemberg (BW) is very interesting. BW is the first federal state in the EU that has introduced a roAEM within the regional agri-environmental program under Council Regulation 1257/1999 in 2000. This example has shown that such an approach is in line with the current institutional framework of the EU's Common Agricultural Policy (CAP). The objective of the AEM titled "Rewarding of a great variety of plant species on grassland" is to support the protection and maintenance of species-rich, extensively and traditionally managed grassland.

In our chapter we give three examples of how roAEM can be designed and implemented in AEPs under Council Regulation 1698/2005. We developed these approaches for the federal state of Brandenburg in Germany. Two examples deal with the issue of biodiversity on grassland, and one deals with N-non-point pollution and the issue of water quality.

Approaches for result-oriented AEM in Brandenburg

Case study region

The federal state of Brandenburg is situated in the northeastern German lowlands, which are dominated by landscapes formed in the Pleistocene epoch (see Figure 13.1). Brandenburg has a total area of 2.9 million hectares with approximately 45 percent agricultural and 37 percent sylvan land use. Seventy-eight percent of agricultural land is arable land and 22 percent grassland. Diluvial sandy soils dominate the landscape; alluvial loamy soils and bogs are limited mostly to the riverside areas. The long-term mean annual precipitation varies between 450 mm in the southeast and 650 mm annually in the northwest. The region is characterized by varied and relatively sparsely populated rural areas (43 inhabitants per km^2).

In Brandenburg, agri-environmental measures have been applied since the beginning of 1990. The most important measures, in terms of area, are horizontal extensive grassland management and organic farming. In 2004, agri-environmental measures were applied to more than 50 percent of Brandenburg's grassland (Matzdorf *et al.* 2005). During the last planning period (2000–2006), Brandenburg invested 275 million euros for AEM (IACS) and will reach nearly that level during the next period (2007–2013) (MLUV 2007).

The established AEM comprise both horizontal and targeted measures. Some AEM are bound by tighter obligations and can only be conducted in combination with certain "base" measures. These are therefore tagged "top-up" measures.

Figure 13.2 gives an overview of the percentage of horizontal and targeted measures offered in Brandenburg and specifies the AEM for 2004.

The main aim of Brandenburg's AEM is the reduction of fertilizer and pesticide inputs. At least because of the high portion of horizontal AEM, there is
potential to improve the effectiveness of the AEP, especially with regard to the
spatial equivalence (Piorr and Matzdorf 2004). The evaluations have shown a
lack of consideration for biodiversity objectives. More goal-oriented approaches
were recommended to improve effectiveness (Matzdorf *et al.* 2005).

Result-oriented grassland AEM targeting on biodiversity

Weaknesses of the current grassland AEM

The conservation and the enhancement of species-rich grassland as an important
feature of the European cultural landscape is a major goal of many AEM in
Europe as well as in Brandenburg (MLUR 2000). Grassland AEM, including
organic farming management of grassland, cover a vast area. The horizontal
grassland AEM "extensive grassland management" (A1) is supported on 91,592
ha. This is approximately 30 percent of the total grassland in Brandenburg. Sixty

Figure 13.1 Location of the federal state of Brandenburg in Germany.

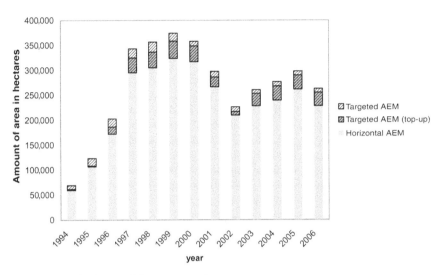

Horizontal and targeted agri-environmental measures (AEM) in Brandenburg

AEM in 2004 (without modulation measures)

	A6	Maintenance of extensive grassland and heath land through grazing
	A7	Maintenance of traditional orchards
	B6	Permanent set-aside of arable land
	A3	Late and restricted mowing
	A4	Small-scale grassland management
	A5	Maintenance of grassland management in "Spreewald"
	A1	Extensive grassland management
	A2	Extensive management and maintenance of wetlands (floodplains)
	B1	Integrated farming (vegetables and fruits)
	B3AL	Organic farming arable land
	B3GL	Organic farming grassland
	B4	Erosion-reducing/ soil-conserving measures
	B5	Conversion of arable land into grassland
	D	Maintenance and conservation of ponds

Figure 13.2 Amount of AEM in Brandenburg implemented from 1994–2006 (source: IACS).

percent of the total expenditure for AEM went to this horizontal AEM. A1 requires the extensive management of grassland areas and is restricted to extensive livestock or mixed farms with a stocking rate of 0.3 to 1.4 livestock units per ha. This measure includes at least one usage per year (mowing, grazing or mulching) and prohibits the use of synthetic chemical fertilizers and pesticides. Since 2004, farmers have had to participate with the whole farm grassland. Farmers can participate in A1 with single grassland fields only in exceptional cases and for nature conservation purposes.

The maintenance of extensively used grassland for landscape diversity reasons was the major goal of A1 in the past. Due to the implementation of cross-compliance into the CAP in 2005, the maintenance of grassland is required to get direct payments (Council Regulation No. 1782/2003 and Council Regulation No. 796/2004). The environmental effects of A1 on the nutrient-input and nutrient-surplus reduction are relatively low compared to conventional farms. Reasons for the relatively low effectiveness of A1 are a low intensive agricultural management, even among conventional farms in Brandenburg, and specific site conditions including climatic conditions (Kersebaum *et al.* 2006). Taking these into account, the conservation and enhancement of species-rich grassland can be seen as the main objective of A1 in Brandenburg.

There is no doubt about the positive impact of extensive grassland management on floral biodiversity objectives[3] in principle (recently, for example, Tallowin *et al.* 2005; Schmitzberger *et al.* 2005; Askew *et al.* 2007; Klimek *et al.* 2007). With regard to AEM, a noteworthy question is whether the most implemented horizontal grassland AEM do this effectively. On the one hand, for instance, Knop *et al.* (2006) and Dietschi *et al.* (2007) emphasize the importance of horizontal grassland AEM to maintain species-rich grassland in Germany and Switzerland. On the other hand, the possibility of enhancing species-rich grassland through this kind of AEM is suspect (Kleijn *et al.* 2006; Herzog 2005). It is argued that species-rich grassland depends essentially on historically extensive use (e.g. Knop *et al.* 2006; Kampmann *et al.* 2008). Furthermore, the temporal aspect has to be considered. Swetnam *et al.* (2004) suggest reminding policymakers that ensuring a successful and maintained reversal of floral decline may take many decades.

Unfortunately, no floristic time series of supported areas was available within the evaluation of the extensive horizontal grassland AEM (A1) in Brandenburg. Some evidence of a light positive influence of A1 is given by a counterfactual comparison (supported and non-supported areas) using numbers of species, number of species indicating extensive grassland use, and number of endangered species as assessment criteria (HUB 2003; Matzdorf *et al.* 2008). Nevertheless, considering the rather long participation of farmers in these AEM, the effectiveness has to improve (Matzdorf *et al.* 2003; Matzdorf *et al.* 2005).

Within the discussion of AEM aimed at biodiversity objectives, the closely linked European Habitats Directive (Directive 92/43/EEC) and Birds Directive (79/409/EEC) have to be considered. Member states have to maintain or restore a favorable conservation status, natural habitats and species of wild flora and fauna of community interest (Article 2, Directive 92/43/EEC). A central element of the Habitats Directive relates to the establishment, safeguarding and management of named Special Areas of Conservation (SAC). Together with the Special Protection Areas (SPA) of the Birds Directive, they form a European network of protected sites – the Natura 2000 network. AEM are important management instruments to achieve the objectives in Natura 2000 areas (COM 2000).

Despite the fact that Natura 2000 sites are nature-conservation target areas, we recommend a different design of result-oriented incentives inside and outside of Natura 2000 areas. Twenty-six percent of the area of Brandenburg is part of the Natura 2000 network (Figure 13.3) with a high proportion of grassland. Our spatial analysis shows that approximately 50 percent of A1 areas were situated in Natura 2000 areas in 2004.

Some natural habitat types of community interest are grassland habitats (see Annex 1 of the Habitats Directive). In Brandenburg, three grassland habitats with relevance for agricultural use have to be considered. Even though these habitat types have specific management requirements, there are no targeted AEM for them within the AEP in Brandenburg.

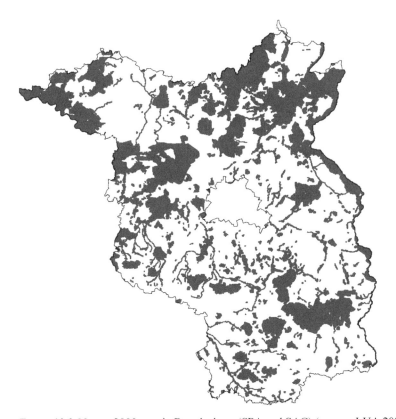

Figure 13.3 Natura 2000 area in Brandenburg (SPA and SAC) (source: LUA 2004).

Supporting species-rich grassland outside of Natura 2000 areas

We recommended, with the update of the mid-term evaluation of the AEP in Brandenburg, replacing A1 outside of Natura 2000 areas with result-oriented AEM (Matzdorf *et al.* 2005). The objectives were:

1   to identify species-rich and agricultural-used grassland areas (relevant for nature conservation);
2   to support only areas with a minimum of nature conservation quality; and
3   to realize the advantages of that kind of approach, especially the higher management flexibility for farmers (see above).

For the design of this AEM we used the successful indicator approach implemented in Switzerland and Baden-Württemberg (BW). The core of these approaches is a list of floristic species that indicates regional typical species-rich grassland. Farmers have to find a minimum number of indicator species each year per field to receive the result-oriented remuneration (Oppermann and Gujer 2003). In BW, farmers are responsible for checking their own eligibility of supported areas.

For Brandenburg, we derived a regionally typical indicator species list by using expert knowledge and statistical crosschecks with a database of over 1,550 pre-existing vegetation samples. In this database we integrated different kinds of existing monitoring data (Matzdorf *et al.* 2008).

First, the database of 1,551 samples was used for an expert-based identification of 318 species that are typical for extensively used grassland in Brandenburg. For the first selection of indicator species, these 318 species were reviewed using the following criteria:

1   high frequency in specific grassland communities (different demands on water supply); and
2   simple identification.

In addition to these positive criteria, poisonousness was used as an exclusion criterion. Finally, a comparison with other existing regional checklists (Baden-Württemberg and Lower Saxony) helped to refine our draft list.

Second, the suitability of this indicator species list was validated by addressing the question of whether the number of our selected indicator species was correlated:

1   with the number of plant species;
2   with the number of species indicating extensive use; and
3   the number of endangered species.

All trend functions are statistically significant (Matzdorf *et al.* 2008).

Table 13.1 Tentative checklist of indicator species for result-oriented grassland AEM in Brandenburg outside of Natura 2000 areas

Species	Moisture value**	Frequency (absolute) in our database (n = 1,547)				
		149	856	518	24	total %
		moderately dry	mesic	damp	wet	
1 Ranunculus acris. R. auricomus	6, x	10	298	186		31.9
2 Carex sp. (tall)*	8–9		120	337	11	30.3
3 Lychnis flos-cuculi	7	1	168	224		25.4
4 Trifolium pratense	x	30	218	51		19.3
5 Cirsium oleraceum	7		112	147		16.7
6 Galium album, G. uliginosum	5, 8	32	116	110		16.7
7 Lathyrus pratensis, L. palustris	6, 8	6	102	137	1	15.9
8 Lotus corniculatus, L. uliginosus	4, 8	13	101	129		15.7
9 Carex sp. (small)*	8–9	7	66	80	2	10.0
10 Lythrum salicaria	8		34	109	4	9.5
11 Achillea ptarmica	8	1	67	69	1	8.9
12 Stellaria palustris, S. graminea	9, 4	1	50	69	2	7.9
13 Campanula patula, C. rotundifolia	5, x	23	86	10		7.7
14 Daucus carota	4	33	71	11		7.4
15 Cardamine pratensis	6		28	67	1	6.2
16 Centaurea jacea, C. scabiosa	5, 3, x	22	62	10		6.1
17 Leucanthemum vulgare	4	6	65	16		5.6
18 Armeria maritima ssp. elongata	3	51	32			5.4
19 Anthoxanthum odoratum*	x	11	42	25		5.0
20 Cnidium dubium	8		33	41		4.8
21 Lysimachia nummularia	6		22	48		4.5
22 Pimpinella saxifrage, P. major	3, 5	15	27	21		4.1
23 Hieracium pilosella	4	32	10	1		2.8
24 Knautia arvensis	4	20	13	1		2.2
25 Inula britannica	7	1	16	17		2.2
26 Silene vulgaris	4	14	16	1		2.0
27 Potentilla erecta	x		10	16	1	1.7
28 Tragopogon pratensis, T. dubius	4	10	13	1		1.6
29 Luzula campestris*	4	2	12	4		1.2
30 Saxifraga granulata	4		7			0.5

Source: Matzdorf *et al.* 2008, slightly changed.

Notes
*Grasses and grass-like plants.
**After Ellenberg *et al.* 1991 gives information on major dissemination with regard to water supply.

In the end, we came up with an indicator checklist (Table 13.1) applicable for the roAEM. Table 13.1 gives a comprehensive overview of the indicator species and species groups. We used only vascular plants and mostly herbs because of their easy recognizability. As shown in Table 13.1, all relevant site types are considered.

Table 13.2 shows the quality of the grassland samples for two different thresholds. Ultimately, the threshold of four indicator species has been recommended. Besides the fact that our findings have shown that this number correlates with grassland of good nature-conservation quality, the recommendation of four species was also a pragmatic decision. Using this threshold, Brandenburg is able to realize a co-finance model within the German federal program "Gemeinschaftsaufgabe Agrarstruktur und Kuestenschutz" (Deutscher Bundestag 2005). However, the definition of a threshold for eligible areas is finally a political decision.

Approximately 30 percent of the total grassland in our database would meet the threshold of four indicator species. The percentage of the areas supported by A1 is a little higher (36 percent). Our results allow us to demonstrate that eligible sites are distributed throughout Brandenburg and on all relevant sites (Matzdorf *et al.* 2008).

These findings are based on a heterogeneous secondary dataset. A method for a simple and robust eligibility check of the indicator species that is suitable for use by farmers has to be defined; to that end, more than 200 field samples were investigated during the summer of 2007 to verify the indicator checklist and to test a proper method for the eligibility check.

In 2008 Brandenburg is introducing a test run of a roAEM using the verified indicator checklist. Admittedly, this roAEM will be offered in addition to the A1. For this reason, this roAEM could be helpful for farmers who are unable or unwilling to use their whole grassland in line with the A1 requirements. These farmers can participate with single grassland fields so long as the fields exhibit the required quality.

Table 13.2 Quality criteria corresponding with two thresholds of indicator species

Number of indicator species	Site group	Number of species	Number of species indicating extensive use	Number of endangered species
3	mesic to moderately	29.4	4.3	0.7
4		32	5.5	1
	dry			
3		25.6	5.8	1
	damp			
4		29.8	7.5	1.5

Source: own calculation. data source HUB 2003, field sample *n* = 391.

Supporting high-nature-value grassland habitat types inside of Natura 2000 areas

In opposition to our recommendation for areas outside of Natura 2000, we suggest supporting horizontal grassland AEM in terms of A1 within these areas. The Habitats Directive requires not only long-term conservation, but also an enhancement of the nature conservation quality of Natura 2000 areas. In these target areas for nature conservation, society has to accept the risk associated with the potentially lengthy process of enhancing the quality of grassland.

Still, there are very good conditions for using result-oriented incentives as an additional measure. Thanks to the spatial identification and a specific definition of the habitat types of community interest inside of Natura 2000 areas by characteristic species, incentives are easy to design and to implement.

Based on the update of the mid-term evaluation of the AEP in Brandenburg, we recommended implementing a result-oriented top-up AEM (in addition to the horizontal AEM) for the three grassland habitat types of community interest shown in Table 13.3. The objectives of this top-up roAEM are:

1   to preserve and enhance previously identified high-nature-value grassland habitat types that meet the requirements of the Habitats Directive; and
2   to realize individually adapted management systems with high flexibility for farmers.

An extensive use as required in A1 or even in organic farming grassland management is necessary to prevent an intensive use of these typical habitats formed by traditional extensive management systems. However, in order to conserve and enhance these landscape features, specific management is needed (COM 1999; Beutler and Beutler 2002). Standardized management guidelines, typical for action-oriented AEM, do not seem to be an appropriate instrument. In fact, an individually adapted management, considering the current status of each habitat, would be much more effective. The design and implementation of the result-oriented incentives could be linked to the mandatory monitoring systems for these habitat types to reduce transaction costs. Characteristic indicator species for each habitat type are still defined and could be used directly for result-oriented approaches.

Table 13.3 Agriculture-dependant grassland habitat types of the Habitats Directive in Brandenburg

Grassland habitat types	Area in Natura 2000 (ha)
Molinia meadows (# 6410)	889
Alluvial meadows of river valleys of the Cnidion dubii (# 6440)	1,201
Lowland hay meadows (# 6510)	3,728
Total	5,818

Source: LUA 2004.

Designing result-oriented AEM aimed at water quality

Weaknesses of the current support system

The reduction of water pollution is the main objective of the Water Framework Directive (WFD) (Directive 2000/60/EC). In Germany, agriculture has been estimated to contribute 62 percent of non-point-source pollution of surface waters (UBA 2004). WFD aims for a "good ecological status" of surface waters by 2015. For this goal to be realized, integrated river basin management plans need to be in place by 2009. With regard to the reduction of water pollution, legal instruments (command-and-control) play an essential role under consideration of the polluter-pays principle. Cross-compliance links the legal requirements with the subsidy system of the CAP. However, even voluntary AEM can reduce non-point-source pollution and thereby contribute to integrated water management. But there are reasonable doubts about their effective contribution. Baldock *et al.* (2002) question "how far AEPs can contribute effectively to resolving chronic problems of water pollution" (76). On the one hand, horizontal AEM can make a contribution in supporting extensive management systems in a broad area. On the other hand, the effectiveness depends highly on the specific site conditions. To make a serious contribution for the WFD, AEM have to be more target-oriented. Otherwise, the positive impact of horizontal AEM can be seen more as a by-product of the AEM. Our impact assessment of the AEM on water quality in Brandenburg illustrates this issue.

Reducing fertilizer input is a main objective of the AEP in Brandenburg (MLUR 2000). The environmental data show that there is no need for further reduction of agricultural-sourced phosphorus and potassium in Brandenburg (Matzdorf *et al.* 2005). Even though the nitrogen surplus on the agricultural land in Brandenburg is relatively low (Kersebaum *et al.* 2006), the reduction of N-loss from agriculture represents the main environmental objective with regard to water quality (MLUV 2005).

In 2004, subsequent AEM caused a reduction of N-input or a runoff of fertilizer: A1, A2, B1, B3, B4, B5, B6 (for explanation see Figure 13.2). These are 83 percent of all AEM (Matzdorf *et al.* 2005). The portion of both horizontal AEM "extensive grassland management" (A1) and organic farming (B3) on these relevant AEM is 85 percent. The N-reduction effect of A1 amounted to 68 percent and B3 amounted to 72 percent compared to the permitted N-fertilizer input of $170\,kg\ ha^{-1}\ yr^{-1}$, according to the national standard of the "Good Agricultural Practice" (GAP) (Piorr and Matzdorf 2004). In fact, because of the relatively low N-input, even for conventional (not supported) management and animal husbandry in Brandenburg, the effective potential to reduce N-leaching is relatively low. For instance, the average stocking rate was only $0.6\ LU\ ha^{-1}$ (Kersebaum *et al.* 2006). Additionally, climatic conditions in many parts of Brandenburg lead only to small amounts of groundwater recharge, especially in the groundwater-affected areas where the water balance during the summer is sometimes negative. This reduces the overall risk of N-leaching. Taking the site specifics into account, 73 percent of Utilized Agricultural Area (UAA) in Brandenburg have very low or low vulnerability to groundwater pollution (see Figure 13.4). It is not surprising that the percentage of AEM reflects this relation. The spatial analysis on a detailed level shows that only 27 percent of the relevant AEM are implemented on vulnerable areas. Table 13.4 shows that the grassland AEM are less effective, especially when considering the spatial equivalence.

Using simulated nitrate-leaching figures

As we demonstrated in our impact analysis for Brandenburg, there is a high potential for improving AEM aimed at reduction of nitrate leaching. One way to improve such AEM could be a site-specific premium depending on spatial vulnerability. We wanted to go one step beyond and so developed a first example of how to use simulated nitrate-leaching figures for a result-oriented incentive. We used N-leaching figures from the root zone. By doing so, we could integrate the aspects of the N-input reduction potential of different management systems and the site conditions in a flexible premium.

Simulated figures present an opportunity to implement result-oriented approaches for such issues, where a direct link to the desired environmental goals is not possible. Water quality represents such an issue. Because of non-point-source pollution and the time lag, incentives for the reduction of nitrate leaching cannot be directly linked to the water quality.

There is another advantage to the use of simulated figures. With the use of measured environmental indicators, there is always the risk for farmers that indicators are not only dependent on the current agricultural use but also on historical use or even on other users or impact factors (e.g. Lowe *et al.* 1999; Baldock *et al.* 2002). Compared to the application of measured environmental indicators within the incentive design, there is no risk to the farmers when using simulated figures. The incentives depend only on the variable integrated in the

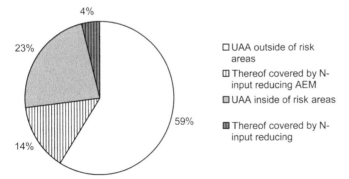

Figure 13.4 N-input reducing AEM of the AEP in Brandenburg in 2004 (source: calculations based on data of Kersebaum *et al.* 2006 and IACS, some UAA are not assessed).

Table 13.4 N-input reducing AEM in groundwater pollution areas in Brandenburg (2004)

Area in %									
N-risk	A1	B3AL	B3GL	A2	B1	B4	B5	B6	Total
very low	80	47	75	88	60	53	51	82	64
low	9	13	9	2	12	14	17	0	11
medium	7	19	10	7	17	13	20	14	13
high	3	21	6	3	11	18	11	0	11
very high	0	1	0	0	0	2	0	0	1

Source: own calculations based on data of Kersebaum *et al.* 2006 and IACS 2004.

model. Naturally, this is an advantage on one hand and a disadvantage on the other. The flexibility of farmers, the potential for innovation, and the dynamic efficiency is not as great when compared with the situation where measured indicators are used.

In our case study the process-oriented model HERMES (Kersebaum 1995) was used for the simulation of N-dynamics. The model requires only a limited number of typically available input data and has been validated on different scales under similar climatic and land-use conditions. The model consists of sub-modules for water balance, N-transport and transformations, crop development, and growth, including N-uptake (Kersebaum and Beblik 2001). The simulation was carried out for four different management systems:

1   extensive grassland management (including grassland management of organic farming);
2   conventional grassland management;
3   organic farming on arable land;
4   conventional farming on arable land.

For arable systems, seven rotations attributed to classes for the soil index (Kersebaum *et al.* 2003) were defined for conventional and organic farming systems separately. This results in ten different soil-attributed crop rotations for each farming system. The crop-management systems for organic farming and the extensive grassland-management system for organic and conventional farming were defined according to the specifications of the agri-environmental measures. Intersections of thematic maps for soils, groundwater level, land use and land parcels result in a map with about 420,000 polygons. To reduce simulation time, the data were aggregated into classes, and the number of different class combinations resulted in 9,600 cases, which were simulated with the model (for more detail, see Kersebaum *et al.* 2006). To identify the spatial distribution of arable and grassland, data from the Integrated Administrative and Control System (IACS) were used at the spatial administrative level of "flur" (a land parcel of approximately 190 ha). Based on simulated N-leaching from the root zone of the four farm management systems, we calculated the possible reduction for three scenarios at the polygon level:

1   converting conventional arable land into extensive grassland;
2   changing conventional arable land into organic arable land (following the current AEM); and
3   changing conventional grassland into organic grassland or extensively used grassland (following the current AEM).

Next, we aggregated the results for each *flur*. Finally, we presented the reduction potential for three different management adaptations for the entire relevant area of Brandenburg (Figure 13.5). The average reduction of N-leaching for all of Brandenburg for the first scenario was 44 kg N ha^{-1}, for the second scenario 20.1 kg N ha^{-1}, and for the last only 5.8 kg N ha^{-1}.

Based on these findings, a result-oriented premium can be designed depending on the reduction of N in kg N ha^{-1}. However, more variety in the management adaptations (more than three) would increase the flexibility of farmers and increase the advantages of roAEM. In principle, the implementation could be relatively easy to realize. It seems to be of importance that the entire farm area is included. A starting point could be the definition of a reference figure for N-leaching at the farm level based on simulated figures under conventional production and under consideration of the legal requirements. Depending on management adaptations, farmers would be remunerated for the reduction of kg N ha^{-1} at the farm level. Using geo-referenced simulated N-leaching figures, the calculations require little effort and transaction costs are proportional. Since 2005, the IACS has been linked to geographic information systems at the level of "agricultural parcels" which support such a site-specific approach. These agricultural parcels can be used to assess the site potential for N-leaching of relevant management adaptations at a very detailed level. In Brandenburg, for example, the average size of IACS land parcels is 19 ha. Even more important is that all supported areas within the CAP are administered at this level.

Discussion and conclusion

This chapter has given examples of how current AEM could be enhanced and designed more efficiently with regard to specific environmental objectives. We took the assessment and discussion of horizontal "broad and shallow" AEM as a starting point to introduce examples of result-oriented incentives within the AEP.

In cases where horizontal AEM are ineffective, it is primarily due to the fact that they do not target specific environmental objectives and that they seek a high level of participation. Analyzing the impact of such AEM for specific environmental objectives such as biodiversity or water quality, has shown that these AEM are quite often less effective than they would be if more specific objectives were targeted. The question has been: how can AEM be designed in such a way that farmers have incentives not only to participate but also to produce environmental goods? We argued that one of the interesting sources for improving AEM is to increase the flexibility for farmers and give them more responsibility to

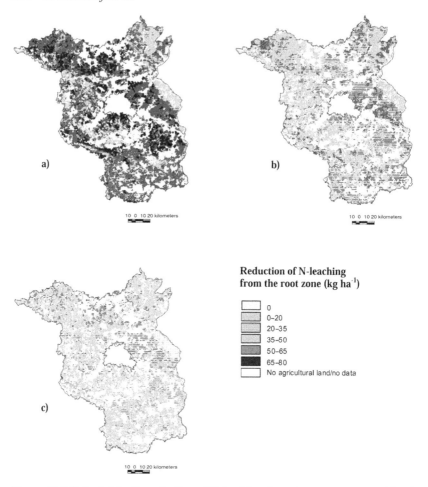

Figure 13.5 Potential for the reduction of N-leaching from the root zone caused by three different AEM: a) Conversion of conventional arable land into extensive grassland; b) organic farming on arable land; c) extensive grassland management (including organic farming on grassland).

reach the desired environmental goals. Results-oriented incentives should meet these requirements. The main challenge is to operationalize environmental objectives useable for result-oriented incentives in practice. By giving three examples dealing with the issue of biodiversity and water quality we wanted to focus the research on the development of those types of incentive instruments.

In our first example, we adapted an existing approach (Oppermann and Gujer 2003) to develop roAEM for ordinary, extensively used grassland outside of Natura 2000. We showed the development of a suitable indicator set to remunerate the production of species-rich grassland outside of nature conservation areas. An adapted approach is used within the regional AEP in Brandenburg during the current planning period (2007–2013). In Germany, this kind of roAEM will also be implemented in other federal states, e.g. Lower Saxony and Schleswig-Holstein. For Lower Saxony, Wittig *et al.* (2007) developed a similar indicator-based approach.

Contrary to arguments made by Baldock *et al.* (2002) concerning the implementation of broad and shallow AEM, we recommend replacing the horizontal A1 (see Figure 13.2) outside of nature conservation areas with a roAEM. In Brandenburg, the question that arose within the horizontal grassland AEM was whether and why society should take over the risk of ineffectiveness in areas of no specific interest.

In our second example we looked at Natura 2000 areas as the most important instrument in the context of biodiversity policy in Europe. Some of the target habitat types are cultivated grassland habitats which need a specific extensive-grassland management. Using the mandatory monitoring efforts, roAEM could be designed and implemented quite easily using the characteristic indicator species of the habitat types. In the framework of the existing instruments in Brandenburg, we recommend an additional incentive to design a result-oriented top-up premium.

With our third example we wanted to broaden the discussion about roAEM by using simulated environmental figures for this approach. One of the main problems of roAEM is the risk for farmers that the outcome depends not only on the farmers' efforts but also on outside influences such as weather conditions or even time lags in the cause-and-effect chain (e.g. Lowe *et al.* 1999; Baldock *et al.* 2002). An important issue in this context is water quality. In most cases, the water quality does not only depend on the management of a single farmer, and time lags are typical in this field. By using simulated nutrient leaching the issue of non-point pollution can be solved for our problem. We introduced in our chapter an example of how simulated nitrate-leaching figures can be used to design result-oriented incentives. The relevance of that kind of incentive is increasing due to the implementation of the Water Framework Directive during the next few years. Our approach can be used as a starting point to think about the introduction of nutrient trading systems instead of AEM.

We did not discuss the problem of how to calculate the premium for roAEM. At present, payments for farmers are determined by reference to the compensation required to cover the loss of income incurred by complying with specific environmental restrictions and the management cost of required actions. The concept of result-oriented incentives fits much better with willingness-to-pay or even willingness-to-accept methods. However, in part because of WTO negotiation, there is a problem with using these methods in the framework of the CAP. Nevertheless, the premium for roAEM can be calculated using a suitable reference management system.

There is no question that the result-oriented approach is only one option to enhance the effectiveness and efficiency of AEM. This kind of incentive is not suitable for all environmental issues. Additionally, the possibility of implementation depends on the specific agri-environmental program, the whole environmental and social objectives, and the institutional framework. Considering the question of acceptance, broad and shallow AEM can be helpful for the agri-environmental policy. The combination of broad and shallow AEM with a top-up result-oriented incentive can be an especially interesting alternative to gain more practical experiences.

Notes

1 The principle of subsidiarity is defined in Article 5 of the Treaty establishing the European Community. It is intended to ensure that decisions are taken as closely as possible to the citizen and that constant checks are made as to whether action at Community level is justified in the light of the possibilities available at national, regional or local level. Specifically, it is the principle whereby the Union does not take action (except in the areas which fall within its exclusive competence) unless it is more effective than action taken at national, regional or local level. It is closely bound up with the principles of proportionality and necessity, which require that any action by the Union should not go beyond what is necessary to achieve the objectives of the Treaty (source: http://europa.eu/scadplus/glossary/subsidiarity_en.htm).
2 Since 1992 the program MEKA (a governmental instrument for environmental protection and the reduction of agricultural overproduction) has been running in Baden-Württemberg under the auspices of the European Union. This program supports the use of mulch-seeding and catch crops in order to reduce soil erosion (source: http://natres.psu.ac.th/Link/SoilCongress/bdd/symp31/2044-t.pdf).
3 Biodiversity is used as a nature-conservation concept.

References

Askew, N.P., Searle, J.B. and Moore, N.P. (2007) "Agri-environment Schemes and Foraging of Barn Owls Tyto Alba," *Agriculture Ecosystems & Environment*, 118: 109–114.

Baldock, D., Dwyer, J. and Sumpsi-Vinas, J.M. (2002) "Environmental Integration and the CAP," Report, the Commission of the European Union DG Agriculture, Institute for European Environmental Policy.

Baylis, K., Rausser, G.C. and Simon, L.K. (2005) "Including Non-trade Concerns: the Environment in EU and US Agricultural Policy," *Int. J. Agricultural Resources, Governance and Ecology*, 4(3/4): 262–276.

Beutler, H. and Beutler, D. (2002) "Katalog der Natürlichen Lebensräume und Arten der Anhänge I und II der FFH-Richtlinie," *Naturschutz und Landschaftspflege in Brandenburg*, Jg. 11, Heft 1, 2.

Buller, H. (2000) "Regulation 2078: Patterns of Implementation," in Buller, H., Wilson, G. and Höll, A. (eds.) *Agri-environmental Policy in the European Union*, Aldershot: Ashgate.

COM (Commission of the European Communities) (1999) "The Interpretation Manual of European Union Habitats," Scientific reference document, version 2, was adopted by the Habitats Committee on October 4, 1999.

COM (Commission of the European Communities) (2000) "Managing Natura 2000 Sites," the provisions of Article 6 of the "Habitat" Directive 92/43/EEC, Luxemburg: Office of Official Publications of the European Commission.

COM (Commission of the European Communities) (2003) "Rural Development in the European Union," Fact Sheet, Luxemburg: Office for Official Publications of the European Commission.

COM (Commission of the European Communities) (2005a) "Agri-environment Measures – Overview on General Principles, Types of Measures, and Application," Directorate.

COM (Commission of the European Communities) (2005b) "Communication from the Commission on Simplification and Better Regulation for the Common Agricultural Policy," 509 final.

COM (Commission of the European Communities) DG Agriculture (2004) "Impact Assessment of Rural Development Programmes in View of Post 2006 Rural Development Policy," final report, Brussels: EPEC.

Commission Regulation No. 796/2004 (April 21, 2004) "Laying Down Detailed Rules for the Implementation of Cross-compliance, Modulation and the Integrated Administration and Control System Provided for in *Council Regulation (EC) No 1782/2003* Establishing Common Rules for Direct Support Schemes Under the Common Agricultural Policy and Establishing Certain Support Schemes for Farmers," *Official Journal of the European Union.*

Council Directive 2000/60/EC of 23 (October 2000) "Establishing a Framework for Community Action in the Field of Water Policy."

"Council Directive 79/409/EEC of 2 on the Conservation of Wild Birds" (April 1979).

Council Directive 92/43/EEC of 21 (May 1992) "The Conservation of Natural Habitats and of Wild Fauna and Flora."

Council Regulation (EC) No. 1257/1999 (May 17, 1999) "Support for Rural Development from the European Agricultural Guidance and Guarantee Fund (EAGGF) and Amending and Repealing Certain Regulations."

Council Regulation (EC) No. 1782/2003 (September 29, 2003) "Establishing Common Rules for Direct Support Schemes Under the Common Agricultural Policy and Establishing Certain Support Schemes for Farmers."

Council Regulation (EC) No. 1698/2005 (September 20, 2005) "Support for Rural Development by the European Agricultural Fund for Rural Development (EAFRD)."

Deutscher Bundestag (2005) "Rahmenplan der Gemeinschaftsaufgabe Verbesserung der Agrarstruktur und des Küstenschutzes," für den Zeitraum 2005 bis 2008. Drucksache 15/5820.

Dietschi, S., Holderegger, R., Schmidt, S.G. and Linder, P. (2007) "Agri-environment Incentive Payments and Plant Species Richness Under Different Management Intensities in Mountain Meadows of Switzerland," *Acta Oecologica*, 31: 216–222.

Ellenberg, H., Weber, H.-E., Düll, R., Wirth, V., Werner, W. and Paulißen, D. (1991) "Zeigerwerte von Pflanzen in Mitteleuropa," *Scripta Geobotanica*, 18.

Falconer, K., Dupraz, P. and Whitby, M. (2001) "An Investigation of Policy Administrative Costs Using Panel Data for the English Environmentally Sensitive Areas," *Journal of Agricultural Economics*, 52: 83–103.

Feehan, J., Gillmor, D.A. and Culleton, N. (2005) "Effects of an Agri-environment Scheme on Farmland Biodiversity in Ireland," *Agriculture Ecosystems & Environment*, 107: 275–286.

Gerowitt, B., Isselstein, J. and Marggraf, R. (2003) "Rewards for Ecological Goods – Requirements and Perspectives for Agricultural Land Use," *Agriculture Ecosystems & Environment*, 98 (1–3): 541–547.

Herzog, F. (2005) "Agri-environment Schemes as Landscape Experiments," *Agriculture Ecosystems & Environment*, 108: 175–177.

HUB (Humboldt-Universität zu Berlin), Landwirtschaftlich-Gärtnerische Fakultät (2003) Wirkung der Grünlandmaßnahmen des KULAP 2000 auf die Pflanzenbestände (Arten- und Habitatvielfalt). Im Auftrag des Ministerium für Landwirtschaft Umwelt und Raumordnung (unpublished), p. 67.

IACS: Data of the Integrated Administration Control System. Applied by the Regional

Ministry (Ministerium für Landwirtschaft, Umweltschutz und Raumordnung des Landes Brandenburg).

JNCC (Joint Nature Conservation Committee) (2007) "Area of Land Under Agri-environment Scheme Management." Online, available at: www.jncc.gov.uk/page-3969 (accessed August 15, 2007).

Kampmann, D., Herzog, F., Jeanneret, Ph., Konold, W., Peter, M., Walter, T., Wildi, O. and Lüscher, A. (2008) "Mountain Grassland Biodiversity: Impact of Site Conditions Versus Management Type," *Journal for Nature Conservation*, 16: 12–25.

Kersebaum, K.-C. (1995) "Application of a Simple Management Model to Simulate Water and Nitrogen Dynamics," *Ecological Modelling*, 85: 145–156.

Kersebaum, K.-C. and Beblik, A.J. (2001) "Performance of a Nitrogen Dynamics Model Applied to Evaluate Agricultural Management Practices," in Shaffer, M.J., Ma, L. and Hansen, S. (eds.) *Modelling Carbon and Nitrogen Dynamics for Soil Management*, Boca Raton: Lewis Publishers, pp. 549–569.

Kersebaum, K.-C., Matzdorf, B., Kiesel, J., Piorr, A. and Steidl, J. (2006) "Model-based Evaluation of Agri-environmental Measures in the Federal State of Brandenburg (Germany) Concerning N Pollution of Groundwater and Surface Water," *Journal of Plant Nutrition and Soil Science*, 169(3): 352–359.

Kersebaum, K.-C., Steidl, J., Bauer, O. and Piorr, H.-P. (2003) "Modelling Scenarios to Assess the Effects of Different Agricultural Management and Land Use Options to Reduce Diffuse Nitrogen Pollution into the River Elbe," *Physics and Chemistry of the Earth*, 28: 537–545.

Kleijn, D., Baquero, R.A., Clough, Y., Diaz, M., de Esteban, J., Fernandez, F., Gabriel, D., Herzog, F., Holzschuh, A., Johl, R., Knop, E., Kruess, A., Marshall, E.J.P., Steffan-Dewenter, I., Tscharntke, T., Verhulst, J., West, T.M. and Yela, J.L. (2006) "Mixed Biodiversity Benefits of Agri-environment Schemes in Five European Countries," *Ecology Letters*, 9(3): 243–254.

Kleijn, D., Berendse, F., Smit, R. and Gilissen, N. (2001) "Agri-environment Schemes do not Effectively Protect Biodiversity in Dutch Agricultural Landscapes," *Nature*, 413: 723–725.

Klimek, S., Kemmermann, A.R.G., Hofmann, M. and Isselstein, J. (2007) "Plant Species Richness and Composition in Managed Grasslands: the Relative Importance of Field Management and Environmental Factors," *Biological Conservation*, 134: 559–570.

Knop, E., Kleijn, D., Herzog, F. and Schmid, B. (2006) "Effectiveness of the Swiss Agri-environment Scheme in Promoting Biodiversity," *Journal of Applied Ecology*, 43: 120–127.

Lowe, P., Falconer, K., Hodge, I., Moxey, A., Ward, N. and Whitby, M. (1999) "Integrating the Environment into CAP-Reform," Research Report, University of Newcastle upon Tyne: Centre for Rural Economy.

LUA (Landesumweltamt) (2004) Daten su den FFH-Lebensraumtypen in Brandenburg. Bewertung des Erhaltungszustandes im Rahmen des Monitorings, Stand 06.07.2004.

Matzdorf, B. (2004a) "Ergebnisorientierte Honorierung ökologischer Leistungen der Landwirtschaft, Vorteile, Voraussetzungen und Grenzen des Instrumentes," *Umweltwissenschaften und Schadstoff-Forschung – Zeitschrift für Umweltchemie und Ökotoxikologie*, 16(2): 125–133.

Matzdorf, B. (2004b) "Ergebnis- und maßnahmeorientierte Honorierung ökologischer Leistungen der Landwirtschaft – eine interdisziplinäre Analyse eines agrarumweltpolitischen Instrumentes," dissertation, Zeitschrift für Betriebswirtschaft, Marktforschung und Agrarpolitik, Sonderheft 179, Agrimedia.

Matzdorf, B., Becker, N., Reutter, M. and Tiemann, S. (2005) Aktualisierung der Halbzeitbewertung des Plans zur Entwicklung des ländlichen Raums gemäß VO (EG) Nr. 1257/1999 des Landes Brandenburg. Ministerium für Ländliche Entwicklung, Umwelt und Verbraucherschutz des Landes Brandenburg, Potsdam. Online, available at: www.zalf.de/home_zalf/download/soz/KULAP2_endbericht_brandenburg.pdf.

Matzdorf, B., Kaiser, T. and Rohner, M.-S. (2008) "Developing Biodiversity Indicator to Design Efficient Agri-environmental Schemes for Extensively Used Grassland," *Ecological Indicators*, 8(3): 256–269.

Matzdorf, B., Piorr, A. and Sattler, C. (2003) "Kapitel 4 – Agrarumweltmaßnahmen (Art. 22–24VO (EG) 1257/999), in ZALF Müncheberg (Projektleitung)," Halbzeitbewertung des Plans zur Entwicklung des ländlichen Raums des Landes Brandenburg: 77–218. Im Auftrag des Ministerium für Landwirtschaft Umwelt und Raumordnung, Potsdam. Online, available at: www.zalf.de/home_zalf/download/soz/KULAP1_endbericht_brandenburg.pdf.

MLUR (Ministerium für Landwirtschaft, Umweltschutz und Raumordnung des Landes Brandenburg) (2000) *Entwicklungsplan für den ländlichen Raum im Land Brandenburg (flankierende Maßnahmen)* – Förderperiode 2000–2006. Potsdam.

MLUV (Ministerium für Landwirtschaft, Umwelt- und Verbraucherschutz des Landes Brandenburg) (2005) *Umweltdaten aus Brandenburg – Bericht 2005*. Online, available at: www.mluv.brandenburg.de/info/berichte.

MLUV (Ministerium für Landwirtschaft, Umwelt- und Verbraucherschutz des Landes Brandenburg) (2007) Entwicklungsplan für den ländlichen Raum 2007–2013. Online, available at: www.mluv.brandenburg.de/cms/media.php/2317/swot.pdf.

OECD (2003) *Mesures Agro-environnementales: Tour d'horizon des évolutions. Groupe de travail mixte sur l'agriculture et l'environnemen*, Paris: Organisation for Economic Co-operation and Development.

Oppermann, R. and Gujer, H.U. (eds.) (2003) "Artenreiches Grünland Bewerten und Fördern – MEKA und ÖQV," in *der Praxis*, Stuttgart: Ulmer.

Piorr, A. and Matzdorf, B. (2004) "The Assessment of Environmental Effectiveness of Agri-environmental Measures Regarding Intensity Impacts and Spatial Equivalence," in University of Natural Resources and Applied Life Sciences (eds.), *Assessing Rural Development Policies of the CAP*: 87th EAAE-Seminar (April 21–23, 2004), Vienna: 1–11.

Primdahl, J., Peco, B., Schramek, J., Andersen, E. and Onate, J.J. (2003) "Environmental Effects of Agri-environmental Schemes in Western Europe," *Journal of Environmental Management*, 67: 129–138.

Rodgers, C. and Bishop, J. (1999) "Management Agreements of Promoting Nature Conservation," London.

Schmitzberger, I., Wrbka, T., Steurer, B., Aschenbrenner, G., Peterseil, J. and Zechmeister, H.G. (2005) "How Farming Styles Influence Biodiversity Maintenance in Austrian Agricultural Landscapes," *Agriculture Ecosystems & Environment*, 108(3): 274–290.

Scrase, I. and Sheate, W. (2002) "Integration and Integrated Approaches to Assessment: What do They Mean for the Environment?" *Journal of Environmental Policy and Planning*, 4(4): 275–294.

Swetnam, R.D., Mountford, J.O., Manchester, S.J. and Broughton, R.K. (2004) "Agri-environmental Schemes: their Role in Reversing Floral Decline in the Brue Floodplain, Somerset, UK," *Journal of Environmental Management*, 71: 79–93.

Tallowin, J.R.B., Smith, R.E.N., Goodyear, J. and Vickery, J.A. (2005) "Spatial and Structural Uniformity of Lowland Agricultural Grassland in England: a Context for Low Biodiversity," *Grass and Forage Science*, 60: 225–236.

UBA (Federal Environmental Protections Agency) (2004) Annual report 2004, Dessau.

Wittig, B., Kemmermann, A.R.G. and Zacharias, D. (2007) "An Indicator Species Approach for Result-orientated Subsidies of Ecological Services in Grasslands – A Study in Northwestern Germany," *Biological Conservation*, 133(2): 186–197.

14 Soil carbon sequestration as an ecosystem service

Madhu Khanna, Hayri Önal, Basanta Dhungana and Michelle Wander

Introduction

Carbon sequestration in agricultural soils in the United States has the potential to remove considerable amounts of carbon from the atmosphere; estimates range from 75 to 208 million metric tons (MMT) annually, representing nearly 8 percent of total US emissions. Studies show that soil sequestration is competitive with other strategies for carbon mitigation, such as afforestation and carbon displacement associated with use of biofuels, but the quantity of carbon sequestered will depend on the price for carbon credits (Antle and McCarl 2002). Several land-use and management practices can be adopted to increase soil carbon sequestration, including conversion from conventionally tilled row crops to conservation tillage to perennial grasses that can be used for forage or for bioenergy production. Two perennial grasses, Switchgrass (*Panicum viragatum*) and Miscanthus (*Miscanthus x giganteus*), have been identified as two of the best choices for low-input bioenergy production in the United States (Lewandowski *et al.* 2003; Heaton *et al.* 2004). We focus here on the use of biomass as a renewable fuel for electricity generation.

The purpose of this chapter is to examine the costs of carbon sequestration in cropland using alternative management strategies and to determine the optimal spatial pattern of land use in a region to achieve given soil carbon sequestration levels. The costs of sequestration depend on the profits foregone and the carbon sequestered by alternative strategies, both of which are expected to vary among those strategies, across space and over time. The potential for soil carbon sequestration varies among strategies with perennial grasses, which have a higher potential to sequester carbon per acre than annual row crops regardless of the tillage applied. Soil carbon sequestration is inherently a dynamic process; the amount of sequestration at any point in time depends on the amount of carbon already present in the soil (West *et al.* 2004). This amount tends to vary spatially depending on land use history and soil and climatic conditions (Tan *et al.* 2006). Moreover, there is an upper limit on the amount of carbon that can be stored in soil with any strategy, and the annual sequestration rate is thought to diminish over time as the soil carbon level approaches an equilibrium established by the land use practice applied (Six *et al.* 2002). Thus accumulation of soil carbon is a non-linear process. This process is also reversible and asymmetric; stored carbon can be released back to the atmosphere if land is reverted back to conventional uses. In this case, rates of soil carbon loss are much higher than rates of accumulation.

The profitability of alternative sequestration-friendly practices relative to the most profitable land use (in the absence of any sequestration considerations) is also likely to vary both spatially (depending on soil conditions, climate and location relative to markets) and temporally (depending on the age of the perennial crops). Additionally, transportation costs can be a significant component of the delivered price of bioenergy and lead to variation in the profitability of growing bioenergy crops across locations depending on their distance from relevant users. In the absence of well-developed markets, the delivered price received by producers is likely to be determined by the price of the fossil fuels they are substituted for and by the policies seeking to promote renewable energy use. Assuming that the price of bioenergy a power plant is willing to pay is the same for all power plants, the farmgate price of biomass is likely to vary spatially, depending on the location of production and the power plant to which the biomass is delivered.

We develop a dynamic framework to investigate the socially optimal pattern of land use in a region that seeks to achieve targeted sequestration levels over a finite time horizon and at the least possible cost. Carbon sequestration dynamics are incorporated by assuming a negative exponential time path of sequestration with saturation limits determined by land use. This time path implies that annual rates of sequestration depend on the initial time of switching to a sequestration-friendly practice. The framework developed here, therefore, incorporates the number of years a land parcel has practiced a sequestration-friendly practice to determine the amount of carbon stored in that parcel. Because landowners have the option to switch in and out of various uses, the soil carbon loss due to a switch from a sequestration-friendly use to a conventional use was also incorporated. We examine the impact of spatial differences in annual sequestration rates on the pattern of land allocation for conservation tillage and bioenergy crops with alternative carbon sequestration targets. The marginal cost of sequestering various levels of soil carbon is determined endogenously and used to develop supply curves for soil carbon sequestration. We use this framework to examine the implications of alternative prices for bioenergy for the marginal cost of carbon sequestration and the optimal allocation of land. As the price of bioenergy increases, the marginal cost of carbon sequestration is expected to decrease. The extent of this decrease depends on the extent to which bioenergy crops contribute to achievement of the carbon sequestration target. We also compare the implications of alternative prices of bioenergy crops and of alternative targets for carbon sequestration for the spatial pattern of land use allocated to either bioenergy crops or conservation tillage practices. We apply this framework using county-level data for Illinois on the costs of producing various crops under alternative rotations and tillage practices and their subsequent contribution to soil carbon sequestration over a 15-year period.

Several economic studies have examined the sequestration potential and costs of afforesting marginal agricultural lands (Parks and Hardie 1995; Alig *et al.* 1997; Plantinga *et al.* 1999; Stavins 1999). Some studies use sector-level analysis to consider sequestration not only through afforestation but also in the agricultural sector by adjusting land uses, crop choices (including biofuels and forestry), and agricultural management practices (McCarl *et al.* 2000; McCarl and Schneider 2001; Lewandrowski *et al.* 2004). These studies analyze the extent to which soil carbon is sequestered at various exogenously given prices in broadly defined regions in the United States. They find that at low carbon payments, conservation tillage would be the dominant strategy for carbon sequestration and that afforestation and biofuels only become viable at higher prices. McCarl and Schneider (2001) do not explicitly consider the dynamics of carbon sequestration and the need for payments over an infinite horizon to maintain carbon permanently in the soil. Lewandrowski *et al.* (2004) compare the implications of payment for permanent carbon sequestration and that of payment for only a 15-year period. They find that the former leads to carbon sequestration levels that are several times greater and with a significantly higher portion provided by afforestation.

In contrast with the above studies, Pautsch *et al.* (2001) and Antle *et al.* (2001) conducted disaggregated studies that focus specifically on examining the economic potential to sequester soil carbon in cropland at various carbon prices in Iowa and Montana. These studies focus on sequestration by changing from conventional to conservation tillage (Pautsch *et al.* 2001) and from crop-fallow systems to grass or continuous cropping (Antle *et al.* 2001). These studies use biophysical models to estimate the carbon accumulated over a 20–30 year period due to a change in land use and convert that to an annual average assuming a linear accumulation function over time. They estimate that at a price of $190 per metric ton of soil carbon, up to one million metric tons (MMT) of additional carbon can be sequestered annually in Iowa (Pautsch *et al.* 2001), and that at a price of $30 per ton of soil carbon, 10.78 MMT of carbon can be stored in 20 years in Montana (see Antle *et al.* 2001). These studies incorporate detailed spatial heterogeneity in costs of sequestration and in sequestration rates, and undertake a static analysis of the potential for soil carbon sequestration at exogenously given prices assuming a constant rate of annual sequestration.

The framework developed here makes several contributions to this literature. First, it accounts for the spatial and temporal variation in the carbon sequestration process by including a carbon accumulation response function. Second, it expands the range of land use options for sequestering soil carbon to include perennial grasses that can be used as a biofuel source for electricity generation. Third, it estimates the marginal costs of sequestration endogenously and analyzes the carbon payments needed to build soil carbon to desired levels at the least cost.

The next section of this chapter discusses the dynamic optimization model, followed by a description of the data used for the numerical simulation in the third section. The results are presented in the fourth section. The final section concludes with a discussion of the policy implications of the empirical findings.

The land use decision model

Our framework is designed to analyze a social planner's land use choices for achieving a predetermined soil sequestration target at the end of a prespecified planning horizon at least cost. Our analysis examines a region that is divided into homogeneous agricultural sub-regions. These sub-regions differ in terms of climate, productivity, relative proximity to power plants, baseline sequestered carbon level, capacity for carbon sequestration and profitability of alternative land uses. Each sub-region is assumed to choose from a pre-specified set of row crops and perennial crops and alternative management practices (rotation and tillage).

Cost and output prices (and therefore, net returns) from row-crop production are assumed to be fixed over time, but to vary spatially. The number of years a land area is continuously under perennial or conservation tillage practice affects the carbon sequestration rate, which varies across sub-regions as explained below. Finally, net returns of production costs and transportation costs from biomass crops also vary spatially since both costs depend on location. The cost of transportation per ton of biomass to a power plant depends on the distance that biomass is shipped. Production costs vary across space and time depending on yields. The price of bioenergy paid by all power plants is assumed to be the same and dependent on the energy content of biomass relative to coal.

The social planner's objective is to allocate land across various crops, rotations and management practices to maximize the sum of discounted aggregate profits over a finite planning horizon of T years and the returns from maintaining the land use achieved in year T permanently, subject to various constraints. The first constraint imposes a target level of soil organic carbon (SOC) sequestration at the end of the planning horizon T. This targeted level is sequestered permanently because land use achieved in year T is maintained permanently. Carbon accumulation depends on each region's site-specific characteristics, specifically the existing level of soil carbon, the long-run equilibrium level of soil carbon, and the natural growth rate of carbon accumulation (as in Arrouays *et al.* 2002). The latter depends on the tillage choice with row crops and on the choice of perennial crop. Carbon accumulation is assumed to increase over time at a diminishing rate and asymptotically approach an upper bound. We also assume that the carbon accumulated on a piece of land is lost and does not contribute to the achievement of the targeted sequestration when that land switches out of the sequestration practice used.

The shadow price of the carbon sequestration constraint represents the discounted present value of foregone profits over the planning horizon to achieve the last unit of sequestered carbon at time T and to maintain that permanently in the soil. It also represents the discounted present value of the marginal cost of achieving a given sequestration target. This is the one-time payment per ton of carbon that would be needed to induce landowners to convert the requisite acres to sequestration-friendly practices to meet the sequestration target. The product of the discounted present value of payment needed and the discount rate is the annualized payment per ton of carbon needed to achieve the given sequestration target. We solve the model repeatedly with different sequestration targets and use the shadow prices associated with these targets to construct a supply function of soil carbon sequestration. The product of the shadow value of carbon and the amount of carbon sequestered by a particular land area (metric tons per hectare) gives the carbon payment per hectare to that land. Although the shadow price of carbon, and thus the marginal cost of carbon sequestration, are uniform over space and time, per-hectare payments for carbon will vary temporally and spatially due to non-linearity in the carbon accumulation function and spatial heterogeneity in the sequestration rate per hectare.

We also include constraints on bioenergy demand and supply. We assume that the market for biomass is constrained by the technical capacities of a coal-based electricity generating plant. Specifically, each power plant can co-fire biomass up to a certain fraction of its capacity to generate electricity. Power plants have the flexibility to acquire biomass from any sub-region. Incorporation of the biomass transportation costs in the objective function implies that each power plant will acquire its biomass input in the least expensive way subject to the sub-region's biomass supplies. Finally, we include a constraint on the total amount of land available and on the ease with which it can be converted from one type of crop or land use to another, to prevent large-scale and abrupt changes in land use. These constraints are partly imposed by the allowable crop rotation possibilities and partly by limits imposed on the extent to which land can be converted from conventional to conservation tillage and from row crops to perennial grasses. The simulation is run in annual time steps for the 15-year period, 2003–2017.

Data description

The framework described above is applied to the state of Illinois using county-level data. The crop choices include four row crops: corn, soybeans, wheat and sorghum; and three perennial grasses: pasture, Switchgrass (*Panicum viragatum*) and Miscanthus (*Miscanthus x giganteus*). The row crops can be grown using either conventional or conservation-tillage practices. We consider 34 different rotation possibilities among these seven crops. The two perennial grasses Switchgrass and Miscanthus not only sequester carbon, but they also provide bioenergy by co-firing with coal to generate electricity at existing power plants in Illinois. Pasture involves a five-year rotation: four years of continuous alfalfa for hay followed by a year of corn for silage. Switchgrass is assumed to have a productive stand life of ten years while Miscanthus is assumed to have a life of 20 years. Five types of data are compiled for these crop choices for each of the 102 counties that comprise approximately 23 million acres of cropland in Illinois (USDA 2003). These include data on crop yields, rotation- and tillage-specific costs of production for row crops, age-specific costs of production for perennials, location and capacity of coal-fired power plants, and annual sequestration rates for soil carbon with conservation tillage and each of the perennial grasses.

The perennial grasses Switchgrass and Miscanthus are warm-season herbaceous crops that have a tolerance for the cool temperatures in the Midwest and can be grown on various types of land with relatively low need for water and fertilizer inputs when using conventional farming practices. The US Department of Energy identified Switchgrass as a "model" crop among 18 other herbaceous crops (not including Miscanthus), and there has been extensive field research on Switchgrass in the United States since 1992 (McLaughlin and Kszos 2005). Miscanthus is a rhizomatous grass that is a native of East Asia and remarkably adaptable to a range of climatic conditions. Research on Miscanthus in Illinois was initiated recently with the establishment of field trials of Miscanthus and Switchgrass at three University of Illinois Agricultural Research and Education Centers (Heaton *et al.* 2006). Field trials show that it has high yields, low fertilizer and pesticide requirements, and high nutrient and water use efficiency.

In the absence of long-term observed yield for Miscanthus in Illinois, we simulate its yield using a process-based crop productivity simulation model, MISCANMOD (Clifton-Brown *et al.* 2004). For Switchgrass, based on the results of field experiments in Iowa and Illinois, we assume an average yield of 9.42 dry tons per hectare for Illinois (see Khanna *et al.* 2008). This is 26 percent of the average yield of Miscanthus predicted by MISCANMOD, and we assume that this ratio remains the same for every county in Illinois. Yields for all row crops and pasture for each county are approximated by their five-year (1998–2002) historical averages obtained from NASS/USDA. We assume that yields do not vary with tillage practice. Finally, when corn is planted on a continuous basis, its yield is assumed to be 12 percent lower than the yield with corn-soybean rotation.

We compiled county-specific construct crop budgets for each row crop and perennial crop. The underlying assumptions are described in Khanna *et al.* (2008). Costs of production differ by tillage practice for row crops. In the case of perennials, costs and revenues are age specific. Transportation costs are calculated using the distance from each county center to each of the 24 coal-fired power plants in Illinois using the great circle distance method and geo-referenced data on location of county centers and power plants (Sinnott 1984).

We used the 2003 loan rates for each county for corn, soybean, wheat and sorghum to estimate the expected revenues from these crops because those prices set the floor price for these crops (FSA/USDA 2003). Other farm subsidies were considered in the form of direct payments decoupled from crop and acreage decisions and based on historical acres under each of these crops. The price of alfalfa was assumed to be uniform across Illinois and set at the average price reported for Illinois in 2003 by NASS/USDA (2005). Since corn silage is typically not marketed, we determined its implicit price by estimating the foregone revenue per acre by growing corn silage instead of corn and the additional cost of fertilizer replacement needed for corn silage (as in Schnitkey *et al.* 2003).

For perennial grasses used for bioenergy production, we assumed that the price a power plant would be willing to pay for co-firing grasses with coal would depend on the cost of coal and the energy content of these grasses. The energy content of Switchgrass and Miscanthus was assumed to be 18 GJ per ton (McLaughlin *et al.* 1996). The average price of coal in Illinois in 2002 was $1.12 per GJ and its heat content was 21.28 GJ per ton of coal (USDOE/EIA 2002). The coal equivalent price that a power plant would be willing to pay for bioenergy is, therefore, $20.22 per delivered dry metric ton (EIA 2004). In practice, this price could be lower if the power plant has to make investments in retrofitting equipment to co-fire grasses or if there is a loss in boiler efficiency with co-firing of grasses. We examined the effect of alternative levels of these prices for bioenergy on the incentives to produce bioenergy crops and on the marginal costs of carbon sequestration. We assumed that use of perennial grasses by power plants is constrained to a maximum of 5 percent of their fuel use, which is determined by their capacity for electricity generation.

To determine the annual sequestration rates for each crop and tillage practice, we first estimated the existing stock of carbon in each county. We obtained estimates of the percentage of soil organic matter (SOM) for each major soil series and hectares in that soil series in each county (including both agricultural and non-agricultural land) in Illinois from an inventory compiled by Alexander and Darmody (1991). This inventory reports the number of acres within each soil series and associated SOM concentrations for each county. We used the data on cropland acreage in each county from 1998–2002 reported in USDA's NASS database and assigned SOM and acreage under each SOM in descending order until the cropland acres were exhausted. Implicit in this is the assumption that land used for agriculture in each county is that with the highest organic matter levels and that land with the lowest SOM is not suitable for agriculture and is being used for other purposes. We then computed a weighted average of the percentage of SOM for cropland in each county. This weighted average of percentage SOM was then converted to the amount of average soil organic carbon using the method employed by Bowman and Peterson (1997). We assumed that about 40 percent of SOM has been lost on currently farmed agricultural land during the last century (Paustian *et al.* 1997; Unger 2001). Recovery of this amount of C is not always achievable because of climatological constraints or changes in hydrology and soil properties. The technically achievable maximum level of SOM, referred to here as the long-run equilibrium level of SOM, was assumed to vary with specific perennial crops, tillage practices, climate, soil types and past land use history (Paustian *et al.* 1997; Six *et al.* 2002). We assumed that conservation tillage and pasture can achieve 70 percent and 75 percent of the maximum capacity, respectively. Switchgrass and Miscanthus are expected to sequester 83 percent and 88 percent of the maximum capacity, respectively. Saturation potentials were based on rates achieved in long-term studies and simulations conducted in the region (see Dhungana 2007).

We updated the county-specific carbon stock from the level in 1991 estimated by Alexander and Darmody (1991) to the level in 2003 due to conservation tillage and pasture by combining data on cropland and pasture from NASS/ USDA and on acreage under conservation tillage from the Conservation Tillage Information Center (CTIC) using methods described by Dhungana (2007). A similar exercise was conducted to allocate duration of time under pasture to the pasture acreage in 2002.

We determined annual sequestration rates for each land use by assuming that carbon accumulation occurs in a non-linear manner with rapid increase in soil carbon in the first ten years and then a gradual leveling off (West *et al.* 2004). The assumptions above imply that annual carbon sequestration rates are higher in a region with higher sequestration potential than in a region with lower sequestration potential. Finally, we assumed that discontinuation of a particular sequestration-friendly land use results in a loss of all accumulated carbon. Our derived rates fall within the range of sequestration rates used in other studies (see Dhungana 2007).

Results

We run the model for a 15-year horizon, namely 2003–2017, for six different levels of sequestration targets ranging between one MMT and 16 MMT in three MMT increments to the business as usual (BAU) level for the fifteenth year. Two alternative bioenergy price levels, namely $1.12 per giga-joule (GJ) and $2.80 per GJ, are coupled with these carbon sequestration targets. The first of these price levels is the coal energy equivalent price that power plants would be willing to pay for bioenergy in the absence of any subsidy. We find that a minimum bioenergy price of $2.40 per GJ will be needed for any biomass to be produced. Prices were then increased in $0.40-per-GJ intervals above this minimum price to examine the land use choices; results are reported here for the $2.80-per-GJ price level. Results are reported in Table 14.1 for the zero and ten MMT and 16 MMT sequestration targets with each of these two bioenergy price levels.

The baseline carbon stock for each county is obtained by projecting the stock of carbon from its estimated level in 1992 to that in 2003, assuming that producers make profit-maximizing land use choices in 2003, and using estimates of the amount of age-specific land under conservation tillage and pasture between 1992 and 2002. The amount of carbon accumulated on land on which conservation tillage was practiced prior to 2003, but not in 2003 (if conservation tillage was not the profit-maximizing land use predicted by the model) is assumed to be released back into the atmosphere and the carbon stock levels on such land revert back to their 1992 level. The BAU carbon stocks at the end of 2003 vary considerably across counties, ranging from 24.5 to 78.6 tons per hectare, and are typically higher in the northeastern and central regions of Illinois. The aggregate baseline carbon stock is estimated to be about 16 MMT in 2003.

Business-as-usual scenario

The BAU scenario assumes no bioenergy subsidy and a carbon sequestration target of zero. The results, displayed in the first column of Table 14.1 show that, in 2017, 45 percent of the 9.4 million hectares of cropland in Illinois would be

Table 14.1 Implications of carbon sequestration targets for land use

Bio-energy price	$1.12 per GJ			$2.8 per GJ		
Carbon sequestration target	None	10 MMT	16 MMT	None	10 MMT	16 MMT
Carbon sequestration over 2003–2017 (million metric tons)	15.85	25.85	31.85	16.77	25.85	31.85
By conservation till (%)	93.53	93.7	94.48	86.88	90.04	91.02
By pasture (%)	6.47	6.3	5.52	6.74	6.29	5.51
By Miscanthus (%)	0	0	0	6.38	3.68	3.46
Land under conservation till (%)	45.07	61.04	70.18	44.61	58.52	67.29
Land under conventional till (%)	52.29	36.33	27.19	51.98	37.83	28.99
Land under pasture (%)	2.64	2.64	2.64	2.64	2.63	2.63
Land under Miscanthus (%)	0	0	0	0.77	1.02	1.09
Marginal cost of carbon sequestration ($/metric ton)	0	130.6	153.62	0	127.39	148.93
Discounted present value of carbon payment to conservation till acres ($M)	0	1,231.25	2,369.98	0	1,001.17	2,046.78
Discounted present value of carbon payment to pasture acres ($M)	0	74.72	87.89	0	72.22	84.43
Discounted present value of carbon payment to Miscanthus ($M)	0	0	0	0	200.53	251.73
Discounted total present value of sequestration C payments for additional above BAU level in 15th year ($M)	0	1,305.97	2,457.87	0	1,273.92	2,382.93
Discounted total present value of C payments for all sequestration above 2003 level ($M)	0	3,574.27	5126	0	3,486.55	4,969.7
Discounted present value of bioenergy subsidy ($M)	0	0	0	496.32	647.38	680.1

under conservation till, less than 3 percent would be under pasture, and the rest would be under conventional tillage. The conservation till and pasture acreages under BAU scenario are 5.6 percent and 10 percent higher, respectively, than their observed values in base year, 2002. As a result of conservation tillage and pasture, the soil carbon level would increase by 16 MMT to 33 MMT in 2017. Of this increase, 93 percent is due to conservation tillage alone. Switchgrass is not profitable at any of the price levels considered here. Land under conservation tillage ranges from 0 to 57 percent of the cropland in individual counties. Counties in central and northeastern Illinois have a relatively high percentage of land under conservation tillage even in the absence of any carbon target or incentive payment for sequestration.

Soil carbon sequestration targets

The impact of imposing a ten MMT and a 16 MMT soil carbon sequestration target to be achieved by 2017 above the BAU level for that year is also reported in Table 14.1. The costs of meeting these targets and their land use implications differ depending on the price of bioenergy. We report the results for two alternative bioenergy prices, $1.12 per GJ (at which there is no biomass production) and $2.8 per GJ (at which some biomass is produced). At the $1.12 per GJ bioenergy price, there is no incentive to produce a biomass crop and the ten MMT carbon sequestration target is achieved by increasing acreage under conservation tillage to 61 percent of cropland. The imposition of a carbon constraint yields a positive shadow price for soil carbon sequestration. For the ten MMT target, this is estimated as $130 per ton and represents the present value of a one-time payment that could be made in 2003 to landowners who adopt practices that contribute to meeting the target in 2017. Alternatively, landowners could be given annualized payments of $5.2 per ton of soil carbon for an infinite horizon to permanently maintain land in a sequestration-enhancing practice.

As the carbon target increases to 16 MMT, acreage under conservation tillage increases to 70 percent and the marginal cost of carbon sequestration increases to $153 per ton. Carbon sequestration targets do not create incentives for producing either Miscanthus or Switchgrass if the bioenergy price is less than $2.4 per GJ.

If the price of bioenergy increases to $2.8 per GJ, it will be economically viable to convert 0.77 percent of the cropland to Miscanthus, which would increase the amount of soil carbon sequestered by one million tons by 2017. This lowers the amount of additional sequestration needed to achieve the targeted level and lowers the cost of sequestration. The imposition of a ten MMT carbon sequestration target would increase the share of cropland under Miscanthus to about 1 percent and raise the share of cropland under conservation tillage to about 60 percent. The contribution of Miscanthus to carbon sequestered is only about 3 percent, while that of conservation tillage is 90 percent. The marginal cost of sequestration of ten MMT and 16 MMT falls by 2–3 percent to $127 per ton and $149 per ton, respectively, with the provision of a bioenergy subsidy.

The above results show that the economic potential for biomass crops like Miscanthus to generate electricity is low (given the low market price of coal-based energy) and remains fairly low even when the contribution to carbon sequestration is valued. Two reasons account for this low potential. The first is a demand constraint: a 5 percent limit for co-firing biomass with coal limits the demand for biomass by power plants even in counties where it is profitable to grow biomass below the price level of $2.8 per GJ. The second reason is the relatively low opportunity cost of sequestering soil carbon through conservation tillage practice. Specifically, with conservation tillage, the average opportunity cost of sequestering one ton of carbon permanently in the soil would be in the range of 55–156 dollars. On the other hand, at the bioenergy price of $2.8 per GJ, the average opportunity cost of sequestering one ton of carbon permanently in the soil through the adoption of Miscanthus would be in the range of 3–824 dollars in the 52 counties where it is profitable to grow it. In 38 counties it is less expensive to sequester carbon through the adoption of conservation tillage than through the adoption of Miscanthus. Thus, meeting low-level targets for soil carbon through conservation tillage is preferred in all of those counties, while only a limited amount of the total cropland needs to be converted to Miscanthus (about 1 percent) in the other counties.

Figure 14.1 shows the marginal cost curve for carbon sequestration in the absence of any biomass production. We find that four MMT of carbon could be sequestered by the fifteenth year at a fairly low price of $40 per ton. The marginal cost rises sharply up to a sequestration target of seven MMT, stays almost flat until the 16 MMT target is achieved, and then rises again as the target is raised to 19 million tons. This indicates that low-cost opportunities for carbon sequestration through conservation tillage are available but limited. The relatively elastic cost curve between the carbon prices $120 per ton and $140 per ton suggests that there is considerable potential for soil carbon sequestration through conservation tillage when prices are in that range. The marginal cost of carbon sequestration depends not only on the sequestration target, but also on the price

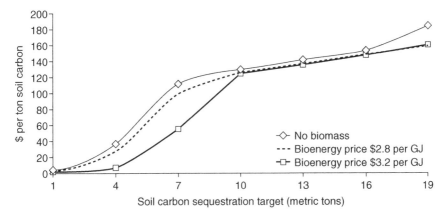

Figure 14.1 Marginal cost of soil carbon sequestration.

of bioenergy. As the price of bioenergy increases to $2.8 per GJ and it becomes more profitable to grow bioenergy crops, the marginal cost of sequestration decreases. Further increase in the bioenergy price to $3.2 per GJ decreases marginal cost even further, particularly in the range between one MMT and ten MMT and for sequestration targets beyond 16 MMT. At very high sequestration targets (beyond 16 MMT), the implied incentive payments per ton of carbon would be high enough to cause a switch to Miscanthus that would be sufficiently large to lower the costs of sequestration. Moreover, the potential for use of conservation tillage to sequester increasing amounts of carbon could be exhausted as practices remain in place and the sequestration target increases. This scenario would make the cost of terrestrial sequestration rise steeply in the absence of a biomass production option.

The land use implications of carbon sequestration targets and bioenergy prices can be seen in Figure 14.2. The acreage under conservation till increases almost linearly as the carbon sequestration target is increased. As the bioenergy price increases, some conservation till acreage would be converted to Miscanthus production. For instance, with the ten MMT carbon sequestration target, the share of cropland under conservation till declines from 61 percent, in the absence of biomass production, to 59 percent with Miscanthus production at a bioenergy price of $2.8 per GJ. Nevertheless, conservation tillage remains the dominant land use strategy for soil carbon sequestration. At any given bioenergy price, the imposition of a carbon sequestration target positively impacts the land area under Miscanthus. At the $2.8 per GJ bioenergy price, Miscanthus acres would increase sharply, particularly as the carbon sequestration target is increased beyond 16 MMT. This is consistent with the finding above, i.e. very high sequestration targets are needed to create significant incentives to grow biomass crops.

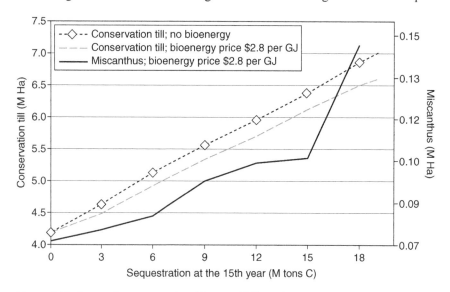

Figure 14.2 Area under conservation tillage and Miscanthus.

The impact of a carbon target on the areas where Miscanthus would be planted is shown in Figures 14.3a and 14.3b. Figure 14.3a shows that Miscanthus production is primarily concentrated in counties that are in close proximity to a power plant. Counties in southern Illinois are likely to have larger acreage devoted to Miscanthus because the yields are higher and production costs are lower in that region. However, transportation costs are also important. The concentration of power plants in northeastern Illinois makes it profitable for some counties there to produce Miscanthus even though the costs of production are relatively high in that region. Figure 14.3b shows that the imposition of a carbon constraint leads to an expansion of the area under Miscanthus in central and northeastern Illinois, often in counties that are bordering those where power plants are located. The incentive payments provided for carbon sequestration make it profitable to grow Miscanthus in areas farther from power plants and incur higher transportation costs to deliver it.

The carbon payment to achieve the sequestration targets considered here also creates incentives to increase the area under conservation tillage. Much of this increase occurs in the northeastern and southern Illinois counties. These are the counties where conservation tillage is unprofitable in the absence of a carbon payment and as a result there is more capacity to sequester carbon in the soil. We find that in three counties (shown with a hatched design) the area under conservation tillage would decline and the land allocation would shift in favor of Miscanthus production in response to the carbon payment.

The total discounted value of carbon payments required to meet the ten MMT sequestration target would be $1,306 million in the absence of any bioenergy subsidy and $1,274 million with a bioenergy subsidy of $1.70 per GJ. Most of these payments would go toward land under conservation tillage. However, the total payments for the ten MMT target would be substantially higher in the presence of biomass production because a direct subsidy (in present value terms) of $647 million would be paid to biomass producers. The carbon payments above are those that are needed to achieve additional sequestration over and above levels that would be achieved under the BAU scenario and are profitable anyway. Difficulties in distinguishing land conversions to sequestration-friendly practices that would have occurred anyway and those that are truly additional might necessitate carbon payments to all farmers that switch to such practices after 2003. In this case the carbon payments required to achieve given sequestration targets would be about two and a half times higher. For example, a ten MMT sequestration target with a $1.12 per GJ bioenergy price would now require carbon payments of $3,574 million instead of $1,306 million.

Sensitivity analysis

The sensitivity of model results to various underlying assumptions is examined with a ten MMT sequestration target and a bioenergy price of $2.80 per GJ. The results are reported in Table 14.2. An increase in the capacity of power plants to utilize bioenergy from 5 percent to 8 percent would increase the land planted under

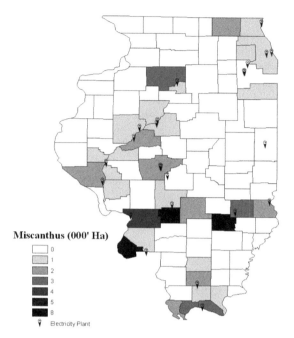

Figure 14.3a Area under Miscanthus with $2.8 per GJ and no carbon constraint.

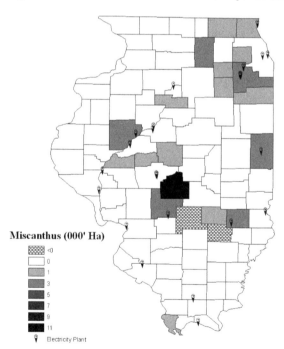

Figure 14.3b Additional area under Miscanthus with $2.8 per GJ and ten million ton carbon constraint.

Table 14.2 Sensitivity analysis[1]

	Increase in power capacity for bioenergy from 5% to 8%	25% increase in biomass production costs	25% decrease in biomass production costs	10% increase in crop yield	25% increase in crop prices	Increase in flexibility of land use changes[2]	Increase in discount rate of 8%	Exclusion of terminal returns to land
Carbon sequestration level in 15 years (Mt)	25.96	25.96	25.96	25.96	25.96	25.96	25.96	25.96
By conservation till (%)	85.44	93.15	83.38	88.85	91.63	86.02	88.93	89.35
By pasture (%)	6.50	6.53	6.50	6.53	6.53	6.92	6.53	6.53
By Miscanthus (%)	8.05	0.31	10.11	4.62	1.83	7.05	4.53	4.11
Land under conservation till (%)	57.67	60.91	57.09	59.09	60.31	58.27	60.49	74.22
Land under conventional till (%)	38.30	36.41	38.74	37.46	36.67	37.82	36.05	22.39
Land under pasture (%)	2.63	2.64	2.63	2.64	2.64	2.75	2.64	2.64
Land under Miscanthus (%)	1.40	0.04	1.55	0.81	0.38	1.16	0.83	0.76
Biomass supply (Mt with 15% moisture)	3.54	0.11	3.75	2.25	1.02	2.87	2.10	1.94
Electricity generated with bioenergy (%)	4.6	0.1	4.8	2.9	1.3	3.7	2.7	2.5
Maximum distance for transportation of biomass (miles)	38.78	10.56	80.75	35.32	26.33	37.85	32.94	32.94
Marginal cost of carbon sequestration ($ t[-1])	126.19	130.60	123 87	139.21	129.53	123.87	51.65	32.69

Notes
1 Bioenergy price: $2.8 per GJ; carbon sequestration target: ten MMT; co-firing limit is 5 percent, i.e. the maximum amount of biomass co-firing is constrained by 5 percent of the total coal-based electricity produced by existing power plants in Illinois.
2 Land use changes are limited to +/–15 percent of those in 2003 instead of to +/–10 percent of those in 2003.

Miscanthus slightly, from 1 percent to 1.4 percent, with a negligible impact on the marginal cost of sequestration. A 25 percent increase or decrease in the cost of producing Miscanthus would also have a small impact on Miscanthus acreage and on the marginal cost of sequestration. A 10 percent increase in row crop yields would increase the cost of relying on biomass crops to achieve the sequestration target and reduce their contribution to sequestration while increasing the marginal cost of carbon sequestration by 9 percent. Allowing greater flexibility in land use changes has a negligible impact on the marginal cost of sequestration.

The discount rate used in the objective function and the inclusion of terminal returns to the land in making land use decisions have the largest impacts on the cost of sequestration. An increase in the discount rate from 4 percent to 8 percent affects the marginal cost of sequestration in two ways. First, it leads to higher annual returns from row-crop production than perennials (which have a two-year gestation lag). As a result, acreage under Miscanthus decreases and more of the carbon target is then met by conservation tillage. This tends to increase the marginal cost of sequestration. Second, and more important, the future costs of land use changes to meet the sequestration target in the terminal year are discounted more heavily, which decreases the present value of the marginal sequestration cost substantially. Exclusion of the terminal returns to the land reduces the incentives for farmers to plant a perennial crop such as Miscanthus, which has a productive life longer than the planning horizon of the model. It also results in much lower marginal costs of sequestration. The marginal costs of sequestration of ten MMT in this case would be much lower ($33 per ton of carbon) than that with permanent sequestration ($127 per ton). However, short planning horizons for carbon sequestration create incentives for temporary carbon sequestration and a reversion to conventional practices at the end of the planning horizon. They are not conducive to investment in perennial grasses that involve high costs of establishment and long payback periods.

Conclusions

This chapter analyzed the costs of soil carbon sequestration in Illinois using dynamic optimization and incorporating a non-linear carbon accumulation function. It considered the potential of both conservation tillage and perennial grasses to sequester carbon. While perennial grasses have a larger technical potential to sequester soil carbon than conservation tillage, they are costly to adopt and typically result in higher costs of sequestration than conservation tillage. The magnitude of these costs depends on the price of bioenergy, leading to a trade-off between a bioenergy subsidy to power plants and a carbon payment to landowners.

Our main findings are as follows. First, at the current coal-based energy price, considerably large bioenergy subsidies would be needed to make it profitable for landowners to grow Miscanthus. Even with these subsidies, the contribution of Miscanthus to the soil carbon sequestered in 15 years remains less than 4 percent and conservation tillage continues to be the primary cost-effective mechanism for soil carbon sequestration. Production of Miscanthus is heavily constrained by location of production sources relative to power plants and by the capacity of the power plants to co-fire bioenergy. Second, the costs of carbon sequestration increase fairly rapidly as sequestration targets increase, particularly up to ten MMT, and then more gradually after that. They increase steeply again at very high sequestration targets. Third, we find that biomass crops can lower the costs of carbon sequestration by up to 8 percent, but mainly at very high carbon sequestration targets and with considerably large bioenergy subsidies. Results are very sensitive to the assumed discount rate and whether sequestration is a temporary or a permanent strategy for mitigating climate change.

Our results have several policy implications. They show that with low coal prices, market incentives to divert land from traditional row crops to biomass crops in Illinois, even if one accounts for the carbon sequestration benefits of biomass crops, are likely to be limited, at least under the present technology and market conditions. Large bioenergy subsidies per unit of energy to power plants and carbon payments per ton of carbon sequestered to landowners would be needed to induce landowners to switch even 1 percent to 2 percent of their crop-land to biomass crops that can be used to produce 3 percent to 5 percent of the electricity generated in Illinois. Moreover, we find that soil carbon sequestration is much less costly if it is a short-run strategy for mitigating climate change rather than as a strategy for permanent reduction in carbon. The availability of this option lowers the incentive to switch to perennial grasses.

This chapter focused only on the sequestration benefits provided by perennial grasses. Further research that incorporates the potential for carbon mitigation and air pollution reduction by using bioenergy to displace coal in power plants is needed to examine the extent to which the price of bioenergy should diverge from the level justified by its coal equivalent heating value. Our results show the extent to which policy-makers can promote carbon sequestration by raising the value of perennial grasses by subsidizing power plants that use bioenergy and/or by providing "green payments" to landowners who switch to sequestration-friendly practices. These payments can reward conservation tillage on working lands or induce the retirement of land from crop production and its conversion to perennial grasses that are harvested for bioenergy. Our results therefore have implications for government payments and show the role that energy policy, conservation policy for working lands and land retirement policies can play in achieving given sequestration goals cost-effectively.

References

Alexander, J.D. and Darmody, R.G. (1991) "Extent and Organic Matter Content of Soils in Illinois Soil Associations and Counties," Champaign: University of Illinois at Urbana-Champaign.
Alig, R., Adams, D., McCarl, B., Callaway, J.M. and Winnett, S. (1997) "Assessing Effects of Mitigation Strategies for Global Climate Change with an Intertemporal Model of the US Forest and Agriculture Sectors," *Environmental and Resource Economics*, 9: 259–274.

Antle, J.M. and McCarl, B.A. (2002) "The Economics of Carbon Sequestration in Agricultural Soils," in T. Tietenberg and H. Folmer (eds.) *The International Yearbook of Environmental and Resource Economics 2002/2003: A Survey of Current Issues*, Northampton, MA: Edward Elgar, 278–310.

Antle, J.M., Capalbo, S.M., Mooney, S., Elliot, E.T. and Paustin, K.H. (2001) "Economic Analysis of Agricultural Soil Carbon Sequestration: an Integrated Assessment Approach," *Journal of Agricultural and Resource Economics*, 26(2): 344–367.

Arrouays, D., Balesdent, J., Germon, J.C., Jayet, P.A., Soussana, J.F. and Stengel, P. (2002) "Mitigation of the Greenhouse Effect. Increasing Carbon Stocks in French Agricultural Soils," French Institute for Agricultural Research (INRA). Online, available at: www.inra.fr/actualites/rapport-carbone/synthese-anglais.pdf.

Bowman, R.A. and Peterson, M. (1997) "Soil Organic Matter Levels in the Central Great Plains," USDA-ARS and NRCS, *Conservation Tillage Fact Sheet #1–96*. Online, available at: www.akron.ars.usda.gov/fs_soil.html (accessed January 15, 2004).

Clifton-Brown, J.C., Stampfl, P.F. and Jones, M.B. (2004) "Miscanthus Biomass Production for Energy in Europe and Its Potential Contribution to Decreasing Fossil Fuel Carbon Emissions," *Global Change Biology*, 10(4): 509–518.

CTIC, C. T. I. C. Online, available at: http://ctic.purdue.edu.

Dhungana, B.D. (2007) "Economic Modeling of Bioenergy Crop Production and Carbon Emission Reduction in Illinois," PhD thesis, Urbana-Champaign: University of Illinois, Department of Agricultural and Consumer Economics.

EIA (2004) "State Electricity Profiles 2004," Energy Information Administration.

FSA/USDA (2003). Online, available at: www.fsa.usda.gov/dafp/psd/LoanRate.htm.

Heaton, E.A., Long, S.P., Voigt, T.B., Jones, M.B. and Clifton-Brown, J. (2004) "Miscanthus for Renewable Energy Generation: European Union Experience and Projections for Illinois," *Mitigation and Adaptation Strategies for Global Change*, 9(4): 433–451.

Heaton, E.A., Voigt, T.B. and Long, S.P. (2006) "Miscanthus X Gigantus: The Results of Trials Alongside Switchgrass (Panicum Virgatum) in Illinois," Plant Science Department, Urbana-Champaign, IL: University of Illinois at Urbana-Champaign. Online, available at: www.ilcfar.org/research/display.cfm?project_id=409.

Khanna, M., Dhungana, B. and Clifton-Brown, J. (2008) "Costs of Producing Switchgrass and Miscanthus for Bioenergy in Illinois," *Biomass and Bioenergy*, 32(6): 482–493.

Lewandowski, I., Scurlock, J.M.O., Lindvall, E. and Christou, M. (2003) "The Development and Current Status of Potential Rhizomatous Grasses as Energy Crops in the U.S and Europe," *Biomass and Bioenergy*, 25(4): 335–361.

Lewandrowski, J., Peters, M., Jones, C., House, R., Sperow, M., Eve, M. and Paustian, K. (2004) "Economics of Sequestering Carbon in the US Agricultural Sector," Economic Research Service TB-1909, Washington, DC: US Department of Agriculture.

McCarl, B.A. and Schneider, U. (2001) "The Cost of Greenhouse Gas Mitigation in US Agriculture and Forestry," *Science*, 294(5551): 2481–2482.

McCarl, B.A., Adams, D.M., Alig, R.J. and Chmelik, J.T. (2000) "Competitiveness of Biomass-Fueled Electrical Power Plants," *Annals of Operations Research*, 94(1): 37–55.

McLaughlin, S.B. and Kszos, L.A. (2005) "Development of Switchgrass (Panicum Virgatum) as a Bio-Energy Feedstock in the United States," *Biomass and Bioenergy*, 28: 515–535.

McLaughlin, S.B., Samson, R., Bransby, D.I. and Weislogel, A. (1996) "Evaluating Physical, Chemical, and Energetic Properties of Perennial Grasses as Biofuels," paper presented at the Bioenergy 96 conference, September 15–20, 1996, in Nashville.

NASS/USDA (2005) Online, available at: http://nas.usda.gov/statisticsbystate/Illinois?Publications/Farm_Reports/2005/ifr0504.pdf.

Parks, P.J. and Hardie, I.W. (1995) "Least-Cost Forest Carbon Reserves: Cost Effective Subsidies to Convert Marginal Agricultural Land to Forests," *Land Economics*, 71(1): 122–136.

Paustian, K., Collins, H.P. and Paul, E.A. (1997) "Management Controls on Soil Carbon," in K. Paustian, E.T. Elliot, E.A. Paul and C.V. Cole (eds.) *Soil Organic Matter in Temperate Agroecosystems*, Boca Raton: CRC Press.

Pautsch, G.R., Kurkalova, L.A., Babcock, B. and Kling, C.L. (2001) "The Efficiency of Sequestering Carbon in Agricultural Soil," *Contemporary Economic Policy*, 19(2): 123–134.

Plantinga, A.J., Mauldin, T. and Miller, D.J. (1999) "An Econometric Analysis of the Costs of Sequestering Carbon in Forests," *American Journal of Agricultural Economics*, 81(4): 812–824.

Schnitkey, G., Lattz, D. and Siemens, J. (2003) "Machinery Cost Estimates: Forage Field Operation," Farm Business Management Handbook, University of Illinois at Urbana-Champaign: Department of Agricultural and Consumer Economics. Online, available at: www.farmdoc.uiuc.edu/manage/pdfs/Mach_forages_2003.PDF.

Sinnott, R.W. (1984) "Virtues of the Haversine," *Sky and Telescope*, 68(2): 159.

Six, J., Conan, R.T., Paul, E.A. and Paustian, K. (2002) "Stabilization Mechanisms of Soil Organic Matter: Implications for C-Saturation of Soils," *Plant and Soil*, 241(2): 155–176.

Stavins, R.N. (1999) "The Costs of Carbon Sequestration: a Revealed Preference Approach," *The American Economic Review*, 89(4): 994–1009.

Tan, Z.X., Liu, S.G., Johnston, C.A., Liu, J.X. and Tieszen, L.L. (2006) "Analysis of Ecosystem Controls on Soil Carbon Stock–Sink Relationships in the Northwest Great Plains," *Global Biochemical Cycles*, 20(4).

Unger, P.W. (2001) "Total Carbon, Aggregation, Bulk Density, and Penetration Resistance of Cropland and Grassland Soils," in R. Lal (ed.) *Soil Carbon Sequestration and the Greenhouse Effect*, Madison: Soil Science Society of America, Special Publication (57): 72–92.

USDA (2003) "Data and Statistics," National Agricultural Statistics Service, US Department of Agriculture. Online, available at: www.nass.usda.gov/Data_and_Statistics.

USDOE/EIA (2002) "State Electricity Profiles 2002," Energy Information Administration, US Department of Energy. Online, available at: www.eia.doe.gov/cneaf/electricity/st_profiles/illinois.pdf.

West, T.O., Marland, G., King, A.W., Post, W.M., Jain, A.K. and Andrasko, K. (2004) "Carbon Management Response Curves: Estimates of Temporal Soil Carbon Dynamics," *Environmental Management*, 33(4): 507–518.

15 Emerging public preferences and the sustainability of farmland preservation

Soji Adelaja, Manuel Colunga-Garcia, Melissa A. Gibson and Mary Beth Graebert

Introduction

US states have increasingly been adopting farmland preservation as a cornerstone of their agricultural policies (Hellerstein and Nickerson 2002; Kline and Wichelns 1996). The rationale appears to be greater recognition of the long-term benefits of preserving farmland. While quality-of-life concerns related to ecology, environment, access to farm amenities, sustainability, farm viability and public access are prominent motives of the public (VHCB 2005; Kline and Wichelns 1996; Nelson 1992; Rosset 1999), most state farmland preservation programs, which involve purchase of development rights (PDR), focus largely on protecting agricultural lands for agricultural purposes (see Table 15.1). For PDR programs to be optimally resourced and supported by the public, they must ultimately incorporate the objectives of the non-farming public, who represent the vast majority of the voting public in most states.[1]

Public concern is shifting away from increasing agricultural production and toward protecting and enhancing the quality of the environment (Bromley and Hodge 1990; Miller 2008; Heinz Center 2002). The public is more willing to pay for agricultural endeavors that are environmentally beneficial (Boody and Krinke 2001). Future preservation funding coalitions should therefore include the broader population of state residents, most of whom are also consumers whose views of agriculture likely differ from those of farmers.

In many states, most consumers live in metropolitan areas and have interests in such accessible farm amenities as pick-your-own operations, fresh food supply, inner-city farmers' markets, bed and breakfasts and agro-tourism. If agriculture could provide more of these benefits, it would enjoy greater legislative and policy support. Future designs of farmland preservation programs must consider these important features, and may have to incorporate them into ranking or scoring systems when identifying ideal farms.

This study explores the emerging goals of society with respect to land preservation. A review of the selection criteria of state farmland preservation programs in the United States identifies emerging economic/market, ecological/environmental, land use and social characteristics, which should increasingly be considered for farmland preservation programs to receive broader acceptance.

Table 15.1 Farmland preservation selection criteria by state, 2005

Selection criteria code

State	1	2	3	4	5	6	7	8	9	10	11	12	13	14	15	16	17	18	19	20	21
California	X	X	X			X				X											
Connecticut	X	X	X	X	X				X							X					
Delaware	X		X	X		X	X			X											
Kentucky	X	X	X	X	X	X	X		X			X									
Maine														X							
Maryland	X	X	X	X	X	X	X			X											
Massachusetts	X	X		X	X	X				X					X						
Michigan	X	X	X			X						X	X			X					
New Jersey	X	X	X	X	X	X		X		X						X	X				
New York		X					X														
North Carolina	X	X	X	X	X			X	X		X	X	X	X	X	X					X
Ohio	X	X	X	X	X	X	X	X	X		X	X	X	X	X		X	X			
Pennsylvania	X	X	X	X	X	X	X	X						X			X		X		
Rhode Island	X	X	X	X			X	X											X	X	
Utah	X	X		X	X	X	X	X	X		X		X					X			
Vermont	X	X	X		X	X	X	X	X		X		X								

Key for selection criteria

1. Number of acres
2. Viable agricultural land
3. Proximity to other farms
4. Soil quality
5. Developmental pressure
6. Location
7. Agricultural preservation district
8. Agricultural practices
9. Level of farm management
10. Commitment
11. Natural resources protection
12. Percent of farm acreage in production
13. Gross sales per year
14. NRCS conservation plan
15. Likelihood of intergenerational transfer
16. Cost of preservation
17. Matching funding
18. Farm infrastructure
19. Local comprehensive plan
20. Mortgage
21. Reasonableness and feasibility

Source: Maryland Agricultural Land Preservation Foundation (MALPF) (2005). *Fact sheets about Maryland's Agricultural Land Preservation Program*. Available at www.malpf.info/facts.html.

Drawing on the vast literature on agricultural resilience, a set of farmland preservation priority indicators, termed "resilience indicators," have been identified. These include indicators of public interest in biodiversity, tourism, amenity value of farmland, access to farms and other survival indicators such as market demographics, market ethnic diversity, proximity to consumers, value-added potential and product diversity.

Specific indicators, chosen based on data availability, were used to generate predictions of farmland acreage that would be preserved by county based on preference. The proximity of such lands to population centers were then assessed via two measures:

1   Gini Coefficient (G); and
2   Ten-County Concentration Ratio (CR_{10}).

The application of the method to the state of Michigan, where policy makers are seeking to expand public support and, therefore, state funding for farmland preservation, suggests that farmer and citizen goals may diverge and that the coalition needed to enhance farmland preservation support could become increasingly fragile if amenities important to non-farmers are not addressed.

Status of farmland preservation programs

In 1979, Connecticut became the first to implement a state farmland preservation program (Adelaja *et al.* 2006). Today, almost 20 states have such programs with $277 million dollars available annually across the nation.[2] Total funding available annually ranges from $0 in Montana, New Hampshire and North Carolina, to $1.5 million in Michigan and Kentucky, to a high of $127 million in New Jersey. According to the American Farmland Trust (AFT 2004a), some 1.4 million acres had been preserved nationwide through state agencies by 2004. The overwhelming majority of states have adopted bond financing as the funding mechanism (AFT 2004a).

Local farmland preservation programs have complemented state programs (Adelaja *et al.* 2006). Earlier adopters in Maryland and New York (Suffolk County, NY, and Harford County, MD) implemented their programs in the mid 1970s. Since then, county programs across the country have acquired approximately 434,000 acres, at a total cost of $170 million (AFT 2004b). State and local programs are often linked, as participation at the state level typically requires local partnership.

Demand for farmland preservation often exceeds what state, local or federal resources can accommodate (Johnson 2007). Therefore, selection criteria were developed by farmland protection programs to help set priorities and focus resources (Ferguson *et al.* 1991; Pease *et al.* 1994). The range of criteria include *purely agricultural production factors* such as farm size, soil quality, proximity to other farms, percent of farm acreage in production, gross sales per year and farm infrastructure. Other less common features include farm *economic profitability* and *viability factors*: acreage of viable agricultural land, location in an agricultural preservation district, utilization of agricultural management practices, level and quality of farm management, reasonableness and feasibility of preservation and level of farmer commitment. Some states also account for development pressure, location and other *land use factors*. Fewer states account for *ecological, environmental* and *sustainability factors* such as natural resources protection, presence of an NRCS (Natural Resource Conservation Service) conservation plan, likelihood of intergenerational transfer, presence of matching funds, cost of preservation or existence of local preservation plans (see Table 15.1).[3]

For agriculture and farmland preservation to be optimally appealing to the general public and to be sustainable, it must convey clear benefits and be synergistic with the public's goals. Therefore, efforts to protect the land base should consider the range of services that agriculture provides to the non-farming public. Farmers are largely rural or suburban residents whose activities are generally located in sparsely populated areas. However, non-farmers are largely located in cities or near-city suburban locations, which have high population density. Therefore, the more farmland is preserved in or near highly populated areas, the more likely farmland preservation will have widespread support. This, of course, assumes that nearness and proximity are key determinants of public support for farmland preservation (Kline and Wichelns 1996; Nelson 1992). Obviously, other determinants of farmland preservation appeal might include farm-sector voice and political clout, public appreciation of preserved farms at remote locations, and statewide appreciation of the role of agriculture.

To explore this complex conflict, we have identified factors that the public is interested in, using Michigan as a case study. Farmland, statewide, is scored on the basis of our resilience factors. High-ranking lands are identified, based on each factor, in order to observe the spatial distribution of priority farms for preservation under each criterion. Concentration measures are then used to examine the implications of alternative criteria for the spatial distribution of priority farms. The measures allow evaluation of how preservation outcomes might vary as one changes objectives from agro-economic factors toward environmental/ecological, land use, economic/market or social factors.

Methods

In developing a framework for identifying the benefits that the public would typically desire from agriculture, we focused on those amenities and activities that synergistically benefit farmers as well as the non-farming public. Previous work by Holling (1973 and 2001), van der Leeuw (2000) and Milestad and Darnhofer (2003) on resilience provided some guidance on mutually beneficial factors. The literature basically suggests that for farmland preservation to be sustainable, it needs to accommodate public interests and concerns.

Holling (1973, 1994, 1996 and 2001) defined resilience in terms of stability, while Milestad and Darnhofer (2003) defined it in terms of adaptability, self-organization and learning potential, highlighting the capacity to adjust and adapt in the presence of systematic changes in the business, social and policy environments. Van der Leeuw (2000) defined social-ecological resilience as the capacity to lead a continued existence by incorporating structural change.

Resilience is a precondition for sustainability (Milestad and Darnhofer 2003). Sustainability requires the ability to deal with multiple uncertainties while juggling changing objectives. Carpenter *et al.* (2001) identified three characteristics of resilient systems:

1   buffer capacity;
2   organizational capacity; and
3   learning and adaptive capacity.

As described by Milestad and Darnhofer (2003), *buffer capacity* relates to environmental adaptability, product diversity, output flexibility, market flexibility, stewardship, socio-economic management capacity, non-specialization and flexible ability to build relationships. *Organizational capacity* involves local support networks with roots in the local community, which can build the foundation for strong relationships with stakeholders. Infrastructure, such as farmers' markets, bed and breakfasts, farm stands, pick-your-own operations, reliance on local inputs and purchases, and community supported agriculture fall under organizational capacity. Finally, *learning and adaptive capacity* relates to farmers' management approaches and learning ability. In this instance, feedback mechanisms and learning/communication mechanisms become very important. Milestad and Darnhofer (2003) point out that specialization, higher productivity, dependence on imported inputs, dependence on distant markets and suppliers, and isolation from next stage processors can all detract from resilience.

Obviously, resilience is a complex unobserved indicator with many components that are difficult to measure. However, one can at least select factors that contribute to resilience. Efficient food and fiber production is a goal of society, and therefore, a component of resilience, as are quality and safety to consumers. Environmental compatibility is a factor, as agriculture must be non-threatening to the environment and to quality of life to be resilient. Other relevant factors that affect the measurement of resilience include: adequate access to fresh produce for consumers, especially underserved communities; adequate farm profitability and quality of life for farmers; flexibility to withstand market instabilities and uncertainties; and environmental and scenic amenities that the public demands. Supplemental farm income, through ecotourism and farm-based recreation, can enhance flexibility, and, therefore, viability and sustainability. In other words, "resilience factors" are "survival factors." We propose that by targeting these factors, public investment in farmland preservation and the benefits to the farm community can be simultaneously optimized.

Selecting resilience indicators

Based on the above and on previous work by Tulloch *et al.* (2003) and Machado *et al.* (2006), the following resilience factors were identified.

Agricultural factors

Acreage of farmland, soil quality, water availability and climate are important determinants of the basic success and resilience of agriculture. These features are represented in the comprehensive designations of "prime" and "unique" farmland. A state's geography may also present a number of regions that are particularly suited for growing specific crops to their full potential.

Economic/market factors

At the farm level, economic viability translates into net income and the ability of farm operators to support a family and invest in the future (Adelaja and Rose 1988). The ability to create and maintain a profit is a clear indication of economic strength. However, agriculture's long-term economic viability is dependent not only on its production efficiency, but also on its ability to adapt to market and other fluctuations.

Farms producing a diversity of agricultural products can more easily adapt to economic and production-related downturns. Thus, diversity in crop, production methods and farm scale are all characteristics of a resilient agriculture. Innovation in growing and processing is also a positive contributor to economic viability (Adelaja 2000). Many farms are strengthening their bottom line by adding value to farm products through processing and packaging. On-farm markets, you-pick operations and agro-tourism all present additional income-generating opportunities for families farming at the urban fringe. The increasing popularity of ethanol is creating expanded markets for crops, such as corn. However, it is important to note that innovations must be based on realistic expectations of the land. Not every farm in a state is suitable for growing every crop.

Proximity to established users of agricultural products and to emerging markets is desirable. Farms in the immediate vicinity of existing elevators and processors may have an economic advantage due to lower transportation costs. Demand for fresh, locally grown vegetables and fruits, as well as meats, eggs and other specialty farm products, is growing. Increasingly, farmers are finding viable opportunities to market their farm products directly to consumers, thus avoiding the wholesale–retail price gap. Farms in physical proximity to population centers may have advantages in their ability to cost-effectively access direct market and tourism-related opportunities, but may face higher costs due to significantly higher rents.

Land use factors

A resilient agriculture must be capable of maintaining an appropriate land base in the face of developmental pressures. "Appropriate land base" allows for a diversity of farm sizes covering a range of production scales. An appropriate land base also clusters agricultural activities to minimize "right-to-farm" conflicts and maintain necessary supporting infrastructure, such as seed sales, equipment repair and veterinarian services. Threats to this land base include growth pressure from population centers and competition for land use. Growth in the urban/rural population ratio and the presence of rising land values help to identify areas that are in danger of losing farmland to other uses. Commitment at the local and regional level to preserving an agricultural land base through right-to-farm protections and farmland preservation programs can contribute to the resilience of agriculture.

Ecological/environmental factors

Farming is inextricably linked to environmental conditions as well as management practices. The long-term productivity of agricultural systems is also dependent on the natural environment's ability to support the industry's pollution emissions and consumption of natural resources. Both natural and managed ecosystems provide many benefits to society, collectively called ecosystem services (Daily 1997), among which are wildlife habitat, biodiversity and groundwater recharge. Some farming practices can also reduce the ability of ecosystems to provide these services (Tilman *et al.* 2002). Many indicators and methods have been proposed to assess ecosystem services provided by agricultural land and agriculture's impact on the environment (Payraudeau and van der Werf 2005). Environmentally conscious farming practices contribute to the sustainability of ecosystems that, in turn, support agricultural business.

Social factors

The socio-demographic characteristics of a region also play a role in its ability to maintain a viable agriculture. For example, the income and education of the consumer base can influence demand for specialty and value-added agricultural products. Ethnic diversity within the farming community is important due to the need for migrant labor on farms and to the growing evidence that minority business owners are some of the most resilient in the nation, with the most potential for growing the employment base of a community (US Department of Commerce 2001). Agricultural land has greater potential of contributing both ecosystem services and aesthetic benefits in areas where human populations are concentrated in urban centers and along major highways. In addition, areas that are tourism destinations stand a greater chance of sustaining agro-tourism operations that cater to recreational travelers and vacationers.

Basic approach

In evaluating the proximity of preserved farmland to highly populated areas, the primary strategy was to determine the acreage of farmland that would be preserved by location under a range of criteria (from agricultural criteria to economic/marketing, land use, ecological/environmental and social factors) and to evaluate the proximity of such preserved farms to population centers. To do this, we:

1   ranked all counties in our study state by population and population density, in order to create a hierarchy of population concentration;

2   identified the locations and costs of preserved lands based on their rankings by specific indicator or characteristics that the public employs in choosing which farms to preserve (for each of the 22 indicators);
3   developed indicators of nearness (or proximity) of preserved acreage to the highest number of people; and
4   compared these proximity indexes across various preservation criteria to determine the nearness of preserved acreage to population centers.

Two measures were used to evaluate the proximity of preserved land to population centers and the subsequent potential for such lands to benefit a high percentage of people:

1   the Gini Coefficient (G); and
2   the Ten County Concentration Ratio (CR_{10}).

G is generally used to measure equity in the distribution of a variable, but here measures the geographic proximity of preserved farms to population. Hence, it is a measure of equitable distribution or access to preserved land by population. As measured in this study, G is the percentage of land preserved in a county versus the percentage of total state population in that county. Similarly, CR_{10} is calculated as the percentage of land preserved that would lie within the top ten most densely populated counties. CRs have been used extensively to measure industrial concentration.

As shown in Figure 15.1, G is a ratio that ranges from zero to one. Its numerator is the area between the Lorenz curve and the uniform (perfect) distribution line (area A). Its denominator is the area under the uniform distribution line (area $A+B$). Therefore, G is $A/(A+B)$. If the Lorcnz curve is represented by $Y=L(X)$, then the value of B is $G=1-2\int_0^1 L(X)dX$. For a population with values y_i, $i=1$ to n, that are indexed in non-decreasing order ($y_i \leq y_{i+1}$),

$$G = \frac{1}{n}(n+1-2\left(\frac{\sum_{i=1}^n (n+1-i)y_i}{\sum_{i=1}^n y_i}\right). \quad \text{(See note 4, p. 280)}$$

A G of zero represents with perfect equality (i.e., preserved lands by county are in the same proportion as population; hence, preserved lands are closer to population centers) and a G of one corresponds to perfect inequality (i.e., preserved lands are dispersed from population centers). Because farmland tends to be more concentrated outside cities, the estimated G (representing existing distribution of preserved farm acreage) is likely to be closer to zero than to one.

CR_{10}, which is the total percentage of preserved land within the largest ten counties in terms of population, is measured as follows:

$$CR_m = \sum_{i=1}^m s_i$$

where m equals ten. A low CR_{10}, of say one percent, suggests that the top ten most populated counties would receive only one percent of preserved farmland.

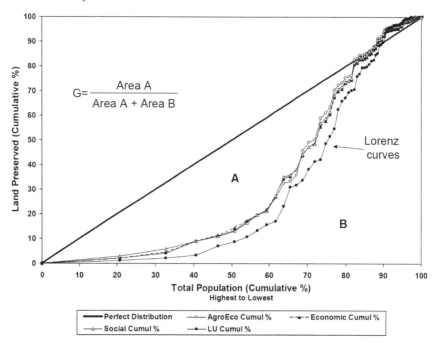

Figure 15.1 Cumulative population and farmland preserved.

This preservation strategy would maximize the benefits to non-urban communities (i.e., most of the preserved farmland is removed from urban cores). However,
a CR_{10} of 100 percent would imply that the leading ten counties maintain 100
percent of preserved land.

Indicators and data management

As revealed above, secondary data on many of the desirable indicators (e.g.,
quality of life for farmers) are non-existent. We therefore used proxies for many
resilience variables. Twenty-two resilience indicators (see Table 15.2 for a complete list and data sources) were selected to prioritize land based on the various
objectives of the farming and non-farming public.

Selected indicators

The unit of analysis, or observational level, utilized in this study was the county.
The indicators chosen were selected to comprehensively reveal the relative resilience of agricultural lands. The raw data for the different indicators were of
various types: numbers of acres, numbers of different species in an ecosystem,
dollars per acre of income, distance ratios, percentages of totals and others.
Within each indicator, a simplified score that ranged from one to ten for each

county was calculated. The scoring revealed where each county lies, with respect to the other counties, for a given indicator. A high score, seven and above, indicates that the county is strong based on a particular resilience measure, and a low score, three or below, indicates the opposite.[5]

Agricultural characteristics

Prime farmland: prime farmland has an adequate and dependable supply of moisture, favorable temperature and growing season, acceptable soil quality, few rocks, is not excessively erosive, rarely floods and is not saturated with water for extended periods of time. All of these characteristics combine to make farming on prime farmland more economically viable and resilient. The percentage of county cropland that is considered prime farmland is selected as an agricultural characteristic, with a high score indicating that a comparatively high percentage of prime farmland is available.

Unique farmland: according to the USDA's definition, unique farmland is land other than prime farmland that is used for the production of specific high-value food and fiber crops. It has the special combination of soil quality, location, growing season and moisture supply needed to produce a sustained high quality and/or high yields of a specific crop in an economic manner. It is difficult to aggregate maps of unique farmland by county in a way that would easily allow the calculation of the proportion of agricultural products that were produced from unique farmland. A crop uniqueness factor (CUF) was used as a proxy for unique farmland, and is measured as the uniqueness of a crop in Michigan based on the number of counties in the state that grow the commodity (CUF = 1-[Number of counties planting a crop (i)/83]), with 83 being the total number of counties, all growing alfalfa hay.[6] We assumed that the fewer the counties that grow a particular crop, the more unique the farmland is in a county that is able to grow this type of crop. All the CUFs in a county were added and the final sum was divided by the number of crops to obtain an average. A high score indicates that a county has a high degree of unique farmland.

Economic/market characteristics

Farm viability: profitability served as a proxy for viability in this study. It was measured as the average net cash receipts per acre for each county. A high score indicates that the average farm in the county is economically viable.[7]

Economic support: measured as government payments per acre of land in the county, this indicator shows the dependence of agriculture on government to achieve viability. A high score indicates that the average farm in the county has a low level of economic support/reliance.

Value-added potential: the potential for a farmer to achieve greater profits by adding value through new processes or products can increase agricultural viability. Value-added potential was measured as the value of a farm's output compared to the value of the intermediate and final goods produced from the crops. It was measured based on the marketing margin in 2000 or 2001, depending on the crop and the year for which the data are available. Farm value share of retail price (percent) for specific crops (when available), or farm value share of retail cost for a commodity group (bakery and cereal products, processed fruits and vegetables, fresh vegetables, fresh fruit) were used as proxies for marketing margin when no data for the specific commodity were available. A high score indicates that the average farm in the county has a high value-added potential.

Product diversity: this indicator measures the variety of agricultural goods produced, including raw commodities, processed goods and products derived from livestock. It was measured as the number of commodities for which a given county had more than 5 percent of the state's total agricultural production in 2002. The commodities for which Michigan is in the top five producers in the nation, as well as traditional cash crops, were included in this study, with a high score indicating that product diversity in the county is high.

Proximity to farmers' markets: this indicator was derived by measuring the proximity of markets to farmland. The first component of this indicator is the number of farmers' markets in the county and surrounding counties, which provides a measure of accessibility of farmers' markets to producers. The second component is the inverse of the average distance to farmers' markets from the county farmland centroid, providing a measure of proximity. The values from these two components were multiplied to obtain a gravity measure of proximity to farmers' markets, with a high score indicating high proximity to farmers' markets in the county.

Proximity to food processors: the first component of this indicator is the number of processors in the county and surrounding counties, providing a measure of accessibility of processors to producers. The second component is the inverse of the average distance to food processors from the county farmland centroid, providing a measure of proximity. These two components were then multiplied to obtain a gravity measure of proximity of farmland to food processors, with a high score indicating high proximity.

Proximity to grain elevators: the first component of this indicator is the number of elevators in the county and its surrounding counties, providing a measure of accessibility to elevators by grain producers. The second is the inverse of the average distance to grain elevators from the county farmland centroid, providing a measure of proximity. These two components were then multiplied to obtain a gravity measure of proximity of farmland to food processors, with a high score indicating high proximity.

Commodity viability: to measure the level of commodity viability in each county, data was collected on the total production of those commodities where Michigan is ranked in the top five nationally. Commodities included three main groups: fruits (tart cherries, sweet cherries, apples, plums, grapes and blueberries), vegetables (cucumbers, celery, asparagus, carrots, squash, tomatoes and pumpkins) and field crops (dry beans and sugar beets). The average price per harvested acre for each commodity group was multiplied by the acreage in that group to obtain the commodity viability measure in dollars, with a high score indicating the county has comparatively high viability by commodity group.

Proximity to customers: this measures the closeness of the farmland or farm products to the customers who generate the final demand for the good. Being close to consumers can cut down on transportation costs and provide greater opportunities for agro-tourism, farm-stand sales and enhanced social networks with the non-farming community. The index of urban influence developed by the USDA ERS was used as the proxy for this indicator. A high score indicates that in the county, the distance between customers and farmland or farm products is comparatively small.

Livestock local demand: this variable is a proxy for the demand for crops to feed livestock and land to dispose of their wastes. It was assumed that greater livestock demand creates a greater demand for cropland, and a greater degree of resilience. For this indicator, data always were collected on the inventories of the following categories:

1　horses and ponies;
2　cattle and calves;
3　beef cows;
4　milk cows;
5　hogs and pigs;
6　sheep and lambs; and
7　chickens (layers and broilers).

Livestock local demand was calculated by multiplying the inventory of each type of livestock by its corresponding "Animal Unit," a proxy for the feed demand and manure production of each animal type. A high score indicates high local livestock demand.

Land use characteristics

Population pressure: this measures the real or perceived threat of the conversion of farmland to other uses, like residential development, as the population of an area grows. As demand for farmland for other uses grows, and land values rise, the farmers are less likely to stay in business (Adelaja and Lake 2005). Population pressure was measured as the change in the ratio of urban to rural population between 1990 and 2000, with a high score indicating high population pressure.

Farm size diversity: this measures flexibility (meeting different kinds of demand) and resilience (surviving different types of economic hardships) of a county's agriculture. The farm size diversity indicator used here was based on the number of farms in different size categories as reported in the US Census of Agriculture (NASS 2002). There are six broad scales (1–9 Acres, 10–49 Acres, 50–179 Acres, 180–499 Acres, 500–999 Acres and 1,000+ Acres) and the degree of disbursement (variation) of farms over all six categories provided a measure of size diversity. A high score indicates high diversity.

Farm contiguity: the more contiguous farm acreage is the better farmers are able to access inputs, share labor and machinery, and avoid right-to-farm conflicts, improving agricultural resilience. Quantification of farm contiguity involves the characterization of the spatial clustering between farm parcels. Due to the lack of an integrated statewide layer of farm parcel information, the clustering of agricultural land use was instead used as an indicator of farm contiguity. Land use clusters of 0.25 miles squared (162 acres) were created from the IFMAP/GAP Michigan Land Cover. Adjacent clusters that contained 10 percent or more of agricultural land were then summed. The estimation of farm contiguity (F) was $F=[P+N]/2$ where P is the size of the largest cluster divided by the total agricultural land and N is the inverse of the number of clusters. Values ranged from zero to one, with a high score indicating high contiguity.

Competition for land use: this refers to the threat of farmland loss due to changes in surrounding land uses (e.g., development encroachment and unfettered growth from residential, commercial and industrial expansion). To measure the degree of competition for land use in a county, the difference between farmland acreage in 1997 and 2002 was used. A high score indicates a high degree of farmland loss, and, thus, competition for land. Michigan counties are very similar in size, therefore there was no need to use the percentage of total acreage converted as a measure.

Current preservation: agricultural land can include crop, range, pasture, forest and other rural land. Current preservation refers to the total farmland in acres that is preserved in the county through two state preservation programs, the Agriculture Preservation Fund Program and the PA 116 Program. A high score indicates a high percentage of farmland being preserved, and a higher resilience factor.

Ecological characteristics

Biodiversity: this refers to the full range of natural variety and variability within and among living organisms and the ecological and environmental complexes in which they occur. A greater degree of biodiversity in a farming community is a measure of agriculture's contribution to natural systems, indicating more sustainable use of the land and provision of environmental services to the surrounding area. To measure the level of biodiversity, data were obtained on the number of species of plants and animals found in each county (MNFI 2001). A high score indicates a large variety of species. The biodiversity score appears correlated with the location of the county.

Social characteristics

Income demographics: this indicator is based on statistical data about the median income of the population by county in Michigan. It is an important indicator because the generation of demand for farmers' products depends on the income demographics of the county's residents. For example, high value organic food is a luxury good, and a change in income causes a larger change in the demand for luxury goods than normal goods. This relatively elastic demand for high value crops presents an opportunity for farmers to take advantage of income demographics and increase agricultural viability. The median household income for each county serves as the proxy for income demographics. A high score indicates a high income.

Ethnic diversity: this refers to the diversity among people in a geographic area according to racial, national, tribal, religious, linguistic or cultural origins. Ethnic diversity was measured by gathering information on minority farm operators, which was used to calculate the ratio of minority farmers to all farm operators. A high score indicates high ethnic diversity.

Tourism: tourism and tourist-related business involvement was measured from information collected on the percentage of market share of pleasure trips from the report *Michigan at the Millennium* (Ballard *et al.* 2003). A high score indicates that tourism opportunities are strong.

Amenity value: amenity value was measured by estimating the proportion of agricultural land in relation to other vegetation. Estimates of buffer areas around roads (0.5 miles) and urbanized areas (five miles) were generated in order to estimate the contribution of agricultural land to visible open space. This indicator is used as a proxy for aesthetic amenities provided by farmland. A high score indicates that agriculture highly contributes to open space values.

Data management

We acknowledge that the data utilized to represent different characteristics of agricultural resilience are not always ideal. For instance, the economic values of the environmental and social benefits of farmland are difficult to quantify.[8] The available data on indicators were ranked using a scoring system ranging from one to ten (one being least preferred, ten being most preferred). Hence, the range of data, from the minimum to the maximum, was divided into ten equal ranges (see Adelaja *et al.* 2006).

The scores were converted into percentages, such that a score of zero indicates that 0 percent of available farmland would be preserved, while one indicates that 100 percent of the available farmland would be protected. That is, the higher a county scored, the higher the percentage of land in the county that would be preserved. This framework obviously ignores local affordability issues, and assumes that funding was fully available for all lands targeted through this methodology. This approach allows us to observe the spatial distribution of acreage to be protected. The projected acres were utilized in the creation of state maps. The maps show where counties score high and low in terms of each characteristic. In looking at these maps, patterns or regions of comparative advantage for different aspects of agriculture can be seen.

The Gini Coefficient and the CR_{10} were used to calculate the concentration of desirable land near more densely populated areas. In using the Gini Coefficient, the trapezoidal approximation method was employed in order to simplify the analysis. Also, for ease of deciphering high and low population communities, the Gini Coefficient is estimated with numbers from high to low.

Empirical results

The application of our method to Michigan data yielded some interesting results.[9] Examine first the total qualified acreage for preservation, statewide, under each criterion, as shown in Table 15.2 (for ease of display, the indicators are grouped into the categories of agro-ecological, economic/marketing, social and land use).

The most acreage that would be preserved would be through a focus on commodity viability (870,000 acres), followed by product diversity (743,000 acres), value-added potential (730,000 acres), amenity value (726,000 acres), prime farmland (710,000 acres), proximity to consumers (706,000 acres), farm contiguity (698,000 acres) and proximity to grain elevators (614,000 acres). The least acreage preserved, statewide, would be through a focus on tourism (192,000 acres), ethnic diversity (299,000 acres), proximity to food processors (316,000 acres), biodiversity (363,000 acres), farm viability (369,000 acres) and current preservation (370,000 acres). That is, viable farms are closest to where the largest concentrations of Michiganders live. The fact that targeting some of the economic and marketing factors would make more land eligible suggests that targeting economic success creates a better win-win situation: more land is eligible while still focusing on farms with a greater chance of financial success. The fact that prime farmland ranks high (at fifth) suggests an abundance of good soils. It is surprising that projected preservation acreage from such factors as proximity to consumers and amenity value scores highly. This is encouraging to those who favor the preservation of amenity values and those who believe that farmland preservation can be more strategically focused on viability.

Figure 15.2 presents the projected farmland acreage, by county, that would be preserved for two indicators (current preservation and tourism).[10] Indicators such as commodity viability and product diversity, which are predicted to preserve the most farmland acreage, have the majority of preservation occurring in the southeastern portion of the state. Indicators such as tourism and ethnic diversity are predicted to preserve the least acreage of farmland; however, tourism acreage would be more concentrated around urban areas, whereas acreage preserved for ethnic diversity would be slightly more dispersed across the state. Nearly all indicators would predict preserving a relatively high number of acres in the "thumb" region of the state, indicating that this farmland is extremely diverse in its amenities and is included in many categories, and that the Saginaw Bay region, in particular, has a high concentration of predicted farmland preservation acreage.

The volume of land preserved only tells a part of the story. Our focus here is distributional equity. The G were estimated using the predicted farmland acreage based on each resiliency indicator (see Table 15.2). A lower G means that the preserved farmland would be more equitably located closer to where the majority of population lives. Higher G, on the other hand, indicate that preserved land is not distributed proportionately to population, and, hence, would be located away from population centers.

Figure 15.2 Concentration of preserved acreage under selected alternative indicator scenarios.

Table 15.2 Projected preserved acreage and concentration measures under 22 preservation scenarios

Category	Indicator	Source	Acres preserved		Gini		CR[10]	
			Acres	Rank	G (%)	Rank	(%)	Rank
Land Use	Current preservation	Farmland and Open Space Preservation Program, MI Dept. of Ag.	369,547	17	64.56	22	12.14	22
Land Use	Farm size diversity	US Census of Ag., 2002, Table 8.	511,482	11	63.79	21	12.42	21
Econ/Mkt	Economic support	US Census of Ag., 2002, Table 5.	445,699	13	63.19	20	13.51	18
Econ/Mkt	Livestock local demand	US Census of Ag., 2002, Tables 11 through 16 and Table 22.	385,318	16	62.79	19	12.73	20
Econ/Mkt	Proximity to food processors	Food Processor Locations (J. Bingen) IFMAP/GAP MI Land Cover.	315,850	20	61.32	18	13.31	19
Econ/Mkt	Commodity viability	US Census of Agriculture, 2002.	869,880	1	60.68	17	14.85	15
Social	Amenity value	IFMAP/GAP Michigan Land Cover. Urbanized areas from US Census Bureau, and MI roads from MI Center for Geographic Info.	725,910	4	60.24	16	14.24	16
Land Use	Farm contiguity	IFMAP/GAP Michigan Land Cover.	698,487	7	60.15	15	13.99	17
Land Use	Competition for land use	US Census of Agriculture 1997 and 2002, Table 8.	544,574	9	60.07	14	16.19	12
Social	Ethnic diversity	US Census of Agriculture, 2002, Tables 41 through Table 50.	299,374	21	59.38	13	17.44	7

Category	Criterion	Source						
Agr/Eco	Prime Farmland	State Soil Geographic Database (STATSGO).	709,630	5	58.96	12	15.50	14
Econ/Mkt	Proximity to grain elevators	Grain dealer locations (J. Bingen), IFMAP/GAP MI Land Cover.	613,678	8	58.38	11	16.09	13
Econ/Mkt	Farm viability	US Census of Agriculture, 1997, Table 4.	369,285	18	58.28	10	18.97	5
Econ/Mkt	Product diversity	US Census of Agriculture, 2002, Tables 24–34.	743,412	2	57.73	9	16.96	11
Econ/Mkt	Value-added potential	US Dept. of Agriculture, Economic Research Service (USDA ERS).	730,925	3	57.70	8	17.05	10
Social	Income demographics	US Census of Population and Housing, 2000.	415,739	15	55.87	7	17.98	6
Econ/Mkt	Proximity to farmers' markets	Farmers' Market Locations (J. Bingen), IFMAP/GAP MI Land Cover.	523,715	10	55.20	6	20.26	3
Land Use	Population pressure	US Census of Population and Housing, 1990 and 2000.	453,569	12	54.94	5	17.28	9
Agr/Eco	Unique farmland	US Census of Agriculture, 2002 (harvested acreage).	443,840	14	54.83	4	20.37	2
Agr/Eco	Biodiversity	MI Natural Features Inventory. *MI County Element Lists. March 2001.*	362,908	19	54.62	3	17.29	8
Econ/Mkt	Proximity to customers	US Dept. of Agriculture, Economic Research Service (USDA ERS).	706,351	6	54.57	2	19.17	4
Social	Tourism	Ballard et al. (2003).	191,937	22	50.04	1	28.92	1

Note
Categories: Land Use, Economic Market (Econ/Mkt), Social, Agricultural/Ecological (Agr/Eco).

As shown in Table 15.2, the current farmland preservation program yields the highest G, and therefore the least concentration of land around population centers. This is not surprising and suggests that as other indicators are brought in, the concentration of preserved land would move toward equitable access to people in more urban communities. The fact that the current program yields the greatest dispersion is cause for concern. This highlights the fact that the current system is still very far from where the general public in Michigan may want it to be. As shown in Table 15.2, some of the agricultural- and viability-oriented indicators yield the highest G. That is, farm size diversity (0.638), economic support (0.632), livestock local demand (0.628), proximity to food processors (0.613) and commodity viability (0.610) yield the least amount of access of farmland to urban residents. On the other hand, using the consumer- and urban-oriented indicators, one gets the most concentrated acreage of land around urban areas (tourism=0.500, proximity to consumers=0.546, biodiversity=0.546, unique farmland=0.548, population pressure=0.549, proximity to farmer markets=0.552, income demographics=0.559 and value-added potential=0.577). These results confirm our hypothesis that the concentration of preserved farmland around population centers is endogenous to the selection criteria. The Lorenz Curve for each indicator category is shown in Figure 15.1. The land-use related indicators yields the highest distribution inequity, while the social related categories yield the highest distribution equity.

Again using the predicted farmland acreage based on each resiliency indicator, the CR_{10} were estimated (see Table 15.2). A high estimated CR_{10} indicates that a high proportion of the land preserved based on the given indicator would be concentrated in the urban parts of the state. As with the G, the current farmland preservation program yielded the least equitable distribution of acreage and therefore the lowest CR_{10}. Tourism, as with the G, yielded the most equitable distribution of acreage and therefore the highest CR_{10}. The pattern observed for the G was very similar to the pattern for the CR_{10}, with a few exceptions.

Conclusions

This chapter evaluated the potential for differences in the priorities of urban residents, vis-à-vis traditional farmland preservation stakeholders, to yield differences in preferred location of preserved farmland. Therefore, it evaluated the implications of an increasing focus on economic/market, land use, ecological/environmental and social priorities for the proximity of selected preserved land to urban populations. The findings are consistent with a priori expectations and the conclusion of Hellerstein and Nickerson (2002) that the design of preservation programs has implications for the spatial pattern of permanently preserved lands, and hence, the location of preserved rural amenities. In other words, traditional proponents of farmland preservation differ from the general public in their priorities, and these differences imply different preferences in terms of where farmland is preserved.

The Gs and the $CR_{10}s$ suggest that as society begins to accommodate the interests of the non-farming public in amenities and direct benefit of agriculture to them, the priorities for farmland preservation will shift away from preserving traditional agricultural characteristics to preserving amenities of importance to the non-farming public. These amenities include factors such as access to tourism, proximity of farms to consumers, biodiversity, unique farmland, population pressure, proximity to farmers' markets, income demographics, value-added potential and product diversity. One implication of this is that farmers must increasingly compromise and strike a balance between their priorities and those of other preservation stakeholders.

A question that therefore emerges is the extent to which state-scoring systems for preserved farmland should be adjusted to accommodate the growing needs of the non-farming public. As indicated by Kline and Wichelns (1996), these programs are already shifting their priorities. The question is how quickly they must adjust to enhance the viability of farmland preservation programs by attracting increased interest of the non-farming public and without compromising too much of their own interests. This raises the issue of a trade-off between the preferences of farmers and their non-farming counterparts, and the relative gains and losses to each as one moves the priorities away from farmers' interests. Obviously, the ranking system and the criteria for farmland preservation are a public choice issue, that decision makers must balance by attempting to optimize the ultimate benefit to society as well as generating optimal support for their actions. The fact that many state farmland preservation management boards have a high concentration of farmers suggests that more input from non-farmers may be beneficial.

Notes

1 Productive and viable farms may only survive or be sustainable if they are compatible with other land uses or are valued by the general public. Therefore, the criteria for preservation must at least consider goals beyond agricultural performance and viability. Today, farmers represent less than 1 percent, and farm families less than 2 percent, of the general public in the United States (US EPA 2006). The coalitions that support funding for farmland preservation tend to have other motivations beyond purely agricultural interests (Kline and Wichelns 1996; Hellerstein and Nickerson 2002).
2 For a complete table of the status of all state and local farmland preservation programs, including year started, acres protected, annual funds and funding source, see *Acreage and Funding Goals for Farmland Preservation in Michigan: Targeting Resiliency, Diversity and Flexibility* (Adelaja *et al.* 2006). Also available is a table presenting information on the level and nature of jurisdiction for state and local farmland preservation programs.
3 For example, Massachusetts recognizes the importance of both land retention and farm viability. Its Farm Viability Enhancement Program couples preservation through non-development covenants with support for the underlying farm infrastructure through guided business planning. Funds are made available to farms that submit successful applications based on specific intergenerational, land mass, economic, diversification, value added, operator experience, environmental and productivity objectives. Professional expertise is then offered to selected farms to help develop and implement a sustainability plan, using funds provided by the state (MDAR 2005).

4 For a discrete probability function $f(y)$, where y_i, $i = 1$ to n are the points with non-zero probabilities and which are indexed in increasing order $(y_i < y_i + 1)$, then $G = 1 - \sum_{i=1}^{n} f(y_i)(S_{i-1} + S_i/S_n)$, where $S_i \sum_{j=1}^{i} f(y_i)y_i$ and $S_0 = 0$. For a cumulative distribution function $F(y)$ that is piecewise differentiable, has a mean μ, and is zero for all negative values of y, $G = 1 - 1/\mu \int_{0}^{\infty} i(1 - F(y))^2_{dy}$.

5 For more complete information on how each variable was compiled, including further explanation of data sources (other than Table 15.2), visit the Land Policy Institute website at www.landpolicy.msu.edu and review the "Acreage and Funding Goals for Farmland Preservation in Michigan: Targeting Resiliency, Diversity and Flexibility" report (Adelaja *et al.* 2006).

6 This measure is based on the assumption that the primary factor that limits the ability to grow a crop is the availability of suitable farmland. Inherent in this assumption is that market price changes do not affect an area's crop mix. While this assumption may be valid in the short run in a competitive industry, such as agriculture, it may not be valid in the long run.

7 Because 2002 was an unusual year in terms of the weather and was marked by large losses of fruit crops, 1997 data were used to generate a more representative measure. Viability is often related to the opportunity costs facing a farmer, especially with respect to development pressure. An indicator of development pressure is accounted for later in the chapter.

8 This framework is based upon a static approach which does not allow for the assessment of how agriculture might be affected in the future by changes in demand, markets, cost of complementary goods and a host of other factors.

9 At $2,000 per acre (the average cost of farmland preservation in 2003), it would cost approximately $20 billion to protect the 10,142,958 acres of farmland in the state. This goal is unattainable.

10 Projected preserved farmland for all 22 resiliency indicators are reported. "The Future of Farmland Preservation Programs, from Retention to Viability to Resiliency" (Adelaja *et al.* 2007), available at www.landpolicy.msu.edu.

References

Adelaja, A.O. (2000) "Agricultural Viability at the Urban Fringe: the Case of New Jersey," paper presented at the New Jersey Agricultural Leadership Development Program, Phillipsburg, New Jersey, June.

Adelaja, A.O. and Lake, M.B. (2005) "Agricultural Viability at the Urban Fringe," selected paper presented at the International Conference on Emerging Issues along Urban/Rural Interfaces: Linking Science and Society, Atlanta, Georgia, March.

Adelaja, A.O. and Rose, K.B. (1988) "Farm Viability Revisited: A Simultaneous-Equation Cash Flow Approach," *Agricultural Finance Review*, 48: 10–24.

Adelaja, A.O., Colunga-Garcia, M., Gibson, M.A. and Lake, M.B. (2007) "The Future of Farmland Preservation Programs: from Retention to Viability to Resiliency," paper presented at the Trans-Atlantic Land Use Conference (TALUC), Washington, DC, September.

Adelaja, A.O., Lake, M.B., Colunga-Garcia, M., Hamm, M., Bingen, J., Gage, S. and Heller, M. (2006) *Acreage and Funding Goals for Farmland Preservation in Michigan: Targeting Resiliency, Diversity and Flexibility*, Land Policy Institute Report Series, 2006–1.

American Farmland Trust (AFT) (2004a) *Status of State PACE Programs*, Farmland Information Center. Online, available at: www.farmlandinfo.org/documents/29942/PACE_State_7–04.pdf (accessed 2005).

American Farmland Trust (AFT) (2004b) *Status of Local PACE Programs*, Farmland Information Center. Online, available at: www.farmlandinfo.org/documents/27749/ PACE_Local_8–04.pdf (accessed 2005).

Ballard, C., Courant, P., Drake, D., Fisher, R. and Gerber, E. (eds.) (2003) *Michigan at the Millennium: A Benchmark and Analysis of its Fiscal and Economic Structure*, East Lansing: Michigan State University Press.

Boody, G. and Krinke, M. (2001) "The Multiple Benefits of Agriculture: An Economic, Environmental and Social Analysis," Land Stewardship Project. White Bear Lake, MN.

Bromley, D. and Hodge, I. (1990) "Private Property Rights and Presumptive Policy Entitlements: Reconsidering the Premises of Rural Policy," *European Review of Agricultural Economics*, 19(2): 197–214.

Carpenter, S., Walker, B., Anderies, J.M. and Able, N. (2001) "From Metaphor to Measurement: Resilience of What to What?" *Ecosystems*, 4: 765–781.

Daily, G.C. (1997) *Nature's Services: Societal Dependence on Natural Ecosystems*, Washington, DC: Island Press.

Ferguson, C.A., Bowen, R.L. and Khan, M.A. (1991) "A Statewide LESA System for Hawaii," *Journal of Soil and Water Conservation*, 46(4): 263–267.

Heinz Center (2002) *The State of the Nation's Ecosystems*, H. Johns Heinz III Center for Science, Economics, and the Environment, Cambridge: Cambridge University Press.

Hellerstein, D. and Nickerson, C. (2002) "Farmland Protection Programs: What Does the Public Want?" *Agricultural Outlook*, Economic Research Services: US Department of Agriculture, May: 1–4.

Holling, C. (1973) "Resilience and Stability of Ecological Systems," *Annual Review of Ecology and Systematics*, 4: 1–23.

Holling, C. (1994) "An Ecologist View of the Malthusian Conflict," in K. Lindahl-Kiessling and H. Landberg (eds.) *Population, Economic Development, and the Environment*, New York: Oxford University Press.

Holling, C. (1996) "Engineering Resilience Versus Ecological Resilience," in P.C. Schulze (ed.) *Engineering Within Ecological Constraints*, Washington, DC: National Academy Press.

Holling, C. (2001) "Understanding the Complexity of Economic, Ecological and Social Systems," *Ecosystems*, 4: 390–405.

Johnson, R. (2007) *Farm Protection Program: Status and Current Issues*, Congressional Research Service Report for Congress: The Library of Congress, code RS22565.

Kline, J. and Wichelns, D. (1996) "Measuring Public Preferences for the Environmental Amenities Provided by Farmland," *European Review of Agricultural Economics*, 23: 421–436.

Machado, E.A., Storms, D.M., Davis, F.W. and Kreitler, J. (2006) "Prioritizing Farmland Preservation Costs Effectively for Multiple Objectives," *Journal of Soil and Water Conservation*, 61(6): 250–258.

Massachusetts Department of Agricultural Resources (MDAR) (2005) *Farm Viability Enhancement Program*, Massachusetts Department of Agricultural Resources. Online, available at: www.mass.gov/agr/programs/farmviability (accessed 2005).

Michigan Natural Features Inventory (MNFI) (2001) *Michigan County Element Lists*, Michigan Natural Features Inventory. Online, available at: http://web4.msue.msu.edu/ mnfi/data/County_lists_2001.pdf (accessed March 2001).

Milestad, R. and Darnhofer, I. (2003) "Building Farm Resilience: The Prospects and Challenges of Organic Farming," *Journal of Sustainable Agriculture*, 22(3): 81–97.

Miller, F.P. (2008) "After 10,000 Years of Agriculture, Whither Agronomy?" *Agronomy Journal*, 100(1): 22–34.

National Agricultural Statistics Service (NASS) (2002) *Census of Agriculture*, Table 4, Net Cash Farm Income of the Operations and Operators. Online, available at: www. nass.usda.gov/census/census02/volume1/mi/st26_2_004_004.pdf (accessed 2002).

Nelson, A.C. (1992) "Preserving Prime Farmland in the Face of Urbanization: Lessons from Oregon," *Journal of the American Planning Association*, 58: 467.

Payraudeau, S. and van der Werf, H.M.G. (2005) "Environmental Impact Assessment for a Farming Region: A Review of Methods," *Agriculture Ecosystems and Environment*, 107: 1–19.

Pease, J.R., Coughlin, R.E., Steiner, F.R., Sussman, A.P., Papazian, L., Joice, A.P. and John, C.L. (1994) "State and Local LESA Systems: Status and Evaluation," in F.R. Steiner, J.R. Pease and R.E. Coughlin (eds.) *A Decade with LESA: The Evolution of Land Evaluation and Site Assessment*, Ankeny, Iowa: Soil and Water Conservation Society.

Rosset, P.M. "The Multiple Functions and Benefits of Small Farm Agriculture: In the Context of Global Trade Negotiations," policy paper prepared for the FAO/Netherlands Conference on the Multifunctional Character of Agriculture and Land: Cultivating Our Futures, Maastricht, Netherlands, September 1999.

Tilman, D., Cassman, K.G., Matson, P.A., Naylor, R. and Polasky, S. (2002) "Agricultural Sustainability and Intensive Production Practices," *Nature*, 418: 671–677.

Tulloch, D.L., Myers, J.R., Hasse, J.E., Parks, P.J. and Lantrop, R.G. (2003) "Integrating GIS into Farmland Preservation Policy and Decision Making," *Landscape and Urban Planning*, 63: 33–48.

US Department of Commerce (2001) *Minority-Owned Firms Grow Four Times Faster than National Average*, Census Bureau Reports: US Department of Commerce News, July.

US Environmental Protection Agency (US EPA) (2006) *Ag 101: Demographics*, US Environmental Protection Agency. Online, available at: www.epa.gov/oecaagct/ag101/demographics.html (accessed August 2007).

van der Leeuw, S. (2000) "Land Degradation as a Socionatural Process," in R.J. McIntosh, J.A. Tainter and S.K. McIntosh (eds.) *The Way the Wind Blows: Climate, History, and Human Action*, New York: Columbia University Press.

Vermont Housing and Conservation Board (VHCB) (2005) *Farmland Preservation Program*, VHCB. Online, available at: www.vhcb.org/Conspage.html (accessed 2006).

Index

Numbers in *italics* refer to illustrations and tables.

*For Product Safety Concerns and Information please contact
our EU representative GPSR@taylorandfrancis.com Taylor & Francis
Verlag GmbH, Kaufingerstraße 24, 80331 München, Germany*

T - #0069 - 230425 - C0 - 234/156/16 - PB - 9780415516884 - Gloss Lamination